# STEPS TO COLLEGE READING

# STEPS TO COLLEGE READING

Dorothy U. Seyler
*Northern Virginia Community College*

**Allyn and Bacon**
Boston   London   Toronto   Sydney   Tokyo   Singapore

*Vice President, Humanities:* Joseph Opiela
*Marketing Manager:* Lisa Kimball
*Editorial-Production Service:* Omegatype Typography, Inc.
*Manufacturing Buyer:* Megan Cochran
*Cover Administrator:* Linda Knowles

Internet: www.abacon.com
America Online: keyword: College Online

**Library of Congress Cataloging-in-Publication Data**

Seyler, Dorothy U.
　　Steps to college reading  /  Dorothy U. Seyler.
　　　　p.　cm.
　　Includes bibliographical references and index.
　　ISBN-0-205-26585-5
　　1. Reading (Higher education).　I. Title.
　LB2395.3.S49　1998
428.4′071′1—dc21　　　　　　　　　　　97-10323
　　　　　　　　　　　　　　　　　　　　　CIP

Printed in the United States of America

10　9　8　7　6　5　4　3　2　1　　02　01　00　99　98　97

Credits are found on pages 485–488, which constitute a continuation of the copyright
page.

# CONTENTS

■ **CHAPTER 14**

*Responding to Persuasive Writing*   427

*Additional Readings*   460

# PREFACE

Are you ready to improve your reading? *Steps to College Reading* is ready to be your guide, to take you—yes—step by step to better reading skills. If you have the desire, *Steps* has the strategies to make you a better reader. But be forewarned. There is no magic wand inside these pages. The only way to improve your reading skills is to *read*. If you just start reading more, your skills will improve. But, if you want to prepare for the reading in your college classes, you do not have time to take the leisurely approach. You need good advice and directed practice. Your instructor and this text will provide both guidance and practice.

*Steps to College Reading* has been constructed on several principles. First, the best way to improve a skill is to understand the "sub-skills" that make it up and to practice each sub-skill separately before integrating them into an overall skill. Second, reading is a process that can be divided into the three basic steps of **Prepare–Read–Respond.** Third, reading is not a passive response to words. Instead, it requires the active engagement of a reader to make meaning from the words. And finally, reading needs a context. Readers need to know the author and the author's purpose, as well as their own purpose in reading.

The text's fourteen chapters comprise four steps to improved reading skills. Chapters 1 through 4 present the "nuts and bolts" of reading. These chapters explain the reading process and introduce strategies for expanding your vocabulary. (Instructors will find that this text's simpler three-step reading strategy is compatible with other reading strategies with which they may be familiar.) Both students and instructors will notice the emphasis on vocabulary in these opening chapters. Improved reading may be said to begin with an expanding vocabulary. Some instructors may choose to start with the vocabulary chapters; others will work in units from those chapters in patterns of their own.

Chapters 5 through 9 offer the next step to improved reading. These chapters guide you through a process of increased awareness of the relationship between main ideas and details and show you how to use a writer's structures and strategies as an aid to understanding main ideas, whether stated or implied. This step ends with a return to vocabulary building and the visual process in reading by working on spelling, on distinguishing between words that look alike, and on improving visual skills.

The next three chapters (Chapters 10–12) move to the step of reading and learning from college textbooks. Included are guidelines for, and practice in, reading graphics, using writing-to-learn strategies, participating in class and preparing for testing, reading more efficiently, and building a college vocabulary. Aids to reading more efficiently focus on how and when to skim and to scan and how to increase reading speed without losing comprehension. Successfully completing the work in these chapters will give you added confidence in your other classes.

A final step, presented in Chapters 13 and 14, reminds you that active reading includes both emotional and analytic responses to what is read. Chapter 13 guides you through a study of connotation, metaphors, and irony—elements of writing that we find in both expressive and persuasive writing. This chapter not only introduces you to some of the kinds of essays you will read in college writing classes, but also prepares you to understand a writer's position in persuasive essays, a step to reading critically. Then Chapter 14 explores the critical reading of persuasive writing and emphasizes the importance of taking a stand on issues. The text ends with four additional selections that can be used as timed readings and for further practice in reading comprehension and reading critically.

In this text you will find clear explanations supported by many examples. You will have the opportunity to practice the skills developed in each chapter by working the many exercises that can be completed in your text. You will be able to practice your reading first with short passages and then apply new skills to longer ones. The chapter's readings come from a range of college textbooks, as well as newspapers and magazines.

*Steps to College Reading* is dedicated to helping you learn to read with understanding and to retain information and ideas from your reading. You have taken the first step by opening the book. Don't stop now. Turn the page and let's get to work!

Fortunately for both authors and their readers, no book is prepared alone. Many colleagues and friends have helped me think about how we read and how we learn. To all of them I am grateful. In particular I want to acknowledge Evonne Jones, Barbara Wilan, Pam Legatt, Pat Hodgdon, and Carol Ischinger for lending books and sharing ideas. I can never complete a book without calling on the gracious support of our reference librarians, especially Marian Delmore and Ruth Stanton. I also want to thank, once again, my most important "first reader," my daughter Ruth. The confidence of my editor, Joe Opiela, that I could do two developmental reading texts has helped me immensely, and for the day-to-day coping with questions and anxieties, no one does it better than Joe's assistant, Kate Tolini. Finally, the following reviewers have contributed many excellent suggestions throughout the development of this text: Leslie K. King, Coordinator of the Learning Skills Center, SUNY College at Oswego; Margaret McClain, Arkansas State University; Jeanne Campanelli, American River College; Elaine M. Fitzpatrick, Massasoit Community College; Janice Beran, McLennan Community College; and Mary Boyles, University of North Carolina at Pembroke.

# STEPS TO COLLEGE READING

# CHAPTER 1

## Getting Started

**In this chapter you will learn:**

- How long-term goals relate to your reading course
- About your reading profile
- The roles of commitment and concentration in reading improvement
- What reading is

In his *Autobiography*, Ben Franklin lists thirteen virtues that he wants to develop. He then explains his specific strategy for success: Work on one at a time until it becomes a habit and then move on to the next. Why did Franklin want to make each virtue a habit? Because he knew that we do more out of habit than from principle. What we actually do—day in and day out—shapes the character that makes us who we are.

Stephen R. Covey, in his popular bestseller *The 7 Habits of Highly Effective People*, asks readers to imagine that they have come to a funeral—their own. They will hear eulogies— talks praising a dead person by family and friends—about themselves. If this were happening to you, what would you like to hear others saying about you and your life?

### EXERCISE 1-1  Who Do You Want to Be?

*I.  Reflect on what you would want others to say about you at the end of your life. Then write a paragraph "eulogy" for yourself—what you hope others would be able to say about you.*

_____

_____

_____

_____

_____

_____

_____

_____

_____

*II. Now organize what you have written into clusters of ideas. Have you said something about personal fulfillment? About lifestyle? About career? About money and possessions? About education? About family life? State the main points about yourself, in phrases, under appropriate headings.*

1. _____

_____

_____

2. _____

_____

_____

3. _____

_____

_____

Do you see your goals and values somewhat more clearly now? We really cannot take charge of our lives until we know what kind of life we want to have, what kind of person we want to be. But just having an idea of the future is not enough to get us there. We must also figure out what steps are needed to achieve our goals. For example, suppose you included a success-ful career in your "eulogy." How do you expect to reach that position? Or, suppose you want to be known as a spiritual person. What steps can you take to achieve that goal?

 **EXERCISE 1-2  What Steps Do You Need to Take?**

*Think about how you can become the person you have written about. List specific steps you need to take to achieve each of the goals you included in Exercise 1-1. (You may want to work with a class partner and help each other with your lists of steps.)*

_____

_____

_____

_____

_____

_____

_____

Did you mention education, either in your "eulogy" or in the steps to achieve your goals? Is it really possible to get to where you want to be with-out a good education? If you seek a career that requires a college degree, you will be busy studying for several years. Suppose one goal is to start your own business. There are books on this subject which guide you through the steps. You will also need to study government regulations and tax codes for small businesses. In addition, there are guides to getting in touch with your inner self, guides to parenting, and guides to maintaining fulfilling relationships. Many people will tell you that learning is a lifelong activity. It does not end when you finish formal schooling.

## ■ YOUR READING PROFILE

What is one way to keep learning and moving toward your goals? **By read-ing!** Will your reading habits and attitudes toward reading help you reach your goals—or hinder you? You are an important part of the reading process. You choose to pick up the book and turn the page. So you need to think about your reading profile—about who you are as a reader.

## EXERCISE 1-3  Your Reading Profile

*I. Mark T (true) or F (false) in the space provided after each statement. The goal is self awareness, so answer truthfully.*

|     |                                                                          | T    | F    |
| --- | ------------------------------------------------------------------------ | ---- | ---- |
| 1.  | I like to read late at night.                                            | ____ | ____ |
| 2.  | I usually have music or the TV on when I read for my courses.            | ____ | ____ |
| 3.  | I often have to go back and reread.                                      | ____ | ____ |
| 4.  | I rarely find time to read the newspaper.                                | ____ | ____ |
| 5.  | I like to read novels but not textbooks.                                 | ____ | ____ |
| 6.  | My favorite place to read is on my bed.                                  | ____ | ____ |
| 7.  | I would like to be a better reader.                                      | ____ | ____ |
| 8.  | I don't need a bigger vocabulary; I just need to read faster.            | ____ | ____ |
| 9.  | Teachers expect students to read too much.                               | ____ | ____ |
| 10. | Good reading skills are needed on the job.                               | ____ | ____ |
| 11. | I like to learn about new subjects.                                      | ____ | ____ |
| 12. | Reading bores me.                                                        | ____ | ____ |

The first six statements are about reading habits. Study your answers to those first. What did you learn? Do you think you have good reading habits? Statements seven through twelve ask you to think about your attitudes toward reading. Study your responses to these statements. Do you like to read? Do you think reading skills are important? Rate yourself on each of the following scales, circling the ratings that are right for you.

|                    | Poor | Average | Good | Very Good |
| ------------------ | ---- | ------- | ---- | --------- |
| Reading Habits     | 1    | 2       | 3    | 4         |
| Reading Attitudes  | 1    | 2       | 3    | 4         |

What is your reading profile? Is there room for improvement? Do you need to develop better reading habits or better attitudes as one strategy for reaching your goals? The following chart sums up three important parts of a good reading profile.

## The "Big 3" of Good Reading Habits

**Commitment:** Develop an *active* desire to read well and benefit from reading. Attitude does matter.

**Concentration:** Give *active* attention to reading; use specific strategies for concentration.

**Knowing about Reading:** Know how language, reasoning, and visual skills are used in *active* reading.

## ■ COMMITMENT

Taking this course is a good first step to improving your reading skills. Still, just signing up for this course will not make you a better reader. Only you can improve your reading skills. And reading is a skill—just like driving a car. How do you improve at any skill? Through a desire to learn, good instruction, and practice, practice, practice. Your instructor will provide good instruction and opportunities for practice. The commitment must come from you. Your desire to improve reading skills will be reflected in how much time you spend reading and building your vocabulary. Commitment shows itself in action.

Connect your desire to improve reading to your goals in life. Use your plans for the future as motivation to keep working when you become anxious or frustrated by reading assignments. Attitude does matter. Negative feelings, whether expressed to others or thought to yourself, get in the way of positive actions. They will not help you build good reading habits.

## ■ CONCENTRATION

If you do not concentrate well when you read, then developing greater concentration will be a necessary step to improving your reading skills. Concentration, like commitment, requires action. Here are some specific steps you can take to improve concentration.

### Steps to Improved Concentration: Before You Begin Reading

1. *Reduce Distractions.* Find a quiet place to read. If you are at home or in a dorm room, turn off the television. Either turn off the stereo or turn it down and choose "quiet" background music. Select a comfortable chair,

but avoid stretching out on a bed or couch. Stretching out invites the body—and the mind—to relax. If your house or dorm is rarely quiet, then read in the library. Select an individual desk in one of the library's quiet zones, not a large table in a busy area.

2. *Choose Good Times to Read.* Do not read late at night or when you are very tired. If you must study late, save work that requires writing as well as reading, such as completing exercises. If you are alert in the morning, read before attending classes. Read in the library or a quiet room between classes.

3. *Let Others Know Your Reading Schedule.* Let roommates or family members know that you will be reading and do not wish to be disturbed. Ask friends not to call or come by during announced study times. Post a "Do Not Disturb" sign on your door. Then ignore those who try to interrupt in spite of your efforts. (If they refuse to get the message, show them this page of your text!)

4. *Keep Your Body in Shape.* Willpower alone cannot keep us going. If you are abusing your body with too little sleep, poor nutrition, or not enough exercise, the body will say "enough." Usually the body speaks to us in the form of a cold or flu, sometimes with more serious problems. So, get enough rest. Eat properly, and that means—beginning with breakfast—plenty of fruits, vegetables, and carbohydrates. (A bag of potato chips is *not* a fruit!) Also schedule time for exercise. You will get more done during the day if you get at least thirty minutes of aerobic exercise every day.

5. *Set Up a Work Plan.* Plan the time you will spend on each reading assignment. If just thinking about a schedule does not keep you focused, then write out one for each day. If you have three classes and three hours for study, spend about an hour on each subject with a ten-minute break. Most experts advise shifting subjects rather than devoting a large block of time to only one subject. Still, you need to read in complete units: an entire article, a complete chapter, or several related sections of a long chapter. If you read only a few pages at one sitting, you will have to reread them when you return to that assignment. This approach does not use time wisely.

6. *Free Your Mind.* Before you read, try to free your mind from nagging details that may distract you. Set aside a time to pay bills, exercise, or make phone calls. You will manage your time better if you make all calls at one time rather than several times during the day or evening. Keep a pad of paper handy for making shopping lists or notes to yourself.

Many counselors advise people to keep a "To Do" list. The idea is to list all of the tasks needing action on a given day, carry the list with you, and cross through each task as it is completed. Often these lists contain more than you can do in a day. Check your progress as the day moves along and make certain to complete the tasks that must be finished that day. (For example, completing an assignment due the next day.) List the unfinished tasks at the beginning of a new work sheet for the next day. Organize your life. Put it in writing. Then, when you start to read, focus on the reading, not on the other parts of your life.

## Steps to Improved Concentration: While You Are Reading

1. *Think Positively.* Try to turn to each reading assignment with some enthusiasm. Think about what you may learn from the reading. Observe the progress you are making through a difficult textbook. Be proud of what you are doing.

2. *Engage Your Memory.* As you begin to read, think about what you already know about the topic. If you are beginning a new chapter in a textbook, think about last week's reading and class discussion. How will the new chapter connect to what you have already learned? Making connections will help you concentrate and get more from your reading.

3. *Read Actively to Keep Focused.* To read actively, ask yourself questions as you go along. Try to visualize (get a mental picture of) what you are reading. Mark the text—if it is yours—or take notes as you read. Then, connect what you are learning with the knowledge you already have. Reading with a pencil in hand will keep you involved.

4. *Take Breaks.* You may find that you concentrate better if you take a short break from reading every hour or so. Reading should not be physical torture. Even if you are reading in the library, you may want to get up and stretch before getting back to work. In your home or dorm room, you can get something to eat or drink. Make certain, though, that your breaks come at logical places to pause. Also be sure that your breaks do not last longer than your reading periods.

5. *Monitor the Loss of Concentration.* When your attention wanders from the reading, try to understand why. Are you thinking about errands you need to run, or are you getting sleepy? If so, then you have not paid attention to the steps for improved concentration before reading. Commit to following more faithfully the steps listed above. If you are getting frustrated by the difficulty of the material, give yourself a "commitment booster." Remind yourself that the course is a requirement and a step toward your goals—and then get back to work.

If you have taken your eyes off the page to think about what you are reading, that's not really a break in concentration. You may want to write down your thoughts. They may lead to good comments or questions you are able to offer in class the next day. Tune into yourself. The more you understand yourself, the better you can direct your reading and study time. The following exercise will increase your awareness of problems with concentration.

 **EXERCISE 1-4 Workshop on Concentration Problems**

*I. With your class partner or in small groups, brainstorm about reasons for poor concentration. List all the reasons your group identifies as causes of poor concentration.*

_____

_____

_____

_____

_____

_____

*II. Draw from the list above to make a list of **your** reasons for concentration problems. Then list specific steps you can take to cope with these problems. Use suggestions in this chapter and your group's discussion.*

**Your Concentration Problems**          **Your Solutions**

_____          _____

_____          _____

_____          _____

## ■ KNOWING ABOUT READING

If someone asked you to define reading, how would you answer? Probably a great many people would answer that reading is being able to recognize or "say" the words on a page. A better answer is that **reading is the process of making meaning from a word or cluster of words.** This statement gives us three key ideas about reading.

First, meaning is found in "clusters of words," not necessarily in complete sentences. In some cases what we call sentence fragments can express meaning. Let's look at the following simple illustration to make the point.

Jason locked his keys in the car. And his bookbag. His wallet, too.

The first statement is a complete sentence, but "and his bookbag" is a fragment. All by itself it would not make much sense. "What about his bookbag?" we ask. And, "Whose wallet?" When the three statements are read together, though, each cluster of words has meaning. We learn that Jason's keys, bookbag, and wallet are in his car and he cannot get them out. We know this if we know the meaning of the word *locked* and if we see how the second and third statements build on the first one.

The second idea about reading in the definition above is that reading involves getting meaning from the words. Reading, then, does not mean simply the ability to say the sounds that the words represent. It also doesn't mean just knowing the definitions of the words on the page. It means understanding the information or ideas or feelings expressed by the words that have been put together in the pattern chosen by the writer. In other words, if we are not getting a message, then we really are not reading. Reading is a thinking activity. We read with our brains, not just with our eyes.

Third, we do not just *understand* a writer's meaning; we, as readers, *make* meaning. On the one hand, readers do strive to understand the writer's meaning. On the other hand, readers must use their knowledge of vocabulary, of sentence structure, and of the writer's subject to *construct* meaning from the words on the page. The more words we know, and the more we know about sentence patterns, the easier reading will be. In addition, the more we know about the writer's subject, the easier reading will be, because we will be able to make connections between statements and see how ideas fit together. The more unfamiliar the words, the more complicated the sentences, and the less we know about a subject, the more difficult reading will be.

Think back to the statements about Jason's belongings locked in his car. Suppose you read those statements in a letter from your mother, and suppose Jason is your brother. Now think about how much more you actually know from those sentences than you did merely reading them in this chapter. Because you know how impatient Jason is, you can imagine how he felt locking his keys in the car. You can also hear your mother's annoyed voice in the letter. And because these people are part of your family, you also have feelings in response to what you have read. Because of your connections, you can make much more meaning out of those clusters of words than others of us could.

Reading is a complex process. As we construct meaning, we draw from our vocabulary, our previous knowledge, our emotions, and also our visual skills. The brain will struggle to construct meaning if the eyes do not process the visual information successfully. Here are some reading difficulties you need to be aware of and, perhaps, to work on solving.

## Visual Distortions

Some readers do not see the actual words. They may read the following sentence:

The sun rose over the still blue lake.

as

The run stole over the rill blue like.

Since the second version makes no sense, the reader has to reread the sentence to try to get meaning from it.

## Regression

Regression occurs when readers complete a sentence, or several sentences, and then realize that they do not know what they have read. Because of visual distortion or lack of concentration or some other difficulty, they did not get meaning from the sentences the first time through. Note: *Going back over a difficult textbook section is not regression.* It is what we need to do to learn from complex material. Regression is frequent rereading of short passages because the eyes did not process well or because the reader used to have some reading problems and has now turned regression into a bad reading habit.

## Vocalization and Subvocalization

As children many of us were taught to read by sounding out the words one by one. Some readers hang on to this habit of saying (vocalizing) the words, resulting in their reading quite slowly. Other readers stop moving their lips as they read, but they continue to "sound" the words in their heads. This is called subvocalization. Some specialists insist that subvocalization slows us significantly and that we should strive to read only with our eyes and brain. Others note that many good readers subvocalize, at least some of the time. The first goal should be to stop vocalization; a secondary goal can be to rely on your eyes more and on subvocalizing less.

## ■ IMPROVING VISUAL SKILLS—1

Rapid word recognition allows readers to attack their reading. A limited vocabulary slows us down and leads to comprehension problems. Because vocabulary is so important both to understanding and to pushing forward, we will devote considerable attention to vocabulary building throughout this text.

For now, you can get "warmed up" with the following drills. These drills are designed to give you practice in concentration, in using your eyes more effectively, and in eliminating regression. Your instructor may time you in class, or you can test yourself and record your times. Relax and make it a game—but also accept the challenge to improve your reading habits.

## EXERCISE 1-5 Word Identification Practice

*Move your eyes quickly across each line. Make a check over each word that is the same as the first word in **bold** type. Complete all 15 lines. Use a stopwatch or a clock with a second hand to time each set. Do not look back over a line. Look only from left to right. Try not to say the words. Just look for each repetition of the word in bold.*

| Set I | Begin timing. | | | | |
|-------|-----|-----|-----|-----|-----|
| 1. **carry** | candy | cradle | curry | candle | carry |
| 2. **load** | loan | load | laid | load | loam |
| 3. **hole** | hold | whole | hole | hold | mold |
| 4. **observe** | obscene | serve | obtain | observe | attain |
| 5. **total** | total | totem | tattle | tell | tattle |
| 6. **aisle** | angel | isle | aisle | aisle | aide |
| 7. **malady** | melody | malady | modem | molar | measly |
| 8. **grown** | clown | grown | grain | grow | ground |
| 9. **sink** | sank | stink | sink | sink | spank |
| 10. **profane** | perform | propane | profile | protect | project |
| 11. **jumble** | jungle | jumble | jingle | thimble | jungle |
| 12. **attest** | test | protest | attest | attain | attest |
| 13. **grasp** | grass | gross | roast | gross | grasp |
| 14. **smoke** | smoke | smack | stoke | smoke | smash |
| 15. **eulogy** | elegy | clergy | useless | eulogy | clergy |

PASSAGE?
BETWEEN

*End timing. Count your checks. Do you have 20? Did you go back over line 10? That line has no repetitions in it.*

Your time: ___1___ Number checked: ___19___

| Set II | Begin timing. | | | | |
|---|---|---|---|---|---|
| 1. **current** | current | currency | courage | current | currants |
| 2. **token** | taken | token | totem | token | total |
| 3. **money** | money | marry | many | money | mostly |
| 4. **bloat** | bloke | blast | battle | bloat | bloat |
| 5. **affect** | effect | aspect | access | affect | effect |
| 6. **flight** | fight | flourish | fought | flight | fight |
| 7. **desert** | dessert | desert | despair | dissent | doesn't |
| 8. **initiate** | initiate | instigate | investigate | initiate | innate |
| 9. **hospitable** | hospital | hospitable | hospice | hopeless | hospitable |
| 10. **mental** | metal | model | module | metal | mental |
| 11. **calculate** | collate | calculate | calcite | collate | cupful |
| 12. **relief** | reef | relate | release | relate | rife |
| 13. **painter** | painter | pointer | picture | pointer | pasture |
| 14. **baffle** | babble | blubber | baffle | babble | rubber |
| 15. **impression** | imposition | immersion | impression | immense | immense |

*End timing. Your time:* ___ l n ___   *Number checked:* ___ 2 l ___

| Set III | Begin timing. | | | | |
|---|---|---|---|---|---|
| 1. **flower** | folder | flour | flower | forever | flour |
| 2. **athlete** | athletic | alleviate | alley | athlete | allegiance |
| 3. **capitol** | capital | capital | capital | captivate | collapse |
| 4. **notary** | notoriety | noteworthy | notation | nation | notary |
| 5. **obsess** | abscess | obsess | abscess | oppress | obsess |
| 6. **expect** | except | accept | expect | respect | expect |
| 7. **optimum** | aptness | openness | option | opine | optimum |
| 8. **stationery** | station | stationary | stationery | stationary | station |
| 9. **hostile** | hostile | hospice | hostile | holster | hamster |
| 10. **momentary** | monetary | momentary | momentous | motion | momentary |
| 11. **insect** | inspect | aspect | insect | insect | inject |
| 12. **accident** | ancient | accidentally | ancient | apposite | accident |
| 13. **penetrate** | perpetrate | penetrate | perpetuate | penetrate | perpetrate |
| MANERS 14. **principle** | principle | principal | postal | principled | principal |
| 15. **illusion** | allusion | illusion | illicit | illusion | immersion |

*End timing. Your time:* _____   *Number checked:* ___ 2 l ___

## ■ BE AN ACTIVE READER

The chart on the "Big 3" in reading stresses the word *active* in each sentence. There are a number of important steps in the reading process, enough to take up all of Chapter 2, but you can start active reading by drawing from the ideas in this chapter as you read the following article. You will be aided by questions and exercises that come before and after each reading selection in this text. The questions preceding each reading selection will guide you to think about the author and the work, to think about what you already know about the subject, and to think about what you might learn from the selection. In some cases, you will find questions that interrupt the reading selection to guide your thinking at that point. You will also find questions at the beginning of each of the following chapters in this text. These questions will help you become an active reader of your textbook.

## Dr. Franklin's Tips for Staying Well

by **Thomas V. DiBacco**

Thomas DiBacco is a historian at American University. He wrote the following article for the *Washington Post*'s Health Section. The article was published January 30, 1996.

*Answer the following questions before reading the selection.*

1. What is important to note about the author?

   _____

2. After thinking about the title and the facts of publication, what do you expect to read about?

   _____

3. Write down what you already know about the topic.

   _____

   _____

   _____

4. List two questions you would like to have answered from reading this selection.

_____

_____

_____

1    The more things change, the more they stay the same. One of colonial America's most senior citizens, Benjamin Franklin (1706–1790), whose birthday is celebrated in January, had medical views regarding a long life that in many cases agree with contemporary professional advice.

2    Of course, Franklin was not a medicine man. But the self-educated American became a scientist noted for practical accomplishments (such as devising bifocals and a catheter and employing electrical treatments for paralysis). He was awarded a doctor of laws degree from Scotland's University of St. Andrews at age 53. Therefore it was not unusual that "Dr. Franklin," as he was henceforth addressed, would continually dabble in medical science, often by coping with his own blues and blahs.

3    Franklin was better known to his contemporaries for fighting colds than for his role in the American Revolution. He advised staying away from people with the malady: "People often catch cold from one another when shut up together in close rooms, coaches, etc., and when sitting near and conversing so as to breathe in each other's transpiration; the disorder being in a certain state."

4    Franklin also believed that colds and "too full living, too little exercise" went hand in hand. To be sure, he wasn't a diet or fitness freak (as the contour of his paunch would attest). But he was still using dumbbell weights at age 66, taking 40 hoists at a time. He walked a lot and recognized that a "greater quantity of some things may be eaten than of others, some being of lighter digestion than others."

5    Franklin took issue with a widespread belief at the time that cold weather and high humidity increased the likelihood of catching colds. "Traveling in our severe winters," he wrote fellow American Benjamin Rush, a physician, on July 14, 1773, "I have suffered cold sometimes to an extremity only short of freezing, but this did not make me catch cold. And, for moisture, I have been in the river every evening two or three hours for a fortnight together, when one would suppose I might imbibe enough of it to take cold if humidity could give it; but no such effect ever followed.

6    "Boys never get cold by swimming. Nor are people at sea, or who live at Bermudas, or St. Helena, small islands, where the air must be

**Benjamin Franklin**

Did Franklin agree or disagree with the idea that cold and humidity increase the chance of catching a cold?

ever moist from the dashing and breaking waves against their rocks on all sides, more subject to colds than those who inhabit part of a continent where the air is driest."

7   Franklin delighted in a form of indoor streaking: "I rise almost every morning and sit in my chamber without any clothes on whatever, half an hour or hour, according to the season, either reading or writing. This practice is not in the least painful, but, on the contrary, agreeable. . . ."

What is streaking?

8   He would have agreed wholeheartedly with recent medical studies that advocate moderation in drink. He was one of the first Americans to make a study of the effects of excessive drinking on people. Quiet

individuals, he noted, often became extroverts, the religious sometimes used profanity, and people of modest learning were not infrequently experts on "all arts and sciences."

9    On choosing eyeglasses: "I send you," he wrote to Mrs. Jane Mecom on July 17, 1771, "a pair of every size [lens] from 1 to 13. To suit yourself, take out a pair at a time, and hold one of the glasses first against one eye, and then against the other, looking on some small print. . . . I advise your trying each of your eyes separately, because few people's eyes are fellows, and almost everybody in reading or working uses one eye principally, the other being dimmer or perhaps fitter for distant objects. . . ."

10    Short cures (from Franklin's "Poor Richard's Almanack"):

- "Don't go to the doctor with every distemper, nor to the lawyer with every quarrel, nor to the pot with every thirst."
- "He's a fool that makes his doctor his heir." → IN HERE
- "Pain wastes the body; pleasures, the understanding."
- "Discontented minds, and fevers of the body, are not to be cured by changing beds or business."
- "He that would travel much, should eat little."
- "He's the best physician that knows the worthlessness of the most medicines."

11    Franklin slept soundly in his four score plus four years.

How many years did Franklin live? 84 years

12    He knew good sleep and heavy suppers don't mix ("Nothing is more common in the newspapers than instances of people who, after eating a hearty supper, are found dead abed in the morning"). And that fresh air in the bedroom is a must.

13    He even had a remedy for the person who wakes in the middle of the night. Get out of bed, first of all, and turn the pillow. Then take off your nightgown and shake it about 20 times. Draw back the covers to cool the bed. Walk around the bedroom naked for several minutes. "When you begin to feel the cold air unpleasant, [put on your bedclothes], then return to your bed, and you will soon fall asleep, and your sleep will be sweet and pleasant. All the scenes presented to your fancy will be, too, of the pleasing kind. I am often as agreeably entertained with them as by the scenery of an opera."

14    Of course, good sleeping, according to Franklin, is ensured by one other ingredient. He called it "a good conscience."

888 words

## Comprehension Check

*Answer the following with a, b, or c, to indicate the phrase that best completes each statement.*

_____ 1. Ben Franklin was called Dr. Franklin because he
   a. was a medical doctor.
   b. liked the title.
   c. was given an honorary doctor of laws degree.

_____ 2. Ben Franklin was the inventor of
   a. bifocal glasses.
   b. medicine.
   c. the Polaroid camera.

_____ 3. Franklin believed that people can catch colds from
   a. other people.
   b. overeating of rich foods.
   c. both a and b.

_____ 4. Franklin argued that people do not get colds from
   a. swimming.
   b. cold weather.
   c. both a and b.

_____ 5. Franklin understood that people often
   a. have one eye that is better than the other.
   b. benefit from excessive drinking.
   c. benefit from eating late at night.

_____ 6. Franklin's version of streaking involved
   a. sitting in his room without any clothes on.
   b. running through Philadelphia without any clothes on.
   c. swimming without any clothes on.

_____ 7. Franklin believed that the best way to get back to sleep at night is to
   a. read for an hour.
   b. walk around the room undressed until you are chilly.
   c. put more covers on the bed.

_____ 8. The best way to be sure of getting a good night's sleep, according to Franklin, is to
   a. have a big dinner.
   b. have a few drinks before bedtime.
   c. have a good conscience.

_____  9.  The author thinks that Franklin

    a.  had some crazy ideas.

    b.  understood a great deal about health.

    c.  was not important to the American Revolution.

_____  10.  The best statement of the main point of the essay is

    a.  Franklin was an important inventor.

    b.  Franklin's views on health are similar to what doctors would advise today.

    c.  Franklin did not understand medicine.

## ▪ Expanding Vocabulary

*Match each word or phrase in the left column with its definition in the right column by placing the correct letter in the space next to each word. When in doubt, read again the sentence in which the term appears. The numbers in parentheses identify the paragraph in which the word appears.*

| | |
|---|---|
| _d_ henceforth (2) | a.  illness |
| _f_ dabble (2) | b.  belly |
| _a_ malady (3) | c.  drink |
| _i_ contour (4) | d.  from now on |
| _b_ paunch (4) | e.  bad language |
| _k_ attest (4) | f.  explore a subject without going into great depth |
| _j_ took issue with (5) | g.  to argue in favor of |
| _c_ imbibe (5) | h.  awareness of one's right conduct |
| _g_ advocate (8) | i.  outline of a figure |
| _e_ profanity (8) | j.  disagreed with |
| _h_ conscience (13) | k.  supply evidence for |

✦ *Use five of the vocabulary words (those in the left column) in a sentence of your own.*

1. _____

_____

2. _____

_____

3. _____

_____

4. _____

_____

5. _____

_____

## For Discussion and Reflection

*Think about these questions and have answers prepared for class discussion. (Your instructor may ask you to write briefly on one of the questions, so be prepared.)*

1. What are two new pieces of information you learned about Franklin? How do they affect your view of him?
2. What is the most interesting information or idea you learned from this article? Why do you find it interesting?
3. Do you think Franklin would have been a fascinating person to know? Why or why not?

## Your Reading Assessment

*Evaluate your reading by answering the following questions.*

1. How many of the comprehension questions did you answer correctly?

_____

2. How many vocabulary words could you match? How many did you use correctly in a sentence? _____

3. How would you describe the reading of this passage? Circle the correct word for you.   Easy   Okay   Hard   Very Hard

4. Were you able to respond to the discussion questions? _____

5. How accurately did you predict what you would read about?

_____

6. Did the article answer your questions? _____ If not, why do you think that it did not?

_____

7. What parts of your reading need work?

Predicting what the reading will cover? _____

Comprehension? _____

Vocabulary? _____

Reflection? _____

## ▌ Chapter Review Quiz

*Complete each of the following statements.*

1. According to Ben Franklin, people act more out of _____ than

_____.

2. What does planning for your future require? _____

_____

3. Commitment is not just an attitude; it requires

_____.

4. Three steps you can take to improve concentration before reading include:

a. _____

b. _____

c. _____

5. Three steps you can take to improve concentration while reading include:

a. _____

b. _____

c. _____

6. Reading is a _____ activity.

7. Before reading, active readers think about:

a. _____

b. _____

c. _____

*The following words have appeared in the chapter or in the reading selection. Circle the letter next to the word (or phrase) that is the best definition of the word.*

1. eulogy
   a. litany of the dead
   b. tribute to a dead person
   c. euphony

2. commitment
   a. a pledge of oneself
   b. blend together
   c. express sympathy

3. concentration
   a. concede the point
   b. compromise
   c. direct one's thoughts

4. profile
   a. vulgar
   b. plan or scheme
   c. brief outline or side view of a person

5. focused
   a. fascination with
   b. concentrated on
   c. fancy

6. brainstorm
   a. propose ideas
   b. intellectual ability
   c. headache

7. imbibe

 a. drink
 b. inhibit
 c. stumble

8. advocate

 a. admit
 b. argue in favor of
 c. explain in detail

9. profanity

 a. bad language
 b. bad food
 c. unhealthy

# Chapter 2

## Developing a Reading Strategy

**In this chapter you will learn:**

- Why a reading strategy improves reading

- Steps in the **Prepare–Read–Respond** strategy

- How to be an active reader

- How to monitor your reading comprehension

- Why reflecting and reviewing are part of a reading strategy

## ■ Prepare to Read

Read and reflect on the chapter's title and objectives. Glance through the chapter, observing headings, to see what is covered. Now answer these questions:

1. What do you expect to learn from this chapter?

_____

_____

2. What do you already know about the chapter's topic?

_____

_____

3. What two or three questions do you want answered from reading this chapter?

_____

_____

_____

_____

In Chapter 1 you learned that reading is a thinking activity and that good readers are actively engaged with the text. You were also given questions to answer before reading. So, you have already begun to practice a reading strategy. This chapter will introduce specific steps in a complete reading plan and give you practice in "grooving" your new strategy.

## ■ WHY HAVE A READING STRATEGY?

Why should you have a reading plan? Reading is intellectual work, and for work to be productive, most people need a plan, a strategy for doing a good job.

A good reading strategy is one that:

• guides you to prepare adequately before reading,

• helps you read in ways to improve comprehension, and

• guides you to respond in ways to retain information and fulfill your purpose in reading.

If you make a habit of using the three-step plan of **Prepare–Read–Respond,** you will become a better reader.

## ■ PREPARE–READ–RESPOND: HOW THE STEPS CONNECT

The diagram in Figure 2.1 shows how the three steps in your reading strategy divide into three stages: before reading, during reading, and after reading. Each major step involves several activities. The several activities involved in **preparing** to read make you an active reader. Then, as you **read** actively, you need to mark the text to support your reading, and you need to keep monitoring (checking) your comprehension. Finally, you are not finished until you **respond**—until you reflect on the reading and review so that you can remember what you have read.

Notice in the diagram that the first and third steps overlap the middle step. The diagram shows you that the three steps of your reading strategy are not completely separate. As you read, you may discover that some of your predictions about the work were not accurate, so you will need to revise your thinking. Also, with a difficult work, you may have to review in sections rather than waiting until you complete a chapter. You may continue to question as you read and stop at times to reflect on what you have just learned. So, your reading strategy can be described as a three-step plan, but the stages also overlap to create an interrelated process.

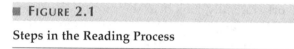

■ FIGURE 2.1

**Steps in the Reading Process**

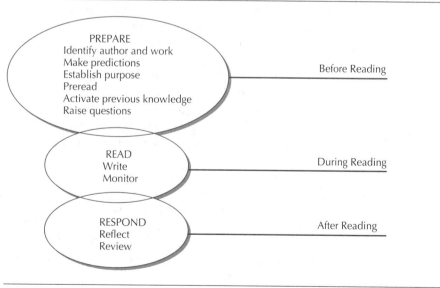

## ▧ PREPARE

Most readers prepare in some way before they begin to read even if they do not think of it as a planned step in reading. You probably do not select a novel to read unless you have heard, perhaps from a friend, that it is a good book. When facing new—and sometimes difficult—material, you need to prepare in a planned and specific way to get the most out of your reading.

## Identify the Author, Type of Work, and Subject to Make Predictions

*Learn about the Author.* Begin by learning all you can about the author (or authors) of the reading material. Identifying means more than just finding the author's name on the page. You want to learn about the writer's education, position, or experiences, the facts that explain why this author's writing on a particular subject has been published. Most books and magazine articles provide some information about the author. Editorials are one exception. They are frequently unsigned and usually represent the views of the editorial staff of the newspaper or magazine.

*Learn about the Work.* Next, take a few minutes to *see* what you can learn about the work. Literally, look over the reading to get an idea of the kind of work it is and the way the material will be presented. For example, how do you know when you are going to read a poem? (By the way the words are arranged on the page.) A poem *looks* different than prose (see those in Chapter 13). Novels and textbooks don't look the same either. Visualize—picture in your mind—a novel you have read. How are the words organized and presented? Probably the book is just page after page of words. Often novels are divided into chapters, but many times the chapters just have numbers, not titles. Still, because you know that the book is a novel, you expect to read a narrative, a story about several characters who are created by the author. In short, because you know the kind of work you are about to read, you can **predict** both **how** the work will be presented and **what** the writer's purpose is.

Now picture one of your textbooks. It is probably a large book, with chapters divided into many subsections. It probably contains many pictures, charts, and diagrams. It may also have "boxes," brief sections set off from the main text by lines or a colored background. Boxes focus on a related subject or provide an application of the subject matter. Magazine articles also frequently contain boxed inserts. Why are so many different strategies used in a textbook? Because the primary purpose is to provide information, and to teach that information to readers. The various graphics and the boxed inserts help explain and clarify the material presented in the text.

*Learn about the Subject.* In addition to looking at the work you are about to read, you need to **preview** or **preread** the selection. Prereading gives you an idea of the author's subject and strategies for covering that subject. One way to decide if you are interested in—or ready for—a particular course is to preview the text for the course. Borrow a friend's or look at one in the bookstore before you buy. Alternatively, when you have registered for a course, buy and preread the textbook before reading any specific assignment. To preread a textbook, follow these guidelines.

## Guidelines for Prereading a Textbook

1. **Read and think about the title. Learn about the author(s) and observe the date of publication.**
2. **Read the preface or introduction.** Here the author explains the book's focus and gives some key ideas that have guided his or her approach to the subject.
3. **Study the table of contents.** This will give you an idea of the specific topics covered. It will also give you an overview of the course you are about to take. Write down questions or thoughts about the topics as you read.
4. **See if the book has any appendices, notes, bibliography, or a glossary.** Many textbooks will have all of these additional sections at the end of the book. Appendices contain additional information; notes document borrowed information and a bibliography guides you to other works on the same subject; the glossary lists and defines key terms used in the book.

Your preview of the text provides important information for your upcoming studies. Each time you read a chapter or section assignment, or read an article, you also need to preread. Some understanding of the work you are about to study is essential to good comprehension. For chapters and articles follow these guidelines.

## Guidelines for Prereading a Chapter or Article

1. **Read and think about the title.** Also read the subtitle, if there is one. Sometimes authors choose catchy titles and then clarify their subject in a subtitle. The title contains the author's first words to you; pay attention to them.

2. **Read the opening and concluding paragraphs.** Authors usually state their main points at the beginning and then again at the end of their writing. Glance at the opening sentences of each paragraph. Often the main idea of a paragraph is stated in the first sentence.

3. **Look through the chapter or article to note headings, subheadings, and words in italics or bold type.** Many books and articles guide readers through the material with visual signposts revealing organization and the subjects covered.

4. **Also look at any graphics—diagrams, charts, pictures.** The author has carefully chosen accompanying graphics not only to add interest but to clarify the subject matter. Looking at the graphics will give you a good sense of the work's subject.

*Make Predictions.* You conclude this first step in the **Prepare** stage of your reading strategy by making some predictions about the material you are going to read. When you are examining a work, do not linger. Push yourself through your previewing, keeping in mind that your goal is an overview, not thorough knowledge of the material. That will come with **Reading** and **Responding.** Still, you are not finished with your previewing until you can talk to yourself about the work, commenting on the writer's subject and purpose and general approach to the subject. Here is an example.

For your speech class you have been assigned the textbook *Mastering Public Speaking,* in its second edition, by George L. Grice and John F. Skinner. When you first purchase your text, you note on the title page that both authors are college professors. You also conclude that the text has been well received because it is in a second edition—and your instructor has selected it for your use. You read the authors' preface, look through the table of contents to see what the book covers, and observe that there are several appendices, including a collection of famous speeches.

When you are ready to read, you turn to the first chapter to preview. You look at several charts and pictures and note that the chapter ends with a summary, exercises, and notes. Here are the chapter's title, headings and subheadings:

# AN INTRODUCTION TO PUBLIC SPEAKING

**Why Study Public Speaking?**
Personal Benefits
Professional Benefits
Public Benefits

**Definitions of Communication**

**Levels of Communication**
Intrapersonal Communication
Interpersonal Communication
Group Communication
Public Communication
Mass Communication

**Components of Communication**
Linear Model of Communication
Interactive Model of Communication

**Your First Speech**
Understand the Assignment
Develop Your Speech Content
Organize Your Speech
*Organize Your Speech Introduction*
*Organize the Body of Your Speech*
*Organize Your Speech Conclusion*
Word Your Speech
Practice Your Speech
*Prepare Your Notes*
*Practice Productively*
Deliver Your Speech
Evaluate Your Speech

**The Public Speaker as Critical Thinker**

What do the headings and subheadings tell you about the contents of the chapter? As you read through them, you might have some thoughts—and questions—such as the following:

- The chapter will explain reasons for learning how to give a speech.
  [If it answers the question "why," it gives reasons.]

- It will explain what communication is.
  [Student has not noted that "definitions" is plural.]

- It will talk about different kinds of communication—going from one person to larger groups.
  [Student has noted the organization of this section.]

- It will explain about the parts of communication—I don't know what these models are all about.

  [Student understands the basic idea of the section, but will also be reading about some new ideas.]

- It gives steps to get you through your first speech.

  [This might be a particularly important section.]

- What does "public speaker as critical thinker" mean?

  [Again, student acknowledges new material.]

Note two key elements in this student's brief analysis of the chapter. First, the student does not just repeat headings. The student talks to herself in her own words—and states the *idea* of each section. Second, the student acknowledges terms or concepts that are new—but also reinforces her understanding of the way sections are organized.

## EXERCISE 2-1  Workshop on Prereading and Predicting

*With a class partner or in small groups, read the title and headings of Chapter 4 of **Mastering Public Speaking** and then answer the questions that follow.*

**Listening**

**The Importance of Listening**

**Listening vs. Hearing**

   *Listening Is Intermittent*
   *Listening Is a Learned Skill*
   *Listening Is Active*
   *Listening Implies Using the Message Received*

**The Process of Listening**

   Receive
   Select
   Interpret
   Understand
   Evaluate
   Resolve

**Obstacles to Effective Listening**

   Physical Distractions
   Physiological Distractions
   Psychological Distractions
   Factual Distractions
   Semantic Distractions

**Promoting Better Listening**
   Desire to Listen
   Focus on the Message
   Listen for Main Ideas
   Understand the Speaker's Point of View
   Withhold Judgment
   Reinforce the Message
   Provide Feedback
   Listen with the Body
   Listen Critically

1. Briefly explain what each major section is going to cover. Use your own words, and use questions when you are confused.

   _____

   _____

   _____

   _____

   _____

   _____

   _____

   _____

2. Why do you think the author has included a chapter on listening in a text on public speaking?

   _____

3. Which is the more important skill, hearing or listening? In what key way do hearing and listening differ?

   _____

4. How might someone "listen with the body"?

   _____

## Identify What You Already Know

Studies have shown that knowledge of the topic does more to raise scores on reading tests than do general reading skills. The more you know, the better you read. This really makes sense when you remember that reading is a thinking skill. But interest in learning about new subjects also helps. You will remember more from your reading and build your storehouse of knowledge if you are eager to learn.

You may actually know more about a topic than you think you do. If you can apply the knowledge you already have, you will understand and remember more of what you read. The key is to identify what you already know. The best way to do this is to jot down some information or ideas related to the subject. You want to *activate* your knowledge so that you have a context in which to read the material.

### EXERCISE 2-2  What Do I Already Know?

*I. You have just preread a chapter on listening. Write down what you already know about listening.*

_____

_____

_____

_____

_____

_____

*II.   Write down what you know about the subjects of each of the following textbook chapter or section titles.*

a. "Ethics and Public Speaking" (from *The Art of Public Speaking*)

_____

_____

_____

b. "How Congress Works" (from *American Government: Roots and Reform*)

_____

---

---

   c. "Energy Balance and Weight Control" (from *Nutrition: Concepts and Controversies*)

---

---

---

## Raise Questions to Fulfill Your Purpose in Reading

Why are you reading? That's a good question to ask yourself before you start to read a particular work. You read a novel for pleasure, but also for insight into human life and experience. You read the newspaper to keep informed on current events—and to see what's on sale. When approaching new or difficult material, you will benefit from reminding yourself of your reading purpose. If you are reading a textbook, or other assigned reading for a course, keep in mind that your purpose is not just to complete an assignment. Your purpose may be to learn the material for testing—and to master the knowledge you will need on the job.

   One important **PREPARE** strategy to help you fulfill your reading purpose is to raise questions that can be answered by the reading. If you seek answers to questions, you will read more purposefully. As you preread, ask yourself what you will be learning by turning titles and section headings into questions. So, instead of just reading the heading "Obstacles to Effective Listening," create questions such as:

   What are some obstacles to effective listening?

   What are some ways to remove obstacles to effective listening?

Or, instead of merely reading "Health in the United States: A Nation of Contrasts," ask yourself:

   What health issues will be discussed?

   What are the contrasts in health in the United States?

As you ask these questions, others may occur to you: Will contrasts be between different groups such as the young and the elderly? Or people living in the country or in cities? Keeping in mind *why* you are reading and *raising questions* as you preread will prepare you to organize and remember specific information and to think about the writer's ideas.

## Exercise 2-3  Turning Headings into Questions

*Turn each of the following titles or section headings into at least two questions.*

1. "Computer Crime" (from Fuller and Manning's *Computers and Information Processing*)

   _____

   _____

   _____

2. "The Roles of Proteins in the Body" (from Sizer and Whitney's *Nutrition: Concepts and Controversies*)

   _____

   _____

   _____

3. "Sources of Stress: The Common and the Extreme" (from Wood and Wood, *The World of Psychology*)

   _____

   _____

   _____

4. "The Effects of the Automobile" (from Henslin, *Sociology*)

   _____

   _____

   _____

## ■ READ

This entire book is about ways to become a more skilled reader. So here we will examine the two activities you need to include with your reading step—annotating and monitoring comprehension—not the activity of reading itself.

## Annotate

Chapter 11 presents several ways to use writing to learn. This section will examine only annotating because it is probably the most used strategy. Studies have shown that writing is an essential aid to reading comprehension. When you write, you are more likely to concentrate and be an active reader. Also, writing pushes you to note what is important and to think about the material.

When you **annotate,** you mark up the text, underlining and making notes in the margins. Now, before you say to yourself that you cannot write in books, let's stop and think about this. Of course you cannot mark up the books that are not yours, but you can annotate your textbooks and other books and magazines that belong to you. What have you gained by keeping your texts spotless if you end up not doing well in the course? You need to learn to annotate and to use this strategy regularly when reading. Here's how to do it.

### Guidelines for Annotating

1. After you read a section, underline key sentences (or important parts of sentences). Underline what seems to be the most important idea in each paragraph.

2. Remember: Underlining highlights by contrast, so underline only what is important.

3. When you look up a word's definition, write the definition in the margin next to the word.

4. Try to separate ideas from examples. Write "ex" in the margin next to an example. If several examples (or points or reasons) are given, label them and then number each one in the margin. This will help you see how many examples (or points or reasons) the author provides.

5. If the selection provides a list, note what the list is about and then circle each item in the list.

6. Draw arrows to connect each example to the idea it illustrates. Draw pictures to illustrate concepts—whatever will help you understand and remember.

7. Make whatever other notes in the margins that will help you concentrate on your reading.

## An Example of Annotating

As you read the following selection, observe the usefulness of the annotations and the extent of reader involvement they show. As you read add your own marginal notes.

*Characteristics*

*1. no limits to storage*

*2. lasts a long time*

***Long-Term Memory: As Long as a Lifetime***   Some information from short-term memory makes its way into long term memory. **Long-term memory** (LTM) is our vast storehouse of permanent or relatively permanent memories. There are no known limits to the storage capacity of long-term memory, and long-term memories last a long time, some of them for a lifetime.

*Def—LTM*

When we talk about memory in everyday conversation, we are usually referring to long-term memory. Long-term memory holds all the knowledge we have accumulated, the skills we have acquired, and the memories of our past experiences. Information in long-term memory is usually stored in semantic form, although visual images, sounds, and odors can be stored there as well.

*What is in long-term memory?*

*How to:*

*1. rehearsal better*

*2. relate new info to old & make connections*

But <u>how</u> does this vast store of information make its way from short-term memory into long-term memory? We seem to remember some information with ease, almost automatically, but other kinds of material require great effort. Sometimes, through mere repetition or rehearsal, we are able to transfer information into long-term memory. Your teachers may have used drills to try to cement the multiplication tables and other material in your long-term memory. This rote rehearsal, however, is not necessarily the best way to transfer information to long-term memory (Craik & Watkins, 1973). When you relate new information to the information already safely tucked away in long-term memory and then form multiple associations, you increase the chance that you will be able to retrieve the new information.

Wood and Wood, *The World of Psychology*

### EXERCISE 2-4  Annotating a Selection

*Read the following excerpt, another selection from Wood and Wood's **The World of Psychology,** and, using the Guidelines for Annotating, annotate the selection. Compare your work with that of classmates and discuss any differences.*

# The Three Processes in Memory: Encoding, Storage, and Retrieval

What must occur to enable us to remember a friend's name, a fact from history, or an incident from our past? The act of remembering requires the successful completion of three processes: encoding, storage, and retrieval, The first process, **encoding,** involves transforming information into a form that can be stored in memory. Sometimes we encode information automatically, without any effort, but often we must do something with the information in order to remember it. For example, if you met someone named George at a party, you might associate his name with George Washington or George Bush. Such simple associations can markedly improve your ability to recall names and other information. The careful encoding of information greatly increases the chance that you will remember it.

The second memory process, **storage,** involves keeping or maintaining information in memory. For encoded information to be stored, some physiological change in the brain must take place—a process called **consolidation.** Normally consolidation occurs automatically, but if a person loses consciousness for any reason, the process can be disrupted and a permanent memory may not form. That is why a person who has been in a serious car accident could awaken in a hospital and not remember what has happened.

The final process, **retrieval,** occurs when information stored in memory is brought to mind. Calling George by name the next time you meet him shows that you have retrieved his name from memory. To remember, we must perform all three processes—encode the information, store it, and then retrieve it. Memory failure can result from the failure of any one of the three.

Similar steps are required in the information processing of computers. Information is encoded (entered in some form the computer is able to use), then stored on disk, and later retrieved on the screen. You would not be able to retrieve the material if you had failed to enter it, if a power failure occurred before you could save what you had entered, or if you forgot which disk or file contained the needed information. Of course, human memory is far more complex than even the most advanced computer systems, but computer processing provides a useful analogy to memory, if not taken too literally.

## Monitor Comprehension

As you interact with the writer's ideas by annotating, you also need to be thinking about how well you are reading. Are you comprehending? And if not, what are you going to do about it? As an active reader, you need to be both player and coach. You are participating in the reading activity, but at the same time you are monitoring how well the activity is going. When you monitor your own performance, you can step in and redirect your attention when problems develop.

What are some clues that warn us of trouble with reading? First, here are some behavior clues to watch for:

You find yourself gazing out the window.

You keep going back to reread passages.

You take a second break in only ten minutes.

You realize that you are frowning as you read.

Can you think of other behavior clues? What do these actions tell you? First, that you have lost concentration. Second, that you are struggling with comprehension.

Now think about the conversations we have with ourselves that signal problems. What do the following verbal clues tell you?

"I've just read three pages, but I don't know what I've read."

"None of this makes any sense."

"I'll never understand this stuff!"

Can you think of other verbal clues?

If you are monitoring your reading, you can tell from such actions and thoughts that all is not going well. The first step to monitoring is recognizing—or admitting—that just continuing to turn pages will not work. The next step is to find a way to remove the difficulty so that you can once again make progress. Here are some suggestions for fixing comprehension problems. Find the solutions that work for you.

### Guidelines for Fixing Comprehension

1. *Monitor your concentration.* Your comprehension problem may be the result of a loss of concentration. Review the guidelines for concen-

tration in Chapter 1 and respond appropriately. (For example, move from a noisy room to a quiet place to complete the reading.)

2. *Redo the* **Prepare** *steps.* Perhaps you forgot to **Prepare** and just started to read, only to get confused. If so, go back and identify the work and subject, preread, identify what you know, and raise questions about the material.

3. *Connect the material to previous reading.* If your comprehension problems occur in the middle of a section or chapter, go back and review the material in the previous section or chapter. You may need to review a good bit to activate your knowledge before moving forward.

4. *Fill in the gaps.* A specific passage may be a problem because there are key words you do not know. If you cannot figure out the meaning from context, you will need to obtain the definitions before continuing to read. Perhaps the definitions can be found in a previous section of the text. Find them and copy them into the margin. Next, try the text's glossary, if there is one. Finally, use your dictionary.

5. *Reread the material.* Accept that some material is difficult and may require a second reading for full comprehension. Be sure that you are annotating as you read.

6. *Go to additional sources for help.* If the solutions listed above don't work, you may need to find help outside the reading material and your monitoring efforts. Try the library for other, simpler books on the subject, or ask your instructor to recommend other books or study guides. Find a classmate to study with or obtain a college-sponsored tutor.

## EXERCISE 2-5  **Monitoring Reading Comprehension**

*Read the following selection, monitoring your comprehension. Then list strategies you would use to fix any comprehension problems you had or that you think other readers might have. Compare your list of strategies with classmates.*

The sequences of amino acids that make up a protein molecule are specified by heredity. For each protein there is only one proper amino acid sequence. If a wrong amino acid is inserted, the result may be disastrous to health.

Sickle-cell disease, in which hemoglobin, the oxygen-carrying protein of the red blood cells, is abnormal, is an example of an inherited mistake in the amino acid sequence. Normal hemoglobin contains two kinds of chains. One of the chains in sickle-cell hemoglobin is an exact copy of that in normal hemoglobin. But in the other chain, the sixth amino acid, which should be glutamine, is replaced by valine. The protein is so altered that it is unable to carry and to release oxygen. The red blood cells collapse into crescent shapes instead of remaining disk shaped, as they normally do. If too many abnormal, crescent-shaped cells appear in the blood, the result is illness and death. One way to detect the disease is to observe the altered red blood cells under the microscope.

Sizer and Whitney, *Nutrition: Concepts and Controversies*

_____

_____

_____

_____

_____

_____

_____

## ■ RESPOND

Responding to your reading is just as important as preparing to read. You need to both reflect and review, activities that overlap to some extent.

## Reflect

Psychologists studying the memory process have found that we have trouble remembering material that seems random or disconnected from anything else. Random numbers, or lists of words, for example, are difficult to remember. If you can connect what you are reading to something else in your life, the material will not seem random. Reflecting on how new information and ideas connect to what you already know and to what is important in your life will improve your chances of remembering what you have read.

Take, for example, information about memory. We do not have to be psychologists to be interested in how our memories function. Just wanting to understand how your own brain works is reason enough to reflect on the passages in this chapter on memory and relate their ideas to your life.

To be certain that your reflection is focused on the reading, you may want to ask yourself specific questions. If you develop the habit of reflecting as a strategy for improving reading skills, you may become a more reflective person generally. This new dimension to your life will bring you pleasure.

What kinds of questions can you ask to aid reflection? Here are some general questions that can be applied to many different readings.

## Questions to Aid Reflection

- How does the selection relate to the course? Why has the instructor assigned (or recommended) it?

- How does this work relate to other courses I'm taking? Am I studying a similar time period? Similar ideas? Subjects that are closely related?

- How can I use this information in my career? Will it make me better trained? Or better informed? Or more understanding of people with whom I will be working?

- How does this material help me better understand myself? My family relationships? People who are different from me? The natural world of which I am a part? How do I feel about this new knowledge?

### EXERCISE 2-6  Reflecting on What You Read

*Reread the two selections on memory (p. 36 and p. 37) and then reflect on their connections with your courses, your career plans, and your learning about life. Write some of your reflections in the space below.*

_____

_____

_____

_____

_____

_____

_____

## Review

Reviewing what you have read can be done several ways, including the time spent reflecting. What is essential is that you review *immediately* and then *periodically.*

The best time for your first review is *immediately* after you finish reading. Resist celebrating the completing of a long reading assignment until after you have taken time for reflecting and reviewing. How does reviewing aid learning? Consider: If you want to remember the names of people introduced to you, repeat their names when you greet them. This repetition is called *rehearsing.* After this initial repetition, say the names to yourself several times, and then use them again in conversation. Chances are good that you will remember the names.

Note that you reviewed the names immediately and then periodically thereafter. Even with an immediate review, some information will not be remembered unless you continue to go over it. You need to review several times rather than just prior to a test. When studying for your courses, a good strategy is to review what you have most recently read before reading further. So, review Chapter 1 before reading Chapter 2, review Chapter 2 before reading Chapter 3, and so on. Each time you relearn the material, you will remember more of it.

Your immediate review may include several strategies. First, redo the prereading step. Second, look over your annotations. Third, answer the questions you raised as a part of your **Prepare** step. Also, if you are reading a textbook, answer any discussion or review questions in the text. Finally, integrate reflection with reviewing.

Now, practice your **Prepare–Read–Respond** strategy on the following selections.

## Megacities, Megachallenges

by the **Editors,** the *Washington Post*

The following editorial was printed in the *Washington Post* on April 22, 1996.

### Prepare

1. Identify the authors and work. What do you expect the authors' purpose to be?

> ★ THEY WOULD TALK OBOT THE CONDITIONS WE
>
> FACE TO MAKE THE CITIES BETTER.

2. Preread to identify the subject and make predictions. What do you expect to read about?

_THE TROUBLE THAT CITIES FACE. MY_

_PREDICTION IS ABOUT THE ENVIROMENT_

3. What do you already know about the subject?

_* IT HAS SOMETHING TO DO WITH THE CITIES_

_AND THEIR PROBLEMS (THEY) HAVE TO FACE_

4. Raise two questions that you expect the article to answer.

_* ( WHAT CHALLENGES FACE THE CITIES?_

_* ( HOW SERIOS IS THIS PROBLEM FOR THE_

_PEOPLE?_

■ **Vocabulary Alert**

The title contains two words, each with the same beginning: *mega. Mega* means large or great. Here are some other words you will find in the editorial.

urbanization (1): process of making more urban (city) areas

subset (1): part within a larger unit

formidable (1): difficult to conquer

literacy (3): ability to read and write

indicators (3): signs

squalor (4): filthy and wretched condition

squatter (4): one who settles on unoccupied land without owning it

biennial (5): every two years

1 Twenty years ago, about 1.5 billion people lived in cities. Today, 2.6 billion do. Thirty years from now, more than five billion people likely will be city dwellers. This rapid urbanization, especially in the developing world, is an important subset of the rapid population growth, which is likely to continue into the middle of the next century at least. Some-

time around the end of this century, more than half of the world's population will live in cities for the first time. This poses formidable challenges in health care and the environment, in both the developed and developing world.

2      The United Nations will hold a conference on urbanization this June in Turkey (urban population today: 43 million; predicted urban population in 2025: 79 million). The world may be suffering from U.N.-conference fatigue. But a report published this week, "World Resources 1996–97: The Urban Environment," leaves no doubt as to the importance of dealing with these issues now.

3      The report points out that urbanization is not all bad; one reason so many people move to cities, after all, is to earn a better living. Literacy, opportunities for women, health indicators and living standards all tend to be higher in cities, on average, than in rural areas.

4      But the phrase "on average" is key. The urban poor in many developing countries live in squalor unlike anything they left behind, and many of their health problems—often including violence—are also new. In Caracas, more than half the total housing stock is squatter housing. In Bangkok, the regional economy is 2.1 percent smaller than it otherwise would be because of time lost in traffic jams. The megacities of the future pose huge problems for waste management, water use and climate change. In 1950, there were only two megacities of eight million or more, London and New York. By 2015, there will be 33, 27 in the developing world.

5      One encouraging note, given its past inattention to environmental questions, is the World Bank's decision this year to join with U.N. agencies and the nonprofit World Resources Institute to publish their Biennial report on the global environment. The bank's commitment to help local communities solve their environmental problems will promote what is called sustainable development—economic growth, that is, which does not come at the expense of future generations. Leaders and communities everywhere must make a similar commitment, so that the stresses of rapid urbanization don't overwhelm the benefits of city living.

421 words

■ Comprehension Check   .

*Fill in the blank with the word or phrase that best completes each sentence.*

1. Today about _____2.6 billion_____ people live in cities.

2. In thirty years the world will have _____5 billion_____ people.

3. Rapid population growth is likely to continue until the

_____midle century_____.

4. City living offers many people a better

way of living_____.

5. By the year 2015 there will be 33 megacities, most of them in

_____their developing_____.

6. The urban poor live in conditions that are _____squalor_____ than what they left behind in the rural areas they came from.

7. The _____Worlds Bank_____ is joining the United Nations and the World Resources Institute to help communities solve environmental problems.

8. Sustainable development means economic growth that does not hurt

_____at the expense of future generations_____.

9. The editors are _____in favor of_____ [in favor of/opposed to] the work of the U.N., the World Bank, and other agencies that address the problems of rapid urbanization.

## Expanding Vocabulary

*Use each of the following words in a sentence you create.*

**urban:** _____OUR URBAN CITIES WOULD BECOME MORE POPULATED ———> IN THE FUTURE._____

_____

**literacy:** _____THE LITERACY OF ONE WILL BENEFIT THE SUCCESS IN THE FUTURE._____

_____

**squalor:** _SYNCE THE DOG CAME HERE, MY N_
_DEPARTMENT IS SQUALOR._

**formidable:** _A FORMIDABLE IDEA TO DETER_
_POPULATION FROM COMING TO CITIES IS_
_BY HELPING THEM PROGRESS IN THEIR OWN_
_PLACE S, OR_
_AREAS_

## For Discussion and Reflection

1. What two new pieces of information did you learn from reading this editorial? What is your reaction to this information? Are you surprised? Bothered? Unconcerned?

2. Do you want to live in a big city after completing school? Why or why not?

3. What suggestions do you have for making cities more livable? For improving the quality of life for poor people?

## Your Reading Assessment

1. How accurately did you predict what you would read about?

   _★ I PREDICTED CLOSE BUT I DIDN'T EXPECT_
   _THE CONDITIONS BY WHICH IT FACE THE CITIES._

2. Did the selection answer your questions? _____ YES

   If not, why do you think that it did not?

   _____

3. What comments or questions do you have in response to your reading?

   _THIS CASE IS SURIUS FOR OUR CITIES._
   _IF MORE PEOPLE COME TO THEM, MORE PROBLEMS_
   _WE WOULD FACE IN OUR ECONOMY AND_
   _HEALTH_

## The Signs of Life

by **Helena Curtis and N. Sue Barnes**

The following selection is an excerpt from the introduction to *Invitation to Biology* (4th ed., 1985). Both authors are college professors who have written other books in addition to *Invitation to Biology*.

### ▮ Prepare

1. Identify the authors and work. What do you expect the authors' purpose to be?

_____

_____

2. Preread to identify the subject and make predictions. What do you expect to read about?

_____

_____

3. What do you already know about the subject?

_____

_____

_____

4. Raise two questions that you expect the article to answer.

_____

_____

_____

_____

1    The first characteristic of living things is that they are highly organized. In living things, atoms—the particles of which all matter, both living and nonliving, is composed—are combined into a vast number of very large molecules called macromolecules. Each type of macromolecule has a distinctive structure and a specific function in the life of the organism of which it is a part. Some macromolecules are linked with other macromolecules to form the structures of which the organism's body is composed. Others do not have a structural role but instead participate in the dynamic processes essential for the continuing life of the organism; among the most significant are the large molecules known as enzymes. Enzymes, with the help of a variety of smaller molecules, regulate virtually all of the processes occurring within living matter. The complex organization of both structures and processes is one of the most important properties by which an object can be identified as living.

2    The second characteristic is closely related to the first: living systems maintain a chemical composition quite different from that of their surroundings. The atoms present in living matter are the same as those in the surrounding environment, but they occur in different proportions and are arranged in different ways. Although living systems constantly exchange materials with the external environment, they maintain a stable and characteristic internal environment. This important property is called homeostasis, which means simply "staying the same."

3    A third characteristic of living things is the capacity to take in, transform, and use energy from the environment. For example, in the process of photosynthesis, green plants take light energy from the sun and transform it into chemical energy stored in complex molecules formed from water and the carbon dioxide in the air. The energy stored in these molecules is used by plants to power their life processes and to build the characteristic structures of the plant body. Animals, which can obtain this stored energy by eating plants, change it into still other forms, such as heat, motion, electricity, and chemical energy stored in the characteristic structures of the animal body.

4    Fourth, living things can respond to stimuli. Bacteria move toward or away from certain chemical substances; green plants bend toward light; mealworms congregate where it is damp; cats pounce on small moving objects. Although different organisms respond to widely varying stimuli, the capacity to respond is a fundamental and almost universal characteristic of life.

5    Fifth, and most remarkably, living things have the capacity to reproduce themselves so that, generation after generation, organisms produce more organisms like themselves. In each generation, however, there are slight variations between parents and offspring and among offspring. As we shall see, the slight variations between parents and offspring provide the raw material for evolution.

6    Some living things, primarily very small organisms such as bacteria, amoebas, and some types of algae, reproduce by simply dividing in two. The offspring are usually identical to the parent. Most organisms, however, have a sixth characteristic: they grow and develop. For example, before hatching, the fertilized egg of a frog develops into the complex, but still immature, form that we recognize as a tadpole; after hatching, the tadpole continues to grow and undergoes further development, becoming a mature frog. Throughout the world of living things, similar striking patterns of growth and development occur.

7    A seventh characteristic of living things is that they are exquisitely suited to their environments. Moles, for instance, are furry animals that live underground in tunnels shoveled out by their large forepaws. Their eyes are small and almost sightless. Their noses, with which they sense the worms and other small animals that make up their diet, are fleshy and enlarged. This most important characteristic of living things is known as adaptation.

8    These characteristics of living things are intimately interrelated, and each depends, to a large extent, on the others. At any given moment in its life, an organism is organized, maintains a stable internal environment, transforms energy, responds to stimuli, and is adapted to its external environment; the organism may or may not be reproducing, growing, and developing, but it possesses the capacity to do so.

690 words

## Comprehension Check

*Answer the following with a, b, or c to indicate the phrase that best completes the statement.*

_____ 1. The best statement of the main idea of the passage is
   a. Living things are highly organized.
   b. Living things share certain characteristics that separate them from nonliving things.
   c. All matter is made up of atoms that combine into macromolecules.

_____ 2. Living things have
   a. complex structures.
   b. complex processes.
   c. both a and b.

_____ 3. Living things have a chemical composition that is
   a. the same as their environment.
   b. different from their environment in proportion and arrangement.
   c. without atoms.

_____ 4. The process by which plants take in and transform the sun's energy is called

    a. photosynthesis.
    b. homeostasis.
    c. enzymes.

_____ 5. The most remarkable characteristic of living things is that they

    a. have offspring that are different from the parents.
    b. are made up of atoms.
    c. can reproduce themselves.

_____ 6. The _____ characteristics of living things are interrelated.

    a. five
    b. seven
    c. eight

*Respond to the following statements with either a T (true) or an F (false).*

|  | T | F |
|---|---|---|
| 7. Living things cannot transform energy from their environment. | ___ | ___ |
| 8. Living things can respond to stimuli. | ___ | ___ |
| 9. Living things adapt to their environment. | ___ | ___ |
| 10. Few living things are able to grow and develop. | ___ | ___ |

## ▋ Expanding Vocabulary

*Match each word in the left column with its definition in the right column by placing the correct letter in the space next to each word. When in doubt, read again the sentence in which the word appears.*

_____ molecules (1)        a. ability to adjust to environment

_____ distinctive (1)        b. a living being

_____ organism (1)        c. general makeup

_____ dynamic (1)        d. ability to maintain internal equilibrium

_____ enzymes (1)        e. process of plants that uses light to synthesize carbohydrates

_____ composition (2)        f. beautifully designed

_____ homeostasis (2)        g. marked by continuous change or activity

_____ photosynthesis (3)        h. ability

_____ transform (3)

_____ capacity (4)

_____ exquisitely (7)

_____ adaptation (7)

i. smallest particle an element or compound can be divided into without changing its properties

j. change significantly

k. separate, marking it as different

l. proteins that function as catalysts

## For Discussion and Reflection

1. What organization do the authors use in this passage to present their information? Did your annotation of the passage make that organization clear? If not, reread the guidelines for annotating.

2. Select your favorite animal and illustrate each of the seven characteristics of living things for that animal. For example, if you were to select a cat, then for the fifth characteristic, you would list that cats can have kittens.

3. With your class partner, do the same list for a nonliving thing of your choice to show why that thing does not qualify as a living thing. You may want to do 2 and 3 together in a chart form.

## Your Reading Assessment

1. How accurately did you predict what you would read about?

_____

2. Did the selection answer your questions? _____

    If not, why do you think that it did not?

_____

3. What comments or questions do you have in response to your reading?

_____

_____

_____

## ■ Chapter Review Quiz

*Complete each of the following statements.*

1. The three major steps in your reading strategy are:

    1. _____

    2. _____

    3. _____

2. Because reading is a complex process, the three steps in your reading strategy may _____.

3. It is important to know something about the author and the work because

    _____.

4. When prereading a textbook chapter or article, be sure to read or look at:

    a. _____

    b. _____

    c. _____

    d. _____

    e. _____

5. Identifying what you already know about a topic before reading about it will help you _____.

6. Annotating a text means that you _____.

7. When monitoring comprehension, you may discover that you have lost

    _____.

8. To review successfully, you need to review _____

    and _____.

*The following words have appeared in the chapter or in one of the reading selections. Circle the letter next to the word (or phrase) that is the best definition of the word.*

1. monitor

    a. drive
    b. check
    c. mold

2. glossary

    a. list of specialized words and their definitions
    b. list of glassware makers
    c. glassy

3. megacities

    a. small cities
    b. large cities
    c. old cities

4. urbanization

    a. the making of utilities
    b. moving to the country
    c. the making of cities

5. biennial

    a. happening every second year
    b. happening annually
    c. happening between two groups

6. organism

    a. a nonliving thing
    b. a living thing
    c. a thing that was once alive

7. adaptation

    a. adoption by a new family
    b. adherence to one's family
    c. adjustment to the environment

8. transform

    a. change significantly
    b. transfer to a new place
    c. go beyond, exceed

# CHAPTER 3

## Word Power 1: Using Context Clues and Building Vocabulary

**In this chapter you will learn:**

- Why building vocabulary is important

- How to understand the meaning of unfamiliar words by using context clues

- Strategies for building your vocabulary

- About some good magazines and books to read

### ■ PREPARE TO READ

Read and reflect on the chapter's title and objectives. Glance through the chapter, observing headings to see what is covered. Now answer these questions:

1. What do you expect to learn from this chapter?

_____

_____

2. What do you already know about the chapter's topic?

_____

_____

3. What two or three questions do you want answered from reading this chapter?

_____

_____

_____

_____

What would happen if you tried to play a piano that was missing some of its keys? You would make more noise than beautiful music. You would probably become frustrated and annoyed. Trying to read without a good vocabulary is much the same. You may use active reading strategies and still become frustrated because too many words are "missing."

Studies have shown a strong connection between success at both school and work and a good vocabulary. That's why key exams such as the SATs contain sections on vocabulary. And with a limited vocabulary, it is hard to be part of a serious conversation. Let's face it: Everyone needs a strong vocabulary. The best way to build a strong vocabulary is through reading—or, more precisely, through the study of new words you come across in your reading.

## ■ CONTEXT CLUES

Suppose you were to read the following sentence:

Although they clapped after each speech, the audience gave the most applause to the president's *oration.*

Perhaps *oration* is a word somewhat unfamiliar to you. If you think about how it is used in the sentence, you might guess that it is another word for *speech.* How? The sentence tells you that the audience listened to more than one speech and liked the president's *speech (oration)* the best. You have guessed the word's meaning from its *context,* from the words in the sentence (or sentences) surrounding the unfamiliar word.

Often, you can guess at the meaning of an unfamiliar word by examining the clues in its context. Using context clues means that you can continue to read. You don't have to stop to use the dictionary each time you come to a word that is new. The key is to look for clues, to think about how the word is used.

 **EXERCISE 3-1  Workshop on Understanding Words in Context**

*With your class partner or in small groups, study the context for each word in **bold** type. Then circle the word that comes closest to the meaning of the **bold** type word. Also, briefly explain your reasoning from the context. The first one has been completed for you.*

1. When the judge told the prosecutor to continue her **inquiry,** the prosecutor asked more questions of the witness.

   a. lecture                      c. speech
   b. questioning                  d. argument

   Your reasoning: *What does the prosecutor do when told to continue her inquiry? She questions the witness. So an inquiry must have something to do with questioning.*

2. Some elderly people live in such **abject** poverty that they go without meals.

   a. little                       c. miserable
   b. jaded                        d. charming

   Your reasoning: _____

   _____

   _____

3. The librarian directed the student to the **periodicals** section to find *Time* and the *Wall Street Journal.*

   a. newspapers/magazines         c. periods of history
   b. books                        d. microfilm

   Your reasoning: _____

   _____

   _____

4. Although George was a great basketball player, he felt **inept** at parties.

   a. injured
   b. unskilled, awkward

   c. quiet
   d. noisy

   Your reasoning: _____

   _____

   _____

5. The professor **clarified** the idea by giving several examples.

   a. made essential
   b. challenged

   c. undercut
   d. made clear

   Your reasoning: _____

   _____

   _____

6. Sandra tried to **facilitate** the election process by handing out the ballots.

   a. assist
   b. control

   c. alter
   d. falsify

   Your reasoning: _____

   _____

   _____

7. Feeling trapped when in crowds, Joe stayed on the **periphery** of the group.

   a. angle
   b. inside

   c. outside
   d. personality

   Your reasoning: _____

   _____

   _____

How well did your group do? Were you able to reason from the context to select the correct synonym? Most readers can understand more words in context than they can actually define. Writers also help us, using several strategies to clarify words in context. Let's examine them, one at a time.

## Definition

As you have discovered, textbooks and other assigned readings are filled with new terms. Part of the purpose of a first-year text is to introduce students to the terms and concepts—the language—of the subject area. In psychology you will learn about *cognition* and *paranoia.* In biology you will learn about the *ecosystem* and *organisms.* Fortunately for students, writers usually give definitions of key terms. In the following textbook passage, two terms are defined.

> Energy passes from one organism to another along a particular food chain. A *food chain* is a sequence of organisms related to one another as prey and predator. The first is eaten by the second, the second by the third, and so on, in a series of *tropic levels,* or feeding levels.
>
> Helena Curtis, *Biology*

*Formal Definition:* The first type of definition, for *food chain,* is usually called a formal definition. The term is used in the first sentence of the passage. The second sentence states the meaning of the term, and the third sentence further explains the definition.

Formal definitions are the easiest clues to spot as you read. There are several signal words and visual signals that announce a formal definition. Usually the defined term is printed in *italics* or in **bold** type. Sometimes the definition is repeated in the margin of the page near the definition in the text. Most textbooks also contain a glossary. The term *glossary* refers to an alphabetized list of key terms used in the book, together with their definitions. Formal definitions are often introduced by expressions such as "is" or "means," "refers to," or "consists of." (What signals were used to announce the definition of the word *glossary?*)

*Informal Definition:* The second term defined in the passage above is *trophic levels.* This term is defined informally, in the phrase "or feeding levels." Even though the purpose of the sentence is to further define *food chain,* the sentence also explains the new term, *trophic levels.* Be alert to these helpful informal definitions. Sometimes informal definitions follow a comma after the term, as in the example above. Sometimes they are placed in parentheses (like this), or they follow a dash—like this.

## EXERCISE 3-2  Identifying Passages That Define

*In each of the following sentences, underline the words that provide a definition of the word in **bold** type. Circle all signals. Then state whether the definition is formal or informal. The first one has been completed for you.*

1. (**Advertising** is) paid nonpersonal communication from an identified sponsor using mass media to persuade or influence an audience.

   Wells, Barnett, and Moriarty, *Advertising*

   *formal definition*

2. One of the properties of ecosystems is **productivity,** which is the total amount of energy converted to organic compounds in a given length of time.

   Helena Curtis, *Biology*

3. **Fossils,** the remains or traces of prehistoric life, were also essential to the development of the geologic time scale.

   Tarbuck and Lutgens, *The Earth*

4. A **corporate culture** consists of the shared values, norms, and practices communicated to and followed by those working for a firm.

   Evans and Berman, *Marketing*

5. [Some] psychologists see learning as a **generative** process—that is, the learner **generates** (constructs) meaning by building relationships between familiar and unfamiliar events.

   Lefton and Valvatne, *Mastering Psychology*

6. **Insomnia,** a prolonged inability to sleep, is a common sleep disorder often caused by anxiety or depression.

   Lefton and Valvatne, *Mastering Psychology*

7. Today, many people fear not only the computer, a fear called **cyberphobia,** but they also fear that computers will replace workers.

   Fuller and Manning, *Computers and Information Processing*

## Examples

When not providing formal or informal definitions, writers often clarify words by giving examples. For instance, you may not know the word *malapropism* before reading this sentence:

A common *malapropism* in student writing is the use of "conscious" when the writer needs "conscience."

From the example, you may be able to conclude that a malapropism is an incorrect word accidently used instead of the correct word. Here is another example of this type of context clue. After reading the sentence, write a brief definition or synonym for the word in italics.

A writer's *diction* may range from the formality of Lincoln's "Gettysburg Address" to the slang of rap artists.

_____

From the two examples in the sentence you may be able to conclude that the term *diction* is a synonym for *word choice*. The type of language a writer usually uses is that writer's diction. Notice that neither sample sentence provides a definition of the italicized word. But the examples given in each sentence provide clues to each term's meaning. Examples are sometimes introduced by words such as "for example," "such as," and "including." Not all examples are introduced by signal words, though; they are just part of what the sentence is about.

 **EXERCISE 3-3  Using Examples as Context Clues**

*Write a definition or synonym for each word in **bold** type in the following sentences. Then list the example clues. The first has been started for you.*

1. Working in the library and waiting tables at nearby restaurants are two ways to **augment** college scholarships.

   a. **augment** means:   *add to, increase*

   b. clues:  _____

   _____

2. The Department of Motor Vehicles keeps several **databases,** including a driver's license file and a file on vehicle registration.

   a. **databases** means:  _____

b. clues: _____

_____

3. **Autocratic** rulers from Napoleon to Hitler have changed the course of history.

a. **autocratic** means: _____

b. clues: _____

_____

4. By painting the outside and building a deck in the back, the owners **enhanced** their new home.

a. **enhanced** means: _____

b. clues: _____

_____

5. The cotton gin and the steam engine were two inventions that **spurred** the Industrial Revolution.

a. **spurred** means: _____

b. clues: _____

_____

6. Several **phobias,** including fear of heights, fear of flying, and fear of crowds, limited Michael's social life.

a. **phobias** means: _____

b. clues: _____

_____

7. Jane was quite **frugal;** she used coupons at the grocery store and bought all her clothes on sale.

a. **frugal** means: _____

b. clues: _____

_____

8. **Inanimate** objects include rocks and minerals.

   a. **inanimate** means: _____

   b. clues: _____

   _____

9. Laser surgery and computer-assisted surgery are important **innovations** in medicine.

   a. **innovations** means: _____

   b. clues: _____

   _____

10. The oceans **sustain** many forms of life, from algae to whales.

   a. **sustain** means: _____

   b. clues: _____

   _____

## Comparison and Contrast

Writers often use comparison or contrast to organize a passage or an entire essay. They can also use these patterns to organize a sentence. You can use your recognition of these patterns to help understand the meaning of a new word. Suppose you read the following sentence:

> All winter the trees in my neighborhood were without leaves, but now that spring is here they are covered with new **foliage.**

If you do not know the word *foliage,* you may be able to guess from the contrast structure of the sentence that *foliage* means the opposite of *without leaves.* The contrast of winter and spring also helps readers conclude that *foliage* refers to the leaves that have come out on the trees in the springtime. Here is another example:

> It is incorrect to speak as if all secretaries or nurses are women; it is also **erroneous** to speak as if all lawyers or pilots are men.

Although the first part of the sentence is about women and the second part about men, the two parts of the sentence have the same structure. The writer says that each type of reference to jobs is incorrect—or **erroneous.** The word "also" tells us that both kinds of speech are incorrect, so readers can conclude that the word **erroneous** also means incorrect.

Comparisons are sometimes introduced by "just as," "the same as," "alike," "equate," "also," and "similarly." Contrasts may be signaled by words such as "unlike," "differ," "disagree," "although," "but," "while," "yet," and "on the other hand."

### EXERCISE 3-4  Using Comparison and Contrast Clues

*Write a definition or synonym for each word in **bold** type in the following sentences. Then list any signal words that help to reveal the comparison or contrast structure. The first has been started for you.*

1. Abigail wore a neat, professional-looking suit to her interview, while Susan's clothes were **tawdry**; Abigail was given the job.

   a. **tawdry** means:  *not neat, flashy or cheap*

   b. clues: _____

   _____

2. Although Joe never doubted or questioned his professors' lectures, Rachel was often **skeptical.**

   a. **skeptical** means: _____

   b. clues: _____

   _____

3. The history teacher encouraged his students to **emulate** the leaders of the past rather than trying to be like Michael Jordan.

   a. **emulate** means: _____

   b. clues: _____

   _____

4. A good doctor will tell you honestly and directly what you need to do to get well. Wouldn't it be nice if politicians always spoke just as **candidly**?

   a. **candidly** means: _____

   b. clues: _____

   _____

5. Although Bob was quick to give up on difficult tasks, Boris remained **tenacious,** no matter how hard the assignment.

   a. **tenacious** means: _____

   b. clues: _____

   _____

6. Although it is not smart to ignore problems or pretend they don't matter, it is just as unwise to **brood** endlessly over every little problem.

   a. **brood** means: _____

   b. clues: _____

   _____

7. The twins were so different at feeding time. Jill ate everything and liked to try new foods, but Jake was a **finicky** eater.

   a. **finicky** means: _____

   b. clues: _____

   _____

8. The young candidate's speeches were loud and challenging, whereas the mature candidate's style was softer and more **subtle.**

   a. **subtle** means: _____

   b. clues: _____

   _____

9. To make decisions, some business managers study sales figures and other available facts, while others rely more on their **intuition.**

   a. **intuition** means: _____

   b. clues: _____

   _____

10. Most of the first graders clapped and cheered the silly clown, but a few remained **passive.**

   a. **passive** means: _____

b. clues: _____

_____

## Experience/Logic

Not all sentences contain specific clues such as examples or contrast. Still, you can often guess at a word's meaning by using your experience or by reasoning from the information in the sentence. For example, suppose you read the following sentence:

He wished that he could write speeches that were as **eloquent** as Martin Luther King's.

If you have read King's "I Have a Dream" or have heard about his speeches, you can draw on your experience to conclude that **eloquent** means expressive and moving. Another approach is to reason from the context of the sentence. The writer wants to write speeches like King's, so we can guess that King's speeches must be very good. Very good or **eloquent** speeches are effective or moving works.

### EXERCISE 3-5  Using Experience or Logic to Understand New Words

*Write a definition or synonym for each word in **bold** type in the following sentences. Then briefly explain how you decided on the word's meaning. The first one has been started for you.*

1. The judge told the jury to continue talking to try to reach **consensus** on a verdict.

   a. **consensus** means: *agreement*

   b. your reasoning: _____

   _____

2. When the family entered the kitchen, they were nearly overcome by the horrible smell that **pervaded** the room.

   a. **pervaded** means: _____

   b. your reasoning: _____

   _____

3. Although John was somewhat **intimidated** by his new boss, he tried not to show any anxiety in the office.

   a. **intimidated** means: _____

   b. your reasoning: _____

   _____

4. Martha's mother worried about her living in New York City, but Martha loved the excitement of **urban** living.

   a. **urban** means: _____

   b. your reasoning: _____

   _____

5. When the doctor could not **alleviate** Dorothy's pain with medication, he recommended surgery for the tennis star.

   a. **alleviate** means: _____

   b. your reasoning: _____

   _____

6. The students wondered if their backpacks received more **scrutiny** than the other travelers' suitcases because the students were young and wearing jeans.

   a. **scrutiny** means: _____

   b. your reasoning: _____

   _____

7. The crowd's excitement grew as they **anticipated** their team's entrance into the stadium.

   a. **anticipated** means: _____

   b. your reasoning: _____

   _____

8. To express his **adoration,** the young man brought flowers to his lady.

   a. **adoration** means: _____

b. your reasoning: _____

_____

9. Juan remained **disconsolate** because he had dropped his ice cream cone, even though his sister offered to share hers.

a. **disconsolate** means: _____

b. your reasoning: _____

_____

10. Noting the car's **erratic** movements, the police started pursuit.

a. **erratic** means: _____

b. your reasoning: _____

_____

EXERCISE 3-6 **Using Context Clues When Reading Paragraphs**

*Write a brief definition or synonym for each word in **bold** type in the following paragraphs. Use context clues to help you. Compare your responses with classmates.*

## Paragraph 1

In time, your college experiences and activities will change you as well as your life. They will increase your knowledge and **competence,** and influence your attitudes and values. They will add **conspicuously** to your career opportunities and **modify** your **avocational** interests. Your plans for the future will change. The experiences you **encounter,** the **diverse** persons you meet, all will have an impact on the kinds of friends and types of relationships you enjoy. Your **cultural** and political **sensitivities** and **sophistication** will expand, your ability to **contribute** to your community and to work on other societal issues will grow.

Chickering and Schlossberg, *How to Get the Most Out of College*

1. **competence** _____

2. **conspicuously** _____

3. **modify** _____

4. **avocational** _____

5. **encounter** _____

6. **diverse** _____

7. **cultural** _____

8. **sensitivities** _____

9. **sophistication** _____

10. **contribute** _____

## Paragraph 2

Jefferson, one of the country's greatest **expansionists,** established the Lewis and Clark **expedition** to explore the country west of the Mississippi River. Jefferson believed that the United States's **exploding** population would eventually fill the entire **continent.** In August 1803, Lewis **embarked** on one of the most demanding **exploits** in American history. Lewis picked up Clark and **recruits** for their adventure in October 1803. Lewis and Clark worked well together; never quarreling, they **complemented** one another's personalities. Surviving their journey into the unknown, they returned to **recognition** but not the fortune their journey **warranted.** Lewis was **inept** as governor of the Louisiana Territory, began drinking heavily, and killed himself in 1809. Clark was finally able to get their *Journals* published, but without all their descriptions of new animals and plants.

1. **expansionists** _____

2. **expedition** _____

3. **exploding** _____

4. **continent** _____

5. **embarked** _____

6. **exploits** _____

7. **recruits** _____

8. **complemented** _____

9. **recognition** _____

10. **warranted** _____

11. **inept** _____

## Paragraph 3

Broadly speaking, **offensive** language is that which **denigrates** people because of gender, race, **ethnicity,** class, sexual preference, age or **disability.** It also includes **obscene** or sexually **explicit** language. Common to all offensive language is intent: to put down those who are different or less fortunate than others. Whether a racial **slur,** a **sexist** statement, or a **demeaning stereotype,** most people agree that such language is obvious and ugly. And most would agree that the **habitual** use of it **perpetuates** damning and **subjugating** attitudes toward its victims.

Gary Goshgarian, *Exploring Language,* 7th ed.

1. **offensive** _____

2. **denigrates** _____

3. **ethnicity** _____

4. **disability** _____

5. **obscene** _____

6. **explicit** _____

7. **slur** _____

8. **sexist** _____

9. **demeaning** _____

10. **stereotype** _____

11. **habitual** _____

12. **perpetuates** _____

13. **subjugating** _____

## Paragraph 4

The climatic **equilibrium** of our planet is now **threatened** by the greenhouse effect of carbon dioxide **accumulating** in the atmosphere. The carbon dioxide comes partly from burning of coal and oil and partly from destruction of forests. Fortunately, there is a remedy. The **quantity** of carbon in the atmosphere is about equal to the quantity in living trees. This means that the problem of the greenhouse is **essentially** a problem of forest management. A large-scale international program of **reforestation** could hold the greenhouse in check, besides producing many other economic and environmental benefits. The cost of growing enough trees to **nullify** the greenhouse is not **prohibitive.** Only the will and the international **consensus** required to do the job are at present lacking. But we shall probably see the will and the consensus **emerge,** as soon as the climatic effects of the greenhouse become more **severe.** When that happens, the whole world will begin planting trees.

Freeman Dyson, *From Eros to Gaia*

1. **equilibrium** _____

2. **threatened** _____

3. **accumulating** _____

4. **quantity** _____

5. **essentially** _____

6. **reforestation** _____

7. **nullify** _____

8. **prohibitive** _____

9. **consensus** _____

10. **emerge** _____

11. **severe** _____

## ■ LEARNING NEW WORDS

Using context clues to aid understanding of a word helps make reading easier, but context can't help readers all the time. Also, the meaning you figure out from one context may not help when you find the word in another context. Then, too, there is a difference between having enough clues to a word's meaning to be able to continue reading and knowing the word so well that you can use it in speaking and writing. To really know a word, you have to *overlearn* it. Words that are truly a part of your working vocabulary are words that you can use and that you can get meaning from quickly as you read. How can you build your word power? Here are some strategies to use.

## Keep a Vocabulary Notebook

To expand your working vocabulary, you need to study new words in an organized way. One method is to make a list of new words to learn either in a section of your notebook for this class or in a separate vocabulary notebook. To make your notebook list a useful study tool, follow these steps.

### A Vocabulary Notebook: Guidelines

1. Use a looseleaf (not a spiral) notebook so that you can remove pages for studying.

2. Draw a line down each page about one-third of the way from the left margin.

3. Write each word to be learned in a list down the left side of the page. If you are not sure how to pronounce the word, write the phonetic spelling under the word. (You will find the phonetic spelling in a dictionary immediately after the initial entry word. See Chapter 4 for information on pronunciation guides in the dictionary.)

4. On the right side of the page, across from each vocabulary word, write the word's definition(s). Include a sentence in which the word is used, but draw a line where the word would go instead of writing it in the sentence. You may also want to include a synonym of the word. You will need several lines on the ~ight side of the page for each word listed on the left. (See Figure 3.1 for a sample vocabulary notebook page.)

5. Now you can study the words in one of two ways. First, fold back the right side of the page so that you can see only the words. See if you can state each word's definition and use each one in a sentence. Sometimes study the words by folding back the left side of the page. By looking at the definition, the sentence (with the word missing), and a synonym, can you name the word? Whenever you are stuck, check the information on the folded-back part of the page. Study with a classmate whenever possible.

■ FIGURE 3.1

**Sample Vocabulary Notebook Page**

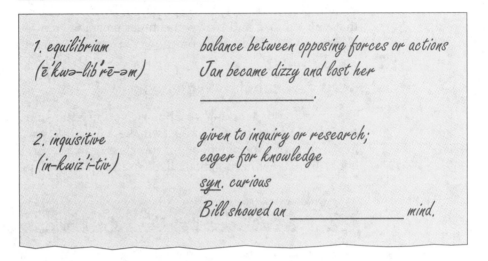

1. equilibrium          balance between opposing forces or actions
(ē'kwə-lib'rē-əm)       Jan became dizzy and lost her
                        _____.

2. inquisitive          given to inquiry or research;
(in-kwiz'i-tiv)         eager for knowledge
                        syn. curious
                        Bill showed an _____ mind.

## Make Vocabulary Cards

Many students have learned the value of flash cards for learning information that can be divided into small segments. You can make your own flash cards to learn new words by using a set of 3" × 5" index cards. Follow these guidelines.

### Vocabulary Cards: Guidelines

1. Make one card for each new word. Start the cards either when you come across new words or later from the words you have circled in your reading.
2. Write each word on one side of a card. If you have trouble pronouncing the word, add the word's phonetic spelling to this side of the card.
3. Find the meaning(s) of the word in your dictionary and write the definition(s) on the other side of the card. Note any word parts (which you will study in Chapter 4) and their meanings, for example: AUTO = self. Also include examples or synonyms of the word and a sentence in which you use the word (but put a line in the sentence where the word would go.)

4. Now you can test yourself in one of two ways. Look at the word on the front of the card and say its definition to yourself. Also try to use it in a sentence. Then turn to the back of the card to see if you have defined and used the word correctly. You can also study the definitions and sample sentences on the back to see if you can name the word on the front of the card.

5. After you think you have really learned some of the words, divide your stack of cards into two piles: one for the words you have learned and one for the words you still need to study. Continue to practice with the words you do not know and with the new cards you keep adding to your stack.

6. Shuffle the cards after each practice so that you do not go through the words in the same order each time.

7. Every week or so, review the stack of cards you have set aside, just to make sure that you continue to be comfortable with them. Study with a classmate whenever possible. (Sample vocabulary cards are illustrated in Figure 3.2.)

## Learn New Words from Reading

Only you can build your word power. You can begin by circling every word in this chapter that is not now a part of your working vocabulary. Then start a vocabulary notebook or make cards for these words.

■ FIGURE 3.2

**Sample Vocabulary Cards**

inquisitive
(in-kwiz′i-tiv)

(front)

given to inquiry or research;
eager for knowledge
syn. curious
Bill showed an
_____ mind.

(back)

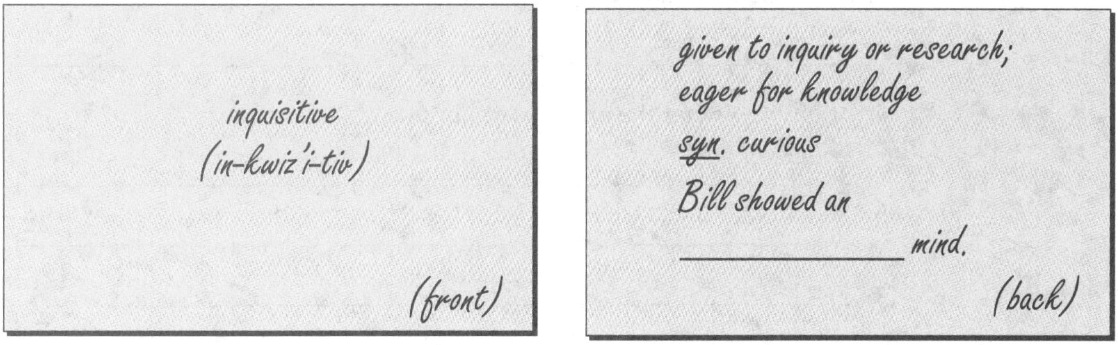

You can also learn new words from your general reading. Try to keep your notebook or cards handy when reading so that you can make a note of new words. When you collect four or five new words to study, look them up in your dictionary to complete entries for them. Then add them to your regular vocabulary study.

What are you reading—in addition to your textbooks? The best way to expand your vocabulary is to develop the habit of regular reading. Try to find at least 45 minutes each day for this activity. Get a morning newspaper that you can read while eating breakfast or between classes. Consider a subscription to one of the weekly newsmagazines: *Time, Newsweek,* or *U.S. News and World Report.* In addition to carrying the week's news, newsmagazines contain interesting cover stories ranging from dinosaurs to artificial intelligence. Look through your library's magazine collection for one related to your hobbies or interests. Or, consider developing a new interest by regularly reading magazines such as *Sports Illustrated, Ebony, Redbook, Discover,* or *Psychology Today.* These are just a few possibilities; your library has hundreds of magazines from which to choose.

### EXERCISE 3-7  Newspaper or Magazine Reading

*Find a newspaper or magazine that you want to read each week. (If you select a monthly magazine, plan to read at least one article each week.) Answer the following questions about the work you have selected.*

1. What is the name of the work you have selected?

   _____

2. Is the periodical published daily, weekly, or monthly?

   _____

3. List the title and author of one article you have read.

   _____

4. Briefly tell what the article was about.

   _____

   _____

   _____

   _____

5. What is one new fact or idea you learned from your reading?

_____

_____

_____

In addition to developing the habit of journal reading, you want to become comfortable reading books. One strategy for pleasurable book reading is to be sure to get a good start into the book. When you begin, read for at least 45 minutes without stopping. This way you will have a better idea of what is happening in the book when you return to it a day or several days later.

## EXERCISE 3-8  Reading a Book

*Select a book from the list that follows this exercise, or one that your instructor approves, and complete the following questions.*

1. What is the name of the book you have selected?

_____

2. Who is the author and when was the book published?

_____

3. Based on reading the first 50 pages, explain what the book is about. If it is a novel, include the characters introduced so far and where the story takes place.

_____

_____

_____

_____

_____

_____

_____

4. When you complete the book, be prepared to summarize and evaluate it in a five-minute talk for classmates.

## ■ A Brief Book List

### Some Classic Novels

Willa Cather, *My Antonia*    The story of an immigrant American farm girl, and of the country she grew up with.

Stephen Crane, *The Red Badge of Courage*    Placed in the Civil War, an important comment on growing up—and on war.

Ernest Hemingway, *A Farewell to Arms*    Drawn from his own experience in World War I, a book about war and love and loss.

George Orwell, *Animal Farm*    Orwell's satiric portrait of a society of animals who seem very much like us.

Mark Twain, *Adventures of Huckleberry Finn*    Adventures of a young boy and a runaway slave on the Mississippi before the Civil War.

Edith Wharton, *Ethan Frome*    The sad tale of stoic Ethan, his sickly wife, and a young cousin who comes to live with them.

### Some Contemporary Novels and Autobiographies

Richard Adams, *Watership Down*    A delightful story about some rabbits—with noticeable human characteristics.

Maya Angelou, *I Know Why the Caged Bird Sings*    A moving autobiography of an African American girl from Arkansas.

Saul Bellow, *A Theft*    A short, engaging tale of Clara Velde and her lost ring.

Sandra Cisernos, *The House on Mango Street*    Growing up in an Hispanic family on a street that does not represent the American dream.

William Golding, *Lord of the Flies*    A group of young boys, alone, try to create their own society.

Richard Harris, *The Fatherland*    Romance and intrigue in Europe after World War II—with Germany winning the war.

James Herriot, *All Creatures Great and Small, All Things Wise and Wonderful, Every Living Thing*    Engaging memoirs of an English veterinarian.

Harper Lee, *To Kill a Mockingbird*    A best-selling novel made into a successful movie, about problems in a small town as seen through the eyes of a young girl.

Alison Lurie, *The Truth about Lorin Jones*    A recently divorced biographer seeks to learn the truth about the life and early death of a young painter—and learns about herself in the process.

Bernard Malamud, *The Natural* A washed-up baseball player makes a comeback.

Mary Mebane, *Mary* Mebane's life growing up in rural North Carolina.

J. D. Salinger, *Catcher in the Rye* The experiences of one of literature's most famous teenagers.

Mark Salzman, *The Soloist* About music, performing, growing up, and knowing oneself.

Jane Smiley, *A Thousand Acres* The relationships among a father, with his desire for a thousand-acre farm, and his three daughters.

Amy Tan, *The Joy Luck Club* Life in an Asian American community in California.

E. B. White, *Charlotte's Web* A wonderful tale of friendship with Wilbur—some pig!

# Naming

by **Rosalie Maggio**

Rosalie Maggio is a textbook editor, a writer of children's stories, and the author of books and articles on language. The following excerpt is from the introduction to her guide *The Dictionary of Bias-Free Usage: A Guide to Nondiscriminatory Language,* which was published in 1991. Maggio reminds us that "language both reflects and shapes society."

## Prepare

1. Identify the author and work. What do you expect the author's purpose to be?

_____

_____

2. Preread to identify the subject and make predictions. What do you expect to read about?

_____

_____

3. What do you already know about the subject?

 

 

 

4. Raise two questions that you expect the article to answer.

 

 

 

1    Naming is power, which is why the issue of naming is one of the most important in bias-free language.

**Self-Definition**

2    People decide what they want to be called. The correct names for individuals and groups are always those by which they refer to themselves. This "tradition" is not always unchallenged. Haig Bosmajian (*The Language of Oppression*) says, "It isn't strange that those persons who insist on defining themselves, who insist on this elemental privilege of self-naming, self-definition, and self-identity encounter vigorous resistance. Predictably, the resistance usually comes from the oppressor or would-be oppressor and is a result of the fact that he or she does not want to relinquish the power which comes from the ability to define others."

3    Dr. Ian Hancock uses the term *exonym* for a name applied to a group by outsiders. For example, Romani peoples object to being called by the exonym *Gypsies*. They do not call themselves Gypsies. Among the many other exonyms are: the elderly, colored people, homosexuals, pagans, adolescents, Eskimos, pygmies, savages. The test for an exonym is whether people describe themselves as "redmen," "illegal aliens," "holy rollers," etc., or whether only outsiders describe them that way.

4    There is a very small but visible element today demanding that gay men "give back" the word *gay*—a good example of denying people the right to name themselves. A late-night radio caller said several times that gay men had "stolen" this word from "our" language. It was not clear what language gay men spoke.

5    A woman nicknamed "Betty" early in life had always preferred her full name, "Elizabeth." On her fortieth birthday, she reverted to Eliza-

In paragraph 4, why are the words "stolen" and "our" in quotation marks?

_____

Does the author agree with the radio caller?

_____

beth. An acquaintance who heard about the change said sharply, "I'll call her Betty if I like!"

6    We can call them Betty if we like, but it's arrogant, insensitive, and uninformed: the only rule we have in this area says we call people what they want to be called.

### "Insider/Outsider" Rule

7    A related rule says that insiders may describe themselves in ways that outsiders may not. "Crip" appears in *The Disability Rag;* this does not mean that the word is available to anyone who wants to use it. "Big Fag" is printed on a gay man's T-shirt. He may use that expression; a non-gay may not so label him. One junior-high student yells to another, "Hey, nigger!" This would be highly offensive and inflammatory if the speaker were not African American. A group of women talk about "going out with the girls," but a co-worker should not refer to them as "girls." When questioned about just such a situation, Miss Manners replied that "people are allowed more leeway in what they call themselves than in what they call others."

### "People First" Rule

8    Haim Ginott taught us that labels are disabling; intuitively most of us recognize this and resist being labeled. The disability movement originated the "people first" rule, which says we don't call someone a "diabetic" but rather "a person with diabetes." Saying someone is "an AIDS victim" reduces the person to a disease, a label, a statistic; use instead "a person with/who has/living with AIDS." The 1990 Americans with Disabilities Act is a good example of correct wording. Name the person as a person first, and let qualifiers (age, sex, disability, race) follow, but (and this is crucial) only if they are relevant. Readers of a magazine aimed at an older audience were asked what they wanted to be called (elderly? senior citizens? seniors? golden agers?). They rejected all the terms; one said, "How about 'people'?" When high school students rejected labels like kids, teens, teenagers, youth, ado-

lescents, and juveniles, and were asked in exasperation just what they would like to be called, they said, "Could we just be people?"

**Women as Separate People**

9    One of the most sexist maneuvers in the language has been the identification of women by their connections to husband, son, or father—often even after he is dead. Women are commonly identified as someone's widow while men are never referred to as anyone's widower. Marie Marvingt, a Frenchwoman who lived around the turn of the century, was an inventor, adventurer, stunt woman, superathlete, aviator, and all-around scholar. She chose to be affianced to neither man (as a wife) nor God (as a religious), but it was not long before an uneasy male press found her a fit partner. She is still known today by the revealing label "the Fiancée of Danger." If a connection is relevant, make it mutual. Instead of "Frieda, his wife of seventeen years," write "Frieda and Eric, married for seventeen years."

10    It is difficult for some people to watch women doing unconventional things with their names. For years the etiquette books were able to tell us precisely how to address a single woman, a married woman, a divorced woman, or a widowed woman (there was no similar etiquette on men because they have always been just men and we have never had a code to signal their marital status). But now some women are Ms. and some are Mrs., some are married but keeping their birth names, others are hyphenating their last name with their husband's, and still others have constructed new names for themselves. Some women—including African American women who were denied this right earlier in our history—take great pride in using their husband's name. All these forms are correct. The same rule of self-definition applies here: call the woman what she wants to be called.

910 words

■ **Comprehension Check**

*Answer the following with a, b, or c to indicate the phrase that best completes the statement.*

_____ 1. Those who don't like people who insist on naming themselves are often

a. their friends.
b. oppressors.
c. traditionalists.

_____ 2. The author argues that the issue over who determines a group's name is an issue of

  a. power.
  b. manners.
  c. language.

_____ 3. The term _exonym_ is used for a name attached to a group by

  a. doctors.
  b. insiders.
  c. outsiders.

_____ 4. The author makes the point that people have a right to

  a. call people gypsies.
  b. oppress others.
  c. name themselves.

_____ 5. An example of an exonym is

  a. homosexual.
  b. Eskimo.
  c. both a and b.

_____ 6. The "insider/outsider" rule states that

  a. outsiders may not always use labels that insiders use.
  b. outsiders should use labels that insiders use.
  c. both a and b.

_____ 7. The "people first" rule reminds us

  a. to put people ahead of animals.
  b. not to label people.
  c. not to use a person's name.

_____ 8. Qualifying words about age, race, or sex should be used

  a. only if they are relevant.
  b. as the best way to identify someone.
  c. just for teenagers.

_____ 9. Today women are

  a. using different forms for their names.
  b. not automatically to be identified by relationship to a man.
  c. both a and b.

_____10. The best way to use language is to

   a. refer to people just as you please.
   b. avoid bias and labeling.
   c. refer to women as girls and teenagers as kids.

## ■ Expanding Vocabulary

*Match each word in the left column with its definition in the right column by placing the correct letter in the space next to each word. When in doubt, read again the sentence in which the word appears.*

| | |
|---|---|
| _____ elemental (2) | a. stuck up, self-important |
| _____ oppressor (2) | b. without knowledge |
| _____ relinquish (2) | c. freedom |
| _____ arrogant (6) | d. knowing as if instinctively |
| _____ insensitive (6) | e. with impatience and annoyance |
| _____ uninformed (6) | f. one who unjustly holds another down |
| _____ inflammatory (7) | g. strategies |
| _____ leeway (7) | h. discrimination based on gender |
| _____ intuitively (8) | i. give up, release |
| _____ exasperation (8) | j. arousing strong feelings |
| _____ sexist (9) | k. fundamental, basic |
| _____ maneuvers (9) | l. relating to marriage |
| _____ etiquette (10) | m. unfeeling |
| _____ marital (10) | n. good manners |

## ■ For Discussion and Reflection

1. What does the author provide to make her points clear to readers? Is she effective? That is, after you read each section, do you understand what she is writing about?

2. Do you think that people, including yourself, should be called by the names they choose? Why or why not?

3. Do you belong to a group (racial, ethnic, age, religious) for which others have unkind labels? If so, how do those labels make you feel? Can "names" hurt us?

## Your Reading Assessment.

1. How accurately did you predict what you would read about?

   _____

2. Did the selection answer your questions? _____

   If not, why do you think that it did not?

   _____

3. What comments or questions do you have in response to your reading?

   _____

   _____

   _____

## Chapter Review Quiz.

*Complete each of the following statements or answer the questions.*

1. What are the advantages of a good vocabulary?

   _____

2. One way to guess the meaning of new words is to study their

   _____.

3. A word's context refers to

   _____.

4. What visual signals do textbooks often use for terms that will be defined?

   _____

5. What are three strategies for recognizing words in their contexts?

   _____

6. What are two strategies for studying vocabulary words?

_____

7. Most adults build their vocabularies from _____.

*The following words have appeared in the chapter or in the reading selection. Circle the letter next to the word or phrase that is the best definition of the word.*

1. context

   a. a writer's word choice
   b. a speech
   c. the words surrounding another word

2. facilitate

   a. falsify
   b. assist
   c. alter

3. fossils

   a. remains of prehistoric life
   b. feeding levels
   c. leftovers

4. diction

   a. a writer's draft
   b. a speech
   c. a writer's word choice

5. innovations

   a. invitations
   b. new procedures
   c. traditions

6. embarked

   a. set out
   b. embargo
   c. exploded

7. inquisitive

   a. equilibrium
   b. curious, eager for knowledge
   c. inaction

8. exonym

    a. pseudonym
    b. name applied to students
    c. name applied to a group by those not in the group

9. relinquish

    a. rekindle
    b. release
    c. rename

*Write a brief definition or synonym for each word in **bold** type in the following paragraph. Use context clues to help you.*

> We find reasons to be **optimistic,** if cautiously so, about the future of Russia, **despite** the **pessimism** that seems to be the order of the day. Russia has many resources, including an educated, creative, and technologically **proficient** population. We do not **underestimate** the enormously difficult problems Russia faces and the pressures and conflicts that **constrain** choices. But we do not think that Russia is necessarily **poised** to break up; at least, strong forces exist that will **counteract** a movement toward **dissolution.**

> Daniel Yergin and Thane Gustafson, *Russia 2010*

1. **optimistic** _____

2. **despite** _____

3. **pessimism** _____

4. **proficient** _____

5. **underestimate** _____

6. **constrain** _____

7. **poised** _____

8. **counteract** _____

9. **dissolution** _____

# CHAPTER 4

## Word Power 2: Recognizing Word Parts and Knowing Your Dictionary

In this chapter you will learn:

- How a knowledge of word parts can help you understand new words

- The meanings of some common roots, prefixes, and suffixes

- How to read a dictionary entry

- Strategies for pronouncing new words

- The kinds of information available in a dictionary

### ■ PREPARE TO READ

Read and reflect on the chapter's title and objectives. Glance through the chapter, observing headings to see what is covered. Now answer these questions:

1. What do you expect to learn from this chapter?

_____  _____

_____

2. What do you already know about the chapter's topic?

_____

_____

3. What two or three questions do you want answered from reading this chapter?

_____

_____

_____

_____

In Chapter 3 you learned how to use context clues to make good guesses about a word's meaning. Using context clues lets you keep reading through a passage without having to look up words in a dictionary. But suppose the context alone does not help you with an unfamiliar word. You have another strategy to use before turning to the dictionary. You can study the word's parts.

## ■ COMPOUND WORDS

You probably already study the parts of compound words—those made up of two words—to get their meaning. There are many compound words in English, words such as:

| | |
|---|---|
| **over/flow** | to flow over the top |
| **sea/shore** | land by the sea |
| **sales/person** | one who sells merchandise |
| **farm/land** | land suitable for farming |
| **good/hearted** | kind, generous |

### EXERCISE 4-1 Workshop on Compound Words

*With your partner or in small groups, make compound words using each of the words in the following list. In some cases, you may be able to think of more than one. List all the compound words you can make. Briefly define each compound word you make.*

**sky/** _____

**over/** _____

**watch/** _____

**back/** _____

**news/** _____

Think of how many words you know that are actually made up of two separate words. Of course compound words are not always spelled as one word. They can be written as two words (ice cream) or hyphenated (mother-in-law). But since we are concerned with "seeing words within words," we have looked only at compound words written as one word. When you come to an unfamiliar word, if you can recognize that it is made up of two smaller words, you may be able to figure out its meaning.

## ▥ LEARNING FROM WORD PARTS: PREFIXES, ROOTS, AND SUFFIXES

We also make words by combining parts that do not, by themselves, make a word. Or, we can attach a word part to a complete word to make a new word.

Word parts that are placed at the beginning of a word (or word part) are called *prefixes*. Word parts that carry the primary meaning of a word are called *roots*. And, word parts that are placed at the end of a word (or word part) are called *suffixes*. Consider the root *mort* (or *mor*). It means death. If we add a suffix, we can make the word *mortal*. (We are only *mortal* because we will die.) If we add the prefix *im*, meaning not, to *mortal*, we can make the word *immortal*. *Immortal* refers to one who is not mortal.

| Prefix | Root | Suffix |
|--------|------|--------|
| im | mort | al |

We can add another suffix and make the noun *immortality*, the state or condition of being immortal. *Immortality* may seem at first glance to be a challenging word, but if we see the parts that make up the word, and know their separate meanings, then we can figure out what the longer word means.

Many roots and prefixes come from Latin; others come from Greek. If you can learn to recognize twenty or so roots—and learn the meanings of the most common prefixes and suffixes that can alter those roots—you will build your word power by hundreds of words. The key is to recognize the root, even though it may have more than one spelling, and to understand what the prefix (or suffix) does to alter the root. Look, for example, at the root *vis* (or *vid*) which means *see*. This root gives us the word *vision*. Can you find the root in each of the following words and decide on the word's meaning? Divide the word into its parts and then define it. The first has been done for you.

video     *vid/eo   visual portion of a television show*
_____

visibility  _____

revise  _____

invisible  _____

To define these three words, you need to know the root meaning, but you also need to understand the effect of two suffixes and two prefixes on that root. We will begin with a study of prefixes, but first some important reminders.

### Remember:

1. You cannot learn every word part at once; some practice and drilling may be necessary.
2. You are already familiar with many of the word parts on the following lists.
3. Not all words have a prefix or suffix, even though they may begin or end with letters that can make a prefix or suffix. For example, *mis/take* begins with the prefix *mis*, but *missile* does not begin with a prefix.
4. Words can have more than one prefix or root or suffix, as do some of the "*vis*" words you just studied.
5. Some word parts change spelling when they combine with other word parts, so they may be difficult to recognize at first. You have already seen that *vis* and *vid* are two spellings of the same word part.

## Prefixes That Express Time or Place

Here is a list of the most common prefixes that express an idea of time or place. Study the prefixes and their meanings for a few minutes and then complete the exercise that follows.

| Prefix | Meaning | Example |
|---|---|---|
| circum | around | circumference |
| de | away, undo | depart |
| ex | from, out of | export |
| inter | between | interchange |
| intro/intra | within, in | intramural |
| post | after | postgraduate |
| pre | before | prefix |
| re | back, again | regain |
| retro | backward | retroactive |
| sub | under | submarine |
| super | above | supernatural |
| trans | across, over | transatlantic |

## Exercise 4-2 Working with Time and Place Prefixes

*I. Fill in the blank with the appropriate prefix to make a word that fits the context of the sentence.*

1. Jane spends some time each day in quiet _____spec-tion.

2. The instructor asked students to _____view their notes for the next quiz.

3. The meeting was _____poned until Thursday so that all committee members could attend.

4. Grade school teachers need to help students with their _____ personal relationships.

5. As the plane approached the airport, it began to _____crease its speed, or _____celerate.

6. It is important to _____serve our natural resources.

*II. Fill in the blanks to complete the statement or answer the question.*

7. When Magellan *circumnavigated* the world, what did he do?

_____

8. When the actress puts a *superhuman* effort into her role, has she performed well or poorly? _____

9. When the cowboy *subjugated* the wild horse, he

_____.

10. If *gress* means to step, then to *transgress* means to

_____.

11. If the vacation *revitalized* the tired executive, how does the executive feel now?

_____

12. If *spect* means to look at or see, then *retrospect* means

_____.

## Prefixes That Create a Negative or Reversal

What follows is a list of some key prefixes that express a negative concept or reverse the meaning of the root. For example, when you add *dis* to the word *agree,* you reverse the meaning; you no longer agree. Similarly, if you are not settled in your new home, then you are *un*settled. Notice the several spellings that have the same meaning as *in.* The spelling of this prefix is affected by the first letter of the root to which it is attached. We say *inactive* but *illicit.* Study the prefixes and their meanings, and then complete the exercise that follows.

| Prefix | Meaning | Example |
|---|---|---|
| a | not | asymmetrical |
| anti | against | anticlimax |
| contra | against | contraception |
| dis | apart, not | disagree |
| in/il/ir/im | not, into | inactive |
| mis | wrong | misrepresent |
| non | not | nonfiction |
| un | not | unsettled |

**EXERCISE 4-3 Working with Negative Prefixes**

*Fill in the blank with the appropriate prefix to make a word that fits the context of the sentence.*

1. The protestor's signs made clear their _____war feelings.

2. The players objected to the change of match time as highly _____regular.

3. Heroes have _____common abilities.

4. Michael Johnson's running skill is truly _____typical.

5. The accountant argued that the error was a _____take.

6. The magician made the rabbit _____appear.

7. The manager insisted that her decision was _____reversible.

8. Jane thought that Peter's argument was _____logical.

9. During the meeting, James felt that he had to _____dict his colleague and present a different explanation of the problem.

10. Ruth enjoyed reading biography and other _____fiction works.

## Additional Prefixes

Here are a few more prefixes you should know. Study them and then complete the exercise that follows.

| Prefix | Meaning | Example |
|--------|---------|---------|
| auto | self | autograph |
| bi | two, twice | bimonthly |
| hetero | different | heterogeneous |
| mono | one, single, alone | monorail |
| poly | many | polygraph |
| semi | half, partial | semidarkness |

 **EXERCISE 4-4 More Work with Prefixes**

*Fill in the blanks to answer each of the following questions.*

1. If the conference is held *semiannually,* how many times a year is it held?

   _____

2. *Gam* is a root for marriage. Those who practice *polygamy* have what kind of marriage?

   _____

3. A *heterosexual* relationship describes what kind of sexual relationship?

   _____

4. If *lateral* refers to a side, then *bilateral* means

   _____.

5. Why are cars called *automobiles?*

   _____

   _____

6. If you talk in a *monotone,* how are you talking?

   _____

## Suffixes

Suffixes, word parts placed at the end of words, have two functions. Sometimes a suffix changes the word's part of speech and therefore how the word is used in a sentence. For example:

Martha showed *sympathy* for her brother. (noun)
Martha has a *sympathetic* feeling for her brother. (adjective)
Martha spoke *sympathetically* to her brother. (adverb)

You probably already know that you can turn many adjectives into adverbs by adding the suffix *ly* (angry/angrily; beautiful/beautifully).

Suffixes can also make new words, or alter the meaning of a root. For example, the adjective *kind* becomes a noun referring to the state of being kind when "ness" is added: *kindness.* When "er" is added to the verb *teach,* we have "one who" teaches, a *teacher.* More than one suffix can be added to many words, and some new words are made by adding two suffixes to a root word. The following table organizes suffixes by the way they alter a word. Study the table, add your example, and then work the exercise that follows.

■ **Common Suffixes**

| Suffix | Example | Your Example |
|---|---|---|
| *Suffixes meaning "one who":* | | |
| -an | comedian | |
| -ant | communicant | |
| -ee | employee | |
| -eer | pamphleteer | |
| -er | teacher | |
| -ist | tourist | |
| -or | sailor | |
| *Suffixes meaning "referring to":* | | |
| -al | seasonal | |
| -ship | ownership | |
| -hood | bachelorhood | |
| -ward | backward | |
| *Suffixes establishing a condition, doctrine, or quality:* | | |
| -able/ible | audible | |
| -ance/ence | excellence | |
| -ic | angelic | |
| -ion/tion | election | |
| -ish | babyish | |
| -ism | realism | |
| -ity | inferiority | |
| -ive | restive | |
| -less | worthless | |
| -ness | meanness | |
| -ous | fabulous | |
| -ty | eternity | |
| -y | cloudy | |

## Exercise 4-5  Working with Suffixes

*Fill in the blank with an appropriate suffix to make a word that fits in the sentence.*

1. When Barbara saw improve_____ in her tennis game, she began to practice harder.

2. Anyone planning to become an engin_____ has many years of schooling ahead.

3. The union lead_____ rallied the factory work_____.

4. The train slowed at the crossing and then lurched for _____.

5. Angela was fam_____ for her gourmet cooking.

6. If you study nineteenth-century literature, you will study romantic-_____.

7. In spite of the doctor's efforts, the patient became less and less re-spons_____.

8. Margaret threatened to quit unless she was given part owner-_____ of the shop.

9. The cruel_____ and vicious_____ of the murders frightened the community.

10. The committee thought the mayor's solutions were worth _____.

*By adding suffixes, make two new words from each of the following. Note: Sometimes you need to delete a letter before adding a suffix.*

1. boy _____

2. capital _____

3. operate_____

4. prevent_____

5. form _____

## Roots

As you have seen, prefixes and suffixes can be added to words to make new words. *Agree* becomes *disagree* with the prefix *dis*; the verb *teach* becomes the noun *teacher* with the suffix *er*. Roots are the main parts of words. They may be complete words to which a prefix or suffix is added (*agreement*). Or, they may be word parts that are completed with a prefix or suffix or another root (*biography*). At the beginning of the discussion of word parts, you were introduced to two roots: *mor/mort* and *vis/vid*. Here are eighteen more roots, divided into two groups, for you to study. Study each group and then complete the exercise that follows.

■ **Common Roots**

| Root | Meaning | Example |
|------|---------|---------|
| aster/astro | star | astronomy |
| dict/dic | say, tell | dictate |
| graph/gram | write | autograph |
| path | feeling, suffering | pathos |
| phon/phono | sound | symphony |
| script/scrib | write | manuscript |
| sen/sent | feel | sentiment |
| tact/tang | touch | tactile |
| terr/terre | land, earth | terrain |

## EXERCISE 4-6  Working with Roots

*Fill in the blanks to complete the statement or answer the question.*

1. The suffix *-ible* refers to a condition or quality; what does *tangible* mean?

   _____

2. What kind of physics does an *astrophysist* study?

   _____

3. Celestial refers to the sky or heavens. What word can you make that refers to or is "of the land"?

   _____

4. A *dictator* is a ruler with absolute power. Explain how the parts of the word lead to that definition.

   _____

   _____

5. By adding suffixes, make two more words from *sentiment*.

   _____

6. Journalists have been described as "ink-stained scribblers." Explain why the expression is appropriate.

   _____

   _____

7. What two roots in the list can be put together to make a word?

_____

8. *Logy* means the study of, as in *biology*. What does *pathology* mean?

_____

■ **More Common Roots**

| Root | Meaning | Example |
|------|---------|---------|
| cess/cede | go, move, yield | cessation |
| cred | belief | credence |
| dic/duct/duce | lead, take | ductile |
| mit/miss | send, let go | missile |
| port | carry | transport |
| psych | mind | psychoanalysis |
| spec/spect | look at, watch | spectacle |
| ven/vent | come | convene |
| voc/vok | call | vocation |

**EXERCISE 4-7 More Work with Roots**

*Fill in the blanks to complete the statement or answer the question.*

1. If your story lacks *credibility*, will anyone believe you?

_____

2. The prefix *con* (*com/col*) means together or jointly. If the candidate *concedes* victory to his opponent, which person has won the election?

_____

3. The word for study of the mind is _____.

4. By adding suffixes, make two words from the word *vocal*.

_____

5. If exercise is *conducive* to weight loss, will exercise help or hinder weight loss? _____

6. After overloading her suitcase, Joan found that it was no longer _____able.

7. If you are an observer at an event, you are a

_____.

8. A judge who *commits* you to jail has done what to you?

_____

9. A *missionary* is one who

_____.

 EXERCISE 4-8  **Quiz on Word Parts**

*Put one line under each prefix and two lines under each suffix in the following words. Then define each word. Do not look back in the chapter. See how much you have learned about word parts. The first one has been completed for you.*

1. interpersonal___*that which is between people*_____

2. amorality _____

3. benediction _____

4. microbiology_____

5. monogamy _____

6. autobiography _____

7. mortician _____

8. dispassionate _____

9. inaudible _____

10. nonparticipant _____

## ■ KNOWING YOUR DICTIONARY

Most of the time we use a dictionary to check the spelling of a word. But dictionaries give us other important information. To illustrate, let's look at the following dictionary entry.

■ FIGURE 4.1

**Dictionary Entry for "Murder."**

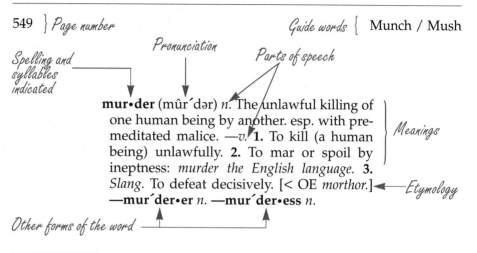

## Guide Words

The two words at the top of the page, on the same line as the page number, tell you that the first word on page 549 is *munch* and the last word is *mush*. Since dictionaries list words in alphabetical order, we know that *murder* will be found between *mun-* and *mus-*.

## Entry Word

Each entry word is listed in bold type with dots separating the word into its syllables. The syllables show how to divide the word at the end of a line of writing. They also help you see what parts make up the word.

## Pronunciation

Immediately after the entry word comes the information needed to pronounce the word. This phonetic spelling of the word, given in parentheses, uses special marks to indicate the word's pronunciation. These marks or symbols are explained in a pronunciation guide in the opening pages of your dictionary. (A shorter version also appears at the bottom of each page of some dictionaries.) We will return to the pronunciation guide shortly.

## Parts of Speech

Preceding the meanings listed for each entry word is an abbreviation, in *italic* type, of the word's part of speech. For words that function in more than one part of speech, definitions are grouped by each part of speech. In our example above, you can see that *murder* is both a noun (*n.*) and a verb (*v.*).

## Meanings

The definitions of *murder* follow after the part of speech abbreviation. When more than one definition is given, the definitions are numbered and listed (usually) from the most common to the least common meaning. Definitions of some words are specialized; the meaning is special to a particular area or field. Special meanings are indicated by a word (or abbreviation) in italics, such as *Mus.* or *Law.*

## Etymology

A word's etymology—its history or origin—concludes most entries. It is placed in square brackets [like this]. Various abbreviations are used; these are listed and explained in the opening pages of your dictionary. We will return to these.

## Other Forms of the Word

Some entries conclude with other forms of the word—and their parts of speech. Our example above includes the noun *murderer,* formed by adding the suffix *-er* to *murder.* Because the word *murderer* is given with the entry word *murder,* it is not listed separately as an entry word. Dictionaries save space by including several forms of a word under one entry word. Keep this in mind when you are looking up words.

## Plurals and Principal Verb Forms

When a noun forms its plural in an irregular way, or when a verb's principal parts are irregular, this information is also included. For example, the entry for *drink* begins this way:

**drink** (dringk) *v.* **drank** (drangk), **drunk** (drungk), **drinking.**

The irregular past tense (*drank*) and past participle (*drunk*)—and their phonetic spellings—are given, followed by the present participle *drinking.*

# ■ PRONUNCIATION

The second spelling of each entry word—the phonetic spelling that shows how to pronounce the word—will help you with unfamiliar words, if you understand the pronunciation marks. It is important, therefore, to study your dictionary's pronunciation key and to practice the pronunciation of the various sounds. Here is *The American Heritage Dictionary*'s pronunciation guide:

## ■ FIGURE 4.2

**Pronunciation Key**

| Symbols | Examples | Symbols | Examples |
|---|---|---|---|
| ă | pat | p | **pop** |
| ā | pay | r | **roar** |
| âr | **care** | s | **sauce** |
| ä | father | sh | **ship**, **dish** |
| b | **bib** | t | **tight**, stop**ped** |
| ch | **church** | th | **thin** |
| d | **deed**, mil**led** | *th* | **this** |
| ě | pet | ŭ | cut |
| ē | **bee** | ûr | **urge**, **term**, **firm** |
| f | **fife**, **ph**ase, rou**gh** | | **word**, **heard** |
| g | **gag** | v | **valve** |
| h | **hat** | w | **with** |
| hw | **which** | y | **yes** |
| ĭ | pit | z | **zebra**, **x**ylem |
| ī | **pie**, by | zh | vi**s**ion, plea**s**ure |
| îr | **pier** | | gara**ge** |
| j | **judge** | ə | **a**bout, it**e**m, edibl**e** |
| k | **kick**, **c**at, pi**que** | | gall**o**p, circ**us**** |
| l | **lid**, need**le** (nēd´l) | ər | butt**er** |
| m | **mum** | | |
| n | **no**, sudde**n** (sŭd´n) | | **Foreign** |
| ng | thi**ng** | | |
| ŏ | pot | œ | *French* f**eu** |
| ō | **toe** | | *German* sch**ön** |
| ô | **caught**, **paw**, **for**, h**or**rid, | ü | *French* t**u** |
| | h**oar**se* | | *German* **über** |
| oi | n**oi**se | KH | *German* i**ch** |
| o͝o | t**oo**k | | *Scottish* lo**ch** |
| o͞o | b**oo**t | N | *French* bo**n** |
| ou | **out** | | |

Primary stress´ **bi•ol´o•gy** (bī-ŏl´ə-jē)***
Secondary stress´ **bi´o•log´i•cal** (bī´ə-lŏj´ĭ-kəl)***

This key tells you, for instance, that there are three sounds represented by the letter "a," plus one more when "a" is followed by an "r." Simple words are used to illustrate each sound. Pronounce *pat, pay, care,* and *father* to hear the different sounds that "a" can have. Now work through the rest of the key, pronouncing each sample word to hear the sounds and to connect those sounds both to the spellings and to the symbols used to represent the sounds.

In addition to including the symbols used to represent the sounds in some foreign words, this key also indicates the marks used to show where to put the stress (or emphasis) when a word of two or more syllables is pronounced. Some words have only one stress. As the example shows, we put emphasis on the second syllable of *bi•ol′o•gy*. However, when this noun is made into the adjective *bi′o•log′i•cal*, then the first syllable receives a slight stress and the third syllable gets the primary emphasis. Sometimes, with long unfamiliar words, the problem is not sounding out each syllable to determine pronunciation but knowing where to put the stress as we pronounce the word. So, note the stress marks when practicing the pronunciation of new words.

## The Schwa

The symbol that looks like an upside down "e"—ə—is called the schwa. You will find it in the phonetic spelling of many words. The exact sound of the schwa varies somewhat depending upon the letters around it, but it is the vowel or vowels that get the least emphasis in the word. Often the schwa sounds like *uh*—the extra sound we make when we hesitate while speaking: "The keys are in the, uh, kitchen, I think." The schwa is also in the word *kitchen*: kichən!

Pronounce each of the following words:

ə•bord′ (aboard)

ē′vən (even)

səb•skrīb′ (subscribe)

Do you hear the schwa? Or, rather, do you hear how each schwa vowel is barely sounded?

 **EXERCISE 4-9  Working with Pronunciation**

*Pronounce each of the following words and then write the actual spelling of the word in the space provided. Use the Pronunciation Key as your guide to sounding out each phonetic spelling. You may want to check your dictionary for the correct spelling of the word you have written.*

1. en´trəns _____

2. jōōn´yər _____

3. kûr´təsē _____

4. sir´ē-əl _____

5. pər•fôrm´ _____

## Pronouncing Unfamiliar Words

In your reading, you will find some words that you have trouble pronouncing. Sometimes, if you can pronounce an unfamiliar word correctly, you may recognize it. That is, you will remember having heard the word before, and you may be able to understand the word's meaning. So, pronouncing the word correctly can be helpful. The key is to pronounce each syllable separately at first, using your dictionary's pronunciation key as a guide. Then pronounce each one again, running them together to form the word. Remember to place the stress on the correct syllable.

To use this method with unfamiliar words, you need to be able to separate each word into its syllables. Each syllable in a word has a separate or distinct sound. Each syllable is composed of at least one of the vowels (*a, e, i, o, u,* and sometimes *y*) and often one or more consonants (any of the rest of the letters of the alphabet). Pronounce each of the following words, listening carefully to hear each separate syllable. How many syllables do you hear in the last two words?

| periodical | 5 syllables |
| tenacity | 4 syllables |
| expatriate | _____ syllables? |
| impressionist | _____ syllables? |

The following guidelines for dividing words into syllables will help you with unfamiliar words. Remember, though, that there will be exceptions to these guidelines.

## Guidelines for Dividing Words into Syllables

1. Divide a word between two consonants coming together.
   Examples: frus/trate   dan/gle   ner/vous

2. Divide a word between a vowel and a single consonant, unless the consonant is *r*.
   Examples: re/port   a/bort   de/mand   BUT: per/use

3. Divide a word between two vowel sounds coming together.
   Examples: vi/a/ble   fi/as/co   mu/se/um

4. Divide a word between its prefix (word beginning) and root (core part).
   Examples: Prefix   Root      Prefix   Root
             im / moral         sub / marine

5. Divide a word between its root (core part) and suffix (word ending).
   Examples: Root   Suffix      Root   Suffix
             final / ly         amaz / ing

## Exercise 4-10  Using Syllables for Pronunciation

*Divide each of the following words into syllables by putting a slash in each appropriate place, using the guidelines above. Then, using the pronunciation key, pronounce each word. Finally, check your pronunciation by looking up each word in your dictionary and writing out its phonetic spelling. The first is done for you.*

| Syllables | Phonetic Spelling from Dictionary |
|-----------|-----------------------------------|
| 1. e v/o/l u/t i o n | *ev´-ə-loo´shən* |
| 2. a g g r e g a t e | _____ |
| 3. e u p h o r i a | _____ |
| 4. n e m e s i s | _____ |
| 5. o s c i l l a t e | _____ |
| 6. p a r s i m o n i o u s | _____ |

## ■ Abbreviations Used in Dictionary Entries

You have seen two abbreviations in the entry for *murder:* the *n.* for noun and the *v.* for verb to indicate the word's parts of speech. Additional abbreviations are used to indicate other parts of speech (for example, *adj.* for adjective), to accompany dates (for example, *d.* for died), and to provide information on a word's origin. *Murder,* you learned, comes from (<) an Old French (OF) word. Abbreviations used in a dictionary are listed in the opening pages, along with the pronunciation key. The more abbreviations you understand, the quicker you can obtain the information you need from the dictionary.

## Exercise 4-11  Knowing Dictionary Abbreviations

*Write in the meaning for each of the following abbreviations found in most dictionaries. Complete as many as you think you know and then check your work by studying the list of abbreviations in your dictionary. Complete the exercise by using your dictionary.*

| 1. adv. | _____ | 11. obs. | _____ |
| 2. L | _____ | 12. pl. | _____ |
| 3. ON | _____ | 13. ME | _____ |
| 4. dial. | _____ | 14. Gk. | _____ |
| 5. Fr. | _____ | 15. sing. | _____ |
| 6. G. | _____ | 16. poss. | _____ |
| 7. Heb. | _____ | 17. Skt. | _____ |
| 8. Dan. | _____ | 18. Celt. | _____ |
| 9. var. | _____ | 19. conj. | _____ |
| 10. OE | _____ | 20. + | _____ |

## ■ WORKING WITH WORD MEANINGS

Entries for some words are quite long because the word has several definitions, because it can be used in more than one part of speech, or perhaps because it is used in idiomatic expressions as well. (An *idiom* is an expression with a particular meaning that you can't figure out from knowing each word in the expression; you have to learn the idiom as a whole expression. For example: *fair and square* means honest or just; it has nothing to do with square objects.) When you find more than one definition for a word, you will need to think about which meaning fits the sentence in which you have found the word.

If you can recognize the part of speech of the word in the sentence, then you can eliminate all definitions of the word that apply to other parts of speech. Suppose, for example, that you read the following sentence:

Many cooks like to use vanilla extract.

Uncertain of the meaning of the word *extract,* you look it up and find that it can be both a verb and a noun. In the sentence the word is used as a noun, not a verb, so you need to study only the two possible meanings of the word when it is used as a noun. The two noun meanings are: 1. A literary excerpt. 2. A substance prepared by extracting; essence; concentrate. Since cooks do not generally put part of a literary work in their cooking, the second definition is the one that works in the sentence. Vanilla extract is a liquid concentrate extracted from the vanilla bean. The following exercise will give you some practice with the long entry for the word *side.*

## EXERCISE 4-12  Word Meanings

*Using the dictionary entry for "side," answer the questions that follow.*

**side** (sīd) *n.* **1.** A surface of an object, esp. a surface joining a top and bottom. **2.** Either of the two surfaces of a flat object, such as a piece of paper. **3.** The left or right half in reference to a vertical axis, as of the body. **4.** The space immediately next to someone or something: *stood at her father's side.* **5.** An area separated from another area by an intervening feature, such as a line or barrier: *on this side of the Atlantic.* **6.** One of two or more opposing individuals, groups, teams, or sets of opinions. **7.** A distinct aspect: *showed his kinder side.* **8.** Line of descent. —*adj.* **1.** Located on a side: *a side door.* **2.** From or to one side: oblique: *a side view.* **3.** Minor; incidental: *a side interest.* **4.** Supplementary: *a side benefit.* —*v.* **sid•ed, sid•ing.** To align oneself in a disagreement: *sided with the liberals.* —*idioms.* **on the side.** In addition to the main portion, occupation, or activity. **side by side.** Next to each other. **this side of.** *Informal.* Verging on: *just this side of criminal.* [< OE *sīde.*]

From *The American Heritage Dictionary*, 3rd ed.

1. For what parts of speech can the word *side* be used?

   _____

2. Excluding idioms, how many separate definitions are given for the word? _____

3. What is the word's etymology?

   _____

   _____

4. Explain, in your own words, the meaning of this sentence: *John showed his gentler side.*

   _____

   _____

5. Use each of the following idioms in a sentence:

   a. *on the side:*  _____

   _____

   b. *side by side:*  _____

   _____

6. Explain the meaning of *side* in each of the following sentences:

   a. *After they were stopped on the one-yard line, the momentum shifted to the other* **side.**

   _____

   b. *Joan's red hair comes from her mother's* **side** *of the family.*

   _____

7. Use *side* in three sentences of your own, one for each part of speech.

   a. (*n.*)  _____

   _____

   b. (*adj.*)  _____

   _____

   c. (*v.*)  _____

   _____

## EXERCISE 4-13  Finding Information in the Dictionary

*Use the dictionary entries on the next page to answer the following questions.*

1. Who was Guy Fawkes and what happened to him?

_____

_____

■

**Faust / featherstitch**                                    **308**

nal *adj.* —fau′nal•ly *adv.*

**Faust** (foust) *also* **Faus•tus** (fou′stəs, fô′-) *n.* A magician and alchemist in German legend who sells his soul to the devil for power and knowledge. —**Faust′i•an** (fou′stē-ən) *adj.*

**fau•vism** (fō′vĭz′əm) *n.* An early 20th-cent. movement in painting marked by the use of bold, often distorted forms and vivid colors. [Fr. *fauvisme* < *fauve*. wild animal.] —**fau′vist** *adj.*

**faux pas** (fō′ pä′) *n.*, *pl.* **faux pas** (fō päz′). A social blunder. [Fr.]

**fa•va bean** (fä′və) *n.* See **broad bean**. [Ital. *fava* < Lat. *faba*. broad bean.]

**fa•vor** (fā′vər) *n.* **1.** A gracious, friendly, or obliging act that is freely granted. **2.a.** Friendly regard: approval or support. **b.** A state of being held in such regard. **3.** Unfair partiality: favoritism. **4.a.** A privilege or concession. **b. favors.** Sexual privileges, esp. as granted by a woman. **5.** A small gift given to each guest at a party. **6.** Advantage; benefit. —*v.* **1.** To oblige. See Syns at **oblige. 2.** To treat or regard with approval or support. **3.** To be partial to. **4.** To make easier: facilitate. **5.** To be gentle with. **6.** *Regional.* To resemble: *She favors her father.* —*idiom.* **in favor of. 1.** In support of. **2.** To the advantage of. [< Lat.]

**fa•vor•a•ble** (fā′vər-ə-bəl. fāv′rə-) *adj.* **1.** Advantageous: helpful: *favorable winds.* **2.** Encouraging: propitious: *a favorable diagnosis.* **3.** Manifesting approval: *a favorable report.* **4.** Winning approval: pleasing: *a favorable impression.* **5.** Granting what has been requested. —**fa′vor•a•ble•ness** *n.* —**fa′vor•a•bly** *adv.*

**fa•vor•ite** (fā′vər-ĭt, fāv′rĭt) *n.* **1.a.** One enjoying special favor or regard. **b.** One trusted or preferred above others, esp. by a superior. **2.** A competitor regarded as most likely to win. [< OItal. *favorito*, p.part. of *favorire*, to favor.] —**fa′vor•ite** *adj.*

**favorite son** *n.* A man favored for nomination as a presidential candidate by his own state delegates at a national political convention.

**fa•vor•it•ism** (fā′vər-ĭ-tĭz′əm, fāv′rĭ-) *n.* A display of partiality toward a favored person or group.

**Fawkes** (fôks), **Guy.** 1570–1606. English Gunpowder Plot conspirator: executed.

**fawn**[1] (fôn) *v.* **1.** To exhibit affection or attempt to please, as a dog. **2.** To seek favor or attention by obsequiousness. [< OE *fagnian*, rejoice < *fægen*, glad.] —**fawn′er** *n.* —**fawn′ing•ly** *adv.*

*Syns: fawn, bootlick, kowtow, slaver, toady, truckle* **v.**

**fawn**[2] (fôn) *n.* **1.** A young deer. **2.** *Color.* A grayish yellow brown. [< OFr. *faon*, young animal < Lat. *fētus*, offspring.]

**fax** (făks) *n.* See **facsimile** 2. —*v.* To transmit (printed matter or an image) by electronic means. [Alteration of FACSIMILE.]

**fay** (fā) *n.* A fairy or elf. [< OFr. *fae*. See FAIRY.]

**faze** (fāz) *v.* **fazed, faz•ing.** To disconcert. See Syns at **embarrass.** [< OE *fēsian*, drive away.]

**FBI** *also* **F.B.I.** *abbr.* Federal Bureau of Investigation.

**FCC** *abbr.* Federal Communications Commission.

**FDA** *abbr.* Food and Drug Administration.

**FDIC** *abbr.* Federal Deposit Insurance Corporation.

**Fe** The symbol for the element **iron** 1. [Lat. *ferrum*, iron.]

**fe•al•ty** (fē′əl-tē) *n.*, *pl.* **-ties. 1.** The fidelity owed by a vassal to his feudal lord. **2.** Faithfulness; allegiance. [< Lat. *fidēlitās*, faithfulness.]

**fear** (fîr) *n.* **1.a.** A feeling of agitation and anxiety caused by the presence or imminence of danger. **b.** A state marked by this feeling. **2.** A feeling of disquiet or apprehension. **3.** Reverence or awe, as toward a deity. **4.** A reason for dread or apprehension. —*v.* **1.** To be afraid of. **2.** To be apprehensive about. **3.** To be in awe of. **4.** To expect: *I fear you are wrong.* [< OE *fær*, danger.] —**fear′er** *n.* —**fear′less** *adj.* —**fear′less•ly** *adv.* —**fear′less•ness** *n.*

**fear•ful** (fîr′fəl) *adj.* **1.** Causing or capable of causing fear; frightening. **2.** Experiencing fear; frightened. See Syns at **afraid. 3.** Timid; nervous. **4.** Indicating anxiety or terror. **5.** Feeling dread or awe. **6.** Extreme, as in degree or extent. —**fear′ful•ly** *adv.* —**fear′ful•ness** *n.*

**fear•some** (fîr′səm) *adj.* **1.** Causing or capable of causing fear. **2.** Fearful; timid. —**fear′some•ly** *adv.* —**fear′some•ness** *n.*

**fea•si•ble** (fē′zə-bəl) *adj.* **1.** Capable of being accomplished or brought about; possible. **2.** Used successfully; suitable. [< OFr. *faire, fais-.* do.] —**fea′si•bil′i•ty, fea′si•ble•ness** *n.* —**fea′si•bly** *adv.*

**feast** (fēst) *n.* **1.** A large elaborate meal; banquet. **2.** A religious festival. —*v.* **1.** To entertain or feed sumptuously. **2.** To eat heartily. **3.** To experience something with gratification or delight. —*idiom.* **feast (one's) eyes on.** To be delighted by the sight of. [< Lat. *festum.*] —**feast′er** *n.*

**feat** (fēt) *n.* A notable act or deed, esp. of courage. [< Lat. *factum.*]

*Syns: feat, achievement, exploit, masterstroke* **n.**

**feath•er** (fĕth′ər) *n.* **1.** One of the light, flat, hollow-shafted growths forming the plumage of birds. **2. feathers.** Plumage. **3.** Character, kind, or nature. —*v.* **1.** To cover, dress, or decorate with or as if with feathers. **2.** To fit (an arrow) with a feather. **3.** To turn (an oar blade) almost horizontal as it is carried back after each stroke. **4.** To alter the pitch of (a propeller) so that the chords of the blades are parallel with the line of flight. —*idioms.* **feather in (one's) cap.** An act or deed to one's credit. **feather (one's) nest.** To grow wealthy esp. by abusing a position of trust. **in fine feather.** In excellent form, health, or humor. [< OE *fether.*] —**feath′er•y** *adj.*

**feath•er•bed** (fĕth′ər-bĕd′) *v.* **-bed•ded, -bed•ding.** To employ more workers than are needed for a job.

**feather bed** *n.* A mattress stuffed with feathers.

**feath•er•brain** (fĕth′ər-brān′) *n.* A flighty or empty-headed person. —**feath′er•brained′** *adj.*

**feath•er•edge** (fĕth′ər-ĕj′) *n.* A thin fragile edge.

**feath•er•stitch** (fĕth′ər-stĭch′) *n.* An embroidery stitch that produces a decorative

From *The American Heritage Dictionary*, 3rd ed., 1992 (*paperback edition*).

2. What is the origin of the art term *fauvism?*

_____

3. What are two synonyms for the word *feat?*

_____

4. What does FDA stand for?

_____

5. What meaning of *favor* do you find in this sentence: *I'm in **favor** of your running for class president?*

_____

_____

6. What is a *fax?* _____

   What word does it come from? _____

7. Why are there two entry words for *fawn?* Why not combine all the definitions into one entry, as you find with most words?

_____

_____

8. What is the symbol for the element iron? _____

9. What does the French expression *faux pas* mean?

_____

10. What is the meaning of *feather* in the following sentence: *Only two weeks after her operation, she appeared in fine **feather?***

_____

_____

**EXERCISE 4-14 Workshop on the Dictionary**

*Working with your class partner, use a dictionary to answer the following questions about words.*

1. a. What is the meaning of the word *zeitgeist?*

   _____

   _____

   b. From what language does the word come?  _____

2. a. What is a *triceratops?* _____

   b. What is the origin of the word?

   _____

3. Explain the meaning of the word *zonked* in the following sentence: *Before the end of the party, Jerry was* **zonked***.*

   _____

4. Which gets eaten, *zircon* or *ziti?* _____

5. What is the origin of the word *sandwich?*

   _____

6. Who was Phillis Wheatley?

   _____

7. What does *e.g.* stand for? _____

8. Which meaning of the word *what* is used in the sentence:

   **What** *a fool she is?* _____

9. What does *SIDS* stand for? _____

10. a. How many syllables does the word *epicurean* have? _____

    b. Write out the word's phonetic spelling and pronounce the word.

    _____

c. What kind of person is an *epicurean?*

_____

## Opposing Principles Help Balance Society

by **Sydney J. Harris**

Sydney Harris was both a drama critic and columnist for the *Chicago Daily News.* His columns covered a range of social, political, and philosophical issues. Many were collected into several volumes. The following essay is from the collection *Clearing the Ground,* published in 1986.

### Prepare

1. Identify the author and work. What do you expect the author's purpose to be?

   _____

   _____

2. Preread to identify the subject and make predictions. What do you expect to read about?

   _____

   _____

3. What do you already know about the subject?

   _____

   _____

   _____

4. Raise two questions that you expect the article to answer.

   _____

   _____

   _____

1   I devoutly wish we could get rid of two words in the popular lexicon: *liberal* and *conservative*. Both are beautiful and useful words in their origins, but now each is used (and misused) as an epithet by its political enemies.

2   *Liberal* means liberating—it implies more freedom, more openness, more flexibility, more humaneness, more willingness to change when change is called for.

3   *Conservative* means conserving—it implies preserving what is best and most valuable from the past, a decent respect for tradition, a reluctance to change merely for its own sake.

4   Both attributes, in a fruitful tension, are necessary for the welfare of any social order. Liberalism alone can degenerate into mere permissiveness and anarchy. Conservatism alone is prone to harden into reaction and repression. As Lord Acton brilliantly put it: "Every institution tends to fail by an excess of its own basic principle."

5   Yet, in the rhetoric of their opponents, both *liberal* and *conservative* have turned into dirty words. Liberals become "bleeding hearts"; conservatives want "to turn the clock back." But sometimes hearts should bleed; sometimes it would profit us to run the clock back if it is spinning too fast.

6   *Radical*, of course, has become the dirtiest of words, flung around carelessly and sometimes maliciously. Today it is usually applied to the left by the right—but the right is often as "radical" in its own way.

7   The word originally meant "going to the roots" and was a metaphor drawn from the radish, which grows underground. We still speak of "radical surgery," which is undertaken when lesser measures seem futile. The American Revolution, indeed, was a radical step taken to ensure a conservative government, when every other effort had failed.

8   Dorothy Thompson was right on target when she remarked that her ideal was to be "a radical as a thinker, a conservative as to program, and a liberal as to temper." In this way she hoped to combine the best and most productive in each attitude, while avoiding the pitfalls of each.

9   Society is like a pot of soup: It needs different, and contrasting, ingredients to give it body and flavor and lasting nourishment. It is compound, not simple; not like wine that drugs us, or caffeine that agitates us, but a blend to satisfy the most divergent palates.

10  Of course, this is an ideal, an impossible vision never to be fully realized in any given society. But it is what we should aim at, rather than promoting some brew that is to one taste alone. It may take another thousand years to get the recipe just right. The question is: Do we have the time?

439 words

## Comprehension Check

*Answer the following with a, b, or c to indicate the phrase that best completes the statement.*

_____ 1. The best statement of Harris's main idea is

    a. *Radical* is a dirty word today.
    b. Both *liberal* and *conservative* are misused.
    c. We should understand what the terms *liberal* and *conservative* really mean because society needs both attributes.

_____ 2. The term *liberal* means

    a. anarchy.
    b. openness, flexibility, and humaneness.
    c. bleeding hearts.

_____ 3. The term *conservative* means

    a. preserving what is good from the past.
    b. anarchy.
    c. repression.

_____ 4. The term *radical* comes from a comparison to

    a. radical surgery.
    b. revolutionaries.
    c. radishes, which grow underground.

_____ 5. Any institution or philosophical position can destroy itself by

    a. its own excesses.
    b. mislabeling political enemies.
    c. not understanding how to use language.

_____ 6. The American Revolution was a

    a. liberal step.
    b. conservative step.
    c. radical step.

_____ 7. The American journalist Dorothy Thompson thought it was good to be

    a. a radical thinker.
    b. a liberal in temper.
    c. both a and b.

_____ 8. Today radicals can be found on

    a. the political left.
    b. the political right.
    c. both a and b.

_____ 9. Harris believes that society is

    a. going to the dogs.
    b. like a pot of soup.
    c. like wine that drugs us.

### Expanding Vocabulary

*Match each word in the left column with its definition in the right column by placing the correct letter in the space next to each word. When in doubt, read again the sentence in which the word appears.*

| | | |
|---|---|---|
| _____ lexicon (1) | a. decline in quality |
| _____ epithet (1) | b. put down by force |
| _____ humaneness (2) | c. with a desire to harm others |
| _____ degenerate (4) | d. style of speaking or writing |
| _____ anarchy (4) | e. different |
| _____ repression (4) | f. vocabulary |
| _____ rhetoric (5) | g. abusive term used to characterize someone |
| _____ maliciously (6) | h. shakes or disturbs |
| _____ futile (7) | i. absence of governmental authority and law |
| _____ agitates (9) | j. tastes |
| _____ divergent (9) | k. kindness, compassion |
| _____ palates (9) | l. useless, unsuccessful |

### For Discussion and Reflection

1. When Harris writes that "society is like a pot of soup," what writing technique is he using?

    _____

    How does this technique help him make his point?

    _____

    _____

2. What does Dorothy Thompson mean when she says she wants to be a "liberal as to temper"? How is she using the word *temper* in this context? (You may want to study the several meanings of this word in your dictionary.) Do you agree with her? Why or why not?

3. Do you agree with Harris that a blend of differing attitudes is best for society? Why or why not?

4. Can you think of situations in our society today that should make our hearts bleed? Can you think of situations that should make us want to turn back the clock?

## Your Reading Assessment

1. How accurately did you predict what you would read about?

   _____

2. Did the selection answer your questions? _____

   If not, why do you think that it did not?

   _____

3. What comments or questions do you have in response to your reading?

   _____

   _____

   _____

## Chapter Review Quiz

*Complete each of the following statements.*

1. A prefix is found at the _____ of a word.

2. A suffix is found at the _____ of a word.

3. Underline the prefixes and circle the suffixes in the following list:

   | able | il | non | pre | ic |
   |------|-----|-----|-----|-----|
   | ant | or | ity | bi | eer |

4. Make two compound words out of each of the following:

under  _____

base  _____

foot  _____

5. Etymology is a word's  _____.

6. The sound of the schwa is usually something like  _____.

7. Divide the word *degenerate* into its syllables:

d e g e n e r a t e.

8. The dictionary abbreviation OE stands for  _____

9. Muthər is the phonetic spelling of the word  _____.

10. Circle each of the following words that would be found on the dictionary page with the following guide words: imply/impressive.

impress     impose     impulse     important

immerse     improve     impotent     impoverish

*The following words have appeared in the chapter or in the reading selection. Circle the letter next to the word or phrase that is the best definition of the word.*

1. invisible

   a. blind
   b. hidden from view
   c. capable of seeing

2. circumnavigate

   a. to go around the Earth
   b. to navigate in traffic
   c. circumstance

3. asymmetrical

   a. not smooth
   b. lacking balance and proportion
   c. a metrical beat

4. semiannual

   a. once every two years
   b. twice a month
   c. twice a year

5. autobiography

   a. work written by one person
   b. life of a person written by that person
   c. history of cars

6. substandard

   a. standing still
   b. above average
   c. not up to standards

7. zeitgeist

   a. a form of pasta
   b. the spirit of a time period
   c. the study of religion

8. liberal

   a. openminded, generous
   b. literate
   c. opposing change

9. conservative

   a. school of music
   b. revolutionary
   c. valuing tradition, the past

# CHAPTER 5

## Distinguishing Between General and Specific Statements

**In this chapter you will learn:**

- To distinguish between general and specific words

- To recognize levels of specificity or generality

- To distinguish between general and specific statements

- How general and specific statements relate in writing

- To understand long, complex sentences

## ■ PREPARE TO READ

Read and reflect on the chapter's title and objectives. Glance through the chapter, observing headings to see what is covered. Now answer these questions:

1. What do you expect to learn from this chapter?

_____

_____

2. What do you already know about the chapter's topic?

_____

_____

3. What two or three questions do you want answered from reading this chapter?

_____

_____

_____

_____

Suppose you came out of a fancy restaurant that provides valet parking. You hand your keys to the attendant and say, "Please bring me my car." Would the attendant be able to get your car? Probably not. Suppose you asked, instead, for "my VW." Now will you get your car? Possibly, but you wouldn't want to count on it. To identify your car to the attendant, you need to be more *specific,* to ask for your "1994 four-door blue Jetta."

On the other hand, if you wanted to discuss various sources of air pollution, you would not talk about four-door blue Jettas. You would discuss the polluting exhaust fumes from cars. That is, you would be more *general.*

## ■ GENERAL AND SPECIFIC STATEMENTS

General statements cover a broad range of subject matter. Specific statements narrow the focus to a smaller range of subject matter. Specific statements exclude and limit possibilities. General statements are broad enough to cause confusion, raise questions, or allow for more than one way to understand the statement. If there are one hundred cars in the parking garage, and I ask simply for "my car," my statement is too general to guide you to the car I have in mind. If I name the make, model, year, color, and style of my car, I have made a much more specific statement, one that should allow you to exclude the other cars in the garage. The following exercises will help you become more alert to general and specific words.

### EXERCISE 5-1 Practice in Generalizing

*For each group of specific items, write a word or phrase general enough to include the group of items. The first has been completed for you.*

1. _works of literature_____

   novels
   plays
   poems
   short stories

2. ___WORK___

pens
chalk
pencils
crayons

3. REASON DEAD PRESIDENTS

Ford
Carter
Bush
Reagan

4. ___SCIENCE FIELD___

chemistry
botany
geology
physics

5. ___FLOWERS___

roses
daffodils
pansies
tulips

6. ___MAGAZINES___

*Sports Illustrated*
*Car and Driver*
*Glamour*
*Newsweek*

7. ___MOVIES___

*Forrest Gump*
*Terminator II*
*Babe*
*Twister*

8. ___FURNITURE___

sofa
lamp
desk
table

9. _____SCHOOL STAFF_____

   coaches
   professors
   deans
   librarians

10. _____SPORTS_____

   football
   baseball
   tennis
   basketball

## EXERCISE 5-2  Workshop on Specifics

*With your class partner, think of three or four specific items that could be included under each of the more general words listed below. The first one has been started for you.*

1. novels

   _The Scarlet Letter_

   _Gone with the Wind_

   _____

   _____

2. professional athletes

   _____

   _____

   _____

   _____

3. trees

   _____

   _____

   _____

   _____

4. college departments

_____

_____

_____

_____

5. party snacks

_____

_____

_____

_____

6. tools

_____

_____

_____

_____

7. types of music

_____

_____

_____

_____

## ■ LEVELS OF SPECIFICITY

In Exercise 5-1 above, what phrase did you use to generalize about the presidents? Did you write "former presidents"? That's a good answer, but you could be more specific and write "recent presidents." "Former presidents" is more general because it includes more items; it covers *all* presidents except the current one. We can also come up with a label that is more general than the one you probably used. We can use the label "former world leaders." The following diagram illustrates the four levels of specificity we have been discussing.

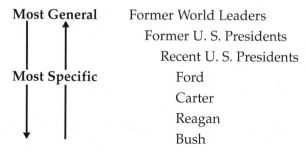

**Most General**  Former World Leaders

Former U. S. Presidents

Recent U. S. Presidents

**Most Specific**  Ford

Carter

Reagan

Bush

Notice that the diagram shows that the four presidents are equally specific, so they are all indented with the same spacing under "recent U.S. presidents." We could list only one of the presidents, or more than one, but we indent them all the same to show that they are equally specific or *parallel* words.

Your question now may be, what do the words *general* and *specific* really mean? The answer is that what they mean is always *relative*. That is, a word (or phrase) is general only in relation to a more specific word (or phrase). Let's go back to cars to illustrate the point. We can be more specific by referring to a *VW Jetta;* we can be more general by creating the category: *forms of transportation.* We can also be more specific than *cars* but more general than the *VW Jetta,* as the following diagram illustrates.

**Most General**

**Forms of transportation** (This includes cars but also includes other forms of transportation such as motorcycles or bicycles or boats.)

**Cars** (This includes all cars, but no other means of transportation.)

**German-made cars** (This includes all cars made by German companies, but excludes cars made by other companies.)

**Volkswagens** (This includes all cars made by one German company, but excludes all other German cars, such as BMWs or Mercedes.)

**Most Specific**   **VW Jetta** (We have finally come to a specific model of car made by Volkswagen. Can you think of an even more specific category than this one?)

Now it is your turn. On the lines below make a similar diagram, beginning with the same first two categories. You add three new items that have the same level of specificity as the last three in the diagram above.

**Most General**  |  **Forms of transportation**
_____

**Cars**
_____

_____

_____

**Most Specific**  |  _____

The following exercises will give you practice with levels of specificity.

 EXERCISE 5-3 **Recognizing Levels of Specificity**

*Each item contains three words or phrases. Rearrange them on the lines to the right to put them in order from most general to most specific. Then briefly explain why the most general is indeed the most general. The first has been completed for you.*

1. my cat Meffie      ___*cats*_____

    cats      _____*Burmese cats*_____

    Burmese cats      _____*my cat Meffie*_____

    Reason: ___*Cats is a category that would include all breeds of cats, so*___

    ____*it is the most general.*_____

2. athletes      _____TENNIS - PLAYERS_____

    Steffie Graf      _____

    tennis players      _____

    Reason: _____

    _____

3. pink damask-covered sofa _____

    furniture      _____

    sofa      _____

    Reason: _____

    _____

4. ballerinas _____DANCER_____

   Kirov ballerinas _____BALLENIRDS_____

   dancers _____

   Reason: _____

   _____

5. textbook _____

   history textbook _____

   *The American Pageant* _____

   Reason: _____

   _____

6. Tom Cruise _____ACTOR_____

   actors _____TOM CRUSE_____

   Hollywood actors _____

   Reason: _____

   _____

## EXERCISE 5-4  Recognizing Parallel Levels of Specificity

*Each item contains four words or phrases. Rearrange them on the lines to the right to put them in order from most general to most specific. Indent the items when you write them to show the two that are equally specific. The first one has been completed for you.*

1. forms of communication  *forms of communication*

   the media  *the media*

   television  *television*

   newspapers  *newspapers*

2. basketball players    _____

   Michael Jordan    _____

   athletes    _____

   Magic Johnson    _____

3. dogs    _____

   my cat Meffie    _____

   cats    _____

   pets    _____

4. writing instruments    _____

   pens    _____

   #2 pencil    _____

   pencils    _____

5. United Airlines    _____

   airlines    _____

   forms of transportation    _____

   US Air    _____

6. Missouri River    _____

   water    _____

   river    _____

   Colorado River    _____

You have been distinguishing between general and specific words and phrases. Words are the building blocks of sentences, and phrases are often used as headings and subheadings in books and articles, especially text-books. You can see how headings show levels of specificity by looking over the following partial chapter outline.

**AN INTRODUCTION TO PUBLIC SPEAKING**
(The chapter title. We know the chapter will be an introduction. What, specifically, will be included?)

**YOUR FIRST SPEECH**
(This is a major section. It will give guidelines for your first speech. What will those guidelines be?)

**Practice Your Speech**
(A subsection under YOUR FIRST SPEECH. One specific guideline is to practice.)

*Prepare Your Notes*
(A subheading under PRACTICE YOUR SPEECH. A specific activity to include in your practice.)

This example shows the importance of levels of specificity in the organizing of textbook chapters and the sections within each chapter.

## ■ RECOGNIZING GENERAL AND SPECIFIC SENTENCES

Words and phrases are important. But most reading involves working with sentences. Sentences are more—or less—general, just as words are. To see how sentences connect to one another in a passage, you first need to be able to recognize the sentences that are more general and those that are more specific. Remember that general statements, just like general words, *include more,* refer to broader ideas or experiences. Specific statements *exclude;* they cover a subject more narrowly. Consider the following sentences, for example.

America has had several presidents who were great leaders.

Abraham Lincoln and Franklin D. Roosevelt were great leaders.

Which is the more general statement? The first one because it does not *specify* particular presidents. If the writer stopped after the first sentence, we would not know which presidents the writer thinks were great leaders. The second sentence is more specific. It mentions two particular presidents who, in the writer's view, were great leaders. It excludes other presidents who might be considered by some to be great leaders.

Here are two more sentences to consider.

Attending college for the first time can be stressful.

Many new students worry about making friends and doing well in their courses.

Which is the more general sentence? The first is because it includes more possibilities. We are not told what situations or activities may cause stress, only that new students may experience it. The second sentence is more specific. It mentions two specific situations that make students anxious and cause them stress.

Now it is your turn. You decide which sentence in each of the following pairs is more general and circle it.

1. a. Probably the greatest factor influencing your longevity is your parents' longevity.
   b. If you are born into a family in which heart disease or cancer is common, you are at greater risk for these life-threatening diseases.

2. a. Children need to be cared for, houses need to be cleaned, and groceries need to be purchased.
   b. Even though more than 50 percent of mothers work outside the home, the work in the home still needs to be done.

3. a. A tomato is a fruit.
   b. A fruit, by definition, is a ripened ovary of a seed-bearing plant.

4. a. The situations you are in can positively influence your behavior.
   b. For example, you are more likely to quit smoking if you work in a smoke-free office.

5. a. Hinduism is the world's third largest religion.
   b. Almost 800 million Indians and about 5 million people elsewhere in the world are Hindus.

6. a. One of the best places to find fossils is the Calvert Cliffs area along the western shore of the Chesapeake Bay.
   b. Many fossils can be found along the coastal plain of Maryland and Virginia.

## Recognizing Levels of Specificity in Sentences

As you can imagine, in long passages of writing, you will find sentences ranging through several levels of specificity. Authors do not write one general and then one specific sentence over and over. They move up and down a scale of three or more levels of specificity, with some sentences at the *same level* and others *more general*, or *more specific*. Here is an example.

| **Most General** | Twenty million years ago a warm sea covered the eastern edge of Maryland and Virginia. |
| **More Specific** | The sea was home to many kinds of marine life. |
| **Most Specific** | Shellfish and corals lived on the sea floor. |
| | Sharks and primitive whales and dolphins swam above. |

Here we have three levels of specificity in four statements. The first sentence identifies a sea to be found at a particular place and time. The second sentence tells us something more specific about that sea: Many kinds of animals and plants lived there. The third and fourth sentences tell us specifically about what lived in the sea. They are at the same level of specificity.

As you read, be alert to an author's use of levels of specificity so that you can see how the sentences connect to one another. The following exercise will give you practice.

## EXERCISE 5-5  Working with Levels of Specificity in Sentences

*Place the letters representing each of the sentences on the lines to the right of the sentences in order from most general to most specific. So, if c is the most general sentence, then the letter c goes on the top line, as in the first item, which has been started for you.*

1. a. Children need to be cared for, houses need to be cleaned, and groceries need to be purchased. _____
   b. Even though more than 50 percent of mothers work outside the home, the work in the home still needs to be done. _____
   c. Some of the changes in today's work force create problems for families and communities. _____c_____

2. a. Almost 800 million Indians and about 5 million people elsewhere in the world are Hindus. _____
   b. About 1.2 million Americans are Hindu. _____
   c. Hinduism is the world's third largest religion. _____

3. a. If you add iron-rich foods to your diet, you will soon feel more energetic. _____
   b. Some foods are rich in iron; others are not. _____
   c. Meat, fish, poultry, and legumes are iron-rich foods. _____

 4. a. Researchers periodically find bones of a fearsome seabird with spikes lining its bill. _____
   b. In spite of many years of searches, scientists still find surprises at Calvert Cliffs. _____
   c. The seabird would have been six feet tall with a wingspan of 18 feet. _____

5. a. Some educators argue that there is a new college crisis. _____
   b. Students are selecting schools based solely on what they can afford. _____
   c. The new crisis is an economic one. _____

6. a. Studies show that students who mark up their textbooks get better grades. _____

b. Active reading produces the best results. _____

c. Students who annotate their texts do better than those who only highlight. _____

7. a. The early Greeks thought the ideal life included excellence in both mental and physical activities. _____

b. The dramatist Sophocles was also a general, a diplomat, and a priest. _____

c. The complete person would be equally active as athlete, philosopher, poet, or judge. _____

8. a. When American children graduate from high school they will have spent twice as much time watching TV as attending school. _____

b. In an average family's home, the TV set is on 11 hours a day. _____

c. U.S. citizens of all ages watch astoundingly large amounts of television. _____

9. a. In 1992 there were almost 2 million violent crimes. _____

b. The U.S. crime rate is many times higher than that of other industrialized countries. _____

c. The U.S. is a violent nation. _____

10. a. The power of the dramatist Sophocles lies in his compassion for his characters. _____

b. An example is his treatment of Oedipus in his play *Oedipus Rex*. _____

c. He makes Oedipus a good-hearted, although headstrong, young man. _____

## Seeing Connections Between Sentences in Writing

Most writing involves a blend of general and more specific statements. Sometimes writers present many specifics—details, examples, statistical data—and then draw conclusions from the specific statements. Their purpose may be to explain the meaning or significance of the specific information. Occasionally conclusions (the more general statements) are implied—suggested, hinted at—rather than stated. But writers who imply conclusions want their readers to understand the general statements that can be drawn from the details. Readers have to think about what general statements can be supported by the specifics.

Sometimes writers want to express and develop ideas—general statements. To make sure that readers understand those general statements, or to convince readers of the soundness of those statements, writers illustrate, explain, and support their general ideas with specifics. To follow a writer's development of ideas, you need to separate the general from the specific and then see how the specific sentences serve to explain or support the general sentences. Here is an excerpt from a textbook on mass media:

> The first successful magazines in the United States, in the 1820s, . . . contributed to a sense of nationhood at a time when an American culture, distinctive from its European heritage, had not yet emerged. The American people had their magazines in common. The *Saturday Evening Post*, founded in 1821, carried fiction by Edgar Allan Poe, Nathaniel Hawthorne and Harriet Beecher Stowe to readers who could not afford books. Their short stories and serialized novels . . . helped Americans establish a national identity.
>
> John Vivian, *The Media of Mass Communications*, 3rd ed.

Observe that the author begins with a general sentence saying that the successful early magazines helped create nationalism in the United States. The second sentence is somewhat more specific. It observes that the new magazines gave Americans something in common. Having something in common will create nationalism. The third sentence is the most specific. It names particular American writers whose works appeared in a particular magazine. In the fourth sentence, the writer comes back to the idea of nationalism, making a connection between the magazine's publications and the development of a national identity.

You have been practicing distinguishing between general and specific statements; you also need to see the connections writers make between their general and specific statements. The following exercises will give you practice.

 ## EXERCISE 5-6  Recognizing Support for General Statements

*For each set of sentences below, circle each letter next to a specific sentence that supports the general statement. Find all statements that support the general statement.*

1. *General statement:* Experts believe that there are several actions we can take to live longer.

   *Specific statements*

   a. Get enough sleep.
   b. Exercise regularly.
   c. Don't be concerned about weight.
   d. Avoid tobacco products.

2. *General statement:* The legend of the cowboy reveals the American desire for action and independence.

*Specific statements*

a. A cowboy's life was filled with loneliness and boredom.
b. Cowboys had to fight Indians and harsh weather.
c. Cowboys faced the constant threat of stampedes.
• d. When they came to town, cowboys played hard and spent money freely.

3. *General statement:* Some argue that television viewing has become an addiction for many Americans.

*Specific statements*

• a. Some people speak of being "hooked on TV."
b. Some people enjoy a few select programs.
c. With TV, viewers can block out the rest of the world.
d. Some viewers will miss activities with family and friends in order not to miss favorite TV programs.

4. *General statement:* Animals adapt to desert life in many ways.

*Specific statements*

a. Polar bears hibernate in the wintertime.
b. Many desert birds and animals get water from the food they eat.
• c. The coyote and other desert animals are nocturnal.
d. The tortoise and other desert animals escape the heat by burrowing into the sand.

5. *General statement:* Psychologists point out several steps we can take to improve the quality of our lives.

*Specific statements*

a. Be kind to others and to oneself.
b. Strive to control all parts of one's life.
c. Maintain good relationships with family and friends.
• d. See mistakes as opportunities to learn.

## EXERCISE 5-7  Finding Specific Statements That Give Support

*For each of the sentences below, write three sentences that give support. You may want to work on this exercise with your class partner.*

1. *General statement:* Abraham Lincoln was a great leader.
   *Specific statements*

   a. _____

   _____

   b. _____

   _____

   c. _____

   _____

2. *General statement:* Attending college for the first time can be stressful.
   *Specific statements*

   a. ____ PROBLEMS ON ENTERING TO COLLEGE ____

   _____

   b. ____ GETTIN LOST AN FINDING THE BUILDINGS

   _____

   c. ____ GET TO KNOW THE CAREER DEPARTMENTS ____

   _____

3. *General statement:* Some situations you may be in can influence your behavior in negative ways.
   *Specific statements*

   a. ____ HANGING WITH UNDISIPLINE FRIENDS, ____

   _____

   b. ____ DO SOMETHING THAT YOU REGRET BECAUSE OF THE PRESSURE
   OF FRIENDS ____

   c. ____ HAVING TOO MUCH CONFIDENCE AROUND
   PEOPLE YOU KNOW. ____

4. *General statement:* Recent movies are filled with violence of one sort or another.

   *Specific statements*

   a. _THE TERMINATOR_____

   _____

   b. _DEPREDATOR_____

   _____

   c. _ALIENS_____

   _____

5. *General statement:* Registering for classes can be complicated and frustrating.

   *Specific statements*

   a. _FIND THE BUILDING WHERE_____

   _YOU HAVE TO GO TO REGISTER CITY COLLEGE._

   b. _FIND THE OFFICES THAT ARE IN_

   _CHARGE TO REGISTER STUDENTS,_

   c. _BRING ALL THE PAPERS THAT PROVES_

   _YOU GRATUATED, HAD YOUR IMMUZINATION,_

   _AND   GREEN CARD (STATUS)_

## EXERCISE 5-8  Generalizing from Specifics

*For each set of specific sentences, write a general statement that can be concluded from or supported by the specific sentences.*

1. a. Benjamin Franklin published several important experiments on electricity.
   b. On his trips across the Atlantic, Franklin tracked the Gulf Stream and studied the ocean's small living organisms.
   c. Franklin wrote wisely on medical and health issues not always understood or accepted in his day.

   *General statement:* ___BENJEMIN'S_ HAS DONE MANY ACHIVMENTS

   _IN HIS LIFE,_

2. a. Less than 10 percent of deaths from lung cancer occur to nonsmokers.
   b. Smokers have a 70 percent higher death rate from stroke than nonsmokers.
   c. About 80 percent of cases of emphysema are related to smoking.

*General statement:* THERE ARE RISK'S WHEN YOU ARE SMOKING A CIGARATE

_____

_____

3. a. Friends respect and trust each other.
   b. Friends help each other.
   c. Friends enjoy one another's company.

*General statement:* WHAT GOOD FRIENDS DOES DO

_____

_____

4. a. Public speaking is more organized than ordinary conversation.
   b. Public speaking uses more formal language than ordinary conversation.
   c. Distracting verbal habits, such as frequently saying "you know," may be acceptable in conversation but not in public speaking.

*General statement:* THE DIFFERENCES BETWEEN

POBLIC SPEAKING

_____

5. a. Much of a college student's learning comes from reading and classroom lectures.
   b. Students can also learn from attending campus events such as a speakers' series or musical productions.
   c. Students also learn from seemingly casual discussions over a meal or in the dorm.

*General statement:* STUDENTS LEARNING ACTIVITIES.

_____

_____

## ▪ UNDERSTANDING COMPLICATED SENTENCES

The exercises on general and specific statements have included single words, phrases, and relatively short sentences. In addition, the exercise sentences usually make just one point. However, in much of the reading you will do for your classes, you will find longer and more complicated sentences.

In textbooks and other required reading, complicated sentences may contain several ideas, or a blend of ideas and specifics. How can you make sure you understand all the general and specific statements within each complicated sentence? You need to isolate the key parts of each sentence and ask yourself questions about what is "going on" in the sentence. Here are some specific strategies to use.

**1. Identify the main idea of each sentence by locating the subject, the verb, and the rest of the predicate.** Every sentence is about someone or something. Years ago, when you practiced finding a sentence's subject, you may have been told to put one line under the subject and two lines under the verb. That's still good advice. Consider the following three sentences.

*Subject*  *verb*  *indirect object*
a. South Africa during the Permian offered the dicynodonts a lush
*direct object*
   realm for feeding.
b. By whatever criterion for success one chooses—numbers of individuals, diversity of species, geographic range, or duration through geological time—the dicynodonts stand out as one of the most successful groups of animals that have ever lived.
c. They also were the first vertebrates to develop sliding jaws for chewing.*

Many sentences, such as sentence (a), begin with the sentence's subject, so it is not too hard to identify. Notice that you can identify the sentence's subject even though you may not know two key words in the sentence. (The *Permian* was a geological period about 250 million years ago. And *dicynodonts* were mammal-like reptiles that lived at the time, a time before the dinosaurs.)

Now, what is the subject of the second sentence? Ask yourself, "who or what is this about?" Remember, too, that you are reading a passage about dicynodonts. If you patiently read through the introductory material, you find that this sentence is also about the dicynodonts. The subject of the third sentence is at the beginning, but it is a pronoun. Pronouns always refer back

---

*These sentences have been adapted from "When the Desert Was Green" by Gillian King (*Natural History,* March 1996).

to a noun, the sentence's "real" subject. Keep track of the passage's subject so that you know who were the first animals to chew.

Next, locate the word or words that tell what the subject does or announce what we will learn about the subject. Ask yourself, "what about South Africa?" The answer is that South Africa "offered." Offered what? "A lush realm for feeding." Offered this to whom or what? Offered it to "the dicynodonts." So, we put two lines under the verb "offered." And we note the rest of the predicate, that is, what South Africa offered and to whom.

Can you locate the verb—the word or words that tell us what the dicynodonts do—in sentence (b)? Put two lines under the verb. In sentence (c) the verb "were" is not an action word. It announces that the rest of the predicate will tell us something about "they." What were "they," the dicynodonts? They were "the first vertebrates to develop sliding jaws for chewing."

**2. If necessary, to locate the subject, mark off the less important parts of the sentence, such as modifying words or phrases, or subordinate clauses.** In sentence (a), the phrase "during the Permian" qualifies the verb "offered," telling us when. It is less important than the key words in the sentence.

Initially marking off the less important parts may be a useful strategy for reading sentence (b). "By" and "for" introduce modifying phrases, so the sentence is not primarily about a "criterion for success." You could put parentheses around these words to show yourself that they are not the main part of the sentence. The next cluster of words have been marked off by the writer to show readers that they are not what the sentence is primarily about. Finally we come to the noun, *dicynodonts,* the sentence's subject.

**3. Observe how any modifying words, phrases, or clauses add to or qualify the information in the main parts of the sentence.** Although you may "mark off" the less important parts of the sentence at first in order to locate the sentence's main idea, you cannot just ignore the rest of the sentence. The subordinate parts add information, often specifics, and sometimes they qualify the sentence in important ways.

In sentence (a), the phrase "during the Permian" is an important time qualifier. The area in South Africa where many dicynodont fossils have been found is, today, a desert. In the Permian period this area was kept lush and green by seasonal rains and wide rivers. What does the long introduction to sentence (b) tell you about the dicynodonts?

**4. Put the sentence in your own words.** The best way to be sure that you understand what you have read is to put the sentence into your own, perhaps somewhat simpler, words. You will probably also want to use several sentences for a really long, complex sentence. When reading complicated sentences, you may need to review right away by saying to yourself the ideas in those sentences. Here, to practice, let's write what we have learned. The first has been done for you. You do sentences (b) and (c).

a. When the dicynodonts lived 250 million years ago, they found lots of food in their home in South Africa.

b.  _THEY were SUCCESSFUL_ _____

_____

_____

_____

c.  _____

_____

## EXERCISE 5-9  Understanding Complicated Sentences*

*Read the clusters of sentences below and answer the questions about them.*

1. Birds are essentially reptiles specialized for flight. Their bodies contain air sacs, and their bones are hollow.

   a. Underline each sentence's subject with one line and each sentence's verb with two lines.

   b. What animals are birds like?  _____

   c. How do birds differ from reptiles?

      _USE AIRSACK_ _____

   d. Whose "bodies" is the second sentence about?  _birds_

   e. Turn the two sentences into three sentences. Put the most general statement first and indent to show levels of specificity and any parallel statements.

      _THEIR BONES ARE HALLOW, THEY HAVE WINGS, THEIR_

      _IS A SACK UNDER THEIR THROUGHTS_

      _____

*These sentences are taken from Curtis and Barnes, *An Invitation to Biology* (Worth, 1985) and from "A Forgotten Naturalist" (*Natural History*, May 1996).

2. The largest known dinosaur, *Brachiosaurus,* <u>was</u> 25 meters in length and weighed, it is estimated, almost 50 metric tons, far larger than any land animal that has succeeded it.

   a. Put one line under the subject and two lines under the verb. (Hint: There are two main verbs in this sentence.)

   b. Who was the largest dinosaur?  _____

   c. What two specifics do you learn about the largest dinosaur?

   _____

   d. What else do you learn about the largest dinosaur?

   _____

   e. On the following lines, write the four pieces of information in the sentence to show levels of specificity and any parallel statements.

   _____

   _____

   _____

   _____

3. When Titian Ramsay Peale died at the age of eighty-five, he left behind an extraordinary body of work—journals, specimens, artifacts, memorabilia, paintings, and drawings based on travels of exploration—that documents natural history in America and abroad in the first half of the nineteenth century.

   a. Put one line under the subject and two lines under the verb.

   b. Who died?  _____

   c. At what age?  _____

   d. Who is the subject of the sentence?  _____

   e. What did the subject do? That is, what is the main idea of the sentence?

   _____

   _____

f. The subject's work grew out of what activities?

_____

g. When did the subject live?

_____

## In the Rain Forest

by **Michael Scott**

_STUDY OF PLANTS_

Michael Scott studied botany and then worked briefly for the World Wide Fund for Nature. He now concentrates on writing and lecturing about nature, and on working for conservation. The following excerpt is from *Ecology*, published in 1995.

### Prepare

1. Identify the author and work. What do you expect the author's purpose to be?

_____

_____

2. Preread to identify the subject and make predictions. What do you expect to read about?

_____

_____

3. What do you already know about the subject?

_____

_____

4. Raise two questions that you expect the article to answer.

_____ d WHAT LEAF's IN THE RAIN FOREST ")

_____

_____

1    In 1832, the great naturalist Charles Darwin was one of the first Europeans to explore the jungle of Brazil. He wrote in his journal, "Delight is a weak term to express the feelings of a naturalist who for the first time has wandered by himself in the Brazilian forest," and added that "nothing but the reality can give any idea how wonderful, how magnificent the scene is."

2    Jungles are known more correctly as tropical rain forests (they are often not as dense and tangled as the name "jungle" suggests). As Darwin had seen, they are incredibly rich in wildlife. For example, the rain forests of South America are home to 30,000 species of flowering plant, and an estimated 30 million species of insect live in the world's rain forests. Altogether, although rain forests cover less than 7 percent of the world's land surface, they hold at least half the world's species of plant and animal.

3    Much of this life lives high in the trees, hidden from anyone walking on the dark, damp forest floor. In fact, the forest is like an apartment building, with many different plants and animals living on each level. This multi-story existence of life partly explains the richness of the forest, but the real key is the climate.

**Rain and cloud**

4    The name "tropical rain forest" perfectly sums up the weather that creates the forest. All rain forests lie close to the equator, where days are uniformly 12 hours long and the climate is warm throughout the year. Typically, the average temperature will only range between 73°F and 87°F throughout the year.

5    The warmth of the land heats the air above, causing it to rise and shed its moisture as rain. Most rain forests, therefore, have at least 98 inches of rainfall a year, and some have twice that amount.

6    This wet, warm world with plentiful sunlight is perfect for plant growth, so dense forest flourishes. The trees grow and flower throughout the year and have evergreen leaves.

7    The trees themselves also affect the climate. They gather water from the soil and pass it out through their leaves through the process of transpiration. This further moistens the air, so that clouds form and hang over the treetops like smoke. This blanket of cloud protects the

■ FIGURE 5.1

**Most rain forests are found within the band of the Tropics, where the climate is constantly mild and there are long hours of sunshine.**

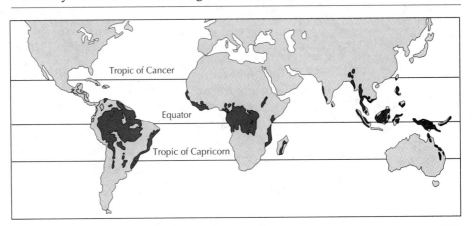

forest from the baking daytime heat and the nighttime chill of nearby desert regions, keeping temperatures within the perfect range for plant growth.

8　　Rain forests slightly farther away from the equator remain just as warm, but they have a dry season of three months or more when little rain falls. Many trees shed their leaves during this dry season, and grow new leaves when the wet season, or monsoon, begins—hence, the name "monsoon forest" for these areas.

9　　Another type of rain forest grows on tropical mountains. It is often called "cloud forest" because clouds constantly hang over the trees, like fog.

**Jungle giants**

10　　The warmth, sunlight, and moisture allow trees of many varieties to flourish in the rain forest. Most are between 130 and 164 feet tall, and their leafy branches interlock to form a continuous, high-level expanse of green, called the canopy. A few taller trees, up to 196 feet tall, tower above the canopy. They are called emergents, because they emerge above the surrounding sea of green. Often there are shorter trees in the gaps beneath the canopy, creating leafy layers below.

11　　All these trees rely for their survival on tiny organisms in the ground. The soil in rain forests is often surprisingly poor in nutrients. However, the mild, damp conditions are perfect for a variety of insects, bacteria, and fungi that live as decomposers. These rapidly break down all the dead plant and animal material that falls to the forest floor, releasing nutrients and minerals in a form that is soon absorbed by the dense network of tree rootlets spreading through the soil. The decomposers work so well in the rain forest that a leaf will disappear completely within six weeks, compared with a year for a leaf in a European oakwood.

### The struggle for life

12  The rain forest is the ideal environment for the growth of many different trees. As many as 200 species can be found in an area of rain forest the size of a football field. The result is fierce competition for living space.

13  This struggle is mainly confined to the first months of a tree's growth. Tree seedlings generally cannot grow in the shade of the forest floor, because there is not enough light for photosynthesis. However, when a canopy tree dies and falls to the ground, the sunlit gap in the forest floor is soon invaded by tree seedlings.

14  Some forest trees produce fruits and seeds in huge numbers. These fruits and seeds can lie on the forest floor for several years before germinating when a tree falls and sunlight reaches them. Other species produce a few large fruits with plenty of stored food to allow their seedlings to establish themselves quickly.

15  Most rain forest trees rely on animals to eat their fruits and spread their seeds. Some fruits are dropped by the animals, spreading the seeds. Others are eaten, and the seeds pass undamaged through the animal's digestive system and are passed out in its droppings.

### Plant hitchhikers

16  Although few plants can grow on the dark forest floor, the regular rainfall allows many plants to grow as "hitchhikers," or epiphytes, on the branches of trees high above the ground. Mosses and ferns are usually first to begin growing there. When these die, their remains form a thin "soil" in hollows and forks in the branches, in which other plants can grow.

17  These epiphytes (literally plants that grow on other plants) get all their water from the falling rain, which also contains the minerals and nutrients they need for growth. Epiphytes are not parasites on the tree; their roots simply wrap around the branches to hold them in place, then dangle down in a thick curtain that helps increase their water absorption.

18  Many orchids, ferns, cacti, and bromeliads grow as epiphytes on rain forest trees. Some of them are torn from the trees and sold in garden centers as "air plants."

19  For anyone walking on the forest floor, the most conspicuous plants are climbers called lianas, which hang from the trees like woody ropes.

These lianas begin life as seedlings on the forest floor, but when a gap in the canopy lets the light in, they shoot up and attach themselves to a young tree. They then grow up with the tree, attached to it by roots, hooks, or coiled threads, or by twining themselves around trunks until they reach the sunlight above. . . .

### In the canopy

20    Most rain forest animals, however, live in the bustling world of the canopy. There flowers, fruits, and leaves provide abundant food throughout the year and the branches form a convenient, high-level walkway.

21    The fruit eaters include a wide variety of monkeys, squirrels, fruit bats, and birds. The strong beaks of parrots and macaws allow them to crack open hard nuts. . . .

22    At any time in the rain forest some trees will have fruit or be in flower, but they will often be far apart. Animals that rely on flowers or fruit for food, therefore, need to move widely in search of a meal. This is not a problem for birds or bats that can fly, but for monkeys it means they must be very swift and agile to move through the branches. To help, some South American monkeys have a prehensile (grasping) tail, which acts like an extra arm or leg and speeds up their movement.

23    Some squirrels and lizards move between trees in another way. They have a flap of skin between their legs that allows them to glide down from high up in one tree to the trunk of a neighboring tree, saving a long climb to ground level. Some snakes can move in the same way by flattening their body and spreading their rib cage to help them glide.

24    All the apes—gibbons, chimpanzees, orangutans, and gorillas—live in the rain forest, eating leaves and fruits. Large adult male orangutans and gorillas can become so large and heavy that trees will not support their weight. They have to live on the ground, moving between clearings where there is plenty for them to eat.

25    Leaf eaters in general do not need to move far in search of food and can afford to be slow-moving, like the sloth. Similarly, many insects spend their young or larval stage grazing on a single tree. Only when they hatch into adults do they fly off to find other trees on which to lay their eggs, ensuring an abundant supply of leafy food for their young. . . .

### Forest hunters

26    The largest predators live on the forest floor, hunting pigs, antelope, and deer. Jaguars, tigers, and smaller cats such as the ocelot are typical of these forest-floor hunters. Other cats, such as the margay and

clouded leopard, are skilled climbers, well able to catch monkeys, squirrels, and birds high in the trees.

27  In the canopy, snakes lie in wait, hidden by their camouflage, to grab any animal that strays too close. Hawks and eagles fly over the canopy, ready to snatch their prey from the branches.

28  All these rain forest animals lead complex, interlocking lives, but all depend ultimately on the climate, which supports the rich plant growth. However, all of their lives are threatened by the destruction of the rain forest by humans. Unless this greed and thoughtlessness can be controlled, most of the rain forest will be destroyed within 10 to 15 years, and what Charles Darwin called the "sublime grandeur" of the rain forest will be lost forever.

1,544 words

## ■ Comprehension Check

*Answer the following with a, b, or c to indicate the phrase that best completes the statement.*

_____ 1. Tropical rain forests receive

   a. no rain.
   b. a lot of rain.
   c. a little rain.

_____ 2. Tropical rain forests have

   a. more plants than in all the rest of the world.
   b. fewer animals than in all the rest of the world.
   c. at least half of the world's plants and animals.

_____ 3. One reason for the many plants and animals is that they

   a. live throughout the large areas of rain forest.
   b. live on many levels of the rain forest.
   c. live in conditions that are too crowded.

_____ 4. Trees contribute to the damp climate by

   a. passing water out of their leaves.
   b. not using much water.
   c. not growing very tall.

_____ 5. Rain forest temperatures keep

   a. varying from very warm to chilly.
   b. consistently cool.
   c. consistently warm.

_____ 6. Emergents are

    a. very tall trees that rise above the forest canopy.
    b. new trees trying to grow.
    c. squirrel-like animals that live in the trees.

_____ 7. Many rain forest plants live

    a. by avoiding sunlight.
    b. by growing on the branches of tall trees.
    c. as parasites on other plants.

_____ 8. Most rain forest animals live

    a. outside the forest and come in only to eat.
    b. on the forest floor where they eat decomposed leaves.
    c. in the canopy where they eat flowers, fruits, and leaves.

_____ 9. Rain forest animals

    a. must be agile to reach all the fruit.
    b. can be slow because they eat only leaves.
    c. both a and b.

_____10. Human greed and thoughtlessness may

    a. destroy the rain forests in 100 years.
    b. destroy the rain forests in 10 to 15 years.
    c. destroy the predators in the rain forest.

## Expanding Vocabulary

*After using context clues and a study of word parts, write a brief definition or synonym for each of the following words.*

tangled (2) _TO BE ADPT-UP_

incredibly (2) _EXTRAORDINARY_

species (2) _____

dense (6) _HEAVY_

invaded (13) _INTRUDE_

germinating (14) _SPREAD_

parasites (17) _FEED BY OTHER ORGANISM_

conspicuous (19) _NOTISABLE_

predators (26) _____ KILLING OTHER ANIMALS _____

camouflage (27) _____ DIS CAYS _____

### Analyzing General and Specific Statements

1. Reread the second, third, and fourth sentences of paragraph 2. Organize some of the statements into three levels of specificity, with one level having parallel items. The first has been started for you.

   _____ *The rain forests are incredibly rich in wildlife.* _____

   _____

2. Reread the first two sentences of paragraph 26. Organize the statements into three levels of specificity, with several parallel items at one level. (Hint: Make the first sentence into two statements.)

   _____

   _____

   _____

   _____

   _____

   _____

### For Discussion and Reflection

1. Have you ever seen a tropical rain forest? If so, how did your response compare to Darwin's? If not, would you like to? Why or why not?

2. Scott uses an interesting comparison between the rain forest and an apartment building. Try to visualize the world he has described. Then, either sketch the scene you are visualizing or write a paragraph describing the sounds you would hear standing in the rain forest.

3. Are you aware of rain forest destruction? Why should we be concerned about this problem?

### Your Reading Assessment.

1. How accurately did you predict what you would read about?

   _____

2. Did the selection answer your questions? _____

   If not, why do you think that it did not?

   _____

3. What comments or questions do you have in response to your reading?

   _____

   _____

   _____

### Chapter Review Quiz

*Complete each of the following statements.*

1. The terms *general* and *specific* are always _____.

2. Textbook chapter headings and subheadings reveal the chapter's organization of material into levels

   _____.

3. On the lines to the right, indicate the order from most general to most specific of the following statements.

   a. Alcohol gets into the cells of the frontal lobe. _____

   b. Alcohol affects the brain in serious ways.     _____

   c. There the alcohol interferes with reasoning    _____
      and judgment.

4. Writers provide specifics to explain or to _____ general statements.

5. To read complicated sentences, begin by finding the

   _____.

6. To test your understanding of a complicated sentence, put the sentence

   _____.

7. Write a general statement that is supported by the following specific statements.

   a. Alcohol first affects reasoning and judgment.
   b. More alcohol impairs speech and vision.
   c. Eventually alcohol affects the brain's control of movement.

   *General statement:* _____

   _____

*The following words have appeared in the chapter or in the reading selection. Circle the letter next to the word (or phrase) that is the best definition of the word.*

1. longevity

   a. longitude
   b. long distance
   c. long life

2. nocturnal

   a. active at night
   b. nightly
   c. noble

3. species

   a. specificity
   b. narrowest category of organisms
   c. group of spectators

4. diversity

   a. diversion
   b. diversify
   c. variety

5. predicate

   a. part of sentence that expresses what the subject is or does
   b. part of sentence that tells where or when something takes place
   c. predictions of the future

6. ecology

   a. study of echoes
   b. study of relationship between organisms and the environment
   c. study of market influences on small businesses

7. dense

   a. thick
   b. dark
   c. dirty

8. parasites

   a. organisms that contribute to growth of other organisms
   b. paralysis
   c. organisms that feed on other organisms

9. predators

   a. those who live by killing other organisms
   b. those who live by predicting the future
   c. predecessors

# CHAPTER 6

## *Understanding Main Ideas*

**In this chapter you will learn:**

▨ To identify a paragraph's topic

▨ To understand the main idea in paragraphs

▨ To understand main ideas in longer passages

▨ To summarize longer passages

## ▨ PREPARE TO READ

Read and reflect on the chapter's title and objectives stated above. Glance through the chapter, observing headings to see what is covered. Now answer these questions:

1. What do you expect to learn from this chapter?

   _I EXPECT TO HAVE A BETTER ABILITY ABOUT_
   _READING._

2. What do you already know about the chapter's topic?

   _UNDERSTANDING PARAGRAPHS, MEANING_
   _AS; ITS TOPIC, THE MAIN IDEA, SUMMIRIZE_
   _POSSAGES._

3. What two or three questions do you want answered from reading this chapter?

> *HOW COULD I IMPROVE MY READING?*
>
> * HOW CAN I FOCUS ON IMPORTAND?
>             THINGS WILD READING
> * I     HOW THE PARAGRAPH SHOW THEIR
>         PASSAGES?

Have you ever tried to tell a joke, but your listener didn't laugh? The listener just "didn't get it." This is a frustrating experience for you and for your listener. A joke makes a point. We laugh when we get the point. If there is no laughter, the point of the joke has not been understood. (Unless, of course, it is just a very bad joke!) What makes this Hagar the Horrible cartoon funny? What is the point or idea developed through the frames? What key words are essential to the joke? Briefly explain the joke in the space below the cartoon.

**HAGAR THE HORRIBLE** DIK BROWNE

Reprinted with special permission of King Features Syndicate

> THE CARTOON REFLECTS A PECULIAR SCENARY, PEOPLE
> TALKING ABOUT THEIR BAD NEWS TO OTHERS. THE FUNNYST
> PART IS WHEN THE BAR TENDER TELLS EVERY ONE THE
> BAD NEWS TO GETOUT OF THE BAR. HE SAYS THIS
> IN NICE WORDS. THE CHARACTER TALKS THE OPPISITE
>             OF THE SITUATION THAT IS IN TH SINE.

Just as we need to understand the idea of a joke or cartoon to see what is funny, so we need to understand the main idea to get the point of what we read. Specific statements lose some of their value if we miss what they add up to, what they mean.

Over lunch with friends, one person observes that professional athletes make too much money. Another responds: "Oh, you mean that Michael Jordan is overpaid." The first speaker is thinking about professional athletes *in general*. The second speaker understands the idea best if it is expressed in the *example* of Michael Jordan. Some people think more readily at a general level, but they may have trouble remembering lots of details. Others are good at the details, but they sometimes have trouble expressing the point of the details.

Reflect for a moment on the previous conversation. Are you more likely to think in general or in specific terms? When working the exercises in Chapter 5, were you better coming up with a general word (or sentence)? Or with specific words (or sentences) to fit under a general category? If you lean one way or the other, then when you read make a conscious effort to work on the part of the process that is less natural for you.

## ■ IDENTIFYING A PARAGRAPH'S TOPIC

One useful way to understand the main idea of a paragraph is to start by identifying the paragraph's *topic*. A paragraph's topic is the subject under discussion. If I write about baseball, basketball, volleyball, and football, what is my topic? Sports, or more precisely, team sports. In Chapter 5 you worked on identifying topics for groups of words. Now you need to apply that practice to paragraphs. When identifying the topic of a paragraph, try to make it general enough to cover the material in the passage, but not so general that the label could apply to many passages. Remember your work on *levels* of specificity. The topic needs to be at the right level of specificity to cover the paragraph.

Let's look at this paragraph to illustrate the points just made.

> Beginning in the late tenth century, many new cities or towns were founded, particularly in northern Europe. Usually, a group of merchants established a settlement near some fortified stronghold, such as a castle or monastery. Castles were particularly favored since they were usually located along major routes of transportation or at the intersection of two such trade routes; the lords of the castle also offered protection. If the settlement prospered and expanded, new walls were built to protect it.
>
> Jackson J. Spielvogel, *Western Civilization*, 2nd ed., Vol. 1

What is this paragraph about? The opening sentence tells us that it is about "cities or towns" in "Europe" in the "tenth century." But, is it about *all* towns in tenth-century Europe? No. As the opening sentence establishes, it is about the *founding* of *new* towns. The rest of the paragraph contains specific details about how (by merchants) and where (near castles and trade or transportation routes) the new towns were established. The paragraph's topic, then, is: the founding of new towns in tenth-century Europe.

Here is another paragraph to study.

> The mass media are expensive to set up and operate. The equipment and facilities require major investment. Meeting the payroll requires a bankroll. Print media must buy paper by the ton. Broadcasters have gigantic electricity bills to pump their messages through the ether.
>
> John Vivian, The Media of Mass Communications, 3rd ed.

Read the following three topic statements and decide which one is the best statement of the paragraph's topic.

    a. the mass media
    b. the costs of broadcasting
    c. the expenses of the mass media

Which one did you select? The first topic is too general. You can find entire books on the mass media. This paragraph is limited to costs. On the other hand, the second topic is too specific. Radio and television broadcasting are only two of a number of mass media. All the media face the costs of equipment, facilities, and payroll. The best choice is c. This paragraph is about (specifically) the expenses of (generally) the mass media.

(*Note:* The word *media* is plural. "The mass media *are*...." "All the media *face*...." The singular form of the word is *medium*. Television is one medium; radio is another medium. When writing on this subject, be sure to pick the correct word and then use the correct verb as well.)

As you work the exercises that follow, keep in mind these points about topics.

## Guidelines for Topics

1. The topic is the subject of the paragraph.
2. You can identify the topic by asking and answering the question, "What or who is this paragraph about?"
3. The topic statement should be general enough to "cover" all the specifics in the paragraph.
4. The topic statement should be specific enough to exclude other paragraphs on related topics.

**EXERCISE 6-1  Selecting the Best Topic Statement**

*After reading each paragraph, circle the letter of the best topic statement. Then briefly explain why you rejected the other two possibilities.*

1. The soil and climate of New England encouraged a diversified agriculture and industry. Staple products like tobacco did not flourish, as in the South. Black slavery, although tried, could not exist profitably on small farms, especially where the surest crop was stones. No broad, fertile hinterland, comparable to that of the South, beckoned men inland. The mountains ran fairly close to the shore, and the rivers were generally short and rapid.

   Bailey and Kennedy, *The American Pageant: A History of the Republic*

   a. the mountains of New England
   b. the effect of New England's geography on agriculture and industry
   c. living and working in New England

   Reason: _THE TOPIC IS READ IN THE FIRST SENTENCE_

   _THIS KEY WORD THAT HELP ME FOUND THE SENTENCE_
   _WAS EN COURAGED_

2. It may be difficult for some of us—particularly those who may have heard or seen him only in his later years—to realize what a great instrumentalist and important American musician Louis Armstrong was. His influence is everywhere. Anyone, anywhere in the world, in any musical idiom, who writes for trumpet is inevitably influenced by what Louis Armstrong and his progeny have shown can be done with the instrument—not only in terms of extending its range, but also in the variety of mutes, half-valve effects, and the like, that have expanded its timbral potential. All of our jazz, real and popularized, is different because of him, and our popular singers of all kinds are deeply in his debt.

   Joseph Machlis, *The Enjoyment of Music*

   a. jazz in the United States
   b. Louis Armstrong
   c. Louis Armstrong's influence on music

   Reason: _HE WAS AN EXAMPLE to SO MANY_

   _PEOPLE WHO WANTED TO BE AS SAME AS HIM._

3. Just as the mass media help to shape our ideas of gender and relationships between men and women, so they also influence our ideas of the

elderly. Like females, the elderly are underrepresented on television, in advertisements, and in the most popular magazines. Their omission implies a lack of social value. The covert message is that the elderly are of little consequence and can be safely ignored.

James M. Henslin, *Sociology*

a. treatment of the elderly by the mass media
b. the mass media
c. underrepresentation of the elderly on television

Reason: _____

_____

4. Minoan Crete must have seemed a fairyland to travelers in 1500 B.C. Magnificent palaces, luxurious villas, and bustling towns sprinkled the mountainous countryside. From its harbors mighty fleets set sail for the far frontiers of the world it knew—Egypt, the Near East, and Greece— laden with timber, pottery, and agricultural goods. Across the Aegean and eastern Mediterranean seas the sailing ships coursed, and they returned to Crete bearing treasures of gold, ivory, and precious stones.

*Mysteries of the Ancient World*, National Geographic Society, 1979

a. Crete in Minoan times
b. the riches of Minoan Crete
c. Minoan ships

Reason: ___THE WORDS "E_____

_____

5. In the United States alone, tens of millions of workers are engaged in marketing-related jobs. They include people employed in the retailing, wholesaling, transportation, warehousing, and communications industries and those involved with marketing jobs for manufacturing, financial and other services, agricultural, mining, and other industries. About 20 million people work in retailing, 6 million in wholesaling, and 4 million in transportation.

Joel R. Evans and Barry Berman, *Marketing*, 6th ed.

a. the number and type of marketing jobs in the United States
b. the number of jobs in the United States
c. the number of retail jobs in the United States

Reason: _____

_____

## EXERCISE 6-2  Stating the Topic

*Write a topic statement for each of the paragraphs below. Follow the guidelines given above for identifying and stating a paragraph's topic.*

1. The Amish are bound by many communal ties, including language (a dialect of German known as Pennsylvania Dutch), a distinctive style of plain dress that has remained unchanged for almost three hundred years, and church-sponsored schools. Nearly all Amish marry, and divorce is forbidden. The family is a vital ingredient in Amish life; all major events take place in the home, including weddings and worship services, even births and funerals. Most Amish children attend church schools only until the age of 13.

   James M. Henslin, *Sociology*

   Topic: _____ LIFE OF THE AMISH BY MANY COMMUN TIES.

2. The baboon must cope with a wide range of behavioral interactions during its lifetime. The relationship between mother and infant, among individuals in a friendship or play group, among males in a dominance hierarchy or among those individuals that cooperate to defend their dominance rank, between the male and female in a consort pair—all produce a complex social environment.

   Robert E. Ricklefs, *Ecology*, 3rd ed.

   Topic: _____ BABON RELATIONSHIPS _____

3. The mining frontier was wasteful in many respects, but there is no doubt that it made a contribution to the development of American life. Aside from the gold and silver it pumped into the nation's financial bloodstream and the wealth or employment it created for a segment of our population, the industry stimulated other economic developments. Gold was the cornerstone; it first brought people to Nevada, Montana, Idaho, and Colorado. But just as the soldier in the field must be supported by those behind the lines, miners required a number of services. Merchants, professional men and women, teamsters, blacksmiths, stockmen, and farmers formed a kind of auxiliary corps in each of the successive mineral rushes. Supply centers grew into thriving cities, and farms appeared near the gold fields.

   Robert G. Athearn, *Winning the West*, Vol. 9,
   *American Heritage Illustrated History of the United States*

   Topic: _____

4. It was in the North that Sojourner Truth gained fame and prominence. At a time when oratory was a fine art, though illiterate, she was one of the best and most famous anti-slavery speakers of her day. . . .With her deep bass voice, her uncanny wit and the eloquence of her speeches, she held her audiences spellbound. She wore across her chest a satin banner bearing the slogan, "Proclaim liberty throughout the land unto all the inhabitants thereof." Often lashing out in her speeches against the evils of slavery, she shamed many people who were apathetic and passive toward the institution of slavery.

George F. Jackson, Black Women Makers of History: A Portrait

Topic: _____ ɪɴ ANTISLAVERY _____

5. In close, rewarding, intimate relationships, partners or friends meet each other's needs. They disclose feelings, share confidences, and discuss practical concerns, helping each other and providing reassurance. They serve as major sources of social support and reinforce our feelings that we are important and serve a purpose in life.

Donatelle and Davis, Access to Health, 4th ed.

Topic: _____ RELATION SHIPS OF FRIENDS _____

## ■ IDENTIFYING MAIN IDEAS

Identifying a paragraph's topic is a good first step to understanding the point of the paragraph, but it isn't exactly the same. The *topic* answers the question: What or who is the paragraph about? The *main idea* answers the question: What does the writer say about the topic? Or, what does the writer want me to understand about the topic?

## Distinguishing Between Topic and Main Idea

To illustrate the difference between a topic and a main idea, let's again consider the four specifics: baseball, football, basketball, and volleyball. What is my topic? Team sports. Now, what main idea could I make about this topic? There are many possibilities. One might be:

> Youngsters are better off playing team sports than individual sports because in team sports they learn cooperation and working in a group.

How does this main idea differ from the topic? The topic refers to a subject, a category into which like items can be put (such as football and basketball). The main idea makes a point; it asserts something about the topic. Notice that topics are stated as words or phrases. Main ideas, though, are complete sentences. Put another way, the main idea is the most general point to be understood from the paragraph. The more specific details within the paragraph explain and support the main idea. Read and identify the topic of the following paragraph.

> We live in an age of statistics. Day in and day out we are bombarded with a staggering array of numbers: Billy Joel has sold over 50 million albums; 12 percent of American children under the age of eighteen suffer from some form of psychological illness; France produces almost 2 billion gallons of wine every year; the literacy rate of Iraq is 71 percent; Americans consume more than 700 million pounds of peanut butter annually.
>
> Stephen E. Lucas, *The Art of Public Speaking*

Topic:  _____ TODAY'S STATISTICS _____

Did you choose statistics as the paragraph's topic? That is a good start, but a more precise topic would be "today's emphasis on statistics" or "the role of statistics in today's society." Either phrase gives you a more precise topic statement for the paragraph. Now, what is the paragraph's main idea? What does the writer want to *say* about statistics? How does he *feel* about them? The answer to these questions can be found in the paragraph's second sentence. The word "bombarded" expresses negative feelings, and the number of available statistics is, for Lucas, "staggering," another negative word. Lucas then "bombards" the reader with a long list of statistics. Is he happy with the emphasis on statistics in today's world? No. We can state his main idea this way:

> Today we are overloaded with, and give too much weight to, statistical information.

Writers often help readers distinguish between a topic and a main idea and identify the main idea for them. In most textbooks and many magazine articles, writers use headings and subheadings. As you have seen, these are topic statements. They announce the section's topic or subject. When writers identify the topic for you, you can concentrate on stating the main idea of each paragraph.

Writers also frequently state a paragraph's main idea in one sentence known as a *topic sentence*. (*Note:* Even though it is called a "topic" sentence, it actually states the paragraph's main idea. Do not be confused by these similar terms.) You will see how to locate the topic sentence as a strategy for identifying the main idea in the next section, but first are guidelines for identifying main ideas and then an exercise to help you distinguish between topics and main ideas.

## Guidelines for Identifying Main Ideas

1. **Use headings.** Headings announce the section's topic. They are usually in **bold** or *italic* type. Identifying the topic is the first step to recognizing the main idea.

2. **Ask questions.** If there are no headings, ask yourself: "What or who is this paragraph about?" to decide on the topic. Then ask, "What does the writer assert—or want me to understand—about this topic?"

3. **List specifics.** If you are having trouble generalizing to identify the topic, make a list of the paragraph's specifics. Then ask: "What do these specifics have in common?"

4. **Read for general statements.** The main idea is a more general statement than the specifics that support it. Underline the most general statements and then ask: "Which statement best represents the main point of the paragraph?"

5. **State the main idea as a complete sentence.** To be certain that you move from topic to main idea, state the main idea in a complete sentence. A word or phrase can state a topic, but only a complete sentence can make a point about the topic.

EXERCISE 6-3  **Distinguishing among Topics, Specific Statements, and Main Ideas**

*For each group of statements, identify the topic, the main idea, and the more specific statement. The first one has been completed for you.*

1.

*topic*    **Composition and Structure of Ceramics**

*specific*    Silicate ceramics, which include the traditional pots, dishes, and bricks, are made from aluminosilicate clay minerals.

*main idea*    Ceramics employ a wide variety of chemical compounds, and useful ceramic bodies are nearly always mixtures of several compounds.

Oxtoby, Nachibrieb, and Freeman, Chemistry: Science of Change

2.

_T_  **The Mass Media: Source of Powerful Symbols**

_S_  Like females, the elderly are underrepresented on television, in advertisements, and in the most popular magazines.

_M_  Just as the mass media help to shape our ideas of gender and relationships between men and women, so they also influence our ideas of the elderly.

James M. Henslin, *Sociology: A Down-To-Earth Approach*

3.

_M_  If you wish to feel greater calmness, behave in a calm way.

_T_  **Act Calm to Feel Calm**

_S_  Evidence suggests that you can bring on certain emotions by behaving as if you were feeling those emotions.

Beebe and Beebe, *Public Speaking: An Audience-Centered Approach*

4.

_M_  Keeping financial accounts, both for the household and the landed estate, alone required considerable financial knowledge.

_S_  Role of aristocratic women in medieval society

_T_  Aristocratic women had numerous opportunities for playing important roles.

Jackson J. Spielvogel, *Western Civilization*, 2nd ed.

5.

_M_  Regular aerobic exercise is beneficial for people of all ages.

_S_  Even preschoolers have been shown to receive cardiovascular benefits from planned exercise.

_T_  **Exercise: Keeping Fit Is Healthy**

Wood and Wood, *The World of Psychology*, 2nd ed.

6.

_T_  **Stress Management**

_S_  We balance rest, relaxation, exercise, nutrition, work, school, family, finances, and social activities.

_M_  Stress management consists primarily of finding balance in our lives.

Donatelle and Davis, *Access to Health*, 4th ed.

7.

_____M_____ Developing mature relationships means being comfortable with and open to persons different from yourself.

_____T_____ **Mature Relationships and Cultural Diversity**

_____S_____ You need to respond to individuals in their own right, not as members of some group.

8.

_____T_____ The role of the atmosphere

_SPECIFIC_ The atmosphere acts like a warming blanket, preventing heat from escaping into space.

_____M_____ The atmosphere plays an important role for all life on Earth.

Michael Scott, Ecology

## Locating the Main Idea in Paragraphs

Your guidelines for identifying the main idea include reading for general statements. When you look for the most general statement in a paragraph, you are looking for its *topic sentence.* **Remember: A paragraph's topic sentence is the paragraph's main idea statement.** See if you can identify the topic sentence—the main idea—in the following paragraph. Underline the paragraph's topic sentence.

> Most experts agree that shifting away from automobiles as the primary source of transportation is the only way to reduce air pollution significantly. Many cities have taken steps in this direction by setting high parking fees, imposing bans on city driving, and establishing high road-usage tolls. Community governments should be encouraged to provide convenient, inexpensive, and easily accessible public transportation for citizens.
>
> Donatelle and Davis, Access to Health, 4th ed.

Did you underline the first sentence? It announces the topic (a shift from cars as the primary source of transportation) and makes the assertion that experts believe this is the only way to reduce air pollution. The next two sentences are more specific. They discuss what has been done and what should be done to reduce our use of cars, the major source of air pollution. The first sentence is the paragraph's main idea and therefore its topic sentence.

Here is another paragraph to study. Read and then underline the topic sentence, or that part of a sentence that states the main idea.

> When we are at the highest level of consciousness, we are fully absorbed, and our thoughts are fixed on the details of our concentration,

such as studying, taking an exam, learning a new skill, and so on. But at such times we are less conscious of other potentially competing stimuli, both external (the noise around us) and internal (whether we are hungry). Athletes at full concentration during a game may be oblivious to pains signaling potentially serious injuries.

Wood and Wood, The World of Psychology, 2nd ed.

Did you underline the first sentence of this paragraph? All of the first sentence? We noted in Chapter 5 that one sentence can combine both a general statement and a more specific statement, such as an example. The first part of the first sentence is the paragraph's main idea, but the examples (studying, taking an exam, learning a new skill) should not be included. Keep in mind that a paragraph's main idea may be stated in part of a sentence that also includes specific details. Also observe, in the paragraph above, the movement from most general (with some specifics) to more specific (what we are not conscious of when fully absorbed) to most specific (the example of athletes).

## Placement of the Topic Sentence

*Topic sentence at the beginning.* You have found, in the two quoted paragraphs, that the topic sentence is the first sentence in each paragraph. The most frequent placement (slightly more than 50 percent) of a topic sentence is as a paragraph's first sentence. To give a visual representation to paragraphs with this pattern, we can use the following diagram:

| topic sentence (main idea) |
|---|
| specific detail |
| specific detail |
| specific detail |

*Topic sentence at the end.* Another placement of the topic sentence is at the end of a paragraph. In this pattern, the topic sentence "sums up" the paragraph; it states what the details "add up to" or prove. Read the following paragraph and then underline the topic sentence.

To meet their expenses, the mass media sell their product in two ways. Either they derive their income from selling a product directly to mass audiences, as do the movie, record and book industries, or they derive their income from advertisers who pay for the access to mass audiences that the media provide, as do newspapers, magazines, radio and

television. In short, the mass media operate in a capitalistic environment, and, with few exceptions, they are in business to make money.

John Vivian, The Media of Mass Communications, 3rd ed.

Did you underline the first or the last sentence in the paragraph? Although
the first sentence sounds like a generalization that could be a topic sentence,
the last sentence is more general. Note also the signal words "in short" that
announce a summary statement: The media are in business to make money.
We can represent paragraphs with topic sentences at the end with this diagram:

| |
|---|
| specific detail |
| specific detail |
| specific detail |
| topic sentence (main idea) |

*Topic sentence in the middle.* Occasionally you will find the topic sentence
in the middle of a paragraph. Often, with this placement, the writer begins
with a transition from the previous paragraph or with specifics to catch the
reader's attention. The writer then states the main idea and follows the topic
sentence with more specifics. Read the following paragraph and then underline the topic sentence.

The average American preschooler watches more than twenty-seven
hours of television per week. This might not be bad if these young children understood what they were watching. But they don't. Up
through ages three and four, most children are unable to distinguish
fact from fantasy on TV, and remain unable to do so despite adult
coaching. In the minds of young children, television is a source of entirely factual information regarding how the world works. There are
no limits to their credulity. To cite one example, an Indiana school
board had to issue an advisory to young children that, no, there is no
such thing as Teenage Mutant Ninja Turtles. Children had been crawl-
ing down storm drains looking for them.

Brandon Centerwall, "Television and Violent Crime"

This paragraph begins with a startling statistic—the number of hours per
week that young children watch TV. It then moves to the even more dis-
tressing fact that these children do not know what they are watching. After
the negative statement, the author restates the idea in a positive structure:
Children believe that what they see on TV is a picture of the real world. The

writer concludes with a specific example to show that children cannot distinguish between fact and fiction on TV. Which sentence is the topic sentence? Sentence 5. We can illustrate this structure with the following diagram:

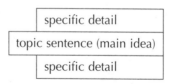

*Topic sentence at the beginning and end.* We should note one more placement of the topic sentence. In some paragraphs the topic sentence appears both at the beginning and at the end. The writer repeats, or more accurately, restates the paragraph's main idea. Sometimes the restatement at the end extends or enlarges upon the first statement of the main idea. Paragraphs with this structure have a nice sense of completeness because the specifics are "wrapped within" the two statements of the main idea. When you aren't sure if the first or the last sentence is the topic sentence, look at them closely to see if they are making essentially the same point in somewhat different words. You may have a paragraph with the topic sentence at both the beginning and the end. Read the following paragraph and underline the topic sentence.

> Media-depicted violence scares far more people than it inspires to violence, and this, according to George Gerbner, a leading researcher on screen violence, leads some people to believe the world is more dangerous than it really is. Gerbner calculates that 1 in 10 television characters is involved in violence in any given week. In real life, the chances are only about 1 in 100 per *year.* People who watch a lot of television, Gerbner found, see their own chances of being involved in violence nearer the distorted television level than their local crime statistics or even their own experience would suggest. It seems that television violence leads people to think they are in far greater real-life jeopardy than they really are.
>
> John Vivian, *The Media of Mass Communications,* 3rd ed.

Which sentence did you underline? The first? The last? Both? The first sentence is a much longer statement of the idea because it includes a reference to researcher George Gerbner, but it and the last sentence make the same point. The author introduces the idea, presents specifics from Gerbner's research, and then restates Gerbner's point, agreeing that the evidence supports Gerbner's idea. We can illustrate this structure with our last diagram:

| topic sentence (main idea) |
|---|
| specific detail |
| specific detail |
| topic sentence (main idea) |

The following paragraphs will give you practice in identifying the paragraph's topic, identifying the paragraph's main idea, and locating the paragraph's topic sentence. Before you begin the exercises, you may want to review the sample paragraphs and the various placements of their topic sentences. You may also want to review the "Guidelines for Identifying Main Ideas." Here is a brief review of the key terms we have been using.

1. The **topic** is the paragraph's subject. It is what the paragraph is about. The topic is usually stated in a phrase.

2. The **main idea** is what the writer wants to say about the topic, what the writer wants us to understand about the topic. The main idea makes an assertion and so needs to be stated as a complete sentence.

3. The **topic sentence** is the sentence in a paragraph that sums up the paragraph's main idea. It is the most general sentence in the paragraph. It may appear anywhere in the paragraph, but is often found at the beginning or at the end of the paragraph.

4. Some paragraphs have no stated topic sentence, so readers must infer the main idea. (More about this in Chapter 8.)

## EXERCISE 6-4 Identifying the Topic and Locating the Topic Sentence

*After reading each paragraph, circle the letter next to the word or phrase that best states the paragraph's topic. Then underline the paragraph's topic sentence. The first one has been started for you.*

1. Most of us pass through two stages in our attitudes toward statistical conclusions. At first we tend to accept them, and the interpretations placed on them, uncritically. In discussion or argument, we wilt the first time somebody quotes statistics, or even asserts that he has seen some. But then we are misled so often by skillful talkers and writers who deceive us with correct facts that we come to distrust statistics entirely, and

assert that "statistics can prove anything"—implying, of course, that statistics can prove nothing.

Wallis and Roberts, *Statistics: A New Approach*

Topic:

(a.) attitudes toward statistical conclusions
b. misleading statistics

2. It is hard to stretch a small vocabulary to make it do all the things that intelligent people require of words. It's like trying to plan a series of menus from the limited resources of a poverty-stricken, war-torn country compared to planning such a series in a prosperous, stable country. Words are one of our chief means of adjusting to all the situations of life. The better control we have over words, the more successful our adjustment is likely to be.

Bergen Evans, *The Word-A-Day Vocabulary Builder*

Topic:

a. control over words
b. the importance of a good vocabulary

3. Harry Truman lived seventy years of his life in Jackson County, Missouri. Think of that. He didn't come to Washington until he was fifty years old. Then he was in Washington as a senator and as Vice President and President for another twenty years. And *then* he went back to Jackson County after he left the White House for another twenty years. So it stands to reason that if you want to understand Harry Truman you'd better know a good deal about Jackson County, Missouri, and you'd better know a good deal about the people there who mattered to him, not just when he was growing up, but during his whole life.

David McCullough, "The Unexpected Harry Truman"

Topic:

a. Harry Truman's years in Washington
b. the influence of Jackson County, Missouri, on Truman

4. By the Louisiana Purchase of 1803, the United States acquired the remote reaches between the Mississippi and the Rockies, but little could be done at once to develop that territory. . . . Although settlement of the Western plains was delayed, the region we call the Midwest was rapidly populated between 1815 and the 1840s. Migration into this region had important influences upon the nation as a whole. It provided a growing market for eastern manufactures and encouraged the rising industrial areas to develop all possible means of transportation to and from the West. Both influences were accelerated when settlers moved

into the treeless plains, where they required outside help to get fencing, lumber, furniture, and hardware. Once the farmer moved to where he could market his crops for cash, his dependence upon manufactures grew fast.

Robert G. Athearn, *The Frontier,* Vol. 6,
*American Heritage Illustrated History of the United States*

Topic:

a. influence of Midwest settlement on manufacturing and transportation
b. settling the treeless plains

5. Galileo was the first European to make systematic observations of the heavens by means of a telescope, thereby inaugurating a new age in astronomy. He had heard of a Flemish lens grinder who had created a "spyglass" that magnified objects seen at a distance and soon constructed his own after reading about it. Instead of peering at terrestrial objects, Galileo turned his telescope to the skies and made a remarkable series of discoveries: mountains and craters on the moon, four moons revolving around Jupiter, the phases of Venus, and sunspots.

Jackson J. Spielvogel, *Western Civilization,* 2nd ed., Vol. 1

Topic:

a. Galileo's observations of the heavens
b. the impact of Galileo's use of a telescope

### EXERCISE 6-5  Stating the Topic, Finding Details, and Identifying the Topic Sentence

*After reading each paragraph, state the paragraph's topic, list one specific detail, and then underline the paragraph's topic sentence. The first one has been started for you.*

1. Even though many who "rushed" to California did not make big fortunes, the California Gold Rush had an important effect on the development of the country. In 1848, San Francisco grew from a village of 800 to more than 20,000 inhabitants. The total population of California increased from 15,000 in 1848 to 250,000 in 1852. The most important effect of the Gold Rush can be found in the number of new settlers in California.

Robert G. Athearn, *Winning the West,* Vol. 9,
*American Heritage Illustrated History of the United States*

Topic: _effect of the Gold Rush on California_

Specific detail: _____

_____

2. Today, most of the books that shape our culture are adapted to other media, which expands their influence. Magazine serialization put Henry Kissinger's memoirs in more hands than did the publisher of the book. More people have seen Carl Sagan on television than have read his books. Stephen King thrillers sell spectacularly, especially in paperback, but more people see the movie renditions. Books have a trickle-down effect through other media, their impact being felt even by those who cannot or do not read them. Although people are more in touch with other mass media day to day, books are the heart of creating American culture and passing it on to new generations.

John Vivian, *The Media of Mass Communications,* 3rd ed.

Topic: _____

Specific detail: _____

_____

3. Although many of the world's volcanoes erupt violently, there are others that erupt quietly. Two of these are Mauna Loa and Kilauea on the island of Hawaii. Mauna Loa, which reaches up some 30,000 feet from the floor of the Pacific, is the tallest mountain in the world and still growing. Every few years an eruption adds more lava to it. When these volcanoes erupt, there is no explosion. Instead, long fissures, or cracks, open up. Fountains of liquid lava spurt into the air, and lava flows slowly from the fissures.

Patricia Lauber, *This Restless Earth*

Topic: _____

Specific detail: _____

_____

4. Leopards are the most intelligent of the cats and the finest feline athletes by far. Their superbly proportioned bodies excel at running, jumping, tree-

climbing, and swimming. Pound for pound, they are remarkably strong: a 120-pound leopard has been known to haul a large giraffe calf up a tree. I have seen a leopard leap at least nine feet vertically and a good twenty-five feet or more horizontally. It would be easy to take the view that no other carnivore has reached such heights of evolutionary adaptation.

P. Jay Fetner, The African Safari

Topic: _____

Specific detail: _____

_____

5. But more than simply reacting against psychoanalysis and behaviorism, humanistic psychologists developed their own unique view of human nature, a view that is considerably more flattering. Human nature is seen as innately good, with a natural tendency toward growth and the realization of one's fullest potential. The humanists largely deny a dark or evil side of human nature. They do not believe that we are shaped strictly by the environment or ruled by mysterious unconscious forces. Rather, as creative beings with an active, conscious free will, we can chart our own course in life.

Wood and Wood, The World of Psychology, 2nd ed.

Topic: _____

Specific detail: _____

_____

## ▪ READING LONGER PASSAGES

To understand main ideas you began distinguishing between general and specific sentences in Chapter 5. In this chapter you have studied main ideas in paragraphs. Although you will rarely read just one paragraph, paragraphs are the building blocks of longer works, so understanding their structure is essential. Now let's apply what you have learned to longer passages.

## Identifying Main Ideas in Longer Passages

Most essays, articles, and textbook sections develop one main idea. To observe this, read the following section from a speech textbook. Annotate as you read, focusing on finding each paragraph's main idea.

**Know How You React to Stress**

(1) . . . nervousness affects different people in different ways. (2) Perhaps you feel that your hands or knees shake uncontrollably as you speak in public. (3) The people sitting next to you may not ever experience those symptoms of nervousness, but they may have difficulty breathing comfortably and feel that their voices are shaky or quivery. (4) Whatever your individual responses to stress, don't wait until you are delivering a public speech to discover them.

(1) Knowing your reactions to stressful situations helps you in two ways. (2) First, this knowledge lets you predict and cope with these physical conditions. (3) Your dry mouth or sweaty palms will not surprise you; instead, you will recognize them as signs that your body is performing well under pressure. (4) Second, since you are anticipating these physical conditions, you will be better able to mask them from the audience. (5) How do you do this? (6) Try these techniques.

(1) If you know that your hands shake when you are nervous, don't hold a sheet of paper during the speech; the shaking paper will only amplify the movement of your hands and will telegraph this sign of nervousness to your audience.(2) If your voice is likely to be thin and quivery as you begin speaking, take several deep, slow breaths before you begin to speak. (3) If you get tense before speaking, try some muscle relaxation techniques: Tense your hands, arms, and shoulders, and then slowly relax them. (4) If you get flustered before speaking, make sure you arrive on time or even a little early—never late. (5) If looking at an audience intimidates you, talk to audience members before class, and when you speak, look for friendly faces in the audience.

Grice and Skinner, *Mastering Public Speaking,* 2nd ed.

Now, look back over paragraph 1. Although sentence 1 is the most general, the paragraph's main idea is stated in sentence 4. Sentence 1 serves as an introduction. Sentences 2 and 3 contain specific examples. And then the practical point is made in sentence 4: Know how you show stress before you make a speech.

Here are questions for you to answer about paragraph 2.

1. What sentence contains the main idea in paragraph 2?

_____ *KNOWING YOUR REACTIONS* _____

2. What words connect to the main idea statement and give the paragraph its structure?

_____

Finally, what about paragraph 3? It contains a list of techniques for hiding nervousness. The idea that controls all of these specifics really comes at the end of paragraph 2.

What, then, is the main idea of the entire section? If we take the section heading and add a second thought, we will have a good main idea statement:

> Know how you react to stress so that you can hide your nervousness from your audience.

## Distinguishing among Details

As you observed in Chapter 5, writers provide specific sentences to illustrate and support more general sentences. Some paragraphs contain a main idea (the topic sentence) and several statements at the same level of specificity. But other paragraphs (such as paragraph 2 above) contain three levels: a main idea (1), two more specific sentences (2 and 4), and one even more specific sentence (3). (The last two sentences are transitions to paragraph 3.) When paragraphs are part of longer passages, then there may be four levels of specificity. The main idea of an essay or article is called its *thesis*. The pattern then shifts to look like this:

**Thesis:** Know how you react to stress so that you can hide your nervousness from your audience. *(main idea of passage)*

**Major Detail:** Knowing your reactions to stressful situations helps you in two ways. *(main idea of paragraph)*

**Minor Detail:** First, this knowledge lets you predict and cope with these physical conditions. *(major detail of paragraph)*

**More Minor Detail:** Your dry mouth and sweaty palms will not surprise you. . . . *(minor detail of paragraph)*

As you read, try to focus primarily on a work's main ideas and major details. Minor details help us visualize the subject and can be quite interesting, but it is the big ideas that we want to be sure to understand. Exception: Some textbook sections, although similar to an essay, contain many minor details that are important. The textbook author has organized an enormous amount of information around a number of topics. Usually much of that information needs to be learned. But, as you can see from the sample passage on stress, there are some minor details that illustrate nervousness that would not have to be learned for a test.

## ■ THE SUMMARY

One good way to review longer passages is to write a summary. A summary helps you prepare for class discussion and makes a useful record for future study. Also, instructors frequently assign summaries because they are good measures of how well you have understood a writer's main ideas. A *summary* is a *brief* restatement of the main ideas of a work. You can summarize a story, an article, a chapter, or section of a text. To make a summary much shorter than the original, you need to include only the main ideas and major details and to leave out minor details. And, to make the summary *your* writing, you need to restate the main ideas in your own words. To be useful, a summary has to be a fair and accurate restatement of the original work.

Read the following passage and then the first summary that follows. Decide if the summary is appropriately condensed, clear, and accurate.

## Social and Economic Structures in Ancient Egypt

Egyptian society had a simple structure in the Old and Middle Kingdoms;* basically, it was organized along hierarchical lines with the god-king at the top. The king was surrounded by an upper class of nobles and priests who participated in the elaborate rituals of life that surrounded the pharaoh. This ruling class ran the government and managed its own landed estates, which provided much of its wealth.

Below the upper classes were merchants and artisans. Within Egypt, merchants engaged in an active trade up and down the Nile as well as in town and village markets. Barter was the primary means by which goods were exchanged. Some merchants also engaged in international trade; they were sent by the king to Crete and Syria where they obtained wood and other products. Expeditions traveled into Nubia for ivory and down the Red Sea to Punt for incense and spices. Egyptian artisans displayed unusually high standards of craftsmanship and physical beauty, while producing an incredible variety of goods: stone dishes; beautifully painted boxes made of clay; wooden furniture, especially of Lebanon cedar; gold, silver, and copper tools and containers; paper and rope made of papyrus; and linen clothes.

By far, the largest number of people in Egypt simply worked the land. In theory, the king owned all the land, but granted out portions of it to his subjects. Large sections were in the possession of nobles and

*[2700–1567 B.C.]

the temple complexes. Moreover, although free farmers who owned their own land had once existed, by the end of the Old Kingdom, this group had disappeared. Most of the lower classes were serfs or common people bound to the land who cultivated the estates. They paid taxes in the form of crops to the king, nobles, and priests, lived in small villages or towns, and provided military service and labor for building projects.

Jackson J. Spielvogel, *Western Civilization,* 2nd ed., Vol. 1

### Summary 1

Ancient Egyptian society had a simple structure. The king was at the top along with nobles and priests. They managed the government and their estates—which produced much wealth. The next group down the social structure were merchants and artisans. Merchants traded along the Nile. Some were international traders with countries such as Crete and Syria where they bought wood. The artisans made many beautiful things such as dishes, furniture, tools, paper, and linen clothes. Most people were in the lowest group who worked the land. They were bound to the land and had to pay the wealthy owners taxes in crops. They also lived in villages and served in the military.

We can agree that the writer of this summary has read and understood the passage. But, the summary contains some details that should be removed (that merchants bought wood), and it needs some ideas added for clarity. For example, since the Egyptian king was considered a god, he really is above the upper class; this is an important distinction. Also, some major details can be grouped into one sentence to shorten the summary. Carefully compare the two versions on the combining of ideas.

### Summary 2

Ancient Egypt had a simple hierarchial social structure. The king, considered a god, was at the top, followed by wealthy nobles and priests who managed both the government and their estates. The next social class included merchants and artisans. Merchants traded along the Nile and with nearby countries including Crete, Syria, and Nubia. Artisans were highly skilled and also produced a great variety of goods from tools to clothes. The largest group of people were lowly farm laborers living in small villages and bound to the land they farmed. They were also in the military and worked on large building projects.

The second version is a clearer restatement of the original and relies less on the wording of the original. From these summaries we can set some guidelines for summary writing.

## Guidelines for Summary

1. Write in your own words, except for key terms that need to be included.
2. Begin with the topic or thesis and then add supporting ideas.
3. Write objectively; do not include your opinion of the original passage. Be careful that your word choice does not misrepresent the meaning of the original.
4. Do not include specific examples or descriptive details. *Do* include important definitions when appropriate.
5. Combine several ideas into one sentence as a way to condense the original.

## EXERCISE 6-6 Summary

*Read the following passage, "The Pyramids," from Jackson J. Spielvogel,* Western Civilization, *Vol. 1. Then, write a brief summary of the passage, keeping your focus on main ideas. Do not write more than one hundred words.*

One of the great achievements of Egyptian civilization, the building of the pyramids, occurred in the time of the Old Kingdom. Pyramids were not built in isolation but as part of a larger complex dedicated to the dead, in effect, a city of the dead. The area included a large pyramid for the king's burial, smaller pyramids for his family, and mastabas, rectangular structures with flat roofs as tombs for the pharaoh's noble officials. In order to hold services for the dead, a mortuary temple was built at the eastern base of the pyramid. From this temple, a causeway led to a valley chapel about a quarter of a mile away near the river bank. This causeway served as a processional avenue for the spirits of the dead. The tombs were well prepared for their residents. The rooms were furnished and stocked with numerous supplies, including chairs, boats, chests, weapons, games, dishes, and a variety of food. The Egyptians believed that the physical body had an etheric counterpart or vital force, which they called the *ka*. If the physical body was properly preserved (hence mummification) and the tomb furnished with all the various objects of regular life, the *ka* could return and continue its life despite the death of the physical body. The pyramid was not only the king's tomb, it was also an important symbol of royal power. It could be seen for miles away as a visible re-

The Sphinx and one of the Pyramids at Giza, Egypt

minder of the glory and might of the ruler who was a living god on earth.

The first pyramid was built in the third dynasty during the reign of King Djoser. The architect Imhotep, a priest of Heliopolis, the center dedicated to the sun cult, was responsible for the step pyramid at Saqqara. Beginning with Djoser, wives and immediate families of the kings were buried in pyramids, nobles and officials in mastabas.

The first real pyramid, in which each side was filled in to make an even surface, was constructed in the fourth dynasty around 2600 B.C. by King Snefru who built three pyramids. But the largest and most magnificent of all was built under Snefru's son Khufu. Constructed at Giza around 2540 B.C., the famous Great Pyramid covers thirteen acres, measures 756 at each side of its base, and stands 481 feet high. Its four sides are almost precisely oriented to the four points of the compass.

The building of the Great Pyramid was an enormous construction project that used limestone blocks as well as granite from Upper Egypt. The Greek historian Herodotus . . . reported the tradition that it took 100,000 Egyptians twenty years to build the great pyramid. But Herodotus wrote two thousand years after the event, and considerable controversy and speculation still surround the construction of the Great Pyramid, especially in view of the precision with which it was built. The interior included a grand gallery to the burial chamber, which was built of granite with a lidless sarcophagus for the pharaoh's body. The Great Pyramid still stands as a visible symbol of the power of Egyptian kings and the spiritual conviction that underlay Egyptian society. No pyramid built later ever matched its size or splendor.

**Your Summary:**

_____

_____

_____

_____

_____

_____

_____

_____

_____

_____

_____

# The Significance of the Frontier

by **Robert G. Athearn**

Professor Athearn earned his doctorate at the University of Minnesota and spent his teaching career at the University of Colorado. He is the author of many books on American history. The following excerpt is from Volume 9 (*Winning the West*) of the *American Heritage Illustrated History of the United States,* a twenty-six-volume series first published in 1963 and published in its latest edition in 1989.

**Prepare**

1. Identify the author and work. What do you expect the author's purpose to be?

    _____

    _____

2. Preread to identify the subject and make predictions. What do you expect to read about?

    _____

    _____

3. What do you already know about the subject?

    _____

    _____

    _____

4. Raise two questions that you expect the article to answer.

    _____

    _____

    _____

1    Before the Mexican War, the country called the West extended from the Appalachian Mountains to a line not far across the Mississippi River. This was the area of settlement and of agricultural development. The land beyond was vaguely called the Far West. It was the haunt of the Indian, the trapper, and the occasional explorer. Economically, it was not yet significant. By the Louisiana Purchase of 1803, the United States acquired the remote reaches between the Mississippi and the Rockies, but little could be done at once to develop that territory. The nation was not ready.

2    Although settlement of the Western plains was delayed, the region we call the Midwest was rapidly populated between 1815 and the 1840s. Migration into this region had important influences upon the nation at large. It provided a growing market for Eastern manufac-

tures and encouraged the rising industrial areas to develop all possible means of transportation to and from the West. Both influences were accelerated when settlers moved onto the treeless plains, where they required outside help to get fencing, lumber, furniture, and hardware. Once the farmer moved to where he could market his crops for cash, his dependence upon manufactures grew fast. He became highly important to Eastern businessmen, who regarded him as a prime prospect.

3      Socially, the great advance of settlement had the effect of increasing the Americanization process typical of the frontier. As the leveling influence touched larger numbers, the nation felt its effect, for by now the West was much more powerful in Congress. Western members thundered their ideologies throughout legislative halls, and the "little people" the length and breadth of the land listened. Thus the social influences of the frontier had their effect upon political growth. The common man, wherever he was, came to demand a greater share in government, and during the Jackson era in particular the movement reached epic proportions.

4      Finally, the growth of the Mississippi and Ohio River Valleys set the scene for the next big move westward. It provided a training ground for those who would go on. Although some adjustments had to be made for the assault upon a new kind of land, where agricultural practices would have to be modified, it was a good place to learn the trade. The nation at large looked on and approved of such successful expansion. When the day came for Americans to make the great leap across the plains to Oregon and California, they would be ready, for by then "westering" had become a part of national tradition.

420 words

## Comprehension Check

*Answer the following with a, b, or c to indicate the phrase that best completes each statement.*

_____ 1. The best statement of the passage's topic is

    a. migration after the Mexican War
    b. the westward movement
    c. the significance of the frontier

_____ 2. The best statement of the passage's main idea is

    a. The country was not ready for the westward movement.
    b. The advance of the frontier changed American politics.
    c. The settling of the Midwest had positive effects on the country.

_____ 3. The Far West in the early nineteenth century was

    (a.) not economically significant.
    b. heavily populated.
    c. important to Eastern businessmen.

_____ 4. Settling the Midwest had positive influences on

    a. the country's economy.
    b. the country's political ideas.
    c. both (a) and (b).

_____ 5. The Jackson era in politics is known for

    a. advancing the political influence of ordinary people.
    b. advancing the influence of the West.
    (c.) both (a) and (b).

_____ 6. The development of the Midwest

    a. helped prepare for the settlement of the Far West.
    b. helped Eastern businessmen.
    (c.) both (a) and (b).

_____ 7. In the development of the country, there were

    a. many negative effects from the frontier.
    b. no frontiers.
    (c.) several frontiers.

## Expanding Vocabulary

*After using context clues and a study of word parts, write a brief definition or synonym for each of the following words.*

haunt (1) ___visit frequently___

migration (2) ___to move one place from another___

accelerated (2) ___increase the speed___

dependence (2) ___support___

prime (2) ___first wrong or importand___

ideologies (3) _____

epic (3) _____

assault (4) ___atlack___

## Analysis of Main Ideas

1. What is the topic sentence in paragraph 3?

   _____

2. What is the main idea in paragraph 4?

   _____

   Where is it stated? _____

3. Write a summary of the passage. Be sure to include a statement of the main idea and the major details. Use your own words and write no more than *five* sentences.

   _____

   _____

   _____

   _____

   _____

   _____

   _____

   _____

## For Discussion and Reflection

1. How did this discussion of the frontier add to your knowledge of U.S. history?

2. Can you picture life in the Ohio area in the 1830s? What are several characteristics of life at that time and place that you can imagine? Would you have enjoyed living on the Midwest frontier in the 1830s? Why or why not?

3. What is the most significant new idea in this passage for you? Why is it significant?

## Your Reading Assessment

1. How accurately did you predict what you would read about?

   _____

2. Did the selection answer your questions? _____

   If not, why do you think that it did not?

   _____

3. What comments or questions do you have in response to your reading?

   _____

   _____

   _____

## Chapter Review Quiz

*Complete each of the following statements.*

1. The _____ is the subject of the paragraph.

2. A topic statement should be _____ enough to cover all of the paragraph's details.

3. The _____ is what the writer asserts about the subject of the paragraph.

4. Two strategies for identifying main ideas include

   _____

   _____

5. When a paragraph's main idea is stated, that sentence is called the

   _____.

6. Topic sentences may be found

   a. _____

b. _____

c. _____

d. _____

7. Read the following paragraph, write the paragraph's topic, and then underline the topic sentence.

The atmosphere is still another thing that makes the earth a planet of life. We could not live without the atmosphere. It is the air we breathe: the source of oxygen for animal life and of carbon dioxide for plant life. It is the source of rain. It is the blanket that traps part of the day's heat from the sun and keeps it from escaping at night. It is the shield that protects us from the sun's ultraviolet radiation and other dangerous rays.

Patricia Lauber, *This Restless Earth*

Topic: _____

8. Read the following paragraph, write the paragraph's topic, and then underline the topic sentence.

Despite dietary improvements, heart disease, certain types of cancer, hypertension (high blood pressure), cirrhosis of the liver, tooth decay, and chronic obesity continue to be major health risks. Why do so many of us have nutritional problems? Much of our preoccupation with food and our tendency to eat the wrong types and amounts of foods stem from our early eating habits.

Donatelle and Davis, *Access to Health,* 4th ed.

Topic: _____

*The following words have appeared in the chapter or in the reading selections. Circle the letter next to the word (or phrase) that is the best definition of the word in bold type.*

1. "the mass **media** help to shape our ideas"

   a. the means of communication
   b. one form of communication
   c. television

2. **topic sentence**

   a. the topic of a paragraph
   b. the most important specific detail of a paragraph
   c. the sentence that states the paragraph's main idea

3. "a **diversified** agriculture"

   a. varied
   b. dense
   c. divided

4. "the sailing ships **coursed** the seas"

   a. courted
   b. moved swiftly over
   c. sunk in

5. "among males in a dominance **hierarchy**"

   a. group
   b. arrangement by family
   c. arrangement by rank

6. "when **oratory** was a fine art"

   a. eloquent public speaking
   b. organization
   c. orientation

7. "athletes . . . may be **oblivious** to pain"

   a. obvious
   b. aware of
   c. unaware of

8. "There are no limits to their **credulity**"

   a. credibility
   b. readiness to believe; gullibility
   c. ability to understand

9. "Books have a **trickle-down** effect through other media"

   a. separate from
   b. transitory
   c. flow slowly down

# CHAPTER 7

## Recognizing Strategies and Structures in Writing

**In this chapter you will learn:**

- Five structures or strategies writers use

- How to annotate each pattern as you read

- Words that signal each pattern or structure

- How to read longer passages that combine several structures or strategies

### ■ PREPARE TO READ

Read and reflect on the chapter's title and objectives. Glance through the chapter, observing headings to see what is covered. Now answer these questions:

1. What do you expect to learn from this chapter?

   _____

   _____

2. What do you already know about the chapter's topic?

   _____

   _____

3. What two or three questions do you want answered from reading this chapter?

_____

_____

_____

_____

You have been studying the basic pattern of good writing: a main idea developed and supported with specific details. Works lacking a main idea, or missing details to illustrate the main idea, are not considered good writing. To organize this most basic pattern of main idea and details, writers use various structures or strategies. As you will see in this chapter, these patterns can be used to organize both paragraphs and longer passages.

There are two good reasons for recognizing these basic structures as you read. First, recognizing a work's structure aids reading comprehension. Understanding the writer's pattern will guide your annotating and help you remember what you read. Second, recognizing a writer's pattern will help you anticipate what is coming. For example, if you read in a history text that World War II was *similar* to World War I, you can expect the passage to develop a comparison of the two wars. Understanding improves when you can predict where the passage is headed.

Writers help readers recognize structures and see how the parts connect by using key words and phrases called *signal words* or *transitions*. For each structure discussed, the most common signal words or transitions will be listed. Learn to recognize them and use them to aid your reading.

## ▥ EXPLAINING BY LISTING

One of the most frequently used patterns to explain a subject is the list. Sometimes items are presented in an actual list: indented and preceded by a numeral (1, 2, 3, etc.) or by bullets (•, •, •, etc.). You have seen such lists in this text, for example, the list of objectives that begins each chapter. Lists are also presented within paragraphs, usually in one of three ways:

1. All of the items are listed in the first sentence and then each is discussed, one at a time, in the following sentences;

2. One item at a time is discussed, with each new item introduced with a signal word such as *second, in addition,* or *also;*

3. An opening sentence announces the number of items to be discussed and then each one is explained in turn.

Usually, a list tells us that all the items are equally important. Sometimes the author signals us that the last item in the list is the most important. If we read: "Finally, and most importantly, salespeople must remember . . . ," then we know that the last item is more significant than the others. When you are studying lists in a textbook, you probably need to learn all of the items.

## Signal Words

Here are the most common signal words to develop lists.

| | | | |
|---|---|---|---|
| also | first | last | next |
| and | furthermore | likewise | second |
| another | in addition | moreover | third |
| finally | | | |

## Basic Structure for Listing

The simple listing pattern has this shape.

## How to Annotate Listings

As always when you are annotating as you read, you want to underline each paragraph's topic sentence and the major details in the paragraph. When the list pattern is used, then each item in the list is a major detail to be underlined. In addition, circle the signal words and then use numbers in the margin to indicate each item in the list. Here is an example:

Basically, human beings have affected the environment in three ways. *①* The first factor is the natural growth of the human species. . . . The second *②* element is the human appetite for natural materials. Coupled with increased population, this need for natural resources has reached a critical point where the depletion of certain goods is a distinct possibility. The *③* third element is the rapid development of technology, which generally has resulted in advances in the standard of living, but often at the cost of the natural environment.

Curran and Renzetti, Social Problems, 3rd ed.

Notice that this paragraph announces the number of items in the opening sentence: There are *three* ways we have affected the environment. The first sentence is the topic sentence, so it has been underlined. The key words for each item have been underlined, the signal words circled, and the items numbered in the margin.

## EXERCISE 7-1  Recognizing and Annotating Listing

*Read and annotate each of the following selections. Then complete the exercise that follows each selection.*

I.  A nutritious diet has five characteristics. One is **adequacy:** the foods provide enough of each essential nutrient, fiber, and energy. Another is **balance:** the choices do not overemphasize one nutrient or food type at the expense of another. The third is **calorie control:** the foods provide the amount of energy you need to maintain appropriate weight—not more, not less. The fourth is **moderation:** the foods do not provide excess fat, salt, sugar, or other constituents. The fifth is **variety:** the foods chosen differ from one day to the next.

Sizer and Whitney, Nutrition: Concepts and Controversies, 6th ed.

1.  What is the paragraph's main idea?

      *NUTRITION DIET HAS FIVE CHARACTERISTICS*

      _____

2.  Briefly state each of the items listed.

      *adequacy, balance, calorie control, modera-*
      *tion, variety*
      _____

      _____

      _____

3.  List the signal words and describe any visual signals used in the paragraph.

      *ONE, ANOTHER, THIRD, FOURTH, FIFTH.*

II. In his book *The Hidden Dimension,* sociologist Edward T. Hall identifies four different distances people assume when conversing. Each of the four distances assures better communication by creating comfort levels. The first of these is *intimate space,* the distance one assumes when speaking to an intimate companion or one's spouse. Intimate space is generally between 6 inches and 18 inches. When conversing with family members or close friends, most people use the 18-inch to 4-foot space that Hall calls *personal space.* In social situations such as parties, or in conversations with people who are not close friends, people maintain a *social space* of between 4 feet and 12 feet. People who put more than 12 feet between themselves and their audience are utilizing *public space.* Use of such broad spaces between speaker and audience often implies that the speaker has something important to say.

Donatelle and Davis, *Access to Health,* 4th ed.

1. What is the paragraph's main idea?

   _____

   _____

2. Briefly explain each item listed.

   _____

   _____

   _____

   _____

   _____

   _____

   _____

3. List the signal words and describe any visual signals used in the paragraph.

   _____

   _____

## ▪ TIME SEQUENCE AND PROCESS

The ordering of information in time sequence is familiar to us from stories. Chronological or time order is also found in histories and biographies and in explanations of how to do something (change a tire) or how a process is accomplished (how water is distilled). You will find the use of time sequence or the explanation of a process in most textbooks, from history and psychology (how the brain functions) to biology and geology (how rocks are formed).

### Signal Words

Here are the most common signal words for time sequence and process.

| | | | |
|---|---|---|---|
| after | first | last | second |
| before | following | next | then |
| finally | later | now | when |
| process | cycle | procedure | |

### Basic Structure for Time Sequence or Process

In time sequence or process, the items relate to one another, not just to the topic being discussed. They relate in chronological order, and sometimes, with process, in a causal order as well. That is, the first step leads to the second step; the second step could not take place without the first step happening. We can illustrate the pattern this way.

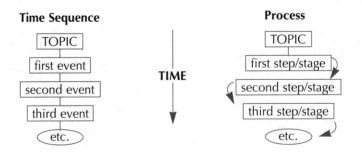

### Annotating the Pattern of Time Sequence or Process

Just as you expect authors to be complete and accurate in the discussion of stages or steps, so you will want to learn the key events of history or all the steps in the process in the correct order.

When reading, annotate to make the stages or steps clear. Underline each topic sentence and the key words in each stage or step. Circle signal words to highlight the time sequence. Indicate steps in a process by numbering. Here is an example:

*1st step* →

*2nd step* →

*3rd step*

*4th step* →

Carbohydrate plays a prominent role in the global carbon (cycle.) Carbon dioxide, water, and energy are combined in plants to form glucose; the plants may store the glucose in the polysaccharide starch. (Then) animals or people eat the plants. In the body the liver and muscles may store the glucose as the polysaccharide glycogen, but ultimately it becomes glucose again. The glucose delivers the sun's energy to fuel the body's activities. (In the process,) glucose breaks down to waste products, carbon dioxide and water, which are excreted. (Later,) these compounds are used again by plants as raw materials to make carbohydrate.

Sizer and Whitney, *Nutrition: Concepts and Controversies,* 6th ed.

## EXERCISE 7-2  Recognizing the Use of Time Sequence or Process

*Read and annotate each of the following selections. Then complete the exercise that follows each selection.*

I. During the time earth and the other planets were being formed, the release of energy from radioactive materials kept their interiors very hot. When earth was still so hot that it was mostly liquid, the heavier materials collected in a dense core whose diameter is about half that of the planet. As soon as the supply of stellar dust, stones, and larger rocks was exhausted, the planet ceased to grow. As earth's surface cooled, an outer crust, a skin as thin by comparison as the skin of an apple, was formed.

Curtis and Barnes, *An Invitation to Biology,* 4th ed.

1. What is the paragraph's topic?

_____

2. State briefly the steps in the process.

_____

_____

3. List the signal words that are used.

_____

II. The first written messages were simply pictures relating familiar objects in some meaningful way—pictographs. Yet there were no images for much that was important to human life. What, for instance, was the image for sorrow or bravery? So from pictographs humans developed ideograms to represent more abstract ideas. An eye flowing with tears could represent sorrow, and a man with the head of a lion might be bravery.

The next leap occurred when the figures became independent of things or ideas and came to stand for spoken sounds. Written figures were free to lose all resemblance to actual objects. Some societies developed syllabic systems of writing in which several hundred signs corresponded to several hundred spoken sounds. Others discovered the much simpler alphabetic system, in which a handful of signs represented the basic sounds the human voice can make.

Don Lago, "Symbols of Humankind"

1. What is the selection's topic?

_____

2. Briefly list the stages described.

_____

_____

_____

_____

3. List the signal words that are used.

_____

## ▪ DEFINITION

Defining terms and concepts is an important part of writing. Essayists devote many paragraphs or even an entire article to defining controversial terms. Textbooks are filled with definitions, because learning about a new subject includes understanding the terms and concepts of that field of study. A formal definition consists of placing the term in a category and then distinguishing it from other, similar items in that category. For example:

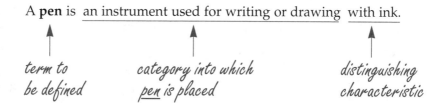

A **pen** is an instrument used for writing or drawing with ink.

*term to be defined*     *category into which pen is placed*     *distinguishing characteristic*

Other items in the category include pencils and chalk. The pen differs because it contains ink. The definition is developed by providing characteristics of the item.

## Signal Words and Other Strategies

In textbooks, the most obvious signal that a definition is coming is that the word is in **bold** or *italic* type. The signal is a visual one. Additionally, the definition may be reprinted in the text's margin, perhaps in a shaded box. Some brief definitions are placed in parentheses ( ) or set off with dashes—. Also look for the use of "that is" and "or" to introduce a definition:

Diction, that is, the writer's choice of language, . . .

Fossils, or the remains of prehistoric life, . . .

## Basic Structure for Definition

The definition strategy can be organized in several ways. When defining complex or debatable terms or concepts, writers often give examples, or contrast the term with others that are similar but not exactly the same, or even give a brief history of the term. You will usually find some, if not all, of the elements illustrated below, but not necessarily in the order shown.

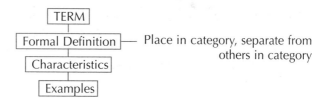

TERM
Formal Definition — Place in category, separate from others in category
Characteristics
Examples

## How to Annotate Definitions

If a formal definition is given, underline it. Note characteristics or examples if they are given. If the term is not highlighted in the text, then underline it twice or circle it, remembering to be consistent in your choice of markings. Here is a chemistry text's definition of *matter*.

*characteristic*

*exs.*

*matter–def.*

The entire universe consists of matter and energy. Every day we come into contact with countless kinds of matter. Air, food, water, rocks, soil, glass, and this book are all different types of matter. Broadly defined, matter is *anything* that has mass and occupies space.

Hein and Arena, Foundations of College Chemistry, 5th ed.

Observe that the formal definition follows the characteristics and examples. Also note that while the term *matter* is not highlighted, the word appears in each of the four sentences.

 ## Exercise 7-3 Recognizing and Annotating Definitions

*Read and annotate each of the following selections. Then complete the exercise that follows each selection.*

I. **Cultural Lag**   Obgurn coined the term **cultural lag** to describe the situation in which some elements of a culture adapt to an invention or discovery more rapidly than others. Technology, he suggested, usually changes first, followed by culture. The nine-month school year is an example. In the nineteenth century, the school year matched the technology of the time, which required that children work with their parents at the critical times of planting and harvesting. Current technology has eliminated the need for the school year to be so short, but the cultural form has lagged severely behind technology.

James M. Henslin, Sociology, 2nd ed.

1. Define the term *cultural lag* in your own words.

   _____

2. List the strategies used in this definition.

   _____

   _____

3. What signals are used to indicate that a definition is being given?

   _____

   _____

II. **Frustration**   When people are hindered from meeting their goals, they often feel frustrated. **Frustration** is an emotional state that is said to occur when any goal—work, family, or personal—is thwarted or blocked. When people feel that they cannot achieve a goal (often due to situations beyond their control), they may experience frustration and stress. When you are unable to obtain a summer job because of a lack of experience, it can cause feelings of stress; when a grandparent becomes ill, you may feel helpless, and this causes stress.

Lefton and Valvatne, Mastering Psychology, 4th ed.

1. Define *frustration* in your own words.

   _____

   _____

2. List the strategies used in this definition.

   _____

   _____

3. Which strategy is most effective in explaining the term, in your view?

   _____

4. What signals are used to indicate that a definition is being given?

   _____

   _____

## ■ COMPARISON AND CONTRAST

When we compare we look at similarities between two items; when we contrast we look at differences between two items. These strategies are widely used because they help make sense of many topics. We can compare or contrast two schools, two books, two jobs, two study methods.

Some writers discuss both similarities and differences in their two items. More typically, writers focus on either similarities or differences, but not both. In fact, the writer's point may be that in spite of apparent similarities, the two items are really quite different. Or, in spite of apparent differences, they are really quite similar.

## Signal Words

Signal words have two roles in the comparison or contrast pattern. Some words or phrases announce the use of the structure: "Comparing . . . views" or "The difference between . . . " announce the strategy that will be used. Other signal words structure the comparison or contrast. They indicate shifts between the two items. Here are some of the most common.

| | | |
|---|---|---|
| both | however | likewise |
| but | in contrast | on the other hand |
| different | in the same way | similarly |
| unlike | | |

## Basic Structure for Comparison or Contrast

The comparison/contrast structure has one pattern if both similarities and differences are given, but another pattern if only comparison or only contrast is used. The following two models show the structure with contrast as the writer's point. What if the writer wanted to compare instead of contrast? The center boxes in the first model would be reversed for comparison. The differences would be briefly mentioned, and the similarities would be compared one by one. The list in the second model would be showing points of similarity for comparison.

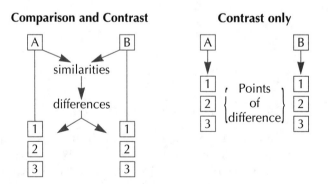

## How to Annotate Comparison or Contrast

When you recognize a comparison or contrast pattern, begin by locating the two items being compared or contrasted. Either underline them twice or circle them. Then note the specific points of similarity or difference, or both.

Underline key words for each point of similarity (or difference) and number each one in the margin. Here is an example.

*Contrast* {

When the American wants to be alone he goes into a room and shuts the door—he depends on architectural features for screening. For an American to refuse to talk to someone is the ultimate form of rejection and a sure sign of great displeasure. The English, on the other hand, lacking rooms of their own since childhood, never developed the practice of using space as a refuge from others. They have in effect internalized a set of barriers, which they erect and which others are supposed to recognize. Therefore, the more the Englishman shuts himself off when he is with an American the more likely the American is to break in to assure himself that all is well.

①
②
①
③

Edward T. Hall, *The Hidden Dimension*

We can summarize the points of difference in this paragraph thus:

| Item A (American) | Item B (Englishman) |
| --- | --- |
| 1. shuts door to be alone | uses a set of barriers (nonverbal messages) |
| 2. uses silence as rejection | uses silence to be alone |
| 3. sees silence as a problem | sees silence as signal to be alone |

## EXERCISE 7-4 Recognizing and Annotating Comparison and Contrast

*Read and annotate each of the following selections and complete the exercise that follows each selection.*

I. A comparison between reading and viewing may be made in respect to the pace of each experience. . . . The pace of reading, clearly, depends entirely upon the reader. He may read as slowly or as rapidly as he can or wishes to read. If he does not understand something, he may stop and reread it, or go in search of elucidation [clarity] before continuing. The reader can accelerate [speed up] his pace when the material is easy or less than interesting, and slow down when it is difficult or enthralling. If what he reads is moving, he can put down the book for a few moments and cope with his emotions without fear of losing anything.

The pace of the television experience cannot be controlled by the viewer; only its beginning and end are within his control as he clicks the knob on and off. He cannot slow down a delightful program or speed up a dreary one. He cannot "turn back" if a word or phrase is not understood. The program moves inexorably [relentlessly] forward, and what is lost or misunderstood remains so. Nor can the television viewer readily transform the material he receives into a form that might suit his particular emotional needs, as he invariably does with material he reads. The images move too quickly.

Marie Winn, *The Plug-In Drug*

1. What are the two items being contrasted?

   _____

2. List the several points of difference.

   _____

   _____

   _____

3. List the signal words that are used.

   _____

II. E-mail may have its advantages in the business world, but it can never match actual letters as the most heartfelt form of communication, especially between parents and their children. While e-mail glows impersonally on a screen, letters come to us wrapped up like small gifts we can hold in our hands, read, re-read and save for later. Yes, e-mail can be printed out. But only as a lifeless facsimile, each copy as tediously similar as the next. Every letter, by contrast, is distinct, original and rich with detail. There is the individuality of the penmanship, whether it flows easily from line to line or scrawls somewhat aimlessly across the page. Even with typed letters, the living hand makes itself known through the signature, as well as any handwritten corrections or additions. . . . [T]he unique personality of the sender shines through.

Andrew Carroll, "Letter to the Editor," *Washington Post*

1. What two items are being contrasted?

   _____

2. List the points of difference.

_____

_____

_____

3. List the signal words that are used. _____

_____

## ■ CAUSE AND EFFECT

The cause/effect pattern is an important tool for writers explaining why something happened (Why did the Roman Empire collapse?), what is causing a current problem (Why is there a greater fear of violence?), and what might happen in the future (Will lowering taxes improve the economy?). Writers can focus on cause or effect, but they are really writing about both. If I describe the effects of smoking on health, I am also explaining the cause of those health problems.

### Signal Words

The best signals of the cause/effect structure are the words *cause* and *effect*. You will often find them in titles, section headings, and opening sentences. "Why" questions also announce that causes will be examined. The following words are also found in cause/effect writing.

| | | |
|---|---|---|
| as a result | due to | impact on |
| because | follows | therefore |
| changes | hence | thus |
| consequently | | |

### Basic Structure for Cause and Effect

Cause/effect structures can take several forms, depending upon the writer's topic. First, a writer can explain how one cause produces one effect:

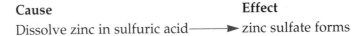

In many cases, one cause produces several effects:

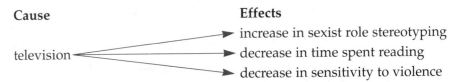

In addition, several causes may work together to produce one effect:

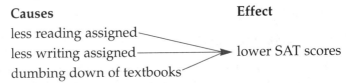

Finally, several causes may produce several effects:

**Causes**                          **Effects**
improved reading skills              { better grades
improved study skills                { more pleasure from school

Remember that in a complicated world we rarely find one simple cause producing one simple effect.

## How to Annotate Cause and Effect

When you recognize that a writer is discussing causes and effects, be sure to understand which is the cause and which the effect. Then, note all the causes, or all the effects, that are given. Underline the topic sentence and the key words that state the cause(s) or effect(s). If there are several, then use numbers in the margin to note each one. Here is an example.

*Effects*

①
②

③

Pleistocene (Ice-Age) glaciers . . . had other, sometimes profound, <u>effects upon the landscape</u>. For example, as the ice advanced and retreated, animals and plants were forced to migrate. This led to stresses that some organisms could not tolerate. Hence, a number of <u>different plants and animals became extinct</u>. Furthermore, <u>many present-day stream courses bear little resemblance to their preglacial routes</u>. The Missouri River once flowed northward toward Hudson Bay, while the Mississippi River followed a path through central Illinois. . . . <u>Other rivers that today carry only a trickle of water but nevertheless occupy broad channels are testimony</u> to the fact that they once carried torrents of glacial meltwater.

Tarbuck and Lutgens, *The Earth: An Introduction to Physical Geology,* 4th ed.

**EXERCISE 7-5 Recognizing and Annotating the Use of Cause and Effect**

*Read and annotate each of the following selections and complete the exercise that follows each selection.*

I. **Alcohol's Effects on the Brain**   When alcohol flows to the brain, it first sedates the frontal lobe, the reasoning part. As the alcohol molecules diffuse into the cells of this lobe, they interfere with reasoning and judgment. With continued drinking, the speech and vision centers of the brain become sedated, and the area that governs reasoning becomes more incapacitated. Still more drinking affects the cells of the brain responsible for large-muscle control; at this point people under the influence stagger or weave when they try to walk. Finally the conscious brain becomes completely subdued, and the person passes out.

Sizer and Whitney, Nutrition: Concepts and Controversies, 6th ed.

1. State the topic of the paragraph so that a cause/effect pattern is indicated.

   _____

2. Briefly list the specific effects.

   _____

   _____

   _____

3. List the signal words that are used.

   _____

II. The Neolithic agricultural revolution had far-reaching consequences. The organized villages allowed a surplus of food and goods to be produced. Trade developed throughout the Near East. Individuals also began to specialize in certain crafts, and a division of labor developed. Pottery was made from clay and fired. The pots were used as containers and for cooking. Thread was made from vegetable and animal fibers, and the resulting flax and wool were being woven into cloth by 6000 B.C. Baskets were also produced. Finally, stone tools became refined as flint blades were turned into microliths that could be used in sickles and hoes, both useful for agriculture.

Jackson J. Spielvogel, Western Civilization, 2nd ed., Vol. 1

1. State the topic of the passage so that a cause/effect pattern is indicated.

   _____

2. Briefly list the effects.

   _____

   _____

   _____

3. List the signal words that are used.

   _____

## EXERCISE 7-6  Distinguishing among Various Structures

_Read, annotate, and then answer the questions that follow each of the selections. Part of your task is to identify the structure or strategy used in each of the selections._

I. **Potential energy** is stored energy, or energy an object possesses due to its relative position. For example, a ball located 20 ft above the ground has more potential energy than when located 10 ft above the ground and will bounce higher when allowed to fall. Water backed up behind a dam represents potential energy that can be converted into . . . electrical or mechanical energy. Gasoline is a source of chemical potential energy.

   Hein and Arena, Foundations of College Chemistry, 5th ed.

1. What is the paragraph's topic sentence?

   _____

2. What structure or strategy is used in this paragraph?

   _____

3. What techniques are used to develop the strategy?

   _____

4. What signals are used in the paragraph?

   _____

II. There is general agreement that the plague began in Europe when Genoese merchants brought it from the Middle East to the island of Sicily off the coast of southern Italy in October of 1347. It spread quickly, reaching southern Italy and southern France and Spain by the end of 1347. Usually, the diffusion of the Black Death followed commercial trade routes. In 1348, the plague spread through France and the Low Countries and into Germany. By the end of that year, it had moved to England, which it ravaged in 1349. By the end of 1349, it had expanded to northern Europe and Scandinavia.

Jackson J. Spielvogel, *Western Civilization*, 2nd ed., Vol. 1

1. What structure is used in the paragraph?

_____

2. What is the paragraph's topic?

_____

3. List three major details from the paragraph in a pattern that reveals the paragraph's structure.

_____

_____

_____

4. What signals are used?

_____

III. Whatever the cause or causes of mass extinctions, their effects on the course of evolution are clear. When entire groups of plants or animals die out, new opportunities are available to other plants or animals that survive. The survivors then diversify and make use of the newly available living space and find new solutions to their problems of survival and development.

adapted from Curtis and Barnes, *An Invitation to Biology*, 4th ed.

1. What is the structure used in the paragraph?

_____

2. What is the main idea? State it to make clear the structure used.

_____

_____

3. What signals are used?

_____

IV. An understanding of the difference between sex and gender is critical to the use of bias-free language.

Sex is biological: people with male genitals are male, and people with female genitals are female.

Gender is cultural: our notions of "masculine" tell us how we expect men to behave and our notions of "feminine" tell us how we expect women to behave. Words like *womanly/manly, tomboy/sissy, unfeminine/unmasculine* have nothing to do with the person's sex; they are culturally acquired, subjective concepts about character traits and expected behaviors. . . .

Sex is an objective biological fact. Gender varies according to culture.

Rosalie Maggio, The Dictionary of Bias-Free Usage:<br/>A Guide to Nondiscriminatory Language

1. What structure or strategy is used in the passage?

_____

Could one say that two patterns are used in this passage? Explain.

_____

_____

2. What is the main idea? State it to indicate the structure used.

_____

_____

3. What signals are used?

_____

V. Most retail companies have their own advertising departments, for several reasons. First, retailers can save money by doing their own advertising instead of contracting out to an advertising agency. Second, retailers often receive advertising materials either free or at a reduced cost from manufacturers and trade associations. Third, retailers operate on a shorter timetable. They often need to put together an advertising campaign in a few days whereas an agency may take weeks or months to complete a project.

adapted from Wells, Burnett, and Moriarty,
*Advertising: Principles and Practice,* 3rd ed.

1. What is the paragraph's main idea?

   _____

2. What structure or strategy is used?

   _____

3. List three ideas from the paragraph in a pattern that reveals the paragraph's structure.

   _____

   _____

   _____

4. What signals are used?

   _____

## ■ MIXED PATTERNS

The longer the essay or textbook section, the more likely you are to find a mix of several patterns. As you read, try to recognize the *primary* structure. This will help you recognize what the passage is about. For example, if you observe a list, but don't see that it is a list of *effects,* you will miss the writer's analysis of cause and effect. As you read and annotate the following example, try to recognize all of the strategies used but also decide which one is the primary strategy.

There are three types of technology. The first is **primitive technology,** natural items that people have adapted for their use such as spears, clubs, and animal skins. Both hunting and gathering societies and pastoral horticultural societies are based on primitive technology. Most technology of agricultural societies is also primitive, for it centers on harnessing animals to do work. The second type, **industrial technology,** corresponds roughly to industrial society. It uses machines powered by fuels instead of natural forces such as winds and rivers. The third type, **postindustrial technology,** centers on information, transportation, and communications. At the core of postindustrial technology is the microchip.

James M. Henslin, *Sociology,* 2nd ed.

The opening sentence announces the topic (types of technology) and signals the use of a list (three types). But is listing the paragraph's primary purpose? Notice the use of **bold** type, often a visual signal of definition. Isn't the author's purpose to define the three kinds of technology? You could also argue that a contrast structure is suggested because the writer distinguishes among the three terms.

Remember to let a recognition of the primary structure guide your understanding of the main ideas of the passage, for comprehension is your purpose in reading. The following passages will give you more practice.

### EXERCISE 7-7  Recognizing and Learning from Mixed Patterns

*Read, annotate, and then answer the questions that follow the selection.*

## Types of Volcanic Mountains

Volcanic mountains have three main shapes. The shape of the mountain is determined by the shape of the vent and the kind of material that pours out of it.

Popocatepetl Volcano, Parque National, Mexico

Some mountains are built chiefly by liquid lava that pours out of long fissures in the sides of the volcano. The lava flows pile up, forming a broad, gently sloping mountain. Such a mountain is called a **shield volcano,** because it is shaped like a shield laid flat on the ground. The Hawaiian volcanoes, which are the largest on earth, are shield volcanoes. There are shield volcanoes in northeastern California and in parts of Oregon. There are many small shield volcanoes in Iceland.

An explosive eruption may pile up a big hill of cinder and ash around the vent. The hill is shaped like a cone with the point cut off and so is called a **cinder cone.** The top of the cone forms a bowl-shaped dent called a crater. The crater takes shape because the explosions tend to blow away material from the vent. While the cone itself is being built of cinder and ash, lava may flow out at its base. Some cinder cones occur alone. Others are found on the sides of bigger volcanoes. Particutin is one of hundreds of cinder cones in the state of Michoacán, Mexico. The western United States has many cinder cones, among them Sunset Crater in Arizona and Mount Pisgah in southern California.

The third type of volcano is built both of lava flows and of cinder and ash. It is called a **composite volcano.** (The name means that it is made of various materials.) A composite volcano develops because more than one kind of eruption occurs. For example, a volcano may start by erupting like a shield volcano, with flows of liquid lava. The next time it erupts, it may erupt like a cinder cone, laying down layers of cinder and ash. Its third eruption may consist of lava flows. Most of the world's famous and beautiful volcanoes are composite volcanoes. Among them are Mounts Hood, Rainier, and Shasta in the United States and Mount Fuji in Japan.

Patricia Lauber, *This Restless Earth*

1. What strategies does the author use?

   _____

2. Which strategy connects to the author's primary purpose in writing?

   _____

3. What signals are used?

   _____

4. Explain, in your own words, how each volcano is formed or how it gets its name.

_____

_____

_____

_____

_____

## The Problem with Moderates

by **E. J. Dionne, Jr.**

E. J. Dionne is a columnist for the *Washington Post* and a senior fellow at the Brookings Institution. He is the author of *They Only Look Dead: Why Progressives Will Dominate the Next Political Year.* The following passage is from a long article on political terms and "positionings," titled "The Labeling Game," which appeared in the *Washington Post Magazine* August 11, 1996.

### Prepare

1. Identify the author and the work. What do you expect the author's purpose to be?

_____

_____

2. Preread to identify the subject and make predictions. What do you expect to read about?

_____

_____

3. What do you already know about the subject?

_____

_____

_____

4. Raise two questions that you expect the article to answer.

_____

_____

_____

1   At some level, we all want to be moderate. It sounds a lot better than being "immoderate," "extreme," "doctrinaire," or just plain wacky. Hell, in a lot of ways, I'm a moderate. This whole article is implicitly "moderate," claiming as it does to describe the problems with everybody else's labels and world views from a perspective that purports to be "fair," if not entirely "objective."

2   But there's a huge problem with moderates, yours truly included. Exactly what is one being moderate about? In 1964, Barry Goldwater[1] got into a lot of trouble for saying: "Extremism in the defense of liberty is no vice. . . . Moderation in the pursuit of justice is no virtue." Well, what really, is wrong with that statement? Do we want to be only "moderately" opposed to slavery or genocide? Do we look very kindly upon those in the past who were? The same critique applies to the word "centrist." Centrist has no meaning until you define the boundaries of "left" and "right." Your definition of where the "center" is might be 100 miles to the left or right of mine.

3   The basic problem with moderation is not dispositional but intellectual. How do you define a moderate? Are there any principles that can be called moderate—or is moderation, almost by definition, unprincipled?

4   Moderates constantly have to choose, and often resist doing so. They especially hate binary choices: yes/no, either/or. Frequently, they are right to do so, since the choices so posed are false. Are you a feminist or do you believe in family values? Well, both. Do you believe in free enterprise or in government? Again, "both" is a reasonable answer. Does poverty lead to crime, or do high crime rates make neighborhoods poorer? Both, of course.

5   But sometimes, "both" is either the wrong answer or not an available choice. It's easy to be ambivalent about abortion, but ultimately you have to decide: Should it be legal or illegal in most cases? Either getting the budget closer to balance is important or it's not. If you decide that it is, you can cut spending or raise taxes or, yes, do a mixture of both, but you have to do something, and your choices will annoy somebody.

6   Historically, it's even easier to see the problems with moderation. The Whigs and the Stephen Douglas Democrats tried to fudge the slav-

[1]Unsuccessful Republican candidate for President in 1964.

ery issue, and some of them, including Douglas, were quite brilliant in justifying their shilly-shallying. But it didn't work. It's worth remembering that Lincoln was both decisive and moderate on slavery—decisive in opposing slavery's spread, but opposed to outright abolition in the South. The Civil War finally forced him to choose abolition.

7    Moderation or centrism can also be a kind of arithmetical proposition that reveals exactly nothing about what someone believes. You might be for abortion rights, for a tax cut, for strong environmental laws and critical of labor unions. Your friend might be opposed to abortion, against tax cuts, critical of environmental laws and pro-labor. Each of you has just taken two "conservative" positions and two "liberal" positions, which presumably makes both of you "moderate" or "centrist." Yet you have just disagreed on every issue on the table.

8    There are really two approaches to moderation or centrism, one of them principled, the other not. The principled moderate is someone who thinks that things are more or less on the right track. The proper approach is therefore to fiddle and adjust and shuffle things here or there, but to avoid radical change. There is a very good case for this kind of moderation. It holds, basically, that government has an important role to play, but can't do everything; that the market more or less works, but needs adjustment and regulation; that the government cannot as the saying goes, "legislate morality," but probably can nudge people a bit in better or worse directions.

9    The unprincipled moderate constantly looks leftward or rightward to see where the balance of opinion lies. If the push is for health care reform, the unprincipled moderate looks to do something, but a little bit less than those pushing for reform. If the push is for slashing government spending, the unprincipled moderate says, yes, yes, cut, but just not quite that much. This sort of moderate is engaged not in *thinking* but in *positioning.*

10    The first kind of moderate can make the system work. The second kind gives moderation a very bad name. So when somebody tells you he or she is a "moderate" or a "centrist," press them hard. Moderates who tell you what *they* think before you tell them what *you* think may be the genuine article.

774 words

## Comprehension Check  ·

_____ 1. The best statement of the passage's topic is
   a. the problem with moderation.
   b. political labels.
   c. the problem with the political label "moderate."

_____ 2. The best statement of the passage's main idea is

    a. There are problems with the moderate label.
    b. Genuine moderates do hold positions.
    c. The author is a moderate.

_____ 3. One problem with the term *moderate* is that

    a. it has meaning only relative to definitions of "left" and "right."
    b. it cannot be defined.
    c. it is always unprincipled.

_____ 4. The basic problem with the term *moderate* is

    a. deciding where it is positioned between left and right.
    b. no one wants to be moderate.
    c. defining the positions the moderate holds.

_____ 5. Unprincipled moderates

    a. do not like to choose positions.
    b. follow political trends but in a limited way.
    c. both (a) and (b).

_____ 6. With some public policy issues

    a. one should not have to make a simple choice.
    b. one needs to make a choice.
    c. both (a) and (b).

_____ 7. There are two ways to be a moderate:

    a. take one position just to the left and the other just to the right of center.
    b. take extreme positions at opposite ends of the political spectrum.
    c. be a principled or an unprincipled moderate.

_____ 8. You can tell principled moderates by

    a. asking for their political positions.
    b. asking for their names.
    c. how they "position" themselves.

_____ 9. When you *shilly-shally,* you

    a. dance.
    b. become a conservative.
    c. keep shifting between positions.

_____10. An *immoderate* person is one who is

    a. doctrinaire.
    b. progressive.
    c. immodest.

**Expanding Vocabulary**

*After using context clues and a study of word parts, write a brief definition or synonym for each of the following words:*

implicitly (1) _____

purports (1) _____

genocide (2) _____

critique (2) _____

dispositional (3) _____

binary (4) _____

ambivalent (5) _____

**Analysis of Structures and Strategies**

1. What is the author's primary strategy?

   _____

2. What is the topic sentence in paragraph 8?

   _____

3. After reading the topic sentence in paragraph 8, what do you expect the rest of the paragraph to be about?

   _____

4. Does the author fulfill your expectations in paragraph 8?

   _____

   How does he complete your expectations?

   _____

   _____

## For Discussion and Reflection

1. What is the most important new idea about political labels that you have learned? Why is it important to you?

2. In paragraph 4, Dionne gives several examples of positions one should not have to choose between. Do you agree with the author that "the choices so posed are false"? Why or why not?

3. In paragraph 5, Dionne gives several examples of positions on which one does have to make choices. Do you agree with the author that one cannot be ambivalent on these issues? Why or why not?

4. In paragraph 8, Dionne lists some moderate principles. Are these the views that you would expect a moderate to hold? Why or why not? Are there other views that you would add to Dionne's list?

## Your Reading Assessment

1. How accurately did you predict what you would read about?

_____

2. Did the selection answer your questions? _____

   If not, why do you think that it did not?

_____

3. What comments or questions do you have in response to your reading?

_____

_____

_____

## Chapter Review Quiz

*Complete each of the following statements.*

1. *Signal words* are words that

_____

2. Three words that signal listing are:

   _____.

3. In textbooks, a typical strategy for signaling a definition is

   _____.

4. Three words that signal a contrast structure are:

   _____.

5. When annotating a passage describing a process, things you should mark in the margin are:

   _____

   _____.

6. When reading about cause or effect, you want to be sure to recognize and label

   _____.

7. Read and annotate the following paragraph and then state the paragraph's structure or strategy.

   [A] typical wave, born of wind and water far out in the Atlantic, . . . [grows] to its full height on the energy of the winds, with its fellow waves forming a confused, irregular pattern known as a "sea." As the waves gradually pass out of the storm area their height diminishes, the distance between successive crests increases, and the "sea" becomes a "swell," moving at an average speed of about 15 miles an hour. Near the coast a pattern of long, regular swells is substituted for the turbulence of open ocean. But as the swell enters shallow water a startling transformation takes place. For the first time in its existence, the wave feels the drag of shoaling bottom. Its speed slackens, crests of following waves crowd in toward it, abruptly its height increases and the wave form steepens. Then with a spilling, tumbling rush of water falling down into its trough, it dissolves in a seething confusion of foam.

   Rachel Carson, *The Sea Around Us,* rev. ed.

   The paragraph's structure: _____

*The following words have appeared in the chapter or in the reading selections. Circle the letter next to the word (or phrase) that is the best definition of the word in **bold** type.*

1. "people maintain a **social space**"

   a. space where a party is held
   b. distance of people who are not social
   c. space between people in social situations

2. "the reader can **accelerate** his pace"

   a. concede
   b. speed up
   c. slow down

3. "each copy as **tediously** similar as the next"

   a. boringly
   b. technically
   c. charmingly

4. "reasoning becomes more **incapacitated**"

   a. intelligent
   b. ignoble
   c. disabled

5. "Whatever the . . . causes of mass **extinctions**"

   a. exits
   b. losses of life
   c. eruptions

6. "government . . . can **nudge** people"

   a. gently push
   b. nourish
   c. judge

7. **ambivalent**

   a. ambiguous
   b. holding opposing feelings about something
   c. the special atmosphere of a place

# CHAPTER 8

## Drawing Inferences and Understanding Implied Main Ideas

**In this chapter you will learn:**

- How to draw inferences

- To distinguish between appropriate and inappropriate inferences

- To state main ideas that are implied

### ■ PREPARE TO READ

Read and reflect on the chapter's title and objectives. Glance through the chapter, observing headings to see what is covered. Now answer these questions:

1. What do you expect to learn from this chapter?

_____

_____

2. What do you already know about the chapter's topic?

_____

_____

3. What two or three questions do you want answered from reading this chapter?

_____

_____

_____

_____

Drawing inferences is an essential part of interacting with the world around us. It is also an essential part of the reading process. The following cartoon will get you started thinking about the process of drawing inferences. Study the cartoon and then answer the following questions.

1. Who are the men in the cartoon? _____

2. Where are they? _____

How do you know the answer to this question?

_____

_____

■ **FIGURE 8.1**

**Laugh Parade, by Bunny Hoest and John Reiner**

**"I'll get it!"**

Reprinted with permission

3. What has just happened?

_____

_____

4. Why does one of the men say "I'll get it!"?

_____

_____

5. Which of these questions are you answering with facts?

_____

Which ones are you answering based on conclusions you are drawing from the details in the cartoon?

_____

## ■ WHAT ARE INFERENCES?

When you look at the cartoon, you see men playing baseball, and you can see that one of them has just hit the ball over the wall. So, your answer to question 3 is a fact, a specific detail that we can see in the cartoon. Your answers to the other questions, though, are inferences. An **inference** is a conclusion based on evidence. An inference is an assumption about something that is _unknown_ based on something that is _known._ Nowhere in the cartoon are the words "prison" or "prisoners." You have inferred this condition based on the details in the drawing. How many details did you list in answer to question 2? If you did not observe the barbed wire around the wall, the watch tower, and the numbers on the prisoner's shirt, you would not be able to draw the inference that this game is being played in prison.

## Drawing Inferences from Life Experiences

Every day you draw inferences about the people and the situations around you. You decide how people are feeling based on their actions and body language in a particular situation. (Remember that 90 percent of communication is _nonverbal._ Often behavior is a better clue to how someone is feeling than what the person actually tells you.) Use the following exercise to increase your awareness of the inferences you regularly draw.

## EXERCISE 8-1 Workshop on Drawing Inferences from Life Situations

*With your class partner or in small groups, answer the questions following each situation.*

1. Walking down the street, you pass a young boy peering down a grate. One pocket of his pants is pulled out; it has a hole in it. As he leans over the grate, his lower lip begins to tremble.

   a. What has happened?

   _____

   _____

   b. How does the boy feel?

   _____

2. As you jog the bike path along the river, you pass a man carrying a metal case and a long pole. He is whistling.

   a. What is the man about to do? _____

   b. Is he looking forward to the activity? _____

3. You move into the left lane to pass a truck. Suddenly a car is on your rear bumper, with lights flashing and horn sounding. As you move quickly around the truck and back into the right lane, the driver of the car behind you goes by, yelling and gesturing in your direction.

   a. What did the driver want to do? _____

   b. What is his attitude toward you?_____

   c. What can you infer about the driver's emotions?

   _____

   _____

4. You overhear the following dialogue at work.

   Barry, stopping by Joan's desk, says, "Let's have lunch today."
   Joan, "I'm sorry. I'm too busy to stop for lunch today."

Barry, "This is the second day this week that I've suggested lunch and you have been too busy."

Joan, "I'm sorry Barry. This McGarvey project is driving me crazy."

Barry, "You just don't want to have lunch with me."

a. What can you infer about Barry's feelings?

_____

b. What inference has Barry made?

_____

c. If Joan really is busy but wants to keep Barry as a lunch partner, what should she say after Barry's last remark?

_____

_____

## ▪ DRAWING INFERENCES FROM READING

Just as we construct meaning by drawing inferences about the situations around us, so when we read we need to construct meaning out of the words on the page. We construct meaning from both what those words say and what they suggest or imply. Sometimes we need to "fill in" information or ideas that are suggested but not stated outright. Other times we need to draw a conclusion from the specifics that have been presented, to infer a main idea that has been implied but not directly stated. Always, as active readers, we need to work with the author to understand what we are reading.

## Why Writers Suggest Rather Than State

Why can't they just write what they mean? I get tired of "reading between the lines" and looking for "hidden meanings," some readers complain. There are good responses to these complaints. First, remember the cartoon at the beginning of the chapter. Reread your answers to the questions about the cartoon. Those answers aren't funny, are they? Humor is almost always suggestive. Second, language that suggests can be more powerful. It draws us in and makes us participants in the construction of meaning. We don't really read "between the lines." Rather, we are actively engaged in getting the point *of* the lines.

## The Role of Knowledge

Perhaps most importantly, how well we read is connected to the knowledge we bring to the reading. Writers assume certain information in their readers and expect them to use that information as they read. Those lacking the assumed knowledge may have trouble drawing appropriate inferences from their reading. For example, think back to the previous exercise. If you have never seen a fishing pole or tackle box, you will not know what the man is about to do in the second situation. You will be puzzled, or perhaps not take much notice of the man, because the details of the situation do not offer you any clues upon which to draw an inference. See what inferences you can draw in the following exercise.

### EXERCISE 8-2 Recognizing the Role of Knowledge in Drawing Inferences

*Read each of the brief selections and then answer the questions that follow.*

1. In addition to saying no to drugs, teenagers today need to spit in Joe Camel's eye.

   a. What does the writer actually want teens to do?

   _____

   _____

   b. To answer (a), what information do you need to have, or what do you need to infer from the statement?

   _____

   _____

2. Pete Townshend of The Who has severely damaged hearing and, in addition, is plagued by tinnitus, an annoying condition in which there is a continuous ringing in the ears.

   Wood and Wood, *The World of Psychology,* 2nd ed.

   a. How did Pete Townshend damage his hearing?

   _____

b. To answer (a), what information do you need to have, or what do you need to infer from the statement?

_____

_____

c. From the reference to Townshend, what point do you infer that the authors want to make?

_____

_____

3. The skeleton of an elephant lies out in the grasses near a baobab tree and a scattering of black volcanic stones. The thick-trunked, gnarled baobab gesticulates with its branches, as if trying to summon help. There are no tusks lying among the bones, of course; ivory vanishes quickly in East Africa.

Lance Morrow, "Africa," Time

a. From the passage, what do you infer about the elephant's probable cause of death?

_____

b. To understand the last statement, what do you need to know—or infer—about ivory?

_____

_____

c. How does the author want readers to feel about the elephant's death?

_____

_____

4. In the Royal Free Hospital was my mother, Sister McVeagh. He married his nurse which, as they both said often enough (though in different tones of voice), was just as well. That was 1919.

Doris Lessing, "My Father" (a biographical essay)

a. Why was it "just as well" that Lessing's father married her mother? What are readers to infer from this passage?

_____

b. What do you infer to be her father's tone of voice?

_____

c. What do you infer to be her mother's tone of voice? (Consider the time period when reflecting on her tone.)

_____

5. They ate economically, but when he got diabetes in his forties and subsisted on lean meat and lettuce leaves, he remembered suet puddings, treacle puddings, raisin and currant puddings, steak and kidney puddings, bread and butter pudding, "batter cooked in the gravy with the meat," potato cake, plum cake, butter cake, porridge with treacle, fruit tarts and pies, brawn, pig's trotters and pig's cheek and home-smoked ham and sausages. And "lashings of fresh butter and cream and eggs." He wondered if this diet had produced the diabetes, but said it was worth it.

Doris Lessing, "My Father"

a. What are readers to infer about the cause of Lessing's father's diabetes?

_____

_____

b. For the details in the paragraph to provide clues to answer the question, what information do readers need to have?

_____

_____

6. Susan Smith came to national fame as a distraught mother, a self-described victim of carjacking and kidnapping. When it all unraveled, and she was taken to court for arraignment, many people lined the streets shouting epithets at her. One woman said it all: "We believed you!" It was strikingly easy to play upon the fear of the stranger.

Ellen Goodman, "Stranger-Danger"

a. What did Susan Smith _say_ had happened to her?

_____

b. Why was she taken to court? What actually happened?

_____

_____

    c. Did you answer (b) from inference or knowledge of the Susan Smith case?

_____

    d. Were you unable to answer (b) because of lack of information?

_____

    e. Do you think the author expects readers to have knowledge of Susan Smith or to infer from the passage?

_____

On what is your answer based?

_____

_____

## ■ CHARACTERISTICS OF APPROPRIATE INFERENCES

An inference, we have noted, is a conclusion based on *evidence.* An inference is not a guess. It is not an idea we make up rather than doing the hard work of studying the evidence. It is not *our* idea on the subject instead of the author's. Your task as a reader is to understand the writer's views on a subject. Once you are clear about the writer's ideas, then you may disagree if you wish. But, while reading for meaning, do not let your views on the subject distort what you are reading. What are appropriate inferences? Appropriate inferences are based on all the details of a passage, do not contradict any of the details, and are not distorted by the reader's views on the subject.

Let's apply these ideas about inferences to the following paragraph.

> When a colonial housewife went to the village well to draw water for her family, she saw friends, gathered gossip, shared the laughs and laments of her neighbors. When her great-great-granddaughter was blessed with running water, and no longer had to go to the well, this made life easier, but also less interesting. Electricity, mail delivery and the telephone removed more reasons for leaving the house. And now the climax of it all is Television.
>
> Boorstin, "Television: More Deeply Than We Suspect, It Has Changed All of Us"

Boorstin's paragraph contains specific details but no topic sentence, no stated main idea. What main idea are we to infer from the details? Here are three possibilities. Circle the one you think is best.

1. Modern conveniences developed over time.
2. Television is a great modern technological achievement.
3. Some technological advances, especially television, separate us from others.

Which one did you circle? If you focus on the paragraph's listing of new conveniences developed over time, you might select the first main idea statement. But the first statement does not "cover" or take account of the paragraph's discussion of the colonial housewife's lifestyle.

If you focus on the word *climax* in the last sentence, you might select the second inference. But the second main idea statement seems to contradict Boorstin's idea that life, with modern conveniences, required less mingling with neighbors and was "less interesting." You may think that television is a great achievement, but Boorstin does not appear to agree with you. Your own views may be getting in the way of reading what Boorstin has to say. The best inference is the third topic sentence because it captures Boorstin's idea that when information comes directly into our homes we become isolated from our community, and this isolation is not a good thing.

## ■ UNDERSTANDING IMPLIED MAIN IDEAS

You have practiced generalizing from specifics in Chapter 5 and reading for main ideas in Chapter 6. In this chapter you have practiced drawing inferences about experience and from reading. You need to make these skills work together to read for implied main ideas. You may find that stating the paragraph's topic will guide you to an appropriate main idea.

Here is another practice paragraph. Circle the best statement of topic and then write a main-idea statement for the paragraph. (Remember: A main idea must be stated as a complete sentence.)

The corner of the office where I work has no windows. The climate is what they call controlled. I can be there all day without knowing if it's hot or cold outside. I commute in a machine on pavement, following the directions of red and green lights. My work day is determined by a clock that remains the same through all tides, moons, and seasons.

Ellen Goodman, "Content to Be in My Place"

Possible Topics:
a. my work day
b. modern life's lack of connection to nature
c. the conveniences of modern life

Main idea: ___THE CORNER OF THE OFFICE WHERE I WORK___

___HAS NO WINDOWS.___

Which topic did you select? Is the intent of the specific details to recount the writer's work day? If so, she has a rather strange way of describing her day. Is the paragraph about modern conveniences? Is Goodman praising air conditioning when she writes that "the climate is what they call controlled"? Does that sound like a statement of praise? No. The best topic is (b). All of the specifics are parts of the work day that disconnect the writer from the "tides, moons, and seasons"—from the rhythms or patterns of nature. Now, ask yourself: How does the writer feel about the topic? Are we lucky to be sealed off from nature during the work day? If you answer the question with a "No," then you can write a main-idea statement for Goodman's paragraph.

The following exercises will give you practice in drawing inferences to determine the implied main idea in paragraphs. But first, review the guidelines for appropriate inferences.

## Characteristics of Appropriate Inferences

They cover all the details in the passage.

They do not contradict any of the details in the passage.

They explain the writer's ideas, not the reader's ideas, about the topic.

### EXERCISE 8-3 Identifying the Best Main-Idea Statement

*After reading each paragraph, circle the best main-idea statement.*

1. A student of botany and geology, John Muir traveled through much of the Midwest and Plains states on foot. He also traveled through Nevada, Utah, and the Northwest to study forests and glaciers. After discovering many glaciers in the Sierra Mountains, Muir explored Alaska, where he also discovered glaciers, one of which was named after him. Throughout his travels he wrote and published his observations, and he called for forest conservation and establishing national parks. He helped with the campaign to create Yosemite National Park and later camped there with then President Theodore Roosevelt. Roosevelt set aside public lands as forest preserves and named a redwood forest in California after Muir shortly before Muir's death in 1908.

   adapted from *American Heritage History of the United States*

   a. Muir explored the United States and discovered many glaciers.

   b. Muir was an important geologist and conservationist who contributed to the development of our national parks.

2. The Nile was responsible for creating an area several miles wide on both banks of the river that was fertile and capable of producing abundant harvests. . . . The river . . . was seen as life enhancing, not life threatening. Although a system of organized irrigation was still necessary, the small villages along the Nile could make the effort. . . . In addition to providing food, it [the Nile] promoted easy transportation and encouraged communication.

Jackson J. Spielvogel, *Western Civilization,* 2nd ed., Vol. 1

a. The Nile River was central to the development of Egyptian civilization.

b. The Nile was a means of transportation from one part of Egypt to another.

3. Young males and females are equally likely to try alcohol, tobacco or illegal drugs. But males, particularly young men 18 to 21 years old, do so more often and in larger quantities.

a. There are some gender differences among young people in behavior that threatens health.

b. Young men are more foolish than young women.

4. H. M. Skeels and H. B. Dye . . . placed thirteen infants whose mental retardation was so obvious that no one wanted to adopt them, in Glenwood State School, an institution for the mentally retarded. Each infant, then about 19 months old, was assigned to a separate ward of women ranging in mental age from 5 to 12 and in chronological age from 18 to 50. The women were pleased with this arrangement. . . . The researchers left a control group of twelve infants, also retarded but higher in intelligence, at the orphanage, where they received the usual care. Two and a half years later, Skeels and Dye tested all the children's intelligence. Their findings were startling: Those assigned to the retarded women had gained an average of twenty-eight IQ points while those who remained in the orphanage had lost thirty points.

James M. Henslin, *Sociology,* 2nd ed.

a. Orphanages should be done away with.

b. Intelligence is at least partly learned through stimulating social interaction.

5. In 1982, scientists in Antarctica discovered that the ozone layer above them was getting thinner. The cause is a buildup in the atmosphere of chemicals called chlorofluorocarbons (CFCs). These are used in aerosol spray cans, foam plastics, refrigerators, and air-conditioning systems. When these products are dumped, the CFCs slowly rise into the atmosphere, and, in the Antarctic winter, they go through complex chemical reactions that destroy the ozone.

Michael Scott, *Ecology*

a. Discarded products containing CFCs are causing serious damage to the ozone layer in the atmosphere above Antarctica.

b. Winter in Antarctica is difficult.

## EXERCISE 8-4 Recognizing Topics and Inferring Main Ideas

*After reading each paragraph, circle the best statement of the paragraph's topic. Briefly explain your choice. Then write a main-idea statement for the paragraph.*

1. [Elephant] babies are eagerly accepted not only by the members of their own groups but by all other elephants as well, including strange bulls— a phenomenon almost unique in animal behavior. There are many well-documented stories about unrelated bulls rescuing young calves in swamps, for example, and under all manner of other circumstances. Moreover, orphans are readily adopted by new families, even for nursing. Unrelated or only distantly related herds will intermingle and mix freely at waterholes, the adults greeting one another with quiet dignity and the youngsters frolicking together.

Fetner, The African Safari

Topics:

a. acceptance of baby elephants

b. social nature of elephants

Explain your choice: _____ THEY TALK ABOUT ALL THE CHARAC-

TERISTICS PEOPLE SAW ELEPHANTS IN THEIR SOCIAL

NATURE TO ADOPT BABY ELEPHANTS.

Main idea BABIES ARE EAGERLY ACCEPTED (#)

---

2. In the Medicare program for Americans over 65, for example, women outnumber men 19 million to 13 million. They depend on Medicare longer, using the program for about 15 years compared on average with 7 years for men. They also outnumber men in the Social Security program; nearly 60 percent of beneficiaries are female.

Abigail Trafford, "Growing Old Is Largely a Job for Women"

Topics:

a. women's dependency on government services for the elderly

b. women's longevity

Explain your choice: ___THEY TALK ABOUT THE WOMEN___

___BEADING MAN IN A LOT OF BENEFISIARY PROGRAMS.___

_____

Main idea ___WOMEN OUTNUMBER MAN___

_____

3. As far back as 500 B.C., when the Nok culture flourished in Nigeria, furnaces were being used to smelt iron. The Nigerian state of Benin exchanged ambassadors with Portugal in 1486. At that time Timbuktu in Mali was a major trading center of international fame. The splendors of the Songhai Empire, which stretched from Mali to Kano, Nigeria, in the fifteenth and sixteenth centuries, were compared by early travelers with those of contemporary Europe. . . . Iron-Age Africans started building stone structures in the area we call Zimbabwe as early as A.D. 1100, and sixteenth-century Portuguese maritime traders found that some West African textiles were superior to anything then being made in Europe.

David Lamb, *The Africans*

Topics:

a. African buildings
b. early cultures in Africa

Explain your choice:_____

_____

_____

Main idea _____

_____

4. The Black Death of the mid-fourteenth century . . . ravaged Europe, wiping out 25 to 50 percent of the population and causing economic, social, political, and cultural upheaval. A Sienese chronicler wrote that "father abandoned child, wife husband, one brother another, for the plague seemed to strike through breath and sight. And so they died. And no one could be found to bury the dead, for money or friendship." People were horrified by an evil force they could not understand and by the subsequent breakdown of all normal human relations.

Jackson J. Spielvogel, *Western Civilization*, 2nd ed., Vol. 1

Topics:

    a. the Black Death in the fourteenth century
    b. the devastation of the Black Death

Explain your choice:_____

_____

_____

Main idea  _____

_____

5. In the past ten years, Miami's population grew only 3.4 percent, but its Spanish-speaking population grew 15 percent, making the city 62 percent Hispanic. Throughout the United States, 83 percent of residents speak English at home, but only 25 percent of Miami residents do so.

Topics:

    a. Hispanic growth in Miami
    b. Hispanic growth in the United States

Explain your choice:_____

_____

_____

Main idea  _____

_____

## ▪ DRAWING INFERENCES AND UNDERSTANDING MAIN IDEAS IN LONGER PASSAGES

The tasks of drawing inferences as you read and understanding implied main ideas are much the same for longer passages as for sentences or paragraphs. The only difference is that you have to stay alert and keep working with the author for a longer period of time. If you stop concentrating before finishing the section or article, you may not "fill in" information that is needed for clarity. Or, you may not keep all the specifics in mind that are needed to recognize the implied main idea of the passage. As you work with longer passages, keep these guidelines in mind.

## Guidelines for Understanding Implied Meanings

1. Annotate carefully as you read.
2. Think about levels of specificity. Focus on major details.
3. Ask yourself, "What does the author want me to learn or understand from this passage?" "What is the author's purpose in writing in this manner about this subject?"
4. State the passage's topic.
5. State the passage's main idea.
6. Check your main idea statement against the details. Have you covered all details? Have you avoided contradicting any details?

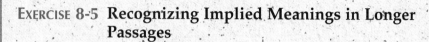

## EXERCISE 8-5  Recognizing Implied Meanings in Longer Passages

*Read and annotate each passage. After reading a passage, complete the exercise that follows.*

I. Exactly what are they teaching in our schools these days? . . . A new national survey suggests that, on average, college graduates today know fewer selected basic facts about government and politics than college graduates did in 1947.

Likewise, today's high school grads appear to know less about government and politics than their educational equals of five decades ago.

For example, a Gallup survey in 1947 found that 77 percent of all Americans surveyed who had graduated from high school but not gone on to college knew which party controlled the U.S. House of Representatives.

Today, barely half—54 percent—of all high school graduates know that the Republicans control the House. . . . [in 1996]

Political knowledge also has slipped among college graduates: 90 percent knew which party controlled the House in 1947, compared to 80 percent in the latest survey.

Richard Morin, "Dumbing Down Democracy"

1. What is the passage's topic?

_____

2. What is implied in the opening question?

_____

_____

3. What are we to infer about the cause or causes for the decline in knowledge about government and politics?

_____

_____

4. What is the author's attitude toward the decline in knowledge?

_____

II. While thousands of businessmen organized corporations, [in the nineteenth century] they all fade from sight in the shadow of the solemn, muscular, well-dressed, and deeply religious person of John Davison Rockefeller. Beginning his career as an accountant, Rockefeller avoided service in the Civil War by hiring a substitute.

■ **FIGURE 8.2**

**John D. Rockefeller and His Attorneys**

He made a small fortune selling provisions to the Union Army, but a small fortune was only an appetizer. Rockefeller had a voracious appetite for riches. Outside of home and Sunday School, which he taught, he talked of little but business. After swinging a lucrative deal as a young man, he danced a two-step jig and exclaimed "Bound to be rich! I'm bound to be rich!"

Rockefeller disapproved of smoking and drinking, in part because of his Baptist faith, but in part because cigars and whiskey cost money that could be invested to make more money. He carefully recorded how he spent every dime; he spent few frivolously. He would remove his stovepipe hat and bend down to pick up a penny.

Joseph R. Conlin, "John D. Rockefeller," The American Past, 3rd ed.

1. What is the passage's topic?

   _____

2. List three traits or personality characteristics of Rockefeller.

   _____

   _____

   _____

3. Do any of these traits seem contradictory to you? If so, which ones? Explain.

   _____

   _____

   _____

   _____

4. Write a main-idea statement for the passage. (Hint: Begin with "John D. Rockefeller was. . . .")

   _____

   _____

   _____

## ■ Figure 8.3

**Amelia Earhart**

## Amelia Earhart

by **Vincent Wilson, Jr.**

A former college instructor, Vincent Wilson has also served as a writer, editor, and historian with the U.S. Government. The following one-page article on Amelia Earhart is part of *The Book of Distinguished American Women* (2nd ed., 1992). Wilson has written several other books in the same American History Research Associates series, including *The Book of the Presidents* and *The Book of Great American Documents.*

### ■ Prepare

1. Identify the author and the work. What do you expect the author's purpose to be?

_____

_____

2. Preread to identify the subject and make predictions. What do you expect to read about?

_____

_____

3. What do you already know about the subject?

_____

_____

_____

4. Raise two questions that you expect the article to answer.

_____

_____

_____

1     Amelia Earhart was the first woman of flight—with an array of first's unmatched in the world. Her daring flights in the 1920s and 1930s captured the imagination of the American public and signaled that women could participate fully in pioneering this new frontier.

2     As a child, Amelia Earhart liked to ride horseback and a miniature homemade roller coaster. After high school, she tried nursing and premedical studies before she first flew—with barnstormer[1] Frank Hawks in Glendale, California, in 1920. Two years later she was flying her own Kinner Canary in California air shows.

3     Amelia Earhart was working in a settlement house in Boston and flying in her free time when publisher George Putnam chose her to fly as a passenger on a transatlantic flight a year after Lindberg's historic crossing. Wilmer Stultz piloted the Fokker trimotor from Newfoundland to Wales; Amelia Earhart kept the flight log. She was the first woman to cross the Atlantic by air, and suddenly she was famous. New York gave "Lady Lindy" a ticker-tape parade. In 1931 Miss Earhart married George Putnam—with an agreement that she have complete freedom to travel. Putnam managed her affairs.

4     On May 21–22, 1932, Amelia Earhart flew solo from Newfoundland to Ireland. In a Lockheed monoplane she flew the 2026 miles in 14

[1]One who tours as a stunt pilot.

hours, 56 minutes, much of it through storms and fog—the first woman to fly the Atlantic alone. She was smothered with honors—among others, the cross of the French Legion of Honor and the U.S. Distinguished Flying Cross. Other first's followed: two transcontinental records and the first non-stop flight from Mexico City to New York.

5    In 1937 a round-the-world flight (another first) was planned, to test long-range performance of crew and aircraft. After an unsuccessful attempt, on June 1st Amelia Earhart and navigator Fred Noonan left Miami, Florida, flying east on an equatorial route that took them across the Atlantic Ocean, Africa, and the Indian Ocean. At Lae, New Guinea, on July 2, they took off to fly 2570 miles to Howland Island, a spot in the Pacific scarcely longer than its runway. They never reached it. Hours after they were due, the Coast Guard cutter *Itaska*, near Howland, received their last voice messages: " . . . gas is running low . . . " and "We are on a line of position. . . ." Sea and air searches found nothing.

6    For years rumors persisted that Miss Earhart had been on an espionage mission and might have been captured by the Japanese. But the facts—including recent (1992) discoveries of possible plane parts in the Howland area—strongly suggest that the plane simply missed Howland and crashed into the sea.

7    Amelia Earhart had a passion for flying—she even wrote verse about it—but she was also deeply committed to the cause of feminism: both as a woman and a flyer, she was a pioneer. She once confided to her husband that, for her, the ideal way to die would be swiftly to go down with her plane.

                                                                496 words

## Comprehension Check

*Answer the following with a, b, or c to indicate the phrase that best completes each statement.*

_____ 1. Amelia Earhart was married to

   a. Lindberg.
   b. Frank Hawks.
   c. George Putnam.

_____ 2. Amelia Earhart was

   a. the first woman to fly alone across the Atlantic.
   b. the first person to fly alone across the Atlantic.
   c. the first female spy.

_____ 3. A Kinner Canary is

    a. a settlement house in Boston.

    b. a type of plane.

    c. the name of an award Earhart won.

_____ 4. On a transcontinental flight, Amelia Earhart

    a. died in New Guinea.

    b. died on the Coast Guard ship _Itaska._

    c. died at sea when her plane crashed.

_____ 5. Amelia Earhart was given many awards including

    a. the Legion of Honor.

    b. the distinguished Flying Cross.

    c. both (a) and (b).

_____ 6. Amelia Earhart

    a. wanted freedom to travel.

    b. was daring from childhood on.

    c. both (a) and (b).

## Expanding Vocabulary

_After using context clues and a study of word parts, write a brief definition or synonym for each of the following words._

smothered (4) _____

equatorial route (5)_____

espionage (6) _____

feminism (7)_____

## Analysis of Main Ideas

1. State the article's topic:

    _____

2. Circle the best main-idea statement:

    a. Amelia Earhart made history in the 1920s and 1930s.

    b. Amelia Earhart was a pioneer for women and in the history of flight.

3. Briefly explain your selection of a main idea.

_____

_____

4. What main idea are we to infer from reading paragraph 2?

_____

_____

5. Why was Earhart called "Lady Lindy" in paragraph 3?

_____

6. Why does the author conclude with Earhart's statement to her husband? What are we to infer from the conclusion?

_____

_____

### For Discussion and Reflection

1. What is the most important new fact you have learned about Amelia Earhart? Why is it important?

2. If you had a chance to go back in time and meet Earhart, what would you talk with her about? Why?

3. Wilson's article about Earhart is one of 50 in his book on distinguished American women. If you were to make such a book, what women would you include? See how long a list of important American women you can make. Remember to consider various fields of endeavor from colonial times to the present.

### Your Reading Assessment

1. How accurately did you predict what you would read about?

_____

2. Did the selection answer your questions? _____

   If not, why do you think that it did not?

_____

3. What comments or questions do you have in response to your reading?

_____

_____

_____

## Chapter Review Quiz

*Complete each of the following statements.*

1. An *inference* is

_____.

2. We draw inferences from both _____

and _____.

3. To draw many inferences we need to "fill in" from our

_____.

4. Three characteristics of appropriate inferences are:

_____

_____

_____

5. Read the following paragraph and then complete the exercise that follows.

   Several years before the Constitutional Convention, James Madison of Virginia read books of political philosophy that Thomas Jefferson sent him from Paris. During the Convention he took the most detailed notes. He also moderated conflicts between George Mason, who believed strongly in individual liberty, and Alexander Hamilton.

   a. Based on the last sentence, what can you infer to be Hamilton's political philosophy?

   _____

   _____

b. Write a main-idea statement for the paragraph.

_____

_____

6. Read the following passage and then complete the exercise that follows.

Tropical rainforests comprise . . . about 8.3 percent of the Earth's total land surface. . . . These remarkable forests . . . have been exploited and devastated at an accelerating pace. . . .

The irony of tropical deforestation is that the anticipated economic benefits are usually illusory. Much of the forest clearing, especially in Latin America, is in response to the social pressure of overcrowding and poverty in societies where most of the people are landless. The governments throw open "new lands" for settlement in the rainforest. The settlers clear the land for crop growing or livestock raising. The result almost always is an initial "nutrient pulse" of high soil productivity, followed in only two or three years by a pronounced fertility decline as the nutrients are quickly leached and cropped out the soil, . . . and erosion becomes rampant.

Much concern has been expressed about tropical deforestation, and some concrete steps have been taken. . . . In 1985 a comprehensive world plan, sponsored by the World Bank, the World Resources Institute, and the United Nations Development Programme, was introduced. It proposes concrete, country-by-country strategies to combat tropical deforestation. It is an $8 billion, five-year project, dealing with everything from fuel-wood scarcity to training extension foresters. Its price tag makes its implementation unlikely.

Meanwhile, the sounds of the axe and the chainsaw and the bulldozer continue to be heard throughout the tropical forest lands.

Tom L. McKnight, *Essentials of Physical Geography*

a. What is the passage's topic?

_____

b. What is one reason that rainforests in Latin America are being cut down?

_____

Is the deforestation usually successful? _____

c. What is the author's attitude toward deforestation?

_____

What clues help you answer the question?

_____

_____

d. Write a main-idea statement for the paragraph.

_____

_____

*The following words have appeared in the chapter or in the reading selections. Circle the letter next to the word (or phrase) that is the best definition of the word in* **bold** *type.*

1. the "gnarled baobab **gesticulates** with its branches"

    a. ensnares
    b. gestures
    c. guesses

2. "**implied** main ideas"

    a. missing
    b. stated indirectly, suggested
    c. implicated

3. "Portuguese **maritime** traders"

    a. sea
    b. war time
    c. market

4. "swinging a **lucrative** deal"

    a. lucky
    b. profitable
    c. illegal

5. "on an **espionage** mission"

    a. spy
    b. special
    c. opinion

# CHAPTER 9

*Word Power 3: Distinguishing among Words*

**In this chapter you will learn:**

- To distinguish among words that sound alike
- To distinguish among words that look similar
- To understand some common idiomatic expressions
- Strategies for improving spelling
- Four basic spelling rules
- The spelling of frequently used words
- To improve visual perception of words

## ■ PREPARE TO READ

Read and reflect on the chapter's title and objectives. Glance through the chapter, observing headings, to see what is covered. Now answer these questions:

1. What do you expect to learn from this chapter?

_____

_____

2. What do you already know about the chapter's topic?

_____

_____

3. What two or three questions do you want answered from reading this chapter?

_____

_____

_____

_____

How well do you see? Just for fun, look at the Figure 9.1 and then write what you see.

_____

The picture in Figure 9.1, often found in psychology texts, is a famous example of the principle that we organize visual stimuli into meaning. In the

■ FIGURE 9.1

**Reversing Figure and Ground**

picture, you may see a white vase against a black background. But you can also reverse the figure and the background and see two black faces, looking at each other (in profile), against a white background. Many people will organize the picture in only one of the possible ways until the other possibility is pointed out.

As we observed in Chapter 1, reading is not only an intellectual skill but also a visual skill. Readers have to process the marks on the page visually first in order to make meaning from those marks. This chapter is all about words—and their meanings—but also about the visual processing of words. One way of processing visual stimuli is by the principle of similarity. Things that look alike are considered to be alike. This principle can get us into trouble when we are reading because many words look much alike (or sound alike) but do not have the same meanings. Also, some words, when put together in particular phrases, no longer have their usual meanings (another blow to the similarity principle). So, readers need to develop skills in seeing (and hearing and understanding) differences.

## ■ WORDS THAT SOUND ALIKE: HOMONYMS

English has a number of sets of words that are pronounced alike, may be spelled alike or differently, but have different meanings. Such words are called *homonyms*. Many of these words—such as *meet* and *meat*—are common words appearing frequently in your reading and writing. You want to be sure of the meanings of each of these "sound alike" words so that you read without confusion and write without mistakes.

### EXERCISE 9-1 Matching Definitions of Homonyms

*For each of the sets of words, match the definitions with the words. Put the letter of the correct definition on the line next to the word. The first one has been started for you.*

| | | |
|---|---|---|
| _a_ | 1. too | a. also |
| ____ | 2. to | b. word for 2 |
| ____ | 3. two | c. toward, against, in front of |
| ____ | 4. its | d. possessive form of it |
| ____ | 5. it's | e. it is |
| ____ | 6. they're | f. possessive form of they |
| ____ | 7. there | g. they are |
| ____ | 8. their | h. at or in that place |

_____ 9. meet         i. to come upon, be introduced to

_____ 10. meat       j. edible flesh of animals

_____ 11. plain      k. a flying machine

_____ 12. plane     l. open to view, clear, simple

_____ 13. whole     m. an opening or gap

_____ 14. hole      n. not divided, complete

_____ 15. hear      o. perceive by the ear

_____ 16. here      p. in this place

_____ 17. do        q. perform, complete, put forth

_____ 18. due       r. payable on demand, owed

_____ 19. waste     s. middle part of human trunk

_____ 20. waist     t. use carelessly

_____ 21. witch     u. what particular one or ones

_____ 22. which     v. a sorceress

## EXERCISE 9-2  Selecting the Appropriate Homonym

_Read each sentence. Then circle the word in **bold** type that best completes the sentence._

1. The school's assistant [**principle / principal**] is in charge of after-school activities.

2. The senator spoke from the [**capital / capitol**] steps.

3. Juan [**through / threw**] the ball in from right field.

4. The choir director decided to [**altar / alter**] the music for the service.

5. The child appeared confused and spoke in a strange [**manor / manner**].

6. As election day approached, we waited eagerly to see [**which / witch**] way the country would vote.

7. The construction workers arrived at the [**sight / site / cite**] for another day in the hot sun.

8. Please let me know [**weather / whether**] you will be attending.

9. Ruth's new [**stationary / stationery**] included her fax number and e-mail address.

10. Some students are seldom [**scene / seen**] by their instructors and class-mates.

## Exercise 9-3  Using Homonyms in Sentences

*Select one word from each of the following pairs of words and use that word in a sentence of your own.*

1. **sale / sail** _____

_____

2. **knew / new** _____

_____

3. **vale / veil** _____

_____

4. **ail / ale** _____

_____

5. **aisle / isle** _____

_____

## ▨ Words That Look or Sound Somewhat Alike: Pseudohomonyms

A *pseudohomonym* is a false (*pseudo:* false) homonym. Real homonyms are pronounced exactly the same. Pseudohomonyms sound similar or look similar and are often confused by both readers and writers, but they are not pronounced exactly the same. When we confuse two words and read—or write—the wrong one, the result is the same, even if the words are not exact homonyms.

To avoid mistakes, you can approach these easily confused words in three ways:

1. Concentrate on hearing differences in pronunciation and make certain that you pronounce the words correctly.

2. Observe differences in spelling and practice spelling the words correctly.

3. Include these words in your vocabulary study. When you *really* know the words, you won't confuse them.

EXERCISE 9-4 **Studying Pseudohomonyms**

*Circle the word in* **bold** *type that completes the sentence. Do all of the sentences without using your dictionary. Compare your answers with classmates. Look up the definitions of words that you missed and add them to your vocabulary study.*

1. The students knew that a test was [**eminent / imminent**].

2. Please do not waste the [**excess / access**] paper; it can be used for another project.

3. The [**personnel / personal**] director prepared to interview eight candidates for the job.

4. Dustin Hoffman's performance as Willie Loman greatly [**affected / effected**] theatergoers.

5. Many teenage girls develop eating disorders as they try to [**lose / loose**] weight.

6. Freud gave the name *superego* to the human [**conscious / conscience**].

7. Margaret had traveled to all European capitals [**accept / except**] Madrid.

8. After the airlines lost his luggage, Carlos had to buy some new [**clothes / cloths**].

9. The Sahara [**desert / dessert**] continues its relentless expansion in Africa.

10. The new boss seems to be a [**descent / decent**] and caring person.

## ■ IDIOMS

An idiomatic expression is a phrase that cannot be understood simply by understanding each word in the phrase. Instead, you have to learn the meaning of the entire phrase. For example, the idiom **call it a day** has nothing to do with "calling." It means quitting or stopping work for that day.

We learn idioms the same way we learn individual words: by hearing them or reading them in context. All languages have idiomatic expressions; idioms are just the way "the natives" speak. Students for whom English is a second language will have some trouble with idioms initially but will learn them with time and practice. Fortunately, many idioms are included in dictionary entries. You will find them included with the key word in the phrase. For example, the idiom **below the belt** can be found under the word *belt*. Here is a list of some common idioms used in the following exercises.

| Idiom | Meaning |
|---|---|
| beat the bushes | make a thorough search |
| on the ball | alert, efficient |
| down the line | later on |
| face the music | accept unpleasant circumstances |
| bite the bullet | face a difficult situation stoically |
| big on | enthusiastic about |
| sit tight | patiently await the next move |
| goes to bat for | supports or defends |
| hand in glove | in close association |
| blow off steam | release anger or emotion |
| to burn | in great amounts |
| calling the shots | be in charge |
| out of line | uncalled for, improper |
| come on board | join a job effort |
| draw a blank | fail to remember something |

 **EXERCISE 9-5 Understanding Idioms**

*After studying the list of idioms, cover the list while you work this exercise. Read each sentence and then answer the questions that follow. Use your own words in the answers, not the words in the sentence. Each idiom is in italics.*

1. The boss told personnel to *beat the bushes* to find the best accountant.
   a. What does the boss want personnel to do?

   _____

   b. How are they to accomplish their goal?

   _____

2. The boss is *big on* the new accountant who has *come on board*.
   a. Is the accountant working for the boss or not?

   _____

b. Is the boss happy or unhappy with the accountant?

_____

3. Others in accounting are worried that the new person will be _calling the shots._

  a. What do the others think the new person may do?

  _____

  b. How do they feel about it?

  _____

4. Others at the company are prepared to _sit tight_ and see if the new accountant is _on the ball._

  a. What are other workers going to do?

  _____

  b. What do they want to see in the new accountant?

  _____

5. Someone in marketing observed that what really matters is how the new guy in accounting manages _down the line,_ and whether or not the boss _goes to bat_ for him.

  a. When, according to the person from marketing, should the new guy be judged?

  _____

  b. What might the boss do to or for the accountant?

  _____

6. Mary, the office manager, complained that the gossipers were _out of line_ and should get back to work or _face the music._

  a. What might happen to the gossipers?

  _____

  b. What does Mary think of their behavior?

  _____

7. The Personnel Director *drew a blank* when asked about the accountant's previous work experience.

    a. What happened to the Personnel Director?

    _____

8. Well, if he is such hot stuff, complained Joan in accounting, I'll bet he will be *hand in glove* with the boss by summer.

    a. Will the new accountant be in good or bad shape with the boss?

    _____

    b. Is Joan happy about the situation?

    _____

9. Now that we have *blown off steam,* observed Mary, we might as well *bite the bullet* and go back to work.

    a. What have the office workers been doing?

    _____

    b. What does Mary think they should do now?

    _____

10. Why don't we go out to lunch, suggests Bill; we have *money to burn.*

    a. Do the workers have money for lunch or not?

    _____

## ■ IMPROVING SPELLING

Language skills—reading, writing, talking, and listening—are all related. Improvement in one skill can lead to improvement in another. The opposite can also be true. For example: If you keep misspelling the word *angle* when you write, you may confuse *angle* and *angel* when you are reading. That's why there is this section on spelling improvement in your reading text. Here are specific steps you can take to improve your spelling skills.

### Use Your Dictionary for Spelling and Pronunciation

Keep your dictionary handy when you are writing—or editing your writing. Do not settle for written work that contains spelling errors. When reviewing class notes, correct misspellings, especially for important terms introduced by your instructor.

Also study the phonetic spelling of words to reinforce correct pronunciation. (Review the discussion of pronunciation in Chapter 4.) You will have trouble spelling words correctly if you are not speaking them correctly. For example, some people pronounce *medicine* (měd´ĭ-sĭn) as if it were spelled *medcine*. The incorrect pronunciation could lead you to spell the word without its first *i*.

## EXERCISE 9-6 Workshop on Pronunciation to Reinforce Spelling

*With your class partner, find the phonetic spellings for each of the following pairs of words. Study the pronunciation key in Chapter 4. Then take turns pronouncing each of the pairs of words. Work on correct pronunciation and on hearing the differences.*

| Words to Pronounce | Phonetic Spelling |
|---|---|
| 1. breath | _____ |
| breathe | _____ |
| 2. since | _____ |
| sense | _____ |
| 3. decent | _____ |
| descent | _____ |
| 4. except | _____ |
| accept | _____ |
| 5. then | _____ |
| than | _____ |

## Use Electronic Aids When You Write

When writing papers, use the spell check on your typewriter or computer. If spelling is a big problem for you, purchase a "spelling only" dictionary or electronic speller for use when you write in class. (Most instructors will approve of these aids for in-class work.) Reminder: Spelling needs to be close to the correct version for the electronic speller to give you the spelling of the word. If your error comes near the beginning of the word, often the electronic speller cannot recognize the word.

## Divide Words into Word Parts or Syllables to Aid Spelling

Recognizing word parts can help you with spelling as well as with understanding the word's meaning. From shorter words to new terms, you can conquer spelling demons if you break the word into smaller units that you can more easily spell. For example, hear all the syllables in math-*e*-ma-tics (not mathmatics), and you will have less trouble spelling the word. Separate *commitment* into its word parts: *commit* and *ment*. You will be less likely to make the common mistake of spelling the word with two *t*'s in the middle. (Review, if necessary, word parts and dividing words into syllables discussed in Chapter 4.)

## Review Basic Spelling Rules

There are many spelling rules—and many exceptions to them. Still, if you can become competent with just four rules, you will eliminate many of the frequent errors with commonly used words. Review each of the following rules, study the examples, and work the exercises. Return to these pages for additional review as needed.

### I. Words with *ie* and *ei*

To conquer most of the *ie* and *ei* words, learn this verse:

> Write *i* before *e*
> Except after *c*
> Or when sounded like *a*
> As in *neighbor* or *weigh.*

The verse is a good spelling guide for words in which the *ie* sound is a single sound pronounced as a long *e*. This is the sound you hear in *believe.*
As the verse reminds us, there are two major exceptions to the *ie* order.

Write *ei* after *c*: receive, perceive.

Write *ei* when the sound is the *a* sound in *neighbor* or *weigh.*

Exceptions include foreign-language words such as *stein* and some common words, including: *height, weird, leisure, seize,* and *either.*

### Exercise 9-7  The *ie/ei* Rule and Exceptions

*Complete the word with the missing letters in each of the following sentences. Each word will have either* ie *or* ei *in it.*

1. The horses pulled the sl_____gh smoothly over the frozen lake.

2. The driver r_____ned in the horses as they approached the barn.

3. The Joneses invited the Cardozas to dinner at _____ [8].

4. The Cardozas were delighted to rec_____ve the invitation.

5. The thief s_____zed the lady's pocketbook and ran across the f_____ld.

6. The ch_____f accountant grabbed his br_____fcase and left the office.

7. She painted the c_____ling black to ach_____ve a modern look.

8. Do not dec_____ve yourself; some people are truly w_____rd.

## II. Final Y

More than one *monkey* is spelled *monkeys*.

More than one *doggy* is spelled *doggies*.

How do you know when to add *s* to make a plural and when to change *y* to *i* and add *es*? Here is the rule:

- When the final *y* is preceded by a vowel (a, e, i, o, u), just add *s: attorney, attorneys*.
- When the final *y* is preceded by a consonant (all the letters that are not vowels), change the *y* to *i* and add *es: ally, allies*.
- Apply the same rule to adding suffixes—with one exception. With any suffix NOT beginning with an *i*, follow the rules stated above:

  employ + er = employer
  empty + er = emptier

  BUT, for any suffix beginning with an *i*, keep the *y* and add the suffix:
  destroy + ing = destroying
  marry + ing = marrying

### EXERCISE 9-8 Practice with Final Y

*Fill in the blanks in each sentence by making a word out of the parts in square brackets.*

1. You should keep _____ [study + ing] until you under-

   stand the new _____ [theory + s].

2. One twin was more _____ [beauty + ful]; the other was

_____ [funny + er].

3. The _____ [alley + s] of many cities are used for drug dealing.

4. The professor _____ [try + ed] to help her students get ready for the next test.

5. The couple offered their _____ [apology + s] for arriving late to dinner.

6. The camel _____ [carry + s] his water with him in his hump.

7. Libraries _____ [category + ize] books by their subjects.

8. _____ [Donkey + s] are animals that get little respect,

whereas almost everyone loves _____ [puppy + s].

9. The _____ [folly + s] of youth are best forgotten.

10. The student complained _____ [angry + ily] about her grade.

### III. Final Silent *E*

Many English words end in a silent *e*. Although the *e* is not pronounced, it changes the way we pronounce the previous vowels. For example, with the silent *e*:

| | | |
|---|---|---|
| *rat* | becomes | *rate* |
| *bit* | becomes | *bite* |
| *us* | becomes | *use* |

The silent *e* affects spelling and pronunciation in these short words. The silent *e* also has an effect on the spelling of words when suffixes are added. Here is the general rule:

- Drop the silent *e* when adding a suffix beginning with a vowel: care + ing = caring
- Keep the silent *e* when adding a suffix beginning with a consonant: care + less = careless

There is an exception to this rule. (It wouldn't be English without an exception!)

- In words with a *c* (pronounced as *s*) or *g* (pronounced as *j*) before the final *e*, keep the *e* when adding ANY suffix.

  notice + able = noticeable
  courage + ous = courageous

Even though each suffix above begins with a vowel, the final *e* is kept because of the sound of the *c* in *notice* and the *g* in *courage*.

## EXERCISE 9-9  Practice with Final *E*

*Fill in the blanks in each sentence by making a word out of the parts in square brackets.*

1. The boys were _____ [hope + ing] to get tickets to the concert.

2. The instructor asked students to do all their _____ [write + ing] in pen.

3. Guests were advised to place all _____ [value + ables] in the hotel safe.

4. The principal came out to the playground to break up the _____ [argue + ment].

5. Hazel assured George that she _____ [true + ly] loved him.

6. The applicant was _____ [nerve + ous] before her interview.

7. Todd _____ [argue + ed] _____ [fierce + ly] to win the debate.

8. London's weather is so _____ [change + able].

9. The flower _____ [arrange + ment] was beautiful.

10. Since the restaurant does not take reservations, it's always _____ [advantage + ous] to arrive early.

### IV. Doubling Final Consonants

> end + ing = ending
> begin + ing = beginning

Why is there a second *n* in *beginning* but not a second *d* in *ending*? The answer is:

> Double the final consonant of a word when all of these conditions apply:
> 1. The word ends in a single consonant preceded by a single vowel.
> 2. The word is one syllable or the last syllable is stressed.
> 3. The suffix begins with a vowel.

Let's see how all the parts of the rule apply.

1. Which of the following words end in one consonant preceded by one vowel?

    > end, begin, resist, plan

    Only *begin* and *plan*, so there is no doubling in *ending* or *resisting*.

2. Which of the following words is one syllable or is stressed on the last syllable?

    > begin, plan, control, junior

    *Plan* is one syllable. *Begin´* and *control´* are stressed on the last syllable, but *ju´nior* is stressed on the first syllable, so the rule would not apply to *junior*.

3. Which suffixes begin with a vowel?

    > -ing, -ed, -ful   so:
    > plan<u>n</u>ing
    > begin<u>n</u>ing
    > contro<u>ll</u>ed
    > cup<u>p</u>ed   BUT   cupful

### EXERCISE 9-10 Practice with Doubling the Final Consonant

*Apply the rule to form words from the following parts.*

1. skip + ing = _____

2. resist + ent = _____

3. ship + ment = _____

4. swim + ing = _____

5. forgot + en = _____

6. faith + ful = _____

7. compel + ing = _____

8. enter + ing = _____

9. commit + ment = _____

10. maintain + ing = _____

## Practice, Practice, Practice!

One of the best ways to become a better speller is through practice. You can begin with the following 280 common words. If you study 20 words a week, you will finish the list in only 14 weeks. (You can test yourself, or your instructor may test you each week.)

| | | |
|---|---|---|
| ability | angle | begin |
| about | angry | behavior |
| absent | animal | believe |
| accept | ankle | between |
| accident | another | bookstore |
| achieve | answer | bottom |
| across | anxious | brake |
| address | apply | break |
| advertise | approve | breathe |
| advice | argue | build |
| affect | argument | business |
| afford | around | capable |
| against | attempt | capital |
| alcohol | attention | careless |
| alien | awful | cashier |
| all right | awkward | 60 celebrate |
| almost | balance | cereal |
| always | 40 bargain | certain |
| alter | beautiful | change |
| 20 although | because | charge |
| among | become | cheap |
| amount | before | chief |

| | | |
|---|---|---|
| children | everything | labor |
| church | examine | 140 language |
| clothing | except | laugh |
| collect | exercise | learn |
| college | expect | length |
| combat | experiment | lesson |
| comfortable | failure | listen |
| company | family | lonely |
| complete | fellow | magazine |
| computer | field | marry |
| condition | flower | match |
| connection | foreign | matter |
| context | friend | measure |
| 80 control | future | medicine |
| converse | garden | middle |
| daily | general | mighty |
| danger | grocery | million |
| daughter | 120 guess | minute |
| death | handy | mistake |
| deceive | happy | money |
| deposit | heard | month |
| describe | heaven | 160 morning |
| different | himself | mountain |
| direction | holiday | necessary |
| distance | house | needle |
| doubt | however | neither |
| dozen | hundred | newspaper |
| during | hungry | noble |
| education | immense | noise |
| effect | instead | nothing |
| either | intelligence | number |
| employment | interest | ocean |
| empty | interfere | offer |
| 100 English | kindergarten | omit |
| enough | kitchen | operate |
| entrance | knowledge | opportunity |

original

ought

painful

peace

pencil

180 perfect

period

person

picture

place

pocket

possible

potato

prepare

president

pretty

proceed

promise

psychology

public

quality

quarter

quick

quiet

quite

200 raise

reading

ready

really

reason

receive

recognize

remember

repeat

response

restaurant

ridiculous

right

salad

sandwich

scene

science

sense

sentence

serious

220 several

should

since

skill

sleep

smoke

something

soul

state

straight

street

stretch

strong

student

study

subject

suffer

summer

sweet

teach

240 telephone

television

thought

thousand

through

ticket

tired

together

tomorrow

tongue

tonight

touch

tough

travel

truly

uncle

understand

until

usual

value

260 variety

vegetable

viewpoint

vision

visitor

vocal

voice

warning

weather

weird

whole

window

wisdom

witch

without

would

writing

yesterday

yield

young

zipper

### ■ IMPROVING VISUAL SKILLS—2

The drills you practiced in Chapter 1 and the ones that follow will help your eye movement and your ability to *see* words without having to *hear* them by subvocalizing. Be sure to time yourself on each set. When you finish, compare these scores to those from Chapter 1 to see if you have improved the visual part of your reading.

 **EXERCISE 9-11  Word Recognition Practice**

*Move your eyes quickly across each line. Make a check over each word that is the same as the first word in* **bold** *type. Complete all 15 lines. Use a stop watch or a clock with a second hand to time each set. Do not look back over a line. Look only from left to right. Try not to say the words. Just look for each repetition of the word in bold.*

| Set I | Begin timing. | | | | |
|---|---|---|---|---|---|
| 1. **sweat** | sweet | sweat | swim | swat | sweat |
| 2. **break** | brake | brash | break | break | brake |
| 3. **maintain** | maintain | mountain | motion | mountain | maintain |
| 4. **locate** | local | cola | locate | local | locate |
| 5. **flower** | flame | framer | flowing | farmer | flowing |
| 6. **plane** | plate | plain | plow | plane | plain |
| 7. **receive** | relieve | receive | receive | believe | relent |
| 8. **thief** | thief | theft | thief | their | theft |
| 9. **sense** | sense | since | since | sense | since |
| 10. **deserve** | deceive | deception | sieve | deserve | deceive |
| 11. **then** | ten | than | then | send | than |
| 12. **steam** | steam | seem | scene | stand | seam |
| 13. **whole** | hole | wall | whole | whole | while |
| 14. **sleigh** | slight | sling | sleigh | slight | sleigh |
| 15. **marry** | marry | money | many | merry | merry |

End timing. Your time: _____  Number checked: _____

| Set II | Begin timing. | | | | |
|---|---|---|---|---|---|
| 1. **simile** | simile | smile | small | simile | smile |
| 2. **broken** | bloke | break | broken | spoken | broken |
| 3. **coarse** | coarse | course | crass | course | coarse |
| 4. **bough** | brown | bough | bought | bought | bough |

| 5. **sing** | sang | sung | sing | sing | sang |
| 6. **swim** | swim | swam | swim | swim | swum |
| 7. **ancient** | accident | ardent | amulet | ancient | ardent |
| 8. **waste** | waist | watch | once | waist | waste |
| 9. **weather** | weather | whether | weather | whether | whether |
| 10. **threw** | throw | thrown | thrift | through | throw |
| 11. **manner** | manner | manor | manor | money | modem |
| 12. **site** | sight | site | sight | cite | sight |
| 13. **knew** | new | knock | knot | new | knew |
| 14. **false** | fast | false | false | flows | flat |
| 15. **result** | reset | receive | rescind | result | reset |

*End timing. Your time:* _____ *Number checked:* _____

---

| *Set III* | *Begin timing.* | | | | |
| 1. **policy** | police | splashy | pansy | policy | police |
| 2. **fester** | faster | fester | foster | fester | faster |
| 3. **skill** | kill | shrill | skull | shrill | skill |
| 4. **polite** | polity | polite | polity | policy | policy |
| 5. **flight** | flown | flight | flight | fight | fight |
| 6. **since** | since | sense | wince | since | sense |
| 7. **either** | either | easier | either | ether | theater |
| 8. **weigh** | way | whoa | wince | way | weigh |
| 9. **allies** | alleys | allay | ally | allies | alleys |
| 10. **wince** | whence | which | once | whence | wench |
| 11. **once** | ounce | once | one | once | ounce |
| 12. **ankle** | angle | angel | uncle | ankle | angel |
| 13. **heard** | heard | herd | herd | heart | heard |
| 14. **hope** | hop | hope | hop | hot | hope |
| 15. **twine** | twin | twit | twine | tight | twin |

*End timing. Your time:* _____ *Number checked:* _____

## EXERCISE 9-12  Word Meaning Recognition

*In the following sets you are looking for a word similar in meaning to the word in **bold** type. Move your eyes quickly across each line. Make a check over the word that has a meaning similar to the word in bold. Do not look back over the line; keep your eyes moving from left to right. Time yourself as you did in the previous exercise.*

*Set I*          *Begin timing.*

| 1. **glance** | glower | shine | grope | look | linger |
| 2. **tired** | famous | fatigued | loud | trained | trite |
| 3. **walk** | wrangle | wink | stole | stroll | wash |
| 4. **aide** | aid | aisle | hope | angel | helper |
| 5. **coat** | wrap | rope | cap | write | cross |
| 6. **help** | hope | cope | aid | keep | heap |
| 7. **giving** | gracious | going | graze | generous | grave |
| 8. **sympathy** | servile | compassion | compete | symphony | pathos |
| 9. **conclude** | concede | impede | question | conscious | infer |
| 10. **twine** | twist | swing | sting | twit | string |
| 11. **direct** | guide | leaden | divine | great | grant |
| 12. **incorrect** | connect | interject | correct | false | facile |
| 13. **vulgar** | vinegar | crude | vocal | crisp | vicious |
| 14. **habitat** | habit | hopeful | dwelling | deception | drapery |
| 15. **likely** | likeable | probable | laughable | possible | probate |

*End timing. Your time:* _____ *Number checked:* _____

*Set II*          *Begin timing.*

| 1. **conflict** | courage | struggle | strength | conflate | course |
| 2. **defeat** | distance | conquest | coast | conquer | deafen |
| 3. **strange** | stranger | unusual | strangle | unlikely | strong |
| 4. **worried** | wondered | worship | able | wrangled | anxious |
| 5. **climb** | ascend | run | attest | lengthen | claim |
| 6. **refill** | remake | replenish | filler | restore | falter |
| 7. **hinder** | hidden | unhappy | thwart | thought | threw |
| 8. **discourteous** | disguise | disrobe | ridicule | rude | religious |
| 9. **right** | regular | correct | remake | connect | relate |
| 10. **irregular** | erotic | erratic | regular | rational | usual |
| 11. **declare** | proclaim | protect | decorate | babble | bashful |
| 12. **alter** | altar | active | charge | change | twist |
| 13. **fire** | force | dismal | failure | discharge | heed |
| 14. **feeling** | sadness | sentiment | forceful | faith | fierce |
| 15. **clamor** | claim | coax | noise | noose | stage |

*End timing. Your time:* _____ *Number checked:* _____

## Choosing an Occupation or Career

by **Gerald Corey**

Gerald Corey has taught teacher preparation, has a private practice in psychology, and gives workshops on counseling. He is the author of many books on teaching and counseling, including *I Never Knew I Had a Choice*, published in its fourth edition in 1990.

**Prepare**

1. Identify the author and the work. What do you expect the author's purpose to be?

   _____

   _____

2. Preread to identify the subject and make predictions. What do you expect to read about?

   _____

   _____

3. What do you already know about the subject?

   _____

   _____

   _____

4. Raise two questions that you expect the article to answer.

   _____

   _____

   _____

1    Making vocational choices is a process spanning a considerable period rather than an isolated event. Researchers in career development have found that most people go through a series of stages in choosing the

occupation or, more typically, occupations that they will follow.... Various factors emerge or become influential during each phase of development. The following factors have been shown to be important in determining a person's occupational decision-making process: self-concept, interests, abilities, values, occupational attitudes, socioeconomic level, parental influence, ethnic identity, gender, and physical, mental, emotional, and social handicaps. In choosing your vocation (or evaluating the choices you've made previously), you may want to consider which factors really mean the most to you. Let's consider some of these factors, keeping in mind that vocational choice is a process, not an event....

### Self-Concept

2    Some writers in career development contend that a vocational choice is an attempt to fulfill one's self-concept. People with a poor self-concept, for example, are not likely to envision themselves in a meaningful or important job. They are likely to keep their aspirations low, and thus their achievements will probably be low. They may select and remain in a job that they do not enjoy or derive satisfaction from, based on their conviction that such a job is all they are worthy of. In this regard choosing a vocation can be thought of as a public declaration of the kind of person we see ourselves as being.

### Occupational Attitudes

3    Research indicates that the higher the educational requirements for an occupation, the higher its status, or prestige (Isaacson, 1986). We develop our attitudes toward the status of occupations by learning from the people in our environment. Typical first-graders are not aware of the differential status of occupations, yet in a few years these children begin to rank occupations in a manner similar to that of adults. Some research has shown that positive attitudes toward most occupations are common among first-graders but that these preferences narrow steadily with each year of school (Nelson, 1963). As students advance to higher grades, they reject more and more occupations as unacceptable. Unfortunately, they rule out some of the very jobs from which they may have to choose if they are to find employment as adults. It is difficult for people to feel positively about themselves if they have to accept an occupation they perceive as low in status.

### Abilities

4    Ability or aptitude has received as much attention as any of the factors deemed significant in the career decision-making process, and it is probably used more often than any other factor. *Ability* refers to your competence in an activity; *aptitude* is your ability to learn. There are

both general and specific abilities. Scholastic aptitude, often called general intelligence or IQ, is a general ability typically considered to consist of both verbal and numerical aptitudes. Included among the specific abilities are mechanical, clerical, and spatial aptitudes, abstract reasoning ability, and eye/hand/foot coordination. Scholastic aptitude is particularly significant, because it largely determines who will be able to obtain the levels of education required for entrance into the higher-status occupations.

5      Interestingly, most studies show little direct relationship between measured aptitudes and occupational performance and satisfaction (Drummond, 1988; Herr & Cramer, 1988). This does not mean that ability is unimportant, but it does indicate that we must consider other factors in career planning.

### Interests

6      Interest measurement has become popular and is used extensively in career planning. Interests, unlike abilities, have been found to be moderately effective as predictors of vocational success, satisfaction, and persistence (Super & Bohn, 1970). Therefore, vocational planning should give consideration to interests. It is important to first determine your areas of vocational interest, then to identify occupations for which these interests are appropriate, and then to determine those occupations for which you have the abilities required for satisfactory job performance. Research evidence indicates only a slight relationship between interests and abilities (Tolbert, 1980). In other words, simply because you are interested in a job does not necessarily mean that you have the ability needed for it.

### Values

7      It is important for you to assess, identify, and clarify your values so that you will be able to match them with your career. There is some merit to following the combination of your interests and abilities as primary reliable guides for a general occupational area. After you have considered how your interests and abilities match with possible career choices, it is then helpful to explore your values. . . .

8      Your work *values* pertain to what you hope to accomplish through your role in an occupation. Work values are an important aspect of your total value system, and knowing those things that bring meaning to your life is crucial if you hope to find a career that has personal value for you. Most career-guidance centers in colleges and universities now offer one or more computer-based programs to help students decide on a career. One popular program is known as the System of Interactive Guidance and Information, or more commonly referred to as SIGI. This program assesses and categorizes your work values.

Taking it will aid you in identifying specific occupations that you might want to explore.

9    You might consider scheduling an appointment in the career-counseling center at your college to participate in a computer-based occupational guidance program. In addition to SIGI, other programs are the Career Information System (CIS), the Guidance Information System (GIS), Choices, and Discover. Each of these programs develops lists of occupations to explore.

903 words

■ **Comprehension Check** .

*Answer the following with a, b, or c to indicate the phrase that best completes the statement.*

_____ 1. Making vocational choices

    a. is a single event.
    b. is a process.
    c. involves a single factor in decision making.

_____ 2. People with low self-esteem

    a. do not think they belong in important jobs.
    b. usually do poorly in their jobs.
    c. keep their feelings private.

_____ 3. Young people learn about job status

    a. from books.
    b. in first grade.
    c. from adults in their society.

_____ 4. As young people grow up, they frequently

    a. reject more occupations as possibilities for them.
    b. choose the same job that a parent holds.
    c. embrace many job possibilities.

_____ 5. Students frequently reject occupations that

    a. have high status.
    b. they may have to select if they want employment.
    c. they would like to have.

_____ 6. The term *aptitude* means

    a. competence.
    b. hand/eye coordination.
    c. ability to learn.

_____ 7. Scholastic aptitude is important in career decisions because

    a. schools test for it.

    b. it determines those who will obtain the education needed for some careers.

    c. it affects happiness in a job.

_____ 8. Vocational interests

    a. are not important.

    b. guarantee success.

    c. are moderate predictors of job satisfaction.

_____ 9. Just because someone is interested in a job does not mean that

    a. the person will get the job.

    b. the person has the ability to do the job.

    c. the person should take the job.

_____10. Assessing one's values is

    a. important as part of the decision-making process.

    b. not important in choosing a job.

    c. more important than abilities and interests in selecting a career.

## Expanding Vocabulary

_Match each word in the left column with its definition in the right column by placing the correct letter in the space next to each word. When in doubt, read again the sentence in which the word appears._

| | | |
|---|---|---|
| _____ spanning (1) | a. sexual category |
| _____ emerge (1) | b. see, imagine |
| _____ ethnic (1) | c. obtain |
| _____ gender (1) | d. believe to be |
| _____ contend (2) | e. covering |
| _____ envision (2) | f. relating to space |
| _____ aspirations (2) | g. guides to the future |
| _____ derive (2) | h. evaluate |
| _____ differential (3) | i. element |
| _____ perceive (3) | j. goals |
| _____ deemed (4) | k. come forth |

_____ spatial (4)          l.  degrees of difference

_____ predictors (6)       m. assert

_____ assess (7)           n.  vital

_____ aspect (8)           o.  puts into different groups

_____ crucial (8)          p.  cultural heritage

_____ categorizes (8)      q.  considered

## Analysis of Structures and Strategies

1. State the article's topic:

   _____

2. Circle the best main-idea statement:
   a. Self concept is a factor in career decision making.
   b. Several factors influence a person's decisions about a career.
3. Does the author believe that computer programs that help students assess interests and values as part of deciding about a career are worth exploring?

   _____

   How do you know the answer to the question?

   _____

4. What is the author's primary organizational strategy?

   _____

## For Discussion and Reflection

1. Have you chosen an occupation or career? If so, how did you go about making your choice? If not, why do you think you are having trouble making a choice?
2. Have you used any career-counseling services? If so, were they helpful? If not, has the author convinced you to do so? Why or why not?
3. Do you agree with Corey that interests and abilities are the most important factors in choosing a career? If you disagree, why?
4. Would you argue that one is more important than the other? If so, which is more important, in your view? Why?

## Your Reading Assessment·

1. How accurately did you predict what you would read about?

   _____

2. Did the selection answer your questions? _____

   If not, why do you think that it did not? _____

   _____

3. What comments or questions do you have in response to your reading?

   _____

   _____

   _____

## Chapter Review Quiz

*Complete each of the following statements.*

1. *Capital* and *capitol* are words that are called _____.

2. *Affect* and *effect* are words that are called _____

   because _____.

3. Phrases that cannot be understood just by understanding each word are
   called _____.

4. Three strategies for improving spelling include:

   _____

   _____

   _____

5. Circle the correctly spelled word in each of the following pairs. Then
   identify the rule that applies.

   a. chief
   b. cheif

   rule: _____

   _____

c. follys
d. follies

rule: _____

_____

e. writting
f. writing

rule: _____

_____

g. loveless
h. lovless

rule: _____

_____

i. judgment
j. judgement

rule: _____

_____

k. shiping
l. shipping

rule: _____

_____

m. perceive
n. percieve

rule: _____

_____

o. travelled
p. traveled

rule: _____

_____

q. factorys
r. factories

rule: _____

_____

s. knowledgeable
t. knowledgable

rule: _____

_____

*The following words have appeared in the chapter or in the reading selection. Circle the letter next to the word or phrase that is the best definition of the word in **bold** type.*

1. **emerge**

    a. emit
    b. come forth
    c. capable

2. **assess**

    a. evaluate
    b. assert
    c. accept

3. **aspirations**

    a. grounds
    b. aspects
    c. goals

4. **deceive**

    a. manage
    b. discipline
    c. mislead

5. **rescind**

    a. take back, cancel
    b. take it
    c. reset

6. **habitat**

    a. drapery
    b. dwelling
    c. hopeful

7. **erratic**

    a. erotic
    b. rational
    c. irregular

# CHAPTER 10

## Reading Graphics

**In this chapter you will learn:**

- The purpose and advantages of graphics or visuals
- Guidelines for reading graphics
- How to understand the information in diagrams, tables, graphs, maps, and charts

### ■ PREPARE TO READ

Read and reflect on the chapter's title and objectives. Glance through the chapter, observing headings, to see what is covered. Now answer these questions:

1. What do you expect to learn from this chapter?

   _____

   _____

2. What do you already know about the chapter's topic?

   _____

   _____

3. What two or three questions do you want answered from reading this chapter?

   _____

   _____

A picture, as the saying goes, is worth a thousand words. Certainly one of the most famous—and powerful—pictures is Tames's photograph of President Kennedy in the Oval Office, shown on page 276. Many graphics (or visuals) appear in textbooks—and in other books, magazines, and newspapers. *Graphics* (or visuals) include pictures, diagrams, maps, tables, charts, and graphs. Even though they are used to aid the reader's understanding, many readers ignore them. This is a mistake. Graphics have three important uses.

- They are aids to learning. They help clarify material that may be difficult to follow in the text alone. They help us *see* relationships.
- They provide information that may be referred to only briefly in the text.
- They add interest, often dramatically so.

Perhaps you have skipped over maps and graphs in the past because you were uncertain how to "read" them. This chapter provides guidelines for reading graphics plus plenty of practice.

## ■ HOW TO READ GRAPHICS

Graphics present a good bit of information in less space than would be needed for an explanation in words only. But words are also part of graphics. First, you will find a reference in the text to every kind of visual except pictures. Second, there is writing connected to the graphic itself—above, below, and even within the visual representation. The first step to reading graphics is to turn to the graphic when it is referred to in the text, or to examine pictures as they appear. Remember: When the author writes "See Figure 10.1," the author wants you to look at that figure at that point in your reading. As you study the following steps to reading graphics, continue to refer to Table 10.1 as your example.

   1. **Locate the particular graphic referred to in the text.** Tables are always labeled Tables; other graphics are labeled Figures, except for pictures, which are not labeled. In books containing many visuals, tables and figures will be numbered, usually by chapter (10) and then by the order in which they appear in the chapter (10.1).

   2. **Read the title or heading of the graphic.** What is the topic of the graphic? How is the topic qualified; that is, what specific information is provided? The topic of Table 10.1 is "Civilian Employees of the Federal

◼ **TABLE 10.1**

**Civilian Employees of the Federal Government, 1816–1991**

| Year | Total Number of Employees | Number Employed in the Washington, D.C. Area |
|---|---|---|
| 1816 | 4,837 | 535 |
| 1821 | 6,914 | 603 |
| 1831 | 11,491 | 666 |
| 1841 | 18,038 | 1,014 |
| 1851 | 26,274 | 1,533 |
| 1861 | 36,672 | 2,199 |
| 1871 | 51,020 | 6,222 |
| 1881 | 100,020 | 13,124 |
| 1891 | 157,442 | 20,834 |
| 1901 | 239,476 | 20,044 |
| 1911 | 395,905 | 39,782 |
| 1921 | 561,142 | 82,416 |
| 1931 | 609,746 | 76,303 |
| 1941 | 1,437,682 | 190,588 |
| 1951 | 2,482,666 | 265,980 |
| 1961 | 2,435,804 | 246,266 |
| 1971 | 2,874,166 | 322,969 |
| 1981 | 2,858,742 | 350,516 |
| 1991 | 3,108,899 | 374,187 |

*Source:* United States Bureau of the Census, *Historical Statistics of the United States, Colonial Times to 1970,* Part 2; pp. 1102–03; U.S. Office of Personnel Management, *Federal Civilian Workforce Statistics: Employment and Trends as of July 1989*; idem, *Employment and Trends as of January 1992.*

Everett C. Ladd, *The American Polity,* 5th ed.

Government." The table is limited in two important ways: (1) it covers the years from 1816 to 1991 and (2) it includes numbers for *civilian* employees only. (What group of government employees is not included in these numbers? _____ )

    **3. Read any notes, description, and the source of information, material that appears at the bottom of the graphic.** In Table 10.1 the information has been compiled from two sources. Many textbooks contain diagrams and charts prepared just for that textbook. Pictures will have a brief description under them, perhaps followed by the name of the photographer or organization owning the original image.

**4. Read the headings for tables and graphs, the legend for maps.** Each column in a table will be labeled to show what it represents. (For example, from Table 10.1: "Year" and "Total number of employees.") A graph will label what is being shown on the vertical line and what is being shown on the horizontal line. A map's legend gives you the scale of the map or what the colors or shadings represent. You cannot draw accurate conclusions from a graphic until you understand exactly what information you have been given. In Table 10.1 we are given the total number of employees and the number of those employees who work in the D.C. area, for each year covered.

**5. Study the information.** Look at the numbers or drawings. Make comparisons. Observe trends or patterns. You might be surprised by the total number of federal employees in 1991—over 3 million. You might be equally surprised by the number who work in D.C., between 350 and 400 thousand.

**6. Draw conclusions.** Think about the information in several ways. First, what does the author want to accomplish by including the graphic? (Our sample table is taken from Everett Carll Ladd's government text *The American Polity.*) Second, what is your reaction to the information provided? What can we conclude from Table 10.1? You might want to reflect, for example, on the fact that in 1931, while the number of federal employees increased, the number working in Washington decreased. How might your knowledge of the time help you explain these numbers? Also, what do you think about such a small percentage of employees actually working in D.C.? What are some types of federal employees who work in other parts of the country?

---

---

Graphics provide information, raise questions, explain processes, make us think. Use this information in your studies. Let's look more closely at each type of graphic.

## ▪ PICTURES AND PHOTOGRAPHS

Many printed materials today include some pictures or photographs. They support the author's discussion and add interest to the text. The reproduction of old paintings or photos in history texts, for example, provides a visual image of important figures and helps us "reach back" to former times. Pictures don't just make a book attractive. They also tell a story. Study them and think about why each one has been selected by the author.

In Ladd's *The American Polity,* he includes the following photograph in his discussion of the presidency. Reflect on it and then answer the questions in the exercise.

■ **The Loneliest Job—President John F. Kennedy in the Oval Office**

New York Times Pictures

 **EXERCISE 10-1  Questions on the Photograph**

1. What details in the photo make it dramatic?

_____

_____

_____

_____

2. What message does the photo send about the job of the U.S. presidency?

_____

_____

_____

_____

# ■ DIAGRAMS

Diagrams are drawings or illustrations that visually capture a concept or process or object under discussion. Textbooks in the sciences and social sciences rely heavily on diagrams to:

1. show and label parts of objects (plants, human cells, the arrangement of the planets), and
2. represent processes that are not visible, or not readily so (the process of photosynthesis, the process of sexual reproduction).

Consider, for example, the following diagram (Figure 10.1) from a biology text. The illustration creates a visual explanation of the process by which carbon moves through the air and is used by both plants and humans. The diagram helps readers to see both the complexity and the importance of the carbon cycle.

## ■ FIGURE 10.1

**The Global Carbon Cycle**
Vast amounts of carbon move through the air, soil, and water  as photosynthesizing autotrophs fix carbon dioxide into organic compounds, and heterotrophs (along with  nonliving combustion processes such as burning) break down those compounds and once again release carbon  dioxide.

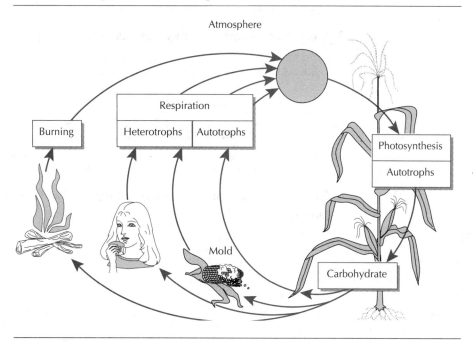

Postlethwait, Hopson, and Veres, *Biology! Bringing Science to Life*

## EXERCISE 10-2 Understanding Diagrams

*Study Figure 10.2—remembering to read the accompanying explanations— and answer the questions that follow.*

1. What is the diagram's subject? What process does it demonstrate?

   _____

   _____

   _____

   _____

2. What three changes in the development of *Equus* are illustrated?

   _____

   _____

   _____

   _____

3. Merychippus comes from what paleontological period?

   _____

   _____

   _____

   _____

4. How many years passed between the period of Hyracotherium and the period of Equus?

   _____

   _____

   _____

   _____

The modern horse and some of its ancestors. Only one of the several branches represented in the fossil record is shown. Over the past 60 million years, small several-toed browsers, such as *Hyracotherium*, were replaced in gradual stages by members of the genus *Equus,* characterized by, among other features, a larger size; broad molars adapted to grinding coarse grass blades; a single toe surrounded by a tough, protective keratin hoof; and a leg in which the bones of the lower leg had fused, with joints becoming more pulleylike and motion restricted to a single plane.

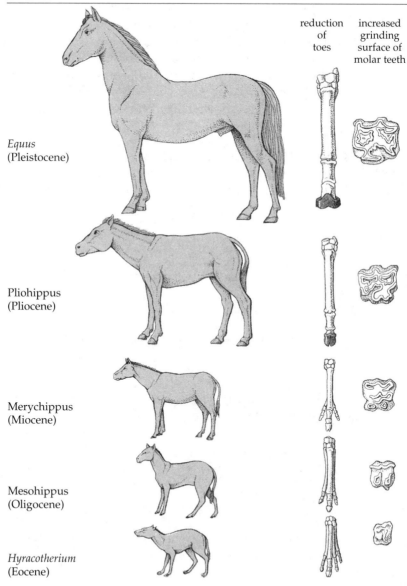

reduction of toes

increased grinding surface of molar teeth

*Equus* (Pleistocene)

Pliohippus (Pliocene)

Merychippus (Miocene)

Mesohippus (Oligocene)

*Hyracotherium* (Eocene)

Illustration by Shirley Baty in Curtis and Barnes, *An Invitation to Biology,* 4th ed.

## ■ MAPS

Maps show geographical areas. Some maps show the entire surface of the Earth, that is, all land masses and oceans, bays, lakes, and rivers. Others are topographical; that is, they show differences in elevations and types of land mass, such as mountains and deserts. Most textbook (and newspaper and magazine) maps, however, focus on one part of the world and show changes or trends—or something about that part of the world at a particular time. The subject presented may be about the Earth itself or about the people living in that part of the world. You would expect to find many maps in history and geography texts. You will also find them used to explain information in the sciences, the social sciences, and current events as well. For example, the map accompanying Michael Scott's selection on tropical rain forests (see p. 142) shows the location of rain forests throughout the world.

 **EXERCISE 10-3  Reading Maps**

*Study the map in Figure 10.3 and answer the questions that follow.*

1. What is the map's subject?

   _____

2. What three economic activities helped develop the West?

   _____

3. In what area of the country did grazing dominate?

   _____

4. What did grazing depend upon for economic development? How is this shown on the map?

   _____

5. Where did most of the mining take place?

   _____

6. No dates are shown on the map. What information helps you place the general time period shown?

   _____

**■ FIGURE 10.3**

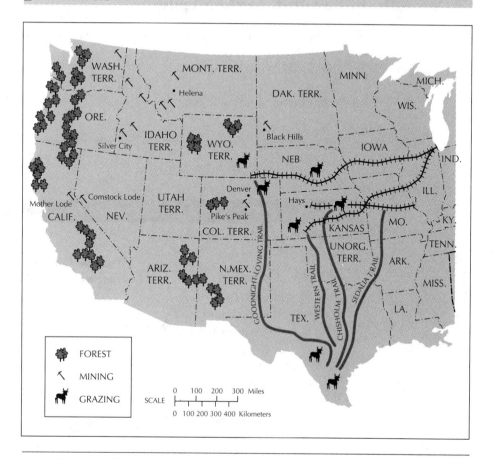

Joseph R. Conlin, *The American Past*, 3rd ed.

## ■ TABLES

As you saw in Table 10.1, a table presents information, in columns, on a given subject. By using columns, tables summarize and focus the information.

When reading the numbers in tables, be sure that you know what the numbers represent. That is, are the numerals showing the actual numbers, or do the numerals represent hundreds or thousands or millions? Or, are the numerals percentages rather than whole numbers? The numerals in Table 10.1 are actual numbers of federal employees. But in a table showing the numbers of residents in the world's largest cities in different years, for example, Tokyo is listed at 16.9 and New York at 15.6. Those numerals are in millions of people; 15.6 million people lived in New York in 1980.

**EXERCISE 10-4  Reading Tables**

*Study each table and then answer the questions that follow.*

I. Caffeine Table (Table 10.2)

1. What is the table's subject?

_____

_____

---

▪ **TABLE 10.2**

**Caffeine Content of Various Products**

| Product | Caffeine Content (average mg per serving) |
|---|---|
| COFFEE (5-oz. cup) | |
| Regular brewed | 65-115 |
| Decaffeinated brewed | 3 |
| Decaffeinated instant | 2 |
| TEA (6-oz. cup) | |
| Hot steeped | 36 |
| Iced | 31 |
| SOFT DRINKS (12-oz. servings) | |
| Jolt Cola | 100 |
| Dr. Pepper | 61 |
| Mountain Dew | 54 |
| Coca-Cola | 46 |
| Pepsi-Cola | 36-38 |
| CHOCOLATE | |
| 1 oz. baking chocolate | 25 |
| 1 oz. chocolate candy bar | 15 |
| ½ cup chocolate pudding | 4–12 |
| OVER-THE-COUNTER DRUGS | |
| No Doz (2 tablets) | 200 |
| Excedrin (2 tablets) | 130 |
| Midol (2 tablets) | 65 |
| Anacin (2 tablets) | 64 |

Donatelle and Davis, *Access to Health*, 4th ed.

2. What five types of products containing caffeine are covered?

_____

_____

3. What do the numbers in the table represent?

_____

4. Which food or drink product contains the most caffeine?

_____

5. Which cola drink would seem to be most appropriately named?

_____

6. According to this table, what is the best drink if you want to limit caffeine intake?

_____

7. What are some other drinks low in caffeine that are not included in this table?

_____

8. Should you use No Doz?  _____

II. Voting Table (Table 10.3)

1. What is the table's precise subject?

_____

2. What do the numbers represent?

_____

3. Voting figures are given for what six categories?

_____

| ■ **TABLE 10.3** | | | | |
|---|---|---|---|---|

**Percentage of Americans Who Vote for President**

| | **1980** | **1984** | **1988** | **1992** |
|---|---|---|---|---|
| *Overall* | | | | |
| Americans Who Vote | 59% | 60% | 57% | 61% |
| *Age* | | | | |
| 18–20 | 36 | 37 | 33 | 39 |
| 21–24 | 43 | 44 | 38 | 46 |
| 25–34 | 55 | 55 | 48 | 53 |
| 35–44 | 64 | 64 | 61 | 64 |
| 45–64 | 69 | 70 | 68 | 70 |
| 65 and up | 65 | 68 | 69 | 70 |
| *Sex* | | | | |
| Male | 59 | 59 | 56 | 60 |
| Female | 59 | 61 | 58 | 62 |
| *Race or Ethnicity* | | | | |
| Whites (non-Hispanic) | 61 | 61 | 59 | 64 |
| African Americans | 51 | 56 | 52 | 54 |
| Latinos | 30 | 33 | 29 | 29 |
| Asian Americans and Pacific Islanders | NA | NA | NA | 50 |
| *Education* | | | | |
| Grade school only | 43 | 43 | 37 | 35 |
| High school dropout | 46 | 44 | 41 | 41 |
| High school graduate | 59 | 59 | 55 | 58 |
| College dropout | 67 | 68 | 65 | 69 |
| College graduate | 80 | 79 | 78 | 81 |
| *Labor Force* | | | | |
| Employed | 62 | 62 | 58 | 64 |
| Unemployed | 41 | 44 | 39 | 46 |
| *Income* | | | | |
| Under $5,000 | 38 | 39 | 35 | NA |
| $5,000 to $9,999 | 46 | 49 | 41 | NA |
| $10,000 to $14,999 | 54 | 55 | 48 | NA |
| $15,000 to $19,999 | 57 | 60 | 54 | NA |
| $20,000 to $24,999 | 61 | 67 | 58 | NA |
| $25,000 to $34,999 | 67 | 74 | 64 | NA |
| $35,000 and over | 74 | 74 | 70[a] | NA |

[a]For 1988, the percentage is an average of $35,000 to $49,900 and over $50,000.

*Source: Statistical Abstract* 1991: Table 450; 1993: Table 454; *Current Population Reports,* Series P-20, vol. 440; U.S. Bureau of the Census, "Voting Registration in the Election of November 1992," no. 466, p. 20.

James M. Henslin, *Sociology* , 2nd ed.

4. Which age group has the best voting record?

_____

5. Which income group has the best voting record?

_____

6. Voting percentages do not change much from 1980 to 1992. Which group in which category has the greatest decrease in voting?

_____

7. Based on this table, what two characteristics have the greatest impact on improving voting behavior?

_____

_____

## ■ GRAPHS AND CHARTS

Graphs show relationships and emphasize comparisons between two or more related items. Some people prefer to use the term _graph_ to refer only to line graphs, and to use _chart_ for pie, bar, and flow charts. Let's look at each type separately.

## Pie Charts

The pie chart is probably the easiest to draw and to read. It is a circle divided into segments to show the relative portion of each part to the whole. You can use pie charts only when you are examining a whole, a complete category. For example, you can divide _all_ students at your college by age groups, or by race, or by parents' income. If you did all three, you would make three separate pie charts.

### EXERCISE 10-5  Reading Pie Charts

_Study the two pie charts and then answer the questions that follow._

1. What is the subject of the charts?

_____

▪ FIGURE 10.4

**Educational Attainment in America, 1970 and 1989 (percentages are of those 25 years of age and older)**

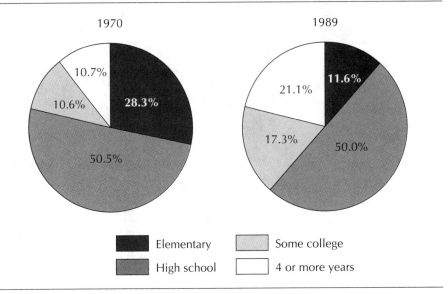

*Source:* U.S. Bureau of the Census, *Statistical Abstract of the United States,* 1991, p. 138. Everett C. Ladd, *The American Policy,* 5th ed.

2. What educational level stayed about the same from 1970 to 1989?

   _____

3. What category shank by more than half?    _____

   Why is this change important? _____

   _____

4. By 1989 what percentage of 25-year-olds had had *at least* some years of college?

   _____

   How much of an increase was this from 1970? _____

5. Which figure surprises you the most? Why?

_____

_____

## Bar Charts

Bar charts are frequently found in textbooks and in periodicals because they show relative proportions in a visually effective way. Bars can extend from either the bottom of the chart (the horizontal line) or the left side of the chart (the vertical line). Colors or shadings are often used to distinguish among the items. Again, be sure to understand what each chart is showing and what the numbers represent.

### EXERCISE 10-6  Reading Bar Charts

_Study each chart and then answer the questions that follow._

I. Income Distribution (Figure 10.5)

1. What, in your own words, is the chart's subject?

_____

■ FIGURE 10.5

**Income Distribution since 1929 (percent of all money income received by lowest 40 percent and highest 20 percent of American families)**

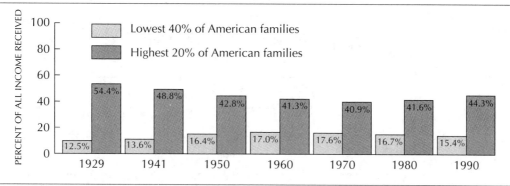

_Source:_ 1929–41: U.S. Bureau of the Census, _Historical Statistics of the U.S.: Colonial Times to 1957,_ p. 166; 1950–70: idem, _Historical Statistics of the U.S.: Colonial Times to 1970,_ p.293; 1980–90: idem, _Current Population Reports,_ Series P-60, No. 174, August 1991, p. 202.

Everett C. Ladd, _The American Policy,_ 5th ed.

2. In what year does the contrast between the richest and the poorest lead to the greatest inequality?

_____

3. In what year did income distribution produce the greatest equality?

_____

4. From 1960 to 1986, have changes resulted in greater or less equality?

_____

II. Unhealthy Behaviors (Figure 10.6)

1. What is the definition of adolescents used in this chart?

_____

2. Which unhealthy behavior is most frequently found among adolescents?

_____

3. Which is the unhealthy behavior that females participate in significantly more than males?

_____

4. Which is the unhealthy behavior that males participate in significantly more than females?

_____

5. Which figure surprises you the most? Why?

_____

_____

## Line Graphs

Line graphs are ideal for showing trends or changes over time or for showing a frequency distribution—a distribution relationship of two variables, such as the number of airline passengers in various age groups. Line graphs can also compare two or more trends on the same chart. Be sure to understand what the horizontal line and the vertical line represent.

■ FIGURE 10.6

**Unhealthy Behavior Among Adolescents***

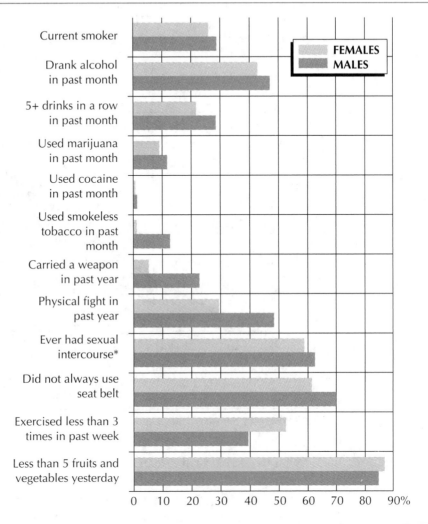

*Ages 14 to 21 and never married.

*Source:* National Center for Health Statistics

 EXERCISE 10-7  Understanding Line Graphs

*Study the graph (Figure 10.7) and then answer the questions that follow.*

■ FIGURE 10.7

**The Gender Pay Gap: The Annual Income of Full-Time Workers and the Percentage of the Men's Income Earned by Women**

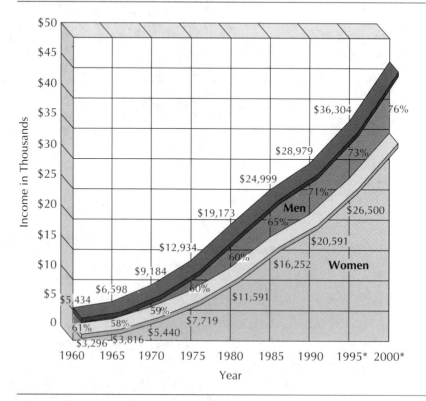

James M. Henslin, *Sociology,* 2nd ed.

1. What two subjects are treated by the graph?

   _____

2. In 1985, what was the average annual income for men?

   _____

3. What percent of men's income in 1985 was earned by women?

   _____

4. During which five-year period did men's incomes increase by the greatest amount?

   _____

5. Does the author's prediction for the future suggest that income equality for women will take place?

## Flow Charts

Flow charts show qualitative rather than quantitative relationships. They are useful for showing steps in a process or a sequence of events or ideas. Usually the flow chart provides a visual summary that reinforces a detailed explanation in the text. They are helpful guides to reviewing for tests.

### EXERCISE 10-8  Reading Flow Charts

*Study the chart (Figure 10.8) and then answer the questions that follow.*

■ FIGURE 10.8

**The Social Transformations of Society**

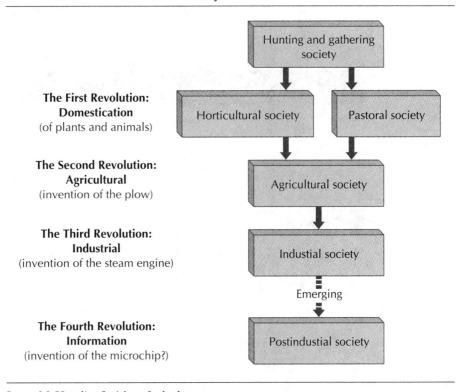

**The First Revolution:**
**Domestication**
(of plants and animals)

**The Second Revolution:**
**Agricultural**
(invention of the plow)

**The Third Revolution:**
**Industrial**
(invention of the steam engine)

**The Fourth Revolution:**
**Information**
(invention of the microchip?)

James M. Henslin, *Sociology,* 2nd ed.

1. What is the subject of the chart?

_____

2. How many steps in the process are there?  _____

3. What event helped bring about the third stage of development?

_____

4. Why is the arrow between Industrial society and Postindustrial society not a solid line?

_____

5. Although the chart shows social, not political, changes, why is it appropriate to use the word *revolution*?

_____

_____

## Graphs Can Lie, Easy as Pie

by **Boyce Rensberger**

Boyce Rensberger is a staff writer for the *Washington Post.* His article on pie charts appeared in the *Post's* "Horizon" learning section on June 12, 1996.

### Prepare

1. Identify the author and the work. What do you expect the author's purpose to be?

_____

_____

2. Preread to identify the subject and make predictions. What do you expect to read about?

_____

_____

3. What do you already know about the subject?

_____

_____

_____

4. Raise two questions that you expect the article to answer.

_____

_____

_____

1   Figures don't lie, but according to an old saying, liars figure. It's still true, and in recent years liars with axes to grind have turned to a new form of technology for help.

2   These are computer graphing programs, software into which you feed a set of figures and choose the style of graph you want—a pie chart, say, or a bar graph. Push a few keys, click the mouse a few times and instantly the computer displays your data in neatly drawn graphical form, complete with color coding and labels.

3   As a tool, graphing programs are wonderful. They are used by virtually all publishers of numerical data, from government analysts and investment brokers to high school students doing papers. Magazines and newspapers publish them in almost every issue.

4   If that were as far as it had gone, there would be no problem. We would all have a better intuitive grasp of the relative sizes of the numbers being compared. But the people who created the graphing programs took an extra step. They decided to let their customers jazz up the appearance of graphs by representing them in what is called 3-D. It isn't really three-dimensional, however, just perspective drawing. But that's not the problem.

■ **Chart 1**

■ **Chart 2**

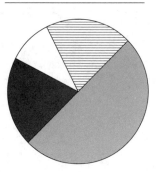

5    The problem is that, when you tip a normally circular pie chart on its side, as is commonly done to make it look "more artistically interesting," you warp the intuitive impact of the relative sizes of the pie slices.

6    Look, for example, at Chart 1, and try to rank the four wedges in order of size. The [gray] part is easily largest, but which is second. Most would pick the [lined] wedge, ranking the [black] a clear third in size, only a little bigger than the [white].

7    Now look at Chart 2. It shows the same data but in an old-fashioned, straight-on, undistorted view. Now it becomes obvious that the [black] and [lined] wedges are equal, each 20 percent of the pie, and the yellow wedge is a much smaller 10 percent.

8    What happened in Chart 1 is what happens to any pie chart tipped and viewed at an oblique angle. Wedges at the top or bottom appear wider, and any wedge at the left or right will look narrower.

9    Both effects are an unavoidable result of perspective drawing, which is what the computer programs do. The numbers guiding the computer are the percentages of the pie assigned to each slice and are the same in both charts. Thus the chart maker can insist that the tipped version is accurate.

10    Might a liar use this distortion to push an unwarranted point?

11    Look at Chart 3. It shows the ethnic composition of the United States. The largest piece of the pie constitutes 76 percent of its area and represents the white, non-Latino population. African Americans, at 12 percent, constitute the second biggest group, followed by Latinos at 9 percent, Asian Americans at 3 percent and Native Americans at 1 percent. The numbers add to 101 percent because of rounding.

12    Suppose you want to promote the view that nonwhites are becoming an unduly large fraction of the American population. You could choose to put the minority groups at the top or bottom of the pie so

■ **Chart 3** 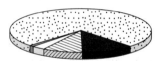 ■ **Chart 4**  ■ **Chart 5**

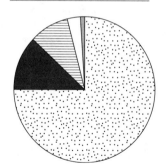

they will benefit from the widening effect, and you would position the white majority slice so it gets as much of the squeezing effect as possible.

13  Now suppose you were pushing the other side, the view that minority groups really are a rather tiny segment of the population. Chart 5 shows the result of shifting them to the squeezed part of the pie.

14  Either way, the tipped pie charts are absolutely truthful representations of the facts. It's just that they have abandoned what was supposed to be the whole point of graphical representations of numerical data, making it easier for people to grasp relative sizes intuitively.

15  Next time you see tipped pie charts, be suspicious. The motive may be entirely artistic, but the point of the message may be quite distorted.

669 words

## Comprehension Check

*Answer the following with a, b, or c to indicate the phrase that best completes the statement.*

_____ 1. Computer graphing programs produce

   a. pie charts.
   b. a color graphic you choose.
   c. axes to grind.

_____ 2. Computer graphing programs are used

   a. by government analysts.
   b. by high school students.
   c. both (a) and (b).

_____ 3. Graphics give readers

    a. a better understanding of relative sizes of comparable numbers.
    b. a better understanding of how to draw.
    c. no understanding of numbers.

_____ 4. Computer graphing programs

    a. are unattractive but accurate.
    b. represent the numbers in 3-D.
    c. use perspective drawing.

_____ 5. When pie charts are tipped on their sides

    a. they become inaccurate.
    b. the relative size of each "slice" is distorted.
    c. the size of each "slice" is enlarged.

_____ 6. When pie charts are tipped on their sides

    a. wedges at top and bottom appear wider
    b. wedges at either side appear narrower.
    c. both (a) and (b).

_____ 7. Tipped pie charts are

    a. accurate but visually distort the numbers.
    b. distorted and inaccurate.
    c. more attractive but inaccurate.

## ▮ Expanding Vocabulary

*After using context clues and a study of word parts, write a brief definition or synonym for each of the following words and phrases.*

axes to grind (1) _____

intuitive (4) _____

jazz up (4) _____

perspective (4) _____

warp (5) _____

undistorted (7) _____

oblique (8) _____

unduly (12) _____

segment (13) _____

### Analysis of Structures and Strategies

1. State the article's topic:

   _____

2. Circle the best main-idea statement:
   a. Computer graphing programs allow users to present numbers in a visually attractive way.
   b. Computer graphing programs, by using perspective drawing, miss the point of graphics because they visually distort relative sizes of comparable numbers.
3. Does the author think that computer graphics software can be helpful?

   _____

   How do you know the answer to the question?

   _____

   _____

4. Does the author think that some users of graphics software may purposely distort data?

   _____

   How do you know?

   _____

   _____

5. What does the author gain by asking readers to rank the sizes of wedges in Chart 1?

   _____

### For Discussion and Reflection

1. Would you have been able to understand Rensberger's points without his use of pie charts for illustration? If so, do the charts make it easier for readers?
2. Did you learn something new about the distortion of perspective drawing? If so, what is your reaction to what you have learned?

3. Should readers be protected in some way from distortions—both visual and in word choice? What is the best protection against the manipulation of others—writers, graphic artists, advertisements?

■ Your Reading Assessment

1. How accurately did you predict what you would read about?

_____

2. Did the selection answer your questions? _____

If not, why do you think that it did not?

_____

3. What comments or questions do you have in response to your reading?

_____

_____

_____

# The Coral Coast

by **Rachel Carson**

A marine biologist who worked for some years at the U.S. Fish and Wildlife Service, Rachel Carson (1907–64) is best known for her popular books, *The Sea Around Us* (1951) and *The Edge of the Sea* (1955), and for her controversial study of chemical pesticides, *Silent Spring* (1962). The following selection comes from *The Edge of the Sea*. The illustrations in the book are by Bob Hines, artist/illustrator for the U.S. Fish and Wildlife Service for more than thirty years.

■ Prepare

1. Identify the author and the work. What do you expect the author's purpose to be?

_____

_____

# ■ The Coral Coast

2. Preread to identify the subject and make predictions. What do you expect to read about?

_____

_____

3. What do you already know about the subject?

_____

_____

_____

4. Raise two questions that you expect the article to answer.

_____

_____

_____

1    I doubt that anyone can travel the length of the Florida Keys without having communicated to his mind a sense of the uniqueness of this land of sky and water and scattered mangrove-covered[1] islands. The atmosphere of the Keys is strongly and peculiarly their own. It may be that here, more than in most places, remembrance of the past and intimations[2] of the future are linked with present reality. In bare and jaggedly corroded rock, sculptured with the patterns of the corals, there is the desolation of a dead past. In the multicolored sea gardens seen from a boat as one drifts above them, there is a tropical lushness and mystery, a throbbing sense of the pressure of life; in coral reef and mangrove swamp there are the dimly seen foreshadowings of the future.

2    This world of the Keys has no counterpart elsewhere in the United States, and indeed few coasts of the earth are like it. Offshore, living coral reefs fringe the island chain, while some of the Keys themselves are the dead remnants of an old reef whose builders lived and flourished in a warm sea perhaps a thousand years ago. This is a coast not formed of lifeless rock or sand, but created by the activities of living

[1]Tropical evergreen tree or shrub with long thin stems.
[2]Subtle suggestions.

things which, though having bodies formed of protoplasm[3] even as our own, are able to turn the substance of the sea into rock.

3    The living coral coasts of the world are confined to waters in which the temperature seldom falls below 70°F. (and never for prolonged periods), for the massive structures of the reefs can be built only where the coral animals are bathed by waters warm enough to favor the secretion of their calcareous skeletons.[4] Reefs and all the associated structures of a coral coast are therefore restricted to the area bounded by the Tropics of Cancer and Capricorn. Moreover, they occur only on the eastern shores of continents, where currents of tropical water are carried toward the poles in a pattern determined by the earth's rotation and the direction of the winds. Western shores are inhospitable to corals because they are the site of upwellings of deep, cold water, with cold coastwise currents running toward the equator.

4    In North America, therefore, California and the Pacific coast of Mexico lack corals, while the West Indian region supports them in profusion. So do the coast of Brazil in South America, the tropical east African coast, and the northeastern shores of Australia, where the Great Barrier Reef creates a living wall for more than a thousand miles.

5    Within the United States the only coral coast is that of the Florida Keys. For nearly 200 miles these islands reach southwestward into tropical waters. They begin a little south of Miami where Sands, Elliott, and Old Rhodes Keys mark the entrance to Biscayne Bay; then other islands continue to the southwest, skirting the tip of the Florida mainland, from which they are separated by Florida Bay, and finally swinging out from the land to form a slender dividing line between the Gulf of Mexico and the Straits of Florida, through which the Gulf Stream pours its indigo[5] flood.

6    To seaward of the Keys there is a shallow area three to seven miles wide, where the sea bottom forms a gently sloping platform under depths generally less than five fathoms.[6] An irregular channel (Hawk Channel) with depths to ten fathoms traverses these shallows and is navigable by small boats. A wall of living coral reefs forms the seaward boundary of the reef platform, standing on the edge of the deeper sea (see diagram).

7    The Keys are divided into two groups that have a dual nature and origin. The eastern islands, swinging in their smooth arc 110 miles from

[3]Semifluid substance in cells of living animals and plants.

[4]Skeletons composed of calcium carbonate or limestone.

[5]Dark, purplish blue.

[6]One fathom measures 6 feet.

■ **The Florida Keys**

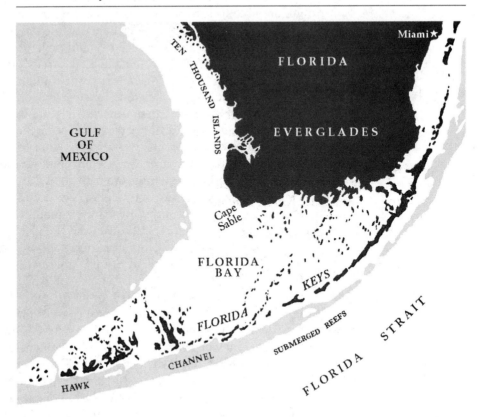

Sands to Loggerhead Key, are the exposed remnants of a Pleistocene[7] coral reef. Its builders lived and flourished in a warm sea just before the last of the glacial periods, but today the corals, or all that remains of them, are dry land. These eastern Keys are long, narrow islands covered with low trees and shrubs, bordered with coral limestone where they are exposed to the open sea, passing into the shallow waters of Florida Bay through a maze of mangrove swamps on the sheltered side. The western group, known as the Pine Islands, are a different kind of land, formed of limestone rock that had its origin on the bottom of a shallow interglacial sea, and is now raised only slightly above the surface of the water. But in all the Keys, whether built by the coral animals or formed of solidifying sea drift, the shaping hand is the hand of the sea.

[7]Geological epoch lasting from 11,000 to 500,000 years ago.

8     In its being and its meaning, this coast represents not merely an un-easy equilibrium of land and water masses; it is eloquent of a continuing change now actually in progress, a change being brought about by the life processes of living things. Perhaps the sense of this comes most clearly to one standing on a bridge between the Keys, looking out over miles of water, dotted with mangrove-covered islands to the horizon. This may seem a dreamy land, steeped in its past. But under the bridge a green mangrove seedling floats, long and slender, one end already beginning to show the development of roots, beginning to reach down through the water, ready to grasp and to root firmly in any muddy shoal that may lie across its path. Over the years the mangroves bridge the water gaps between the islands; they extend the mainland; they create new islands. And the currents that stream under the bridge, carrying the mangrove seedling, are one with the currents that carry plankton[8] to the coral animals building the offshore reef, creating a wall of rocklike solidity, a wall that one day may be added to the mainland. So this coast is built.

9     To understand the living present, and the promise of the future, it is necessary to remember the past. During the Pleistocene, the earth experienced at least four glacial stages, when severe climates prevailed and immense sheets of ice crept southward. During each of these stages, large volumes of the earth's water were frozen into ice, and sea level dropped all over the world. The glacial intervals were separated by milder interglacial stages when, with water from melting glaciers returning to the sea, the level of the world ocean rose again. Since the most recent Ice Age, known as the Wisconsin, the general trend of the earth's climate has been toward a gradual, though not uniform warming up. The interglacial stage preceding the Wisconsin glaciation is known as the Sangamon, and with it the history of the Florida Keys is intimately linked.

10     The corals that now form the substance of the eastern Keys built their reef during that Sangamon interglacial period, probably only a few tens of thousands of years ago. Then the sea stood perhaps 100 feet higher than it does today, and covered all of the southern part of the Florida plateau. In the warm sea off the sloping southeastern edge of that plateau the corals began to grow, in water somewhat more than 100 feet deep. Later the sea level dropped about 30 feet (this was in the early stages of a new glaciation, when water drawn from the sea was falling as snow in the far north); then another 30 feet. In this shallower water the corals flourished even more luxuriantly and the reef grew upward, its structure mounting close to the sea surface. But the drop-

[8]Small plant or animal organisms that float in bodies of water.

ping sea level that at first favored the growth of the reef was to be its destruction, for as the ice increased in the north in the Wisconsin glacial stage, the ocean level fell so low that the reef was exposed and all its living coral animals were killed. Once again in its history the reef was submerged for a brief period, but this could not bring back the life that had created it. Later it emerged again and has remained above water, except for the lower portions, which now form the passes between the Keys. Where the old reef lies exposed, it is deeply corroded and dissected by the dissolving action of rain and the beating of salt spray; in many places the old coral heads are revealed, so distinctly that the species are identifiable. . . .

■ **Shore line of southeastern part of continent during Sangamon interglacial stage, when Florida Keys were forming as offshore coral reef.**

11      Knowing this past, we can see in the present a repetition of the pattern, a recurrence of earth processes of an earlier day. Now, as then, living reefs are building up offshore; sediments are accumulating in shallow waters; and the level of the sea, almost imperceptibly but certainly, is changing.

1,420 words

## Comprehension Check

*Answer the following with a, b, or c to indicate the phrase that best completes the statement.*

_____ 1. The best statement of topic is:

    a. coral reefs in the Florida Keys.
    b. the shaping over time of the Florida Keys.
    c. the Florida Keys.

_____ 2. To live and grow, coral animals need

    a. the Florida Keys.
    b. cold waters and currents.
    c. warm waters.

_____ 3. Coral reefs are found

    a. on eastern shores of continents.
    b. on northeastern shores of Australia.
    c. both (a) and (b).

_____ 4. The Florida Keys

    a. are nearly 200 miles long.
    b. move southwestward from near Miami.
    c. both (a) and (b).

_____ 5. In the United States

    a. the only coral reef is the Florida Keys.
    b. there are no coral reefs.
    c. there are many coral reefs.

_____ 6. Some of the Florida Keys

    a. broke off from the mainland.
    b. are glaciers.
    c. were made from solidifying sea drift.

_____ 7. Off the Florida Keys to the east

    a. new coral reefs are forming.
    b. lies Hawk Channel.
    c. both (a) and (b).

_____ 8. The Florida Keys made from coral

    a. formed during the Sangamon interglacial period.
    b. formed during the Wisconsin glacial period.
    c. formed near the beginning of time.

_____ 9. The coral that formed the eastern Florida Keys

    a. died when people started living on the islands.
    b. died during the Wisconsin glacial period.
    c. died when it was covered with water.

## ▌Expanding Vocabulary

_Match each word in the left column with its definition in the right column by placing the correct letter in the space next to each word._

| | | |
|---|---|---|
| _____ uniqueness (1) | a. | closely |
| _____ corroded (1) | b. | balance |
| _____ desolation (1) | c. | richly abundant |
| _____ counterpart (2) | d. | release of substance from body |
| _____ fringe (2) | e. | materials that settle at the bottom of water |
| _____ remnants (2) | f. | unlike anything else |
| _____ secretion (3) | g. | particular type or kind of animal |
| _____ profusion (4) | h. | taken apart |
| _____ traverses (6) | i. | barely noticeable |
| _____ equilibrium (8) | j. | one closely resembling another |
| _____ eloquent (8) | k. | edge |
| _____ intimately (9) | l. | large quantities |
| _____ luxuriantly (10) | m. | chemically worn down |
| _____ dissected (10) | n. | travels, passes over |
| _____ species (10) | o. | surviving traces |
| _____ sediments (11) | p. | movingly expressive |
| _____ imperceptibly (11) | q. | emptiness |

## Analysis of Structures and Strategies

1. Circle the best main-idea statement:

   a. The making of the Florida Keys from coral and sediment reminds us of the ongoing life and change at the edge of the sea.

   b. The Florida Keys were made from coral and sediment.

2. How has the author used graphics to aid learning and add interest?

   _____

   _____

3. What, for Carson, is especially exciting about the Florida Keys?

   _____

   _____

   How does she convey her excitement to readers?

   _____

   _____

   _____

## For Discussion and Reflection

1. What is the most interesting piece of information you have learned from this selection? Why do you find it especially interesting?

   _____

   _____

## Your Reading Assessment

1. How accurately did you predict what you would read about?

   _____

2. Did the selection answer your questions?  _____

If not, why do you think that it did not?

_____

3. What comments or questions do you have in response to your reading?

_____

_____

_____

## Chapter Review Quiz

*Complete each of the following statements.*

1. *Graphics* refers to:

_____

_____

2. Two uses of graphics include:

_____

_____

3. To understand what a table, graph, or chart is showing, it is really important to understand

_____

_____

4. Flow charts show

_____

_____

5. Three different graphics accompanied an article on the Internet published in the *Washington Post* July 1, 1996. Study the graphics and then answer the following questions.

■ FIGURE 10.9

# Who's on the Internet

**By the year 2000,** *experts project there will be 52 million Internet users worldwide, the majority of them in the United States...*

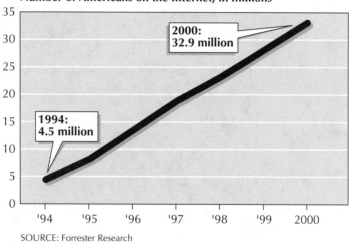

**Number of Americans on the Internet, in millions**

2000:
32.9 million

1994:
4.5 million

SOURCE: Forrester Research

**... While men are projected** *to remain the largest group of Internet users, women and children increasingly will be getting on-line...*

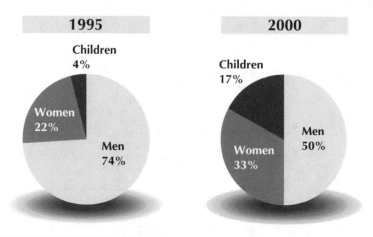

■ **FIGURE 10.10**

**...as the Internet,** *once the domain of university scholars, becomes ever more common at home and at work.*

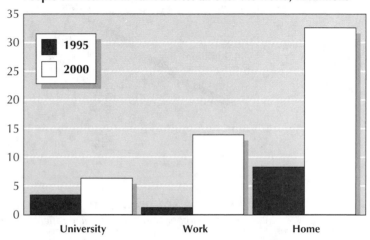

**People on Internet at various sites all over the world, in millions**

Legend: ■ 1995    □ 2000

THE WASHINGTON POST

a. What does the line graph show?

_____

b. Approximately how many Americans were on the Internet in 1996?

_____

c. Among men, women, and children, which group is projected to have the greatest increase in Internet users by 2000?

_____

d. The pie charts show the number of men on the Internet decreasing from 74% to 50% by 2000. Does this mean that fewer men will be using the Internet?

_____

e. In 1995, approximately how many people were using the Internet in their homes?

_____

f. The work site showing the greatest projected increase in Internet use from 1995 to 2000 is:

_____

g. What is one change in Internet use that helps to explain the rate of increase at the busiest site by the year 2000?

_____

# CHAPTER 11

## Reading and Studying for College Classes

**In this chapter you will learn:**

- How to get the most out of your textbook reading

- How to outline, map, and take notes on your reading

- How to get the most out of classroom learning

- How to prepare for testing

## ■ PREPARE TO READ

Read and reflect on the chapter's title and objectives. Glance through the chapter, observing headings, to see what is covered. Now answer these questions:

1. What do you expect to learn from this chapter?

   _____

   _____

2. What do you already know about the chapter's topic?

   _____

   _____

3. What two or three questions do you want answered from reading this chapter?

_____

_____

_____

_____

You are probably using this book because you want to improve your reading skills to do well in your college classes. And that means reading and learning from your college textbooks, books that are often large and rather imposing looking. It also means showing your knowledge both in the classroom and on tests. How do you cope?

In Chapter 2 you were introduced to a reading method **(Prepare–Read–Respond),** and you have been applying this method to this textbook and the reading selections in it. You have also, since studying Chapter 2, expanded your vocabulary, become more aware of levels of specificity and skilled in finding main ideas, and learned about basic strategies for organizing material. Now, let's take your new skills and apply them specifically to reading—and learning from—college textbooks.

## ■ READING TEXTBOOKS

As you practice your **Prepare–Read–Respond** strategy with the following sections from several textbooks, we will also establish additional guidelines for successful reading and learning.

## Prepare

This step in the reading process includes 1) prereading to make predictions, 2) identifying your previous knowledge, and 3) raising questions. When prereading a textbook chapter, remember to:

1. Read and think about the chapter title.
2. Read the opening and concluding paragraphs, or read the chapter objectives and chapter summary.
3. Look through the chapter to observe headings and subheadings.
4. Look at any graphics to get a sense of what the chapter is about.

Consider the third guideline in particular. Most chapters contain major headings and at least one level of subheading. Often, you will find a second level of subheadings. All major headings will use the same type, and perhaps even be in color. All first-level subheadings will be in the same type, but somewhat smaller than major headings. All second-level subheadings will be in the same type, but smaller or in some other way less distinguished than first-level subheadings. For example:

**MAJOR HEADING**
　　**First-level subheading**
　　　*Second-level subheading*

Be sure to observe the patterns that indicate each level so that you will see what material belongs together under major headings. The various headings provide a clear structure for the material and are aids to learning.

　　Look back to pages 30–31 at the outline of a chapter on listening. Examine the various headings and then answer the following questions.

1. How many major headings does the chapter have?  _____

2. In the last major section, how many subheadings are there?  _____

3. How many second-level subheadings are there?  _____

## Read

After completing the **Prepare** stage, you will return to the beginning of the chapter to read actively. Remember that active reading includes annotating as you read and monitoring comprehension. One advantage of annotating is that you can put questions in the margin next to passages that are confusing to you. Here are additional guidelines for reading a textbook chapter.

1. Do not feel that you must read an entire chapter at one time. Some textbook chapters are quite lengthy and dense with information to be learned.

2. Do *always* read a complete section at one time. If you read only a paragraph or two at a time, you will have trouble seeing how the chapter holds together or what is most important to learn.

3. Look for definitions, lists, and other structures (such as process or contrast) as guides to organizing the information in your own mind.

4. Continue to try to anticipate or predict what is coming. Think about what the section (or the chapter) will have to include to complete its treatment of the topic.

5. Note key examples. (They sometimes appear on tests.)

**EXERCISE 11-1  Reading a Textbook Section**

*Read and annotate the following section from the chapter "Listening" from* **Mastering Public Speaking** *by Grice and Skinner. Then answer the questions that follow.*

## LISTENING VS. HEARING

1   Has the following ever happened to you? You are watching *The Late Show with David Letterman,* listening to a new Anita Baker tape, or doing economics homework when one of your parents walks by and tells you to put out the trash. Fifteen minutes later, that person walks back to find you still preoccupied with television, music, or homework, and the trash still sitting by the door. Your parent asks, "Didn't you hear me?" Well, of course you did. You *heard* the direction to put out the trash just as you heard Letterman joking with Paul Shaffer, Anita Baker harmonizing, the dog barking at a passing car, and the air conditioner clicking on in the hall. You heard all of these things, but you might not have been *listening* to any of them.

2   What is the difference between **listening** and **hearing**? Listening differs from hearing in at least four important ways.

3   **Listening Is Intermittent.** Listening is not a continuous activity, but occurs only from time to time when we choose to focus and respond to stimuli around us. Hearing, on the other hand, is a continuous function for a person having normal hearing ability.

4   **Listening Is a Learned Skill.** Listening must be taught and learned. Unless you were born with a hearing loss, however, hearing is a natural capacity for which you need no training. We hear sounds before we are born; fetuses grow accustomed to certain voices, noises, and music. For this reason, pediatricians advise new parents not to tiptoe or whisper around the infant they have just brought home from the hospital. The child is already used to a lot of noise and must grow accustomed to the rest of it. Throughout our lives, we hear sounds even as we sleep.

5   **Listening Is Active.** Hearing means simply receiving an aural stimulus. The act of hearing is passive; it requires no work. Anytime the tiny bones of the inner ear are set in vibration, we are hearing something, and the activity requires no expenditure of energy. We can limit hearing only by trying to reduce or eliminate the sources of sound in the environment or by covering our ears.

6   Listening, in contrast, is active. It requires you to concentrate, interpret, and respond – in short, to be involved. You can hear the sound of a fire engine as you sit at your desk working on your psychology paper. You listen to the sound of the fire engine if you concentrate on its sound, identify it as a fire engine rather than an ambulance, wonder if it is coming in your direction, and then turn back to your work as you hear the sound fade away.

7   **Listening Implies Using the Message Received.** Audiences assemble for many reasons. We choose to listen to gain new information; to learn new uses for existing information; to discover arguments for beliefs or actions; to assess those arguments; to laugh and be entertained; to provide emotional support for a speaker; to celebrate a person, place, object, or idea; and to be inspired.

8    We are attracted to novel ideas and information just because we may have some future use for that data. There are literally thousands of topics you could listen to; for example, characteristics of gangsta rap, converting to electronic currency, the history of blue jeans, adapting Japanese management style to American businesses, the ethics of criminal entrapment, preparing lemon-grass chicken, fantasy league football and baseball, the history of the National Cathedral, and the life of Arthur Ashe. Some of these topics might induce you to listen carefully. Others might not interest you, so you choose not to listen. The perceived usefulness of the topic helps determine how actively you will listen to a speaker. Listening implies a choice; you must choose to participate in the process of listening.

1. What two key terms does the section define?

_____

2. What two key structures are used to define *listening*?

_____

3. In your own words, what are the characteristics of *listening* and how do they differ from *hearing*?

_____

_____

_____

_____

_____

_____

## Respond

Responding consists of both review and reflection. Reflecting on what you have read helps the review process because it makes what you have studied more personally your own. Reflecting may also help your studies by generating questions that you want to ask of the instructor or by helping you see connections with other sections or chapters in the textbook. Still, when you are reading to learn from a textbook, serious review is essential to "fixing" the information in your memory.

One way to review is to read over your annotations: the sentences you have underlined and the notes you have made in the margin. Then, close the book and see if you can recite the key ideas of the section. Open to the section and see if you left out any key ideas. If your reciting was not accurate or detailed enough, reread your annotations and try again.

**EXERCISE 11-2  Prepare—Read—Respond**

*Read the following first section of the chapter "Addictions and Addictive Be-havior" from **Access to Health** by Donatelle and Davis. Annotate, review your annotations, and then answer the questions that follow.*

## *D*EFINING ADDICTION

1    **Addiction** is an unhealthy, continued involvement with a mood-altering object or activity that creates harmful con-sequences. Addictive behaviors initially provide a sense of pleasure or stability that is beyond the addict's power to achieve otherwise. Eventually, the addictive behavior is necessary to give the addict a sense of normalcy.

2    Physiological dependence is only one indicator of ad-diction. Psychological dynamics play an important role, which explains why behaviors not related to the use of chemicals—gambling, for example—may also be addic-tive. In fact, psychological and physiological dependence are so intertwined that it is not really possible to separate the two. For every psychological state, there is a corre-sponding physiological state. In other words, everything you feel is tied to a chemical process occurring in your body. Thus, addictions once thought to be entirely psy-chological in nature are now understood to have physio-logical components.

3    To be addictive, a behavior must have the potential to produce a positive mood change. Chemicals are responsi-ble for the most profound addictions, not only because they produce dramatic mood changes, but also because they cause cellular changes to which the body adapts so well that it eventually requires the chemical in order to function normally. Yet other behaviors, such as gambling, spending, working, and sex, also create changes at the cel-lular level along with positive mood changes. Although the mechanism is not well understood, all forms of ad-diction probably reflect dysfunction of certain biochemi-cal systems in the brain.

4    Traditionally, diagnosis of an addiction was limited to drug addiction and was based on three criteria: (1) the presence of an abstinence syndrome, or **withdrawal**—a se-ries of temporary physical and psychological symptoms that occurs when the addict abruptly stops using the drug; (2) an associated pattern of pathological behavior (deteri-oration in work performance, relationships, and social in-teraction); and (3) **relapse**, the tendency to return to the addictive behavior after a period of abstinence. Further-more, until recently, health professionals were unwilling to diagnose an addiction until medical symptoms appeared in the patient. Now we know that although withdrawal, pathological behavior, relapse, and medical symptoms are valid indicators of addiction, they do not characterize all addictive behavior.

### Habit versus Addiction

5    What is the distinction between a harmless habit and an addiction? The stereotypical image of the addict is of someone desperately seeking a fix 24 hours a day. Con-versely, people have the notion that if you aren't doing the behavior every day, then you're not addicted. The reality is somewhere between these two extremes.

6    Addiction certainly involves elements of **habit**, which is a repetitious behavior in which the repetition may be un-conscious. A habit can be annoying, but it can be broken without too much discomfort by simply becoming aware of its presence and choosing not to do it. Addiction also involves repetition of a behavior, but the repetition occurs by compulsion and considerable discomfort is experi-enced if the behavior is not performed. While many peo-ple consider compulsive eating an addiction, current research shows that it is actually more of a habit...

7    It is helpful not to limit our understanding of addic-tion to the amount and frequency of the behavior, for what happens when a person is involved in the behavior is far more meaningful. For example, someone who drinks only rarely, and then in moderation, may experi-ence personality changes, blackouts (drug-induced amne-sia), and other negative consequences (e.g., failing a test, missing an important appointment, getting into a fight) that would never have occurred had the person not taken a few drinks. On the other hand, someone who has a few martinis every evening may never do anything out of character while under the influence of alcohol but may become irritable, manipulative, and aggressive when un-able to have those regular drinks. For both of these peo-ple, alcohol appears to perform a function (mood control) that they should be able to perform without the aid of chemicals, which is a possible sign of addiction. Habits are behaviors that occur through choice. In con-trast, no one decides to become addicted, even though people make choices that contribute to the development of an addiction.

1. For a behavior to be addictive, what must it have the potential to do?

   _____

2. Addictions involve both physiological dependence and

   _____

3. What is the difference between a habit and an addiction?

   _____

   _____

4. What are four common symptoms of addiction?

   _____

   _____

   _____

## ▪ WRITING-TO-LEARN STRATEGIES

For many students, reviewing their textbook annotations is not enough to help them learn difficult material in the detail necessary for their college classes. It is a good idea to have several strategies for studying and learning from reading and then to choose the best method for each course that you take. You have learned to annotate and to write summaries. Additional strategies include outlining, mapping, and note taking.

## Outlining

Outlining, like summary, is a main-idea strategy. Effective outlining depends upon your recognizing main ideas and levels of specificity under the main ideas. Outlining is a good choice when:

- You cannot annotate because you do not own the book.
- Your text has narrow margins so you cannot do enough annotating.
- You learn better by seeing how the material is organized.

The formal outline depends on a specific pattern of numbers, letters, and indenting to show the relationship of ideas. Here is the pattern:

I. Main idea
   A. Supporting idea
   B. Supporting idea

II. Main idea
   A. Supporting idea
   B. Supporting idea
     1. Major detail
     2. Major detail
       a. Minor detail
       b. Minor detail

III. Main idea

Whenever you are required to turn in an outline, be sure to follow the formal pattern shown here. Your instructor will evaluate the format of the outline as well as the content.

Some works are easier to outline than others. At times, when you are outlining to help yourself learn, you may want to prepare a more informal outline that will meet your study needs. Even an informal outline, though, needs to show the relationship among main ideas and details. You do not want to end up with just a list of points. Reread the selection on addiction and think about how you would outline it. Then compare your possible outline with the one that follows.

*Outline: Defining Addiction*

I. Definition of Addiction
   A. Basic characteristics
     1. Unhealthy
     2. Continued over time
     3. Initial pleasure
     4. Becomes essential to feel normal
   B. Effects
     1. Physiological  }  both affected
     2. Psychological }  closely connected

II. Traditional Criteria Used in Diagnosis
   A. Withdrawal when person stops
   B. Causes pathological behavior
   C. Relapse often occurs
   D. Medical symptoms develop

} Modern view—not all addicts have symptoms.

*III. Contrast between Habit and Addiction*

   *A. Habit*

      *1. Repetitive behavior can be stopped*

      *2. Habits are result of choice*

   *B. Addiction*

      *1. Repetitive behavior is compulsive; discomfort results when stopped*

      *2. Addiction not result of choice*

Notice that the outline follows the basic formal pattern, but notes have been added to stress the connection between physiological and psychological effects. Also notice the main headings that have been created to organize the selection's ideas. The following guidelines include both "rules" and advice for making outlines.

## Guidelines for Outlining

1. Items of the same level (e.g., A and B) are lined up evenly. Use a ruler if necessary (or tab settings if you are typing).
2. Each subdivision needs at least two parts. That means you cannot have an A without a B, or a 1 without a 2.
3. Any subsection can have more than two parts and some sections may not be divided at all.
4. Use your knowledge of writing patterns to help you distinguish between main ideas and supporting details. Pay attention to signal words that announce a list, or steps in a process, or contrast.
5. If you seem to be just making a list, look at what you have written to see how to reorganize the material. You may need to create some headings under which to group points.
6. Add notes to your study outlines when helpful.

## EXERCISE 11-3   Preparing an Outline

*Read (or reread) either Curtis and Barnes's "The Signs of Life" (pp. 47–49) or Scott's "In the Rain Forest" (pp. 140–145) and then prepare an outline in the following space.*

_____

_____

_____

_____

_____

_____

_____

_____

_____

_____

_____

_____

_____

_____

_____

_____

## Mapping

An alternative to outlining is mapping. Mapping, like outlining, shows the relationships between main ideas and supporting details. Mapping differs from outlining by using a visual pattern rather than numbers, letters, and indenting. Some people learn more easily from visuals than from text. If you learn best this way, use mapping to make your own diagrams from which to study.

Probably the most popular map style is one with spokes coming out of a center circle that contains a statement of the topic. But this isn't the only useful style for mapping. You can also use a "flow chart" type of pattern or other possibilities that you create.

Read the following paragraph on advertising and then observe how the information in this paragraph has been mapped in two different patterns.

### The Marketing Role

Marketing is the strategic process a business uses to satisfy consumer needs and wants through goods and services. The particular consumers at whom the company directs its marketing effort constitute the *target market*. The tools available to marketing include the product, its price, and the means used to deliver the product, or the place. Marketing also includes a mechanism for communicating this information to the consumer, which is called *marketing communication*, or promotion. These four tools are collectively referred to as the *marketing mix* or the *4 Ps*. Marketing communication is further broken down into four related communication techniques: advertising, sales promotion, public relations, and personal selling. Thus advertising is only one element in a company's overall marketing communication program, although it is the most visible.

Wells, Burnett, and Moriarty, *Advertising: Principles and Practice*, 3rd ed.

▨ FIGURE 11.1

**Mapping**

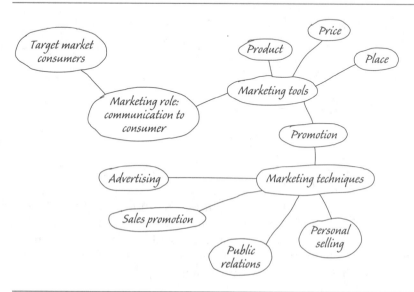

■ FIGURE 11.2

**Mapping**

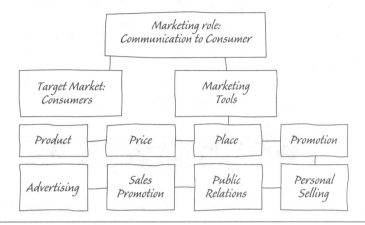

Experiment with different patterns. Use the following guidelines to help you create maps from which you can learn.

## Guidelines for Mapping

1. Decide on the selection's main topic and write it, in a word or phrase, within a circle or box, at the center or at the top of your paper.

2. Place each main idea on a line radiating out from the main circle or box.

3. Use as many levels of lines or boxes as needed to include the information you want to learn.

4. Try to draw your map so that you can read each item without having to turn the paper around.

5. Give yourself enough room so that you can write out the information you need to learn and so that you can read what you have written. (Mapping may not work if the information is too complicated. Know when to choose outlining or note taking instead.)

6. Experiment with different patterns.

## EXERCISE 11-4 Mapping

*On separate sheets of paper, prepare a map for two articles that you have already read, "Listening vs. Hearing," pp. 315–316 and "Defining Addiction," p. 317.*

# Note Taking: The Cornell Method

There are times when neither outlining nor mapping seems the best choice for writing to learn. At these times note taking may be the strategy to choose. For many students, it is their favorite strategy. The notes they take on assigned readings can be placed in the same notebook they use for class notes. Then all notes are together to study for tests.

The Cornell Method is just one way of putting notes on paper so that you have a good study tool when you finish. It was devised at Cornell University and has worked well for many students.

## Guidelines for the Cornell Method of Notes

1. Use 8 ½" by 11" lined paper that will fit into a three-ring notebook. With a ruler, draw a line from top to bottom on each page 2 ½" from the left margin.
2. Write your notes down the page in the 6" section to the right of the line you have drawn. Although the Cornell Method recommends using complete sentences, many students use phrases sometimes.
3. After you finish taking notes on a particular assignment, read through your notes, underlining key words.
4. Write the key words next to the notes on that topic in the smaller space to the left of the line you have drawn. Later, you can cover the notes and use the key words as a way to review.

Reread the paragraph on marketing (p. 322) and then take notes on it using the Cornell Method. Compare your note taking to the sample page of notes that follows.

### Notes on the Marketing Role

| | |
|---|---|
| Marketing—def. | Marketing: planned process to get goods and services to consumers. |
| Target market | Consumers represent target market. |
| Marketing tools—4 | Marketing tools include: product, price, place, and promotion. These are the 4 Ps. |
| Promotion techniques—4 | Promotion—manner of communication. Can include: advertising, sales promotion, public relations, personal selling |
| Advertising—visible | Advertising—most visible form of marketing |

## ■ LEARNING FROM A TEXTBOOK CHAPTER

Let's now put your reading and note-taking strategies to work on the following chapter: "American Government: Roots and Reform." As you first look over this chapter, you may feel that the reading will be difficult. But if you apply your reading strategy, take notes on each section, and answer the questions that will guide your study, you will be successful. Remember that much of your reading success depends upon the knowledge you bring to reading. You already know a good bit about American government and politics. Let your knowledge, the headings and other guides in the text, and your reading and writing strategies work together.

## Prepare

Follow the prereading guidelines on p. 313 to preview the chapter. Then answer the following questions.

1. How many major headings are in the chapter? _____

2. How many paragraphs make up the introduction? _____

3. How many "boxes" (sections enclosed by lines) and "side bars" (narrow strip sections in the margin) add related information to the chapter? ___

4. Is there a summary? _____

5. Are key terms listed at the end of the chapter? _____
   If so, circle each term that you are not familiar with and be alert to its use in the chapter.

6. Does the chapter conclude with review questions? _____
   If so, read them before reading the chapter. If not, think about your own review questions as you read.

7. What two people seem most important in the chapter discussion?

   _____

   How do you know?

   _____

8. Which visual most attracted your attention?

   _____

   Why? _____

   _____

## Read

First, read and annotate the chapter's introductory paragraphs. Then respond to the questions that follow.

# C H A P T E R           1

# American Government: Roots and Reform

WHERE DID OUR IDEAS OF GOVERNMENT COME FROM?

DEVISING A NATIONAL GOVERNMENT

WHY A CAPITALIST SYSTEM?

UNDERSTANDING OUR DEMOCRATIC SYSTEM

*I*t is not only Americans who have wrestled with the problems of creating a government to meet their needs. In 1789, cries of "Liberty, Equality, and Fraternity" rang out in France as members of the working class, inspired by the American Revolution, rose up against King Louis XVI. The king, members of his family, and many French aristocrats were executed. Civil unrest continued and mobs controlled Paris until order was restored through the creation of a provisional government.

In the early 1900s in Russia, the radical Bolshevik Party mobilized citizens who were demoralized by war and who were without jobs or food, to overthrow and ultimately execute Czar Nicholas II and his family. The Bolshevik Revolution was followed by a period of civil war, and the Union of Soviet Socialist Republics was created from the ruins of the Russian Empire. Inspired by the Bolshevik model, Chinese communists similarly established a communist government in the late 1940s after a prolonged period of civil war.

More recently, these once revolutionary communist governments have themselves been faced with revolutionary discontent. In 1989, Chinese students demonstrated for democracy in Tienanmen Square, but to little avail. The communist rulers responded with a massive and bloody show of force that left many dead or injured. These events caused little political change in China. The early 1990s, however, saw the breakup of the Soviet Union. Most of this breakup was spurred by citizen demands, particularly in Eastern Europe, for democratization. In one new Eastern European state after another, citizens have gone to the polls to elect new leaders. Some of the changes have occurred with relatively little violence; others, such as the carving out of Bosnia-Herzogovenia from the former Yugoslavia, have produced all-out war and tremendous personal tragedy.

In each of these situations, whether peaceful or not, men and women have attempted to create new political systems to resolve the classic, age-old question of politics: Who gets what, when, and how?

Even in the short time between when you get up in the morning and when you leave for classes or work, this question pervades your life. The national or state government, for example, sets the standards for whether you wake up on Eastern, Central, or Western Time. The national government regulates the airwaves and licenses the radio or television broadcasts you might tune in to as you eat and get dressed. States, also, regulate and tax telecommunications. Whether the water you use as you brush your teeth contains fluoride is a state or local governmental issue. The federal Food and Drug Administration inspects your breakfast meat and sets standards for the advertising on your cereal box, orange juice carton, and other food packaging. And states set standards for food labelling. Are the elements of your breakfast really "lite," "high in fiber," or "fresh squeezed"? Usually, one or more levels of government is authorized to decide these matters.

How governments get their powers, and what rights their citizens or subjects retain, is a major focus of this book. All governments—whether democracies, such as the United States, Great Britain, and France, or authoritarian regimes such as Iraq under Saddam Hussein—exercise some kind of authority over the daily lives of their people. To understand how the U. S. government and our political system work today, it is critical to understand the philosophies that guided the American colonists as they created a system of governance different from those then in existence. It is also necessary to know how that system evolved and changed in order to understand better how government affects you and the world around you. And, just as important, a thorough understanding of the workings of government will allow you to question and think about the system—the good parts and the bad—and decide for yourself the advantages and disadvantages of possible reforms.

The question of who exercises power, and how and why they acquired it, is important to understanding a political system. As we will see, there is no simple answer to that question. For example, do elected representatives actually represent the people who elect them, or do they respond to other interests? High school civics classes often teach that elected representatives, working through legitimate channels, produce policies and govern. Yet simple explanations such as this one do not hold together. How, for example, could the savings and loan crisis, involving massive failures of numerous savings and loan banks, have occurred? Despite numerous national and state banking

## Spring Forward, Fall Back
♦ ♦ ♦

Daylight Saving Time was introduced during World War I as a measure to save coal, which was used to produce electricity for lighting. In order to provide more natural light at the end of the working day, clocks are advanced one hour. In the United States, Daylight Saving Time begins on the first Sunday in April (clocks are moved ahead one hour) and ends on the last Sunday in October (clocks are moved back one hour). Any state may decide to remain on Standard Time during this period, as do Arizona and Hawaii; Indiana even allows *counties* to decide whether to switch.

*Source:* USA *Today,* April 2–4, 1991: p. 1-A.

laws designed to prevent banks from going under, precisely that happened, often taking the savings of many Americans along with them. Laws were broken, many who were involved got very rich, and few went to jail. Yet, the final "bill" to the American taxpayer was over one hundred and fifty billion dollars.

The public, political parties, interest groups, the bureaucracy, and congressional committees are just part of the answer to the question of who has power, and why and how it is used. Consider, for example, the tobacco industry in the United States. A 1991 draft report from the Environmental Protection Agency concluded that *second-hand* cigarette smoke kills 53,000 nonsmokers annually. The U. S. Surgeon General requires strong warnings on tobacco products concerning the link between tobacco use and cancer. Nevertheless, not only does the government permit smoking, but it also provides *billions* of dollars a year in subsidies to tobacco farmers. At the same time, however, the national, state, and even some local governments tax cigarettes. In 1993 the federal excise tax on cigarettes was 24 cents a pack, and state excise taxes ranged from 2.5 cents in Virginia (a major tobacco-growing state) to 51 cents in Massachusetts. But in spite of the health threat, taxes on cigarettes are lower in the United States than in virtually any other industrialized nation.

In the case of cigarettes, the powerful tobacco lobby, in conjunction with equally powerful senators and representatives from tobacco-growing states, has been instrumental in seeing that the tobacco industry is allowed to flourish. In contrast, red dye number 2, used to add color to certain food products, was banned in the mid-1970s when it, like tobacco, was found to contain cancer-causing agents. Unlike tobacco, it had few supporters (lobbyists) to argue for its continued use in the food industry.

Although all governments have problems, it is important to stress the good they can do in their attempts to decide who gets what, when, and how. In the aftermath of the Great Depression in the United States, for example, the government created the Social Security program, which dramatically decreased poverty among the elderly. Our contract laws and judicial system provide an efficient framework for business, assuring people that they have a recourse in the courts should someone fail to deliver goods or services as promised. And even something seemingly as mundane as our uniform bankruptcy laws help protect both a business enterprise and its creditors if the business collapses.

Just as it is important to recognize that governments serve many important purposes, it is also important to recognize that government and **politics,** the process by which policy decisions are made, are not static. They are part of a never-ending dynamic process of action and interaction. Governmental actions do not occur in isolation. The United States and its people, for example, are actors in a world order that from this nation's beginning has affected and continues to affect our laws, policies, and actions. Undoubtedly, the Framers at the Constitutional Convention in Philadelphia were reacting to what they viewed as the tyrannical rule of King George when they drafted Article II of the Constitution, creating a president of the United States. Similarly, the actions of President George Bush and the U. S. Congress in the Persian Gulf War of 1991 were the product of a series of events and reactions to them. So too were President Bill Clinton's approach to the crisis in Bosnia-Herzogovenia. The unpopular and unsuccessful Vietnam War, the United States need for oil, Iraq's invasion of Kuwait, reelection concerns, and probably even George Bush's desire to be viewed as a strong leader—all contributed to some extent to the final decision to deploy troops and then to commence Operation Desert Storm. Similarly, Bill Clinton's decision not to send ground troops into Eastern Europe, in spite of numerous urgings to do so, was also the product of his perception of the crisis and past events. Thus, many major national and international policy decisions have their roots in the politics and policies of the past. The lessons of history are often in the mind of policy makers as they seek to lead the nation on a sure course.

## Questions on the Introduction.

1. What is the *major focus* of this book?

   _____

   _____

2. What do all governments do?

   _____

   _____

3. To understand how a political system works, what must we know?

   _____

   _____

4. What is the point of the examples in paragraphs 1 and 2?

   _____

   _____

5. What is the point of the examples in paragraph 4?

   _____

   _____

6. What is the point in the example of tobacco?

   _____

   _____

7. How is *politics* defined?

   _____

   _____

8. What is the relationship between politics and government?

   _____

   _____

   _____

Answering these questions will help you take good notes on the introduction. Now complete the page of notes started for you.

*Ch. 1 American Gov't: Roots and Reform—Intro.*

Focus | *Focus of text:* _____

_____

*Government:*

*All have some authority over citizens.*

*Need to know:* _____

_____

*Those with power besides Congress:*

____ *political parties* _____

____ *interest groups* _____

_____

_____

*Gov'ts have* _____

*Gov'ts do* _____

Def—key term | *Politics:* _____

_____

*Gov't and politics are* _____

_____

_____

Now read the first section and complete the questions and note taking that follow. Before reading, reflect on the section heading. How do you think this section will be organized?

## Where Did Our Ideas of Government Come From?

The current American political system did not spring into being overnight. It is the result of an intellectual tradition, as well as trial and error, and even luck. To understand how we came to have the form of government we have today, we must first understand the theories of government that influenced the Framers.

### From Aristotle to the Enlightenment

Aristotle (384–322 B. C.) and the Greeks were the first to articulate the notion of **natural law,** the doctrine that human affairs should be governed by certain ethical principles. Being nothing more nor less than the nature of things, these principles can be understood by reason. In the thirteenth century, the Italian priest and philosopher Thomas Aquinas (1225–1274) gave the idea of natural law a new, Christian framework, arguing that natural law and Christianity were compatible because God created the natural law that established individual rights to life and liberty. In contradiction to this view, throughout Europe, kings continued to rule as absolute monarchs by divine right from God. Thus, citizens were bound by the government under which they found themselves, regardless of whether they had a say in its workings: If government reflected God's will, who could argue with it?

In the early sixteenth century, a religious movement to reform the doctrine and institutions of Roman Catholicism began to sweep through Europe. In many cases, these efforts at reform resulted in the founding of Protestant churches separate from their Catholic source. This Reformation and the resultant growth in the Protestant faith, which promoted the belief that people could talk directly to God without the intervention of a priest, altered the nature of government as people began to believe they could also have a say in their own governance. So did the ideas of philosophers and scientists such as Isaac Newton (1642–1727) during the period called the Enlightenment. Newton and others argued that the world could be improved through the use of human reason, science, and religious toleration. He and other theorists directly challenged earlier notions that fate alone controlled an individual's destiny and that kings ruled by divine right. Together the intellectual and religious developments of the Reformation and Enlightenment periods encouraged people to seek alternatives to absolute monarchy and to ponder new methods of governing.

### A Growing Idea: Popular Consent

In England, when one faction called "separatists" split from the Anglican church, they did so believing that the ability to speak directly to God gave them the power to par-

The Mayflower Compact. While on the Mayflower, English colonists drew up a compact declaring their intention to form a "Civil Body Politick," or government, to preserve order and peace.

ticipate directly in the governing of their own local congregations. In establishing self-governing congregations, the separatists were responsible for the first widespread appearance of self-government in the form of social compacts. The separatists who moved to the English colonies in America brought their beliefs about self-governance with them. The Mayflower Compact, written while that ship was still at sea, reflects this tradition. Although it addressed itself to secular government, the Pilgrims called it a "covenant" (its form was akin to other common religious "covenants"; note the use of this word in the reproduction of the Mayflower Compact above) adopted by Congregationalists, Presbyterians, and Baptists.[1]

Two English theorists of the seventeenth century, Thomas Hobbes (1588–1679) and John Locke (1632–1704), built on conventional notions in proposing a social contract theory of government (see "People of the Past," p. 10). In contrast to Aquinas and the theorists of God-ordained government, they argued that even before the creation of governments, all individuals were free and equal by natural right. This freedom, in turn, required that all men give their consent to be governed.[2]

**Hobbes and Locke.**  In his now-classic political treatise *Leviathan* (1651), Hobbes argued pessimistically that man's natural state was war. In his attempt to make sense

---

[1]  The English and Scots often signed covenants with their churches in a pledge to defend and further their religion. In the Bible, covenants were solemn promises made to humanity by God. In the colonial context, then, covenants were formal agreements sworn to a new government to abide by its terms.

[2]  The term *men* is used here because only males were considered fit to vote.

The title page from Thomas Hobbes's *Leviathan,* 1651.

of King Charles's restoration to the throne, he theorized that life without government was a "state of nature," where, without written, enforceable rules, people would live like animals—foraging for food, stealing, and killing when necessary. To escape the horrors of the natural state, Hobbes argued, men must, in order to protect their lives, give up to government certain rights. Without government, Hobbes warned, life would basically be "solitary, poor, nasty, brutish, and short"—a constant struggle to survive against the evil of others. For this reason, governments had to intrude on people's rights and liberties in order to better control society and provide the proper safeguards for property.

# PEOPLE OF THE PAST

## Hobbes

Thomas Hobbes was born in 1588 in Gloucestershire (Glouster), England and began his formal education at the age of four. By age six he was learning Latin and Greek, and by nineteen he had obtained his bachelor's degree from Oxford University. In 1608, Hobbes accepted a position as a family tutor with the Earl of Devonshire, a post he retained for the rest of his life.

Hobbes was greatly influenced by the chaos of the English Civil War of the mid-seventeenth century. Its impact is evident in his most famous work, *Leviathan* (1651), a treatise on governmental theory that states his views on Man and Citizen. *Leviathan* is commonly described as a book about politics, but it also deals with religion and moral philosophy. Hobbes characterized humans as selfishly individualistic and constantly at war with one another. Without an effective government, argued Hobbes, life would be "solitary, poor, nasty, brutish, and short." People, he claimed, surrendered themselves to rulers in exchange for protection from their neighbors.

Hobbes was quite an energetic man, and at the age of eighty-four he wrote his autobiography in Latin verse. He died at the age of ninety-one.

## Locke

John Locke, born in England in 1632, was admitted to an outstanding public school at the age of fifteen. It was there that he began to question his upbringing in the Puritan faith. At twenty he went on to study at Oxford, where he became a lecturer in Aristotelian philosophy. Soon, however, he found a new interest in medicine and experimental science.

In 1666, Locke met Anthony Ashley Cooper, the first Earl of Shaftesbury, a liberal politician. It was through Cooper that Locke discovered his own talent for philosophy. In 1689, Locke published his most famous work, *Second Treatise on Civil Government,* in which he set forth a theory of natural rights. He used the concept of natural rights to support his "social contract [theory]—the view that the consent of the people is the only true basis of any sovereign's right to rule." Governments exist, he argued, because individuals agree through a contract to form one to protect their rights under natural law. They agree to abide by decisions made by majority vote in the resolution of disputes. Locke died on October 28, 1704 at the age of seventy-two.

Hobbes argued strongly for a single ruler, no matter how evil, to guarantee the rights of the weak against the strong. Leviathan, a biblical sea monster, was his characterization of an all-powerful government. Strict adherence to Leviathan's laws, however encompassing or intrusive on liberty, was but a small price to pay for living in a civilized society, or even for life itself.

In contrast, John Locke—like many other political philosophers of the era—took the basic survival of humanity for granted and argued that government's major responsibility was the preservation of private property, an idea that ultimately found its way into the Constitution of the United States. In two of his works (*Essay Concerning Hu-*

*man Understanding* [1690] and *Second Treatise on Civil Government* [1689]), Locke responded to King James II's abuses of power directed at the Anglican church and Parliament. Locke denied the divine right of kings to govern. More important, he argued that men were born equal and with equal rights in nature that no king had the power to void. Under what Locke termed **social contract theory,** the consent of the people is the only true basis of any sovereign's right to rule. According to Locke, men form governments largely to preserve life, liberty, and property, and to assure justice. If governments act improperly, they break their "contract" with the people and therefore no longer enjoy the consent of the governed. Because he believed that true justice comes from laws, Locke argued that the branch of government that makes laws—as opposed to the one that enforces or interprets laws—should be the most powerful.

Locke believed that a chief executive to administer laws was important, but that he should necessarily be limited by law or by the "social contract" with the governed. Locke's writings influenced many American colonists, especially Thomas Jefferson, whose original draft of the Declaration of Independence noted the rights to "life, liberty, and property" as key reasons to split from England.[3]

[3] Jefferson ultimately and without explanation changed these words to "Life, Liberty, and the pursuit of Happiness," although most of the signers were far more concerned with property.

## Questions on the First Section.

1. What is the primary writing strategy that organizes this section?

   _____

2. In medieval times, governments were believed to reflect

   _____

   _____

   and kings ruled by _____

3. What is the Mayflower Compact?

   _____

   _____

   _____

4. What is meant by *social contract?*

_____

_____

_____

5. What kind of government did Hobbes defend? Why?

_____

_____

_____

6. What kind of government did Locke argue for? Why?

_____

_____

_____

7. In what century did Hobbes and Locke publish their works on government?

_____

_____

_____

8. Who did they influence and which had the greater influence?

_____

_____

_____

Answering these questions will help you take good notes on the first section. Now complete the page of notes started for you.

Section 1. Sources of Ideas of Gov't

Medieval view of gov't: _____

_____

_____

Natural law: _____

_____

Role of science and protestantism: _____

_____

_____

_____

Mayflower
Compact

Social contract

Popular consent: theory of social contract: _____

_____

_____

_____

Hobbes

Leviathan 1651

Hobbes believed: _____

_____

_____

Locke

Locke believed: _____

_____

_____

| Table 1.1 ◆ Types of Government | | |
| --- | --- | --- |
| **TYPES** | **EXAMPLE** | **HOW MANY ARE INVOLVED IN THE GOVERNING PROCESS** |
| *Monarchy* | Eighteenth-century Great Britain | One |
| *Oligarchy* | El Salvador, 1960s<br>Brazil, 1970s | Small number |
| *Aristocracy* | Seventeenth-century Poland<br>Haiti, 1980s | Small number |
| *Indirect Democracy* | United States today | Many |
| *Direct Democracy* | Ancient Athens | Nearly all (free males) |

Now read the second section and then complete the questions and note taking that follow. Before reading, reflect on the section heading. What do you think this section will cover?

## Devising a National Government

Although social contract theorists agreed on the need for government, they did not necessarily agree on the form that a government should take. Thomas Hobbes argued for a single leader; John Locke and Jean-Jacques Rousseau, a French philosopher (1712–1778) saw the need for less centralized power.

As depicted in Table 1.1, the colonists rejected a system with a strong ruler, like the British **monarchy,** as soon as they had declared their independence. Most European monarchical systems gave hereditary rulers absolute power over all forms of activity. Many of the colonists had fled from Great Britain to avoid religious persecution and other harsh manifestations of power wielded by George II, whom they viewed as a malevolent despot. They naturally were reluctant to put themselves in the same position in their new nation.

While some colonies such as Massachusetts originally established theocracies in which religious leaders eventually ruled claiming divine guidance, they later looked to more secular forms of governance. Colonists also did not want to create an **oligarchy,** or "rule by the few," in which the right to participate is conditioned on the possession of wealth or property. Aristotle defined this form of government as a perversion of an **aristocracy,** or "rule of the highest." Again, the colonists were fearful of replicating the landed and titled system of the British aristocracy and viewed the formation of a representative form of government as far more in keeping with the ideas of social contract theorists. But the **democracy** in which we live, as settled on by the Framers, is difficult to define. Nowhere is the word mentioned in the Declaration of Independence or the U. S. Constitution. Like many of our ideas about government, however, the term comes from two Greek words: *demos* (the people) and *kratia* (power or authority). Thus, democracy can be interpreted as a form of government that gives power to the people. The question, then, is how and to which people is this power given?

## The Theory of Democratic Government

As evidenced by the early creation of the Virginia House of Burgesses in 1619, and its objections to "taxation without representation," the colonists were quick to create participatory forms of government in which most men (subject to some landowning requirements) were allowed to participate. The New England town meeting (see "Then and Now," p. 13), where all citizens gather to discuss and decide issues facing the town, today stands as a surviving example of a **direct democracy**, such as was used in ancient Greece when all free, male citizens came together periodically to pass laws and "elect" leaders by lot.

Direct democracies, however, soon proved unworkable in the colonies. Although Rousseau argued that true democracy is impossible unless *all* citizens participate in governmental decision-making, as more and more settlers came to the New World, many town meetings were replaced by a system called **indirect** or **representative democracy.** Ironically, this system of government, in which representatives of the people are chosen by ballot, was considered undemocratic by ancient Greeks, who believed that all citizens must have a direct say in their governance.

Representative or indirect democracies, which call for the election of representatives to a governmental decision-making body, were formed first in the colonies and then in the new Union. Many citizens were uncomfortable with the term "democracy" and used the term **republic** to avoid any confusion between the system adopted and direct democracy. Even today, representative democracies are more commonly called "republics" and the words "democracy" and "republic" often are used interchangeably. Historically, the term "republic" implied a system of government in which the interests of the people were represented by more educated or wealthier citizens. In the early days of America, for example, only those who owned land could vote. But today, those barriers no longer exist.

## What Are the Characteristics of American Democracy?

The United States is an indirect democracy with several distinguishing characteristics. Tremendous value is placed on the individual. All individuals are deemed rational and fair, and endowed, as Thomas Jefferson proclaimed in the Declaration of Independence "with certain unalienable rights." And the individual is deemed more important than the state.

Another key characteristic of our democracy is the American emphasis on political equality, the definition of which has varied considerably over time (as discussed in Chapter 5). The importance of political equality is another reflection of American stress on the importance of the individual. Although some individuals clearly wield more political clout than others, the adage "one man, one vote" implies a sense of political equality for all.

**Popular consent,** the idea that governments must draw their powers from the consent of the governed, is another distinguishing characteristic of American democracy. Derived from social contract theory, the notion of popular consent was central to the Declaration of Independence and its underlying assumption that governments *must* derive their powers from the consent of the governed. A citizen's willingness to vote is thus an essential premise of democracy.

**Majority rule** and the preservation of minority rights are two additional facets of American democracy. Majority rule implies that only policies supported by most of the population will be made into law. This right of the majority to govern themselves is summed up by the term **popular sovereignty.** This term, however, did not come into wide usage until pre-Civil War debates over slavery. At that time, supporters of popular sovereignty argued that the citizens of new states seeking admission to the Union should be able to decide whether or not their states would allow slavery within their borders.

Today, emphasis on majority rule also usually stresses concern with minority rights, although tension between the two concepts still exists. One example of that tension is illustrated by the issues and controversy generated over President Bill Clinton's nomination of his long-time friend and former law school classmate Lani Guinier, a University of Pennsylvania Law School professor, to head the Civil Rights Division of the U. S. Justice Department. When her position on the respective roles of the majority and the minority became public, the controversy was such that Clinton was forced to withdraw her nomination. In a 1991 *Michigan Law Review* article, Guinier attacked a "hostile permanent (white) majority" often unwilling to give minorities in legislatures their share of power. Thus Guinier proposed, among other things, a "minority veto" to allow black legislators the ability to veto measures passed by majorities in cases where minority legislators were unable to make inroads. Once he read her work, even Clinton was unwilling to accept Guinier's ideas or defend them, noting, "I cannot fight a battle . . . if I do not believe in the ground of the battle."[4]

**Personal liberty** is perhaps the single most important characteristic of American democracy. The Constitution itself was written to assure "life" and "liberty." Over the years, our concepts of liberty have changed. Liberty was first considered to be freedom "from." Thus, Americans were to be free from governmental infringements on freedom of religion and speech, from unreasonable search and seizure, and so on (see Chapter 4). The addition to the Constitution of the Fourteenth Amendment and its emphasis on equal protection of the laws and subsequent passage of laws guaranteeing civil rights, however, expanded Americans' concept of liberty to include demands for "freedom to" be free from discrimination. Debates over how much the government should do to guarantee these rights or liberties illustrate the conflicts that continue to occur in our democratic system.

## Who Makes Decisions in America?

How conflicts are resolved, and how much emphasis is placed on any of these characteristics of American democracy, is often determined by how the government is operated, and by whom. Over the years, several theorists have posited widely different points of view in their attempts to answer this important question. No one view completely explains "who gets what, when, and how," although most political scientists of today probably subscribe to the pluralist view (see p. 16).[5] Nevertheless, a knowledge of these divergent perspectives will make it possible for you to analyze political questions from more than one vantage point.

**Elite Theory.**   In *The Power Elite* (1956), American sociologist C. Wright Mills argued that important policies are set by a loose coalition of three groups with some overlap among them. According to his **elite theory,** these three major influencers of policy—corporate leaders, military leaders, and a small group of key governmental leaders—are the true "power elite" in America. (Other elite theorists have argued that the news media should be included as a fourth element in the United States.) These

---

[4] Margaret Carlson, "Where Is 'My Center'?" *Time* (June 14, 1993): 22.

[5] Harold D. Lasswell, *Politics: Who Gets What, When, and How* (New York: McGraw-Hill, 1938).

elite theorists believe that government has become increasingly alienated from the people and is rarely responsive to their wishes.

**Bureaucratic Theory.**   Max Weber (1864–1920), the founder of modern sociology, argued that *all* institutions, governmental and nongovernmental, have fallen under the control of a large and ever-growing bureaucracy. This view is called **bureaucratic theory.** Because all institutions have grown more complex, Weber concluded that the expertise and competence of bureaucrats allows them to wrest power from others, especially elected officials. As we will see in Chapter 8, there is no doubt that in certain policy areas bureaucrats carry increasing amounts of power. Politicians come and go, yet most bureaucrats stay on in their positions for a good part of their working lives.

**Interest Group Theory.**   Political scientist David B. Truman postulated what is termed the **interest group theory** of democracy in *The Governmental Process* (1951). According to Truman, interest groups—not elites, sets of elites, or bureaucrats—control the governmental process.[6]

Truman believes there are so many potential pressure points in the executive, legislative, and judicial branches of the federal government—as well as at the state level—that groups can step in on any number of competing sides, and that government becomes the equilibrium point in the system.

**Pluralist Theory.**   Another, more widely accepted theory about the nature of power is held by those who follow the *pluralist* school of thought. According to political scientists such as Robert Dahl, the structure of our democratic government allows only for a pluralist model of democracy. Borrowing from Truman's work, Dahl argued that resources are scattered so widely in our diverse democracy that no single elite group can ever have a monopoly over any substantial area of policy. In *Who Governs?* (1961), for example, Dahl concluded that political competition and elections coupled with the growing ethnic and socioeconomic diversity of New Haven, Connecticut, led to a situation in which a single elite could never take and hold power legally. James Madison had argued in *Federalist No. 10* that a large number of interests and "factions" clashing in the public arena serve to enhance compromise. Dahl observed this need for compromise in New Haven in the areas of public education, urban renewal, and political nomination.[7]

Adding to this debate, political scientist Theodore J. Lowi has coined the term "interest group liberalism" to describe how political decision-making occurs today. According to Lowi, participants in every political controversy get something; thus, each has some impact on how political decisions are made. Lowi also states that governments rarely say no to any well-organized interests. Thus, all interests ultimately receive some benefits or rewards. Lowi bemoans the fact that the public interest (what is good for the public at large) often tends to lose in this system.[8]

All these theories provide interesting ways to begin to view how policy decisions are made, whether at local, state, or national levels. It could be, as Dahl has argued, that no single group or interest can ever have a monopoly over any issue, let alone over larger policy programs. It also stands to reason that the patterns we discover in the United States may apply to a certain extent in other parts of the world.

[6] David B. Truman, *The Governmental Process* (New York: Knopf, 1951).

[7] See also Robert Dahl, *Dilemmas of Pluralist Democracy: Autonomy vs. Control* (New Haven, CT: Yale University Press, 1982) and Iris Marion Young, *Justice and the Politics of Difference* (Princeton, NJ: Princeton University Press, 1990).

[8] Theodore S. Lowi, *The End of Liberalism* (New York: Norton, 1979), Chapter 3.

### Questions on the Second Section.

1. What three forms of government did the American colonists reject? Define each form.

_____

_____

_____

_____

_____

_____

2. What are two types of *democracy?*

_____

3. Why is the term *republic* appropriate for representative democracies?

_____

_____

4. *Political equality* stems from what American value?

_____

5. What characteristics of American democracy are in tension?

_____

_____

6. What are four theories explaining how decisions are made in our system?

_____

_____

_____

_____

_____

Answering these questions will help you take good notes on the second section. Now complete the page of notes started for you.

Section II. Devising a National Government

Forms of gov't: _____

_____

monarchy

aristocracy

oligarchy

democracy

republic

Characteristics of American democracy: _____

individualism

political equality

majority rule

minority rights

Theories of decision making: _____

Now read the third section and complete the questions and note taking that follow. Before reading, reflect on the section heading. What do you think the section will cover?

## Why a Capitalist System?

In addition to fashioning a democratic form of government, the colonists were also confronted with the dilemma of what kind of role the government should play in the economy. Concerns with liberty, both personal and economic, were always at the forefront of their actions and decisions in creating a new government. They were well aware of the need for a well-functioning economy, and saw that government had a key role in maintaining this. What constitutes a malfunction in the economy, however, and what steps the government should take to remedy it, were questions that dogged the Framers and continue to puzzle politicians and theorists today (see Chapter 17).

The private ownership of property and a **free market economy** are key tenets of the American system called **capitalism.** In contrast to **socialism,** in which the working class owns and controls all means of production and distribution, capitalism favors private control of business and minimal governmental regulation of private industry.

**Capitalism.**   Capitalism is a mode of economic production characterized by private ownership by individuals or groups of land, factories, raw materials, and other instruments of production. It is the economic system found in the United States, Great Britain, and most nations of Western Europe. In capitalist systems, the laws of supply and demand in the marketplace and free trade set prices of goods and drive production.

In 1776, the same year as the signing of the Declaration of Independence, Adam Smith (1723–1790) published *An Inquiry into the Nature and Causes of the Wealth of Nations* (generally known as *The Wealth of Nations*). Smith's book marked the beginning of the modern capitalist era. He argued that free trade would result in full production and economic health. These ideas were greeted with great enthusiasm in the colonies as independence was proclaimed. Colonists no longer wanted to participate in the mercantile system of Great Britain and other Western European nations. These systems bound trade and its administration to national goals and not those of the individual. Smith and his supporters saw free trade as "the invisible hand" that produced the wealth of nations. This wealth, in turn, became the inspiration and justification for capitalism.

Under capitalism, sales occur for the profit of the individual. Capitalists believe that both national and individual production is greatest when individuals are free to do as they wish with their property and goods. The government, however, plays an indispensable role in creating and enforcing the rules of the game. One such rule is the "contract clause" in the U.S. Constitution, which prevents states from extending the time in which debtors can meet their payments or get out of contractual obligations.

From the mid- to late eighteenth century through the mid-1930s in the United States and in much of the Western world, the idea of *laissez-faire* economics (from the French, to let do) enjoyed considerable popularity. While most states regulated and intervened heavily in their economies well into the nineteenth century, the national governments routinely followed a "hands off" economic policy. By the late 1800s, however (as discussed in Chapters 8, 16, and 17) the U. S. government felt increasing pressure to regulate some aspects of the nation's economy. This pressure often arose

## Understanding the "ISMs"
♦ ♦ ♦

These humorous definitions of political systems of the world appeared in an FDR-era farm journal:

> Socialism: You have two cows. The government takes one and gives it to your neighbor because he doesn't have a cow.
>
> Communism: You have two cows. The government takes both and gives you the milk.

> Nazism: You have two cows. The government takes both and shoots you.
>
> New Dealism: You have two cows. The government takes both and shoots one, milks the other and throws the milk away.
>
> Capitalism: You have two cows. You sell one and buy a bull.

*Atlanta Journal-Constitution,* June 20, 1993: A2.

from the difficulties states faced in regulating large multistate industries such as the railroads, and big industry's desire to override the patchwork of regulations produced by the states. Thus, true capitalism ceased to exist.[9] The extent of this trend, however, varied by country and over time. In post–World War II Britain, for example, the extent of government economic regulation in industrial policy and social welfare was much greater than that attempted by American policy makers in the same period.

**Socialism.**   Reaction to the overwhelming wealth of millionaire industrialists and a corresponding exploitation of workers in France, England, and ultimately the United States, led to the development of socialism, a philosophy that advocates collective ownership and control of the means of economic production. Karl Marx (1818–1883), the German socialist and founder of communism, once stated that socialism was a transitional phase between capitalism and communism.

In direct opposition to the ideas of capitalism favored by the Framers, socialists (and communists) call for governmental—rather than private—ownership of all land, property, and industry and, in turn, an equitable distribution of the income from those holdings. In Marx's words, "From each according to his ability, to each according to his needs."[10]

It is important to note that some socialists actually tolerate capitalism as long as the government maintains some kind of control over the economy. Others, including communists, reject capitalism outright and insist on the abolition of all private enterprise. Thus, all communists are socialists, but not all socialists are communists.

Over the years, socialists have been united in their view of concern for all men and women, but have not agreed about the means by which to reach a socialist ideal.

---

[9] Modern disciples of *laissez-faire* are called libertarians. Libertarians adamantly oppose all forms of government regulation and action unless it is critical to the protection of life, liberty, or property. They argue that while governments are at best an evil necessity, governments are best when they govern least.

[10] Karl Marx, "Critique of the Gotha Program," in *Marx Selections,* ed. Allen W. Wood (New York: Macmillan, 1988), p. 190.

Karl Marx

Some, especially in Western Europe, have argued that socialism can evolve through democratic processes. Thus, in nations like Great Britain, certain critical industries or services such as health care or the coal industry have been *nationalized,* or taken over by the state to provide for more efficient supervision and to avoid the major concentrations of wealth that occur when individuals own key industries.

**Communism.** Karl Marx grew up in Germany as the socialist movement developed there and in many other parts of Western Europe. Its influence on him was profound. He came to argue that government was simply a manifestation of underlying economic forces and could be understood according to types of economic production.

According to Marx, all societies went through five stages:

(1) primitive communalism, (2) slavery, (3) feudalism, (4) capitalism, and (5) socialism. He believed that history brought with it an evolving economic and political system in which a class struggle between workers and property owners was inevitable. The clash of the interests of these two classes led to the development of the state or government. In turn, governments were used by rich capitalists, called by the French term *bourgeoisie,* to protect their property in much the same way that, according to Charles Beard, the Framers of the U. S. Constitution were motivated by their personal economic concerns when they drafted the Constitution (see p. 59). In *Das Kapital* (1867), Marx argued that capitalist states would inevitably be replaced by socialist states in which the working class would own the means of production and distribution and would be able to redistribute the wealth to meet its needs.

Ultimately, Marx advocated **communism,** a scheme more radical than socialism. Through communism Marx sought to abolish all class differences and to create a system of common ownership of the means of sustenance and production. In essence, Marx viewed communism as the sixth stage of history, beyond socialism. To achieve communism, Marx believed that capitalist systems would have to be overthrown, no matter how violent the means. The communism espoused by Marx, however, continues to be a theory. It was never fully implemented even in the former Soviet Union. In most countries that still profess communism, such as China, economic and political control are held by a single, frequently authoritarian political party. Moreover, economic growth and planning are overseen by some sort of central authority.

**Totalitarianism.** Whereas socialist and communist systems spread the wealth and control of publicly owned industries and other means of production to all members of society, in a **totalitarian** system governments retain unlimited powers for the benefit of elite rulers. In contrast to systems based on democratic beliefs, totalitarian governments have total authority over their people and their economies. George Orwell's novel *1984* is perhaps the best depiction of what a pure totalitarian regime would be like. The reign of the Ayatollah Ruhollah Khomeini in Iran from 1979 until his death, and that of President Saddam Hussein in Iraq, come close to the "total" control of forms of production, the airwaves, education, the arts, and even sports implied by totalitarianism. Some communist systems also approach totalitarianism.

Because total control by a single ruler or elite requires technological innovations and weapons of mass destruction that only modern science can provide, totalitarianism, even in partial form, did not present itself to the world until well into the 1900s.[11] Even Adolf Hitler's Germany, perhaps the most totalitarian government that has appeared so far, probably lacked the resources to assert complete control over every aspect of life for all citizens.

---

[11] Hannah Arendt, *The Origins of Totalitarianism* (Cambridge, MA: Harvard University Press, 1958).

## Questions on the Third Section.

1. When the Framers drafted the Constitution, what did they want to protect?

_____

2. What are two key elements of the American economic system?

_____

_____

3. What are the chief characteristics of *capitalism?*

_____

_____

_____

4. Who is Adam Smith? Why is he important?

_____

_____

5. What are the key elements of *socialism?*

_____

_____

6. Which are some Western democracies that have elements of socialism?

_____

_____

7. What are the key elements of *totalitarianism?*

_____

_____

_____

8. Who is Karl Marx? What kind of political economy did he advance?

_____

_____

_____

*Section III. Why a Capitalist System?*

*Capitalism:* _____

_____

_____

_____

*private property*

*Adam Smith*

*Socialism:* _____

_____

_____

*in Western*
*democracies*

_____

*Communism:* _____

_____

*Karl Marx*

_____

*Totalitarianism:* _____

_____

_____

_____

Now read the final section of the chapter and then complete the questions and note taking that follow. Before reading, reflect on the section heading. What do you think the section will cover?

## Understanding Our Democratic System

One key to understanding our democratic system is a recognition of the role that history and its lessons have played in the development of the American political system. The lessons of history provide a context in which to understand not only policies of the past but also policies today. Changes in ideas and public expectations about government lead to reform no less than do crisis situations.

**Changes in Ideas and Public Expectations.**   Americans' ideas about and expectations of their government have changed and grown tremendously since colonial times. As ideas about social compacts were adopted and transmitted to the New World, colonists' ideas of government were altered. Once the Declaration of Independence and Constitution were drafted, expectations about the role of government evolved and continue to evolve.

Expectations about the "proper" role of government are often tempered by an individual's (or government's) ideological approach. As discussed in Chapter 10, whether one is "liberal" (by today's definition, generally favoring social and political reform and governmental solutions) or "conservative" (favoring the existing order with less governmental intervention in business or society), may also affect expectations. Although many continue to debate government's proper role, public opinion polls reveal that most Americans have come to expect "big government," and to want the government—especially the national government—to tackle economic and social problems. Thus, while a small percent of Americans are libertarians, those who stress that government should not involve itself in the plight of the people or attempt to remedy any social ills, most Americans today look to government for support in many areas, including education, medical research, and relief from poverty.

In the 1980s, for example, more than 175,000 people became infected with the HIV virus, and 109,000 of them died. Although AIDS was first viewed as a rare disease primarily afflicting homosexual men in California and New York, its demographics have changed, and now AIDS is the most common cause of non-accidental death among large segments of the population, including, for example, women in certain age groups. As more people from all groups and of all ages fall victim to AIDS, pressure on the national government to find a solution to this problem increases. Victims or those in high-risk groups are fighting for federal budget increases for AIDS research in addition to antidiscrimination legislation. Others argue for better screening of the blood supply and for compulsory testing of those in the medical profession. Governmental response was urged by C. Everett Koop, U. S. Surgeon General during Ronald Reagan's presidency, who played a major role in the decision to increase the federal government's effort for AIDS education over the protest of some conservative groups. Thus, as new problems occur, the public increasingly has looked to the government for help and solutions.

**The Lessons of History.**    As historians are fond of noting, history often repeats it-self. Clear cycles can be seen in the evolution of our democratic system. For example, in the mid-1800s, many women's rights activists sought the right to vote on a state-by-state basis and rejected suggestions to seek a constitutional amendment. The same state-by-state approach was used later in the suffrage movement (1890–1920) by a new generation of women who sought the right to vote, but again it proved unworkable as efforts in individual states were costly and often unsuccessful. Women finally de-cided that an amendment to the U. S. Constitution would be the most expeditious way to secure voting rights.

In the 1980s, after a series of decisions indicated an increased willingness on the part of the U. S. Supreme Court to restrict abortion rights, pro-choice forces initially sought to fight for the right to an abortion on a state-by-state basis. But by mid-1991, the National Abortion Rights Action League (NARAL) had admitted that it had lost far more than it had won with this strategy as state after state passed increasingly re-strictive laws. In an effort reminiscent of that adopted by women suffragists in the 1910s, NARAL decided to throw all its efforts behind passage of the national *Freedom of Choice Act* to guarantee a woman's right to an abortion free from any state restric-tions. Thus, an understanding of the difficulty women have encountered historically helps us to understand the effectiveness (and even the adoption) of some political strategies today.

**The Role of Crises and Reform.**    As government at all levels continues to grow, we cannot ignore the role that crises have played. The development of the power of the national government as well as realignments in the powers of the various institutions have also been affected by crises, as will be discussed in succeeding chapters. Crises do not affect only the American state; democracies like Britain have witnessed the shaping of their politics, institutions, and conflicts by unforeseen domestic and inter-national emergencies. The two world wars, for example, placed many new issues on the national agenda—for example, nationalization of industry, social welfare, and eco-nomic planning.

Although the U. S. Civil War and other national crises, such as the Great Depression and even the Watergate scandal (see pp. 264–265), created major turmoil, they demon-strated that our system can survive and even change in the face of enormous political, societal, and even institutional crisis. Often, these crises have produced considerable reforms. The Civil War led to the dismantling of the slavery system and to the passage of the Thirteenth, Fourteenth, and Fifteenth Amendments (see Chapter 5), which led to the seeds of recognition of African Americans as American citizens. The Great De-pression led to the New Deal and the creation of a government more actively involved in economic and social regulation. More recently, the Watergate scandal resulted in stricter ethics laws that have led to the resignation or removal of many elected officials.

In this text we present you with the tools to understand the political system in which you live. We hope that you will approach the study of American politics with an open mind. When you read a daily newspaper or watch a television news program, you are actually engaged in the study of politics. Your study of the processes of government should help you become a better citizen as you become more informed about your government and its operations. We hope that you learn to ask questions. Know who gets "what, when, and how." Learn to understand why a particular law was enacted. Ask, how was it implemented? And make sure your vote counts.

## Summary

To understand how our current system of government works, it is important to understand choices that were made many years ago. To that end, in this chapter we have made the following points:

1. The American political system was based on several notions that have their roots in classical Greek ideas, including natural law, the doctrine that human affairs should be governed by certain ethical principles that can be understood by reason. Also heavily influencing our ideas of how government should work were the ideas of the Reformation, the period when people began to believe that they could talk directly to God without the intermediary of a priest; the Enlightenment, the movement in Western Europe in the 1700s that espoused human reason, science, and religious toleration; and the ideas of social contract theorists John Locke and Thomas Hobbes, who held the belief that people are free and equal by God-given right. In turn, this freedom requires that all men give their consent to be governed.

2. In devising a new national government and a democratic system, the colonists opted for an indirect democracy, or republic, in which citizens may vote for representatives to work on their behalf. Key ideals of this indirect democracy are the value of the individual, political equality, popular consent, majority rule and the preservation of minority rights, and personal liberty.

Several different theories have been offered to explain how decisions are made in an indirect democracy. They include elite theory, the idea that important policies are set by three loose coalitions of groups including the military, corporate leaders, and a small set of government officials; bureaucratic theory, the belief that all governmental and nongovernmental institutions are, in effect, controlled by an all-powerful bureaucracy; interest group theory, the belief that interest groups—not elites, sets of elites, or bureaucrats—control the governmental process; and pluralist theory, in which resources are seen as so widely scattered in our diverse democracy that no single elite group can ever have a monopoly over any substantial area of policy.

3. The system set up by the Framers was capitalism, which advocates private ownership of property and a free market economy. Other nations have opted for socialism, which advocates public ownership and control of the means of economic production, or communism, in which government is seen simply as a manifestation of underlying economic forces, understood according to types of economic production.

4. Three factors are key to understanding our democratic system and its development: (1) changes in ideas and public expectations, (2) the lessons of history, and (3) the role of crisis and reform.

## Key Terms

politics

natural law

social contract theory

monarchy

oligarchy

aristocracy

democracy

direct democracy

indirect (representative) democracy

republic

popular consent

majority rule

popular sovereignty

elite theory

bureaucratic theory

interest group theory

pluralist theory

free market economy

capitalism

socialism

*laissez-faire*

communism

totalitarian

## Suggested Readings

Bentley, Arthur. *The Process of Government.* Chicago: University of Chicago Press, 1908.

Dahl, Robert. *Polyarchy: Participation and Opposition.* New Haven, CT: Yale University Press, 1971.

———*Who Governs?* New Haven, CT: Yale University Press, 1961.

Hobbes, Thomas. *Leviathan.* New York: Everyman (Library Edition), 1914.

Locke, John. *Two Treatises of Government,* ed. Peter Lasleti. New York: Mentor, 1960.

Marx, Karl. *Das Kapital.* Chicago: Regnery, 1970.

Mills, C. Wright. *The Power Elite.* New York: Oxford University Press, 1956.

Schumpeter, Joseph A. *Capitalism, Socialism, and Democracy.* New York: Harper, 1942.

Schlesinger, Arthur M. *The Age of Jackson.* Boston: Little, Brown, 1945.

Truman, David. B. *The Governmental Process.* New York: Knopf, 1951.

Weber, Max. *From Max Weber: Essays in Sociology,* trans. and ed. H. H. Gerth and C. Wright Mills. London: Routledge & Kegan Paul, 1948.

## Questions on the Final Section.

1. We understand our democratic system by understanding the

   _____

   and how _____ lead to reform.

2. What are some examples of crises that have led to change?

   _____

   _____

   _____

3. What is one lesson from history?

   _____

   _____

4. What do most Americans expect of government?

   _____

   _____

5. What do students gain from a study of their political system?

   _____

   _____

Answering these questions will help you take good notes on this final section. Now make your own page of notes.

*Section IV. Understanding Our Democratic System*

   _____

   _____

   _____

_____

_____

_____

_____

_____

_____

_____

_____

_____

_____

_____

_____

You have read, answered questions about, and completed four pages of notes on the first chapter of a challenging college textbook. If you apply your reading strategy and use a writing-to-learn strategy, you can learn complex information.

## Respond

The last step in your reading strategy is to respond by reviewing and reflecting on the material you have read. You will need to review your notes to answer possible test questions later in this chapter. Before continuing to read, reflect on the government chapter you have just studied. Here is one question to aid your reflection: What is the most significant new idea you have learned about American government and why is it important to you?

_____

_____

_____

_____

_____

_____

## Reinforcing Learning In Class

One of the best methods for becoming successful in some activity is to find out what other successful people have done and then copy their methods. We do know the methods of successful students.

### Preparing for Class

Good students almost never miss class, and they go to class prepared. Reading assignments before going to class gives you a *learning context* for the class period. Some students go to class hoping that the instructor will teach them what they need to know so that they will not have to read the textbook. These students have the process backwards. Class lectures and discussions should clarify what you have already read. Even if the reading is difficult, you will gain some knowledge that will allow you to follow the lecture and participate in discussion.

### Participating in Class

Good students participate in class. Active engagement in class includes the following activities.

1. **Sit near the front of the class.** From here you can see the board clearly. You also signal your instructor that you want to learn.

2. **Come with the appropriate materials.** Have needed materials assembled before the instructor begins class. *Good students do not walk in late and then further disrupt class by asking a neighbor what's happening.*

3. **Listen.** Intend to learn. Pay attention to signal words that announce a list or definition or contrast, the same signal words you find in written materials. Really listen to signal words that announce important material (because it will be on the next test!). Some of these signals include:

"This is really important," "I want you all to be clear on this," and "Let me emphasize. . . ."

4. **Participate in class discussions, question periods, and group activities.** Come to class with questions about the reading assignment or the last class lecture. Speak up in class discussions, even if you are shy, because putting the ideas in your own words is an important strategy for learning. Class discussions give you a chance to test your understanding without being graded. (It is those students who are not participating who are being graded—down.)

5. **Take notes.** The Cornell Method of note taking is also ideal for class notes. Take your notes in the space to the right of the vertical line on each page. Add key words and phrases down the left column after class. Label reading notes and class notes at the top of each page and keep them in the same three-ring binder notebook.

   When taking notes, listen for main ideas and get down complete definitions of key terms. Be certain to copy *everything* that is put on the board. Include signal words in your notes: the *causes* of the Civil War or the *differences between* the First and Second World Wars.

6. **Review notes immediately.** You want to fix in your memory as much of the class discussion as possible, so review your notes and add key words as soon as class is finished. If you have another class right away, hurry to that class and then review your notes before the second class begins.

## ■ PREPARING FOR TESTING

The best way to prepare for testing is to learn the material as you go so that you are ready for the test. You learn the material by applying your reading strategy to the textbook, by participating in class, and by reviewing your notes every week of the term.

Keep your focus on the task of learning. You are not learning when you are thinking about the test instead of the subject matter. Successful students spend their time and energy doing the work of the course. Unsuccessful students spend more time thinking about themselves and about their anxieties and past performances, rather than thinking about the subject matter. Plan to model yourself after successful students.

Most instructors describe the format of tests either in class or on the course syllabus. So, you will know if a given test will be multiple choice, fill in the blanks, short answer, or essay format. Remember that any of the short-answer formats will demand knowledge of details. You will not be able to "shoot the breeze" or give personal responses to the material. Short-answer formats may test ideas and inferences as well as facts, though, so you still need to reflect on the subject matter, just as you will need to do for essay testing. First, here are some guidelines for preparing for short-answer forms of testing.

## Guidelines for Short-Answer Testing

1.     **Study from thorough notes.** Make certain that both class notes and reading notes are detailed and complete. Be sure to include key terms and their definitions. You may want to make vocabulary flash-cards for key terms.

2.     **Concentrate on material the instructor has emphasized in class.** Your class notes should reveal what has been stressed in class. Know this material "cold."

3.     **Use chapter review questions or study problems as ways to pre-pare.** Be sure you can answer all the review questions and also work any additional problems at each chapter's end as a way to review and test yourself.

4.     **Do not overlook historical elements in your texts.** Many in-structors care about the history of their field of study and expect stu-dents to learn some of that history. Be prepared for such questions as "Who was the father of psychoanalysis?" in your psychology class.

5.     **Practice naming parts, reciting steps in processes, recounting key examples.** Talk through the material, either to yourself or with a study partner. Cover a page of notes and recite the material. Then check yourself for accuracy before going to another page.

6.     **Be able to spell key terms correctly.** For any test format other than multiple choice, you will need to write. So, practice spelling along with definitions of key terms. Instructors will forgive misspellings of minor words more readily than misspellings of key terms. Can you spell *laissez-faire?*

7.     **Anticipate the questions.** As you study, ask yourself what ques-tions you would use to test someone on the material. Listening in class and using the text's summaries or review questions should help you figure out most of what's coming on the test.

Here are some possible short-answer questions on the chapter you just stud-ied. Review your reading notes and then see how well you would do with these test questions.

## Multiple Choice

_____ 1. In medieval times kings
   a. ruled by divine right.
   b. were loved by their subjects.
   c. were despised by their subjects.
   d. ruled by consent of the governed.

Often with multiple-choice tests, you can eliminate two of the four possible answers immediately. (It is difficult to create tests with four "good" answers.) The answer to the sample question is going to be either (a) or (d). (Obviously some kings were loved and some were despised; the chapter did not discuss medieval kings who were loved or despised.) The right answer is (a). Popular consent is the new idea.

## Fill in the Blank

1. The Mayflower Compact reflects ideas of _____

_____.

Notice that this test item is more difficult than the multiple-choice item. You have to write the answer, not just recognize it. Ask yourself, what was the Mayflower Compact used as an example of? The answer: self-governance. The pilgrims who came here aboard the Mayflower wanted to set up their own self-governing communities.

## True/False

1. American democracy functions entirely on the concepts of political equality and majority rule.

When taking true/false tests, keep in mind that a statement must be _completely_ true to be marked true. If some part of the statement is not true, then you must mark the statement false. Read each statement carefully before deciding how to mark it. The statement above is false because American democracy _also_ functions on the concept of protecting minority rights. Be alert to sweeping words such as "entirely." They usually signal a false statement.

## Short Answer

1. Briefly define the four theories that explain how decisions are made in our system.

With short-answer topics, write to the point. You should be able to answer these questions in just a few sentences if you stay on the topic. You can respond to the topic above right from your reading notes. Devote one sentence to each theory. For example:

> Elite Theory asserts that just a few powerful leaders—from the military, business, government, and possibly the media—make the decisions and run the government.

## Essay Tests

To write a good essay answer, you need the same information for short-answer tests, but you also need to make connections and understand larger issues. In addition, you need to organize your thoughts in a short period of time. You can cope, however, if you prepare properly for essay testing. Here are some guidelines.

**1. Follow the seven guidelines given above for short-answer testing.** Do not think that you can just "write off the top of your head." You still need to know the subject matter and be able to spell key terms.

**2. Anticipate essay questions.** Review your class notes to see how the instructor organized the subject matter and made connections within the chapter and to other parts of the course. Make up some essay questions that *you* would ask about the material.

**3. Read the essay topic carefully and understand what you are asked to write about before you start an answer.** Too many students end up writing off the subject because they start to write everything they know without focusing on the specific topic. Use these strategies to understand essay topics.

a. Turn the statement into a question that you then answer in your essay. For example, suppose you read this topic: Discuss the ideas of Locke that helped shape the American system of government. Ask yourself, "What were the key ideas of Locke?" Jot down key points and then think about how they were used by the Founders of our government.

b. Pay attention to direction words. "Examine," "discuss," and "explain" call for an organized presentation of information. "Interpret" and "evaluate" ask you to make judgments and include your views. "Relate" asks you to make connections, "compare" to note similarities or differences, "trace" to use a time sequence to examine causes or steps in a process.

**4. Organize your answer before writing.** Take time to collect your thoughts and select an organization. Use one sheet of paper or the back of the test to jot down some points in the order you want to discuss them. The instructor expects you to compose an orderly discussion of the topic.

**5. Learn from doing.** Study each test when it is returned to you. Note any questions you did not anticipate. Compare your test to a classmate's to see why you lost points. Did you leave out a key point? Did your essay jump around rather than maintain a clear organization? Apply the knowledge you gain to your study for the next test.

## Chapter Review Quiz

*Complete each of the following.*

1. When previewing a chapter, always look at and think about:

   a. _____

   b. _____

   c. _____

2. To get the most out of classroom learning, be sure to:

   a. _____

   b. _____

   c. _____

3. Mapping differs from outlining by

   _____

   _____

4. The terms "boxes" and "side bars" refer to

   _____

   _____

   _____

5. Answer the following questions on the chapter you studied on American government.

1. Politics is
   a. the process of government.
   b. the process of decision making.
   c. the election of presidents.
   d. taking a government course.

2. Hobbes and Locke published their works on government in the
   a. 16th century.
   b. 17th century.
   c. 18th century.
   d. 19th century.

3. The primary function of governments has been to

   _____

   _____.

4. The Framers of the Constitution were particularly concerned about protecting

   _____.

5. Briefly contrast four types of governments.

   _____

   _____

   _____

   _____

   _____

   _____

   _____

## True/False

|  | T | F |
|---|---|---|
| 6. Locke and Rousseau influenced the American republic more than Hobbes. | ___ | ___ |
| 7. Believing in a capitalist economy, Americans oppose all types of socialism. | ___ | ___ |

# CHAPTER 12

## Reading More Efficiently

**In this chapter you will learn:**

- How to scan for information
- How and when to skim reading material
- To improve visual perception in reading
- To improve reading speed

## ■ PREPARE TO READ

Read and reflect on the chapter's title and objectives. Glance through the chapter, observing headings, to see what is covered. Now answer these questions:

1. What do you expect to learn from this chapter?

   _____

   _____

2. What do you already know about the chapter's topic?

   _____

   _____

3. What two or three questions do you want answered from reading this chapter?

_____

_____

_____

_____

Just as instructors use different teaching strategies in the classroom depending on what they are teaching, so readers need different strategies depending on *what* and *why* they are reading. In previous chapters we have stressed reading for full comprehension and have developed strategies for coping with difficult textbook material. In some reading contexts, though, you can speed up and still accomplish your purpose in reading. One way to be an efficient reader is to know when to read for full comprehension and when to use other reading methods, such as **scanning** and **skimming.**

## ■ SCANNING

**Scanning** involves searching written materials for a particular piece of information. Instead of reading every word on the page, you move your eyes quickly, searching for what you need. You scan when you look up a word in a dictionary, or a phone number in the telephone directory. You don't read all the definitions or all the names; you look just for the word you need or the name of the person you wish to call. Right? Or, do you let your eyes wander around the page instead of aggressively searching for just the information you need? To be an efficient reader, focus on finding just what you are looking for.

How can scanning help you read course materials more efficiently? Instead of looking back over a chapter to find a definition of *superego,* scan the book's index for the pages you need. (You could also scan the book's glossary; that is a faster way to locate just the definition.)

Scanning is also useful when you are doing research. You may need just one piece of information on a table or chart. You will want to scan indexes to possible sources for a research paper, looking just under the headings for works on your topic. Or, scan reference books for just the section you need, reading carefully only what is important to your study. These are just some occasions for using scanning as a reading strategy. They all have in common the need to locate specific information. To be most efficient when you scan, follow these basic guidelines.

## Guidelines for Scanning

1. **Understand the organization of the material.** Is the material organized in columns? (dictionaries; tables) Is it alphabetical? (dictionaries; glossaries; indexes) Are there section headings and subheadings to guide you? (most textbooks) Be clear about the organizational pattern before beginning your search.

2. **Keep focused on what you are looking for.** When scanning material in columns, search with your eyes. Do not read; run your eyes down the columns of the index, looking first for the "s" section, then for the word *superego*. When scanning prose materials, either focus on a key term or phrase (such as *superego*), or ask a question and then scan to find the answer. Visualize the term; hold it in your mind's eye so that you search only for that term and nothing else.

3. **Use whatever clues are available to speed your search.** Section headings are in large print, often in color. Key terms are often in *italic* or **bold** type for easy spotting. At the top of each page of a dictionary are the words that begin and end that page. As you flip pages, look only at those identifying words until you find the page you need.

4. **Confirm your information.** Scan aggressively, but once you think you have found what you are looking for, take time to confirm the information. Is it really *affect* that you want to spell correctly, or *effect?* Read the definition of the word to be sure. When looking for information in tables or charts, be sure to understand how the information is presented so that you can word the information correctly when you use it.

The following exercises will give you practice scanning different kinds of materials.

## Exercise 12-1 Scanning Indexes

*I. Scan the index page shown in Figure 12.1 to answer the following questions about the text* Patterns of Reflection. *Try to complete the questions in less than one minute.*

1. On what pages can you find a discussion of steps to active reading?

■ **FIGURE 12.1**

Index page from *Patterns of Reflection,* 2nd ed.

2. On what pages will you find "The Story of an Hour"?

_____

3. Is Mrs. Zajac a person or the title of a work? _____

How do you know?

_____

4. On what pages will you find information about organization?

_____

*II. Locate some information in one of your library's most used reference works,* The Reader's Guide to Periodical Literature. *If you are unfamiliar with the format and abbreviations used in this index, study the information in Figure 12.2 first. Then scan Figure 12.3 for information to answer the following questions. Once you turn to the index, try to complete the questions in less than one minute.*

1. If you want to find more articles about greenhouses, under what subject heading should you look?

_____

2. How many subject headings will lead to more articles on edible greens?

_____

3. What is the article "To spike or not to spike" about?

_____

4. How many speeches by Alan Greenspan were printed in *Vital Speeches* in 1995?

_____

5. Who wrote "Global warming is still a hot topic" and in what magazine did the article appear?

_____

6. Is the Greenpeace article in *Maclean's* magazine illustrated? _____

On what pages did the article appear? _____

■ FIGURE 12.2

**From *The Reader's Guide to Periodical Literature***

## SAMPLE SUBJECT ENTRY

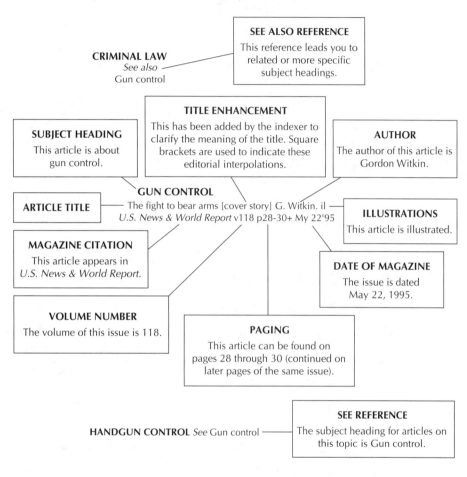

## SAMPLE NAME ENTRY

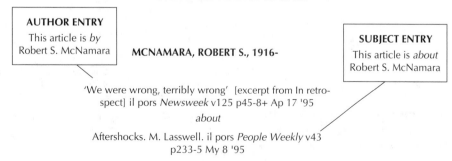

## A Sample Page from *The Reader's Guide to Periodical Literature*

**GREENHOUSE EFFECT**—*cont.*
Rio signatories to negotiate new goals. R. Koenig. il *Science* v268 p197 Ap 14 '95
Robot, build thyself [colonies of self-replicating machines would convert carbon dioxide into carbonate rock; research by Klaus Lackner and Christopher Wendt] T. A. Bass. il *Discover* v16 p64-7+ O '95
Satellite detects a global sea rise [Topex/Poseidon] R. Monastersky. il *Science News* v146 p388 D 10 '94
Scientists see greenhouse, semiofficially [report of the Intergovernmental Panel on Climate Change] R. A. Kerr. il *Science* v269 p1667 S 22 '95
Shifting dominance within a montane vegetation community: results of a climate-warming experiment. J. Harte and R. Shaw. bibl f il map *Science* v267 p876-80 F 10 '95
Simulation of recent global temperature trends. N. E. Graham. bibl il maps *Science* v267 p666-71 F 3 '95
Some like it hot [phytoplankton consumption by salps may be responsible for missing carbon; research by Evgeny A. Pakhomov and Renzo Perissinotto] W. W. Gibbs. il *Scientific American* v273 p28+ D '95
Some like it hot [Republican view of global warming] R. Wright. *The New Republic* v213 p6 O 9 '95
Steady temperatures: greenhouse sign? [work of Thomas R. Karl] *Science News* v148 p255 O 14 '95
Studies say—tentatively—that greenhouse warming is here. R. A. Kerr. il map *Science* v268 p1567-8 Je 16 '95
Temperature rising. L. E. Taylor. il *Canada and the World Backgrounder* v61 p12-15 O '95
Triggering the heat. B. B. Gordon. *Sea Frontiers* v41 p6 Spr '95
Troublesome tidings [changes in sea level recorded by Topex/Poseidon satellite] map *Discover* v16 p16 Ap '95
U.S. climate tilts toward the greenhouse [study by Thomas Karl] R. A. Kerr. il *Science* v268 p363-4 Ap 21 '95
Under the influence of clouds [data from the Earth Radiation Budget Satellite; research by V. Ramanathan] Y. Baskin. il por *Discover* v16 p62-9 S '95
Unintended consequences [saving the ozone could increase global warming] C. Zimmer. il *Discover* v16 p32-3 Mr '95
Vanishing zooplankton [warming ocean off California] J. Kaiser. *Science News* v147 p151 Mr 11 '95
Where's winter? il *Newsweek* v125 p58 Ja 23 '95
Why global warming would be good for you. T. G. Moore. *The Public Interest* no118 p83-99 Wint '95
Will plants profit from high $CO_2$? E. Culotta. il *Science* v268 p654-6 My 5 '95
World climate panel charts path for action. R. Monastersky. *Science News* v148 p293 N 4 '95

### Economic aspects
Time for a reality check [address, May 22, 1995] W. F. O'Keefe. *Vital Speeches of the Day* v61 p654-7 Ag 15 '95

### Seasonal variations
A fickle sun could be altering earth's climate after all. R. A. Kerr. il *Science* v269 p633 Ag 4 '95
Global warming is still a hot topic [arrival of the seasons may show greenhouse effect; views of David J. Thomson] D. A. Schneider. *Scientific American* v272 p13-14 F '95
The seasons, global temperature, and precession. D. J. Thomson. bibl f il *Science* v268 p59-68 Ap 7 '95; Discussion. v271 p1879-83 Mr 29 '96
Sun's role in warming is discounted [work of David J. Thomson] R. A. Kerr. il *Science* v268 p28-9 Ap 7 '95
Warming may disrupt pace of seasons [research by David J. Thomson] R. Monastersky. *Science News* v147 p214 Ap 8 '95

**GREENHOUSES**
*See also*
Cold frames
Green thumb? Get a greenhouse! L. Byczynski. il *Organic Gardening* v41 p34-7 N '94
Preserving a sunny day. H. E. Gibson. il *Flower and Garden* v38 p38-40 D '94/Ja '95

**GREENIAUS, H. JOHN**
*about*
Hit 'em first. J. M. Clash. il por *Forbes* v156 p102-3 Ag 28 '95

**GREENIDGE, V. N.**
The name of the game: consumer power! il *Black Enterprise* v26 p94-6 D '95

**GREENING OF HARLEM (ORGANIZATION)**
Bernadette Cozart: turning mean streets into green streets. D. E. Thigpen. il por *National Wildlife* v33 p14-15 D '94/Ja '95
Greenings from Harlem [work of B. Cozart and B. Barlow] K. Tenusak. il pors *American Forests* v101 p72 Aut '95

### Industries
*See also*
Whaling—Greenland
**GREENLEES, DON**
The Gallic logic behind the tests. *World Press Review* v42 p19-20 N '95
**GREENMAIL**
Is Kerkorian's bid 'a big hoax'? G. G. Marcial. *Business Week* p154 My 1 '95
**GREENMAN, STUART**
*about*
Silence, cunning, exile [drama] Reviews
*New York* v28 p57 Mr 6 '95. J. Simon
*The New Yorker* v70 p28-9 F 6 '95
*The New Yorker* il v71 p112-13 Mr 13 '95. N. Franklin
**GREENMARKETS** *See* Farmers' markets
**GREENNAN, EAMON**
Place [poem] *The New Republic* v213 p42 O 23 '95
**GREENPEACE INTERNATIONAL**
Anti-nuclear passions [opposition to French tests] E. K. Fulton. il map *Maclean's* v108 p26-7 Jl 24 '95
Dead-serious prank: a Greenpeace operation [A. Baker and M. Whiting pilot Ketch La Rebaude near French nuclear test site at Mururoa] J. Skow. il *Time* v146 p86-7 S 18 '95
Greenpeace: a house divided. R. Luyken. *World Press Review* v42 p18-19 S '95
It's not easy being Greenpeace. A. Toufexis. il *Time* v146 p86 O 16 '95
North Sea Shell game [work of T. Bode and Greenpeace in preventing disposal of Royal Dutch/Shell Group rig] T. Paterson. il *World Press Review* v42 p18-19 S '95
The passions of the Greenpeacers [opposition to French nuclear tests in the South Pacific] W. F. Buckley. *National Review* v47 p71 O 9 '95
They cannot sink us all [diary excerpts of protester aboard Greenpeace ship Rainbow Warrior II in French atomic test zone] S. Mills. il pors *Harper's Bazaar* p196-9 D '95
**GREENS, EDIBLE**
*See also*
Celtuce
Cooking—Vegetables
Dandelions
Herbs
Kale
Lettuce
Mustard (Plant)
From our kitchen to yours. K. Adams. il *Southern Living* v30 p184 Mr '95
Grow a rainbow of leafy edibles. J. Poncavage. il *Organic Gardening* v42 p38-43 F '95
Holler for collards [leafy greens may lower risk of macular degeneration; research by Johanna Seddon] M. Munson. *Prevention (Emmaus, Pa.)* v47 p43-5 Mr '95
In search of summer salads. L. T. Chaplin. il *Organic Gardening* v41 p52-7 Jl/Ag '94
**GREENS (GOLF COURSES)**
Distinctive designs: island greens. M. Purkey. il *Golf Magazine* v37 p150-1 Mr '95
Focusing on a grainy picture [effect of putting green grass growth direction on chip shots] il *Golf Magazine* v37 p34 Jl '95
Perfectly precise [Augusta National's greens]; ed. by Mike Purkey. T. Weiskopf. il *Golf Magazine* v37 p44-6+ Ap '95
To spike or not to spike [spiked golf shoes' damage to greens; views of Jim Snow] M. Purkey. il *Golf Magazine* v36 p98-9 Jl '94
**GREENS (GOLF COURSES), ARTIFICIAL**
Backyard birdies [practice greens] J. Grossmann. il *Golf Magazine* v37 p84-5 Ag '95
**GREENSBORO (N.C.)**
### Education
Breaking away from the agrarian school calendar: can 30 more days make a difference? [Brooks Global Studies Extended-Year Magnet School in Greensboro, N.C.] M. A. Tawasha. il *Omni (New York, N.Y.)* v17 p20 Ap '95
### Parks and playgrounds
Greening Greensboro's streams [StreamGreen project] C. Hammond. *Audubon* v97 p112-13 My/Je '95
**GREENSPAN, ALAN**
The Federal Reserve and monetary policy [address, May 16, 1995] *Vital Speeches of the Day* v61 p514-16 Je 15 '95
Key economic issues facing the nation [address, October 19, 1995] *Vital Speeches of the Day* v62 p79-82 N 15 '95
Maintaining stability in the prices of goods and services [address, June 20, 1995] *Vital Speeches of the Day* v61 p586-9 Jl 15 '95

7. What kind of work is Eamon Greennan's "Place"? _____

When and where was it published?

_____

 **EXERCISE 12-2  Scanning Tables, Charts, and Maps**

*I.  Scan the information on weather in foreign cities in Figure 12.4, then answer the questions on p. 370. Try to complete the questions in less than one minute.*

■ **FIGURE 12.4**

**Weather Information for Cities Around the World for September 30, 1996 (from the *Washington Post*)**

# Foreign Cities

| City | Weather Yesterday | Forecast Today | Forecast Tomorrow |
|------|-------------------|----------------|-------------------|
| Acapulco | 93/75 pc | 93/78 t | 89/79 t |
| Amsterdam | 65/58 r | 59/53 r | 54/40 r |
| Athens | 64/55 r | 66/56 pc | 69/59 pc |
| Auckland | 58/46 pc | 60/51 s | 65/57 pc |
| Bangkok | 90/77 r | 87/76 r | 86/74 sh |
| Barbados | 87/75 t | 86/74 t | 86/73 c |
| Beijing | 78/59 pc | 71/52 pc | 67/53 r |
| Berlin | 57/57 r | 70/57 t | 74/44 t |
| Bermuda | 80/73 pc | 81/74 pc | 81/75 pc |
| Bombay | 86/73 pc | 86/73 c | 87/72 pc |
| Brussels | 67/59 c | 64/56 r | 57/42 r |
| Budapest | 64/48 pc | 66/55 c | 71/53 c |
| Buenos Aires | 75/57 s | 77/61 s | 76/60 pc |
| Cairo | 91/66 s | 90/67 s | 95/68 s |
| Caracas | 91/77 c | 92/77 pc | 90/77 pc |
| Casablanca | 88/68 s | 83/63 s | 77/63 s |
| Copenhagen | 55/55 r | 60/48 c | 52/44 r |
| Dakar | 90/79 s | 92/79 s | 90/75 s |
| Dublin | 62/47 r | 53/47 r | 54/49 r |
| Edinburgh | 58/43 c | 53/44 t | 55/42 c |
| Geneva | 67/49 pc | 72/52 pc | 56/39 r |
| Havana | 88/75 pc | 87/75 t | 87/77 pc |
| Helsinki | 49/43 r | 49/42 r | 52/47 c |
| Hong Kong | 83/73 pc | 82/74 pc | 82/75 c |
| Istanbul | 61/50 c | 64/54 pc | 67/56 pc |
| Jerusalem | 81/55 s | 81/54 s | 82/56 s |
| Johannesburg | 78/50 pc | 81/51 s | 85/53 s |
| Karachi | 91/71 s | 91/71 s | 94/74 s |
| Kingston | 91/78 t | 90/77 t | 90/77 pc |
| Lagos | 82/72 pc | 82/72 pc | 81/72 pc |
| Lima | 67/59 c | 67/59 c | 68/60 pc |
| Lisbon | 79/62 s | 74/57 s | 67/57 pc |
| London | 71/58 c | 61/46 r | 59/43 pc |
| Madrid | 88/58 s | 86/55 s | 73/48 pc |
| Manila | 89/75 c | 89/75 t | 89/76 c |
| Mexico City | 63/55 r | 73/55 sh | 72/57 c |
| Montreal | 65/54 pc | 58/41 pc | 66/50 pc |
| Moscow | 39/27 s | 45/35 s | 51/49 c |
| Nairobi | 77/54 pc | 78/60 r | 80/53 pc |
| Nassau | 89/76 t | 90/74 pc | 87/75 pc |
| New Delhi | 101/71 s | 103/72 s | 100/74 s |
| Nice | 72/60 pc | 73/58 pc | 69/54 pc |
| Oslo | 54/41 r | 55/45 r | 54/39 c |
| Ottawa | 64/48 pc | 59/39 pc | 66/49 pc |
| Panama City | 87/75 t | 86/74 t | 89/76 pc |
| Paris | 69/54 pc | 73/54 pc | 55/40 r |
| Port au Prince | 91/73 t | 91/71 pc | 90/72 pc |
| Prague | 55/47 c | 69/54 pc | 74/40 pc |
| Rio de Janeiro | 79/68 pc | 75/64 sh | 74/62 pc |
| Riyadh | 104/67 s | 103/66 s | 103/68 s |
| Rome | 70/56 pc | 75/52 pc | 71/56 pc |
| Santiago | 83/48 s | 75/46 s | 76/53 s |
| Saraievo | 60/37 pc | 65/45 pc | 70/47 pc |
| Seoul | 80/63 s | 79/53 s | 76/51 s |
| Shanghai | 80/65 pc | 80/65 pc | 79/65 pc |
| Singapore | 88/76 t | 88/73 t | 87/73 t |
| Stockholm | 51/46 r | 54/43 pc | 54/45 c |
| Sydney | 74/59 t | 70/53 pc | 63/48 pc |
| Taipei | 85/73 c | 83/73 c | 84/71 r |
| Tokyo | 75/59 pc | 72/61 pc | 72/56 c |
| Toronto | 65/48 pc | 58/43 pc | 68/51 c |
| Vancouver | 62/48 c | 64/44 pc | 57/45 s |
| Vienna | 59/50 c | 73/57 pc | 74/51 pc |
| Warsaw | 56/46 pc | 64/55 c | 74/55 c |
| Winnipeg | 49/32 pc | 48/32 pc | 51/42 c |

Weather abbreviations are: s-Sunny, pc-Partly Cloudy, c-Cloudy, sh-Showers, r-Rain, t-Thunderstorms, i-Ice, sn-Snow. sf-Snow Flurries. All temperatures are given in degrees Fahrenheit.

* For weather updates, phone (202) 334-9000, then enter 9 and the first three letters of the city's name.

For hourly updates of major cities, visit The Post's World Wide Web site at http://www.washingtonpost.com

For weather reports for 2000 U.S. and foreign cities, phone 1-900-HI-OR-LOW from a touch-tone phone (75¢ per min.; average call lasts 2 mins.). Area codes required for U.S. cities.

1. How many foreign cities can expect rain tomorrow [October 1, 1996]?

_____

2. Which city had the highest temperature yesterday [September 29, 1996]?

_____

3. Which city can expect the lowest temperature today [September 30, 1996]?

_____

4. Tomorrow [October 1, 1996] in Cairo, by how many degrees will the temperature vary from low to high?

_____

*II. Scan the map in Figure 12.5 to answer the following questions. Try to complete the questions in less than one minute.*

■ **FIGURE 12.5**

**National Weather Map for September 30, 1996 (from the *Washington Post*)**

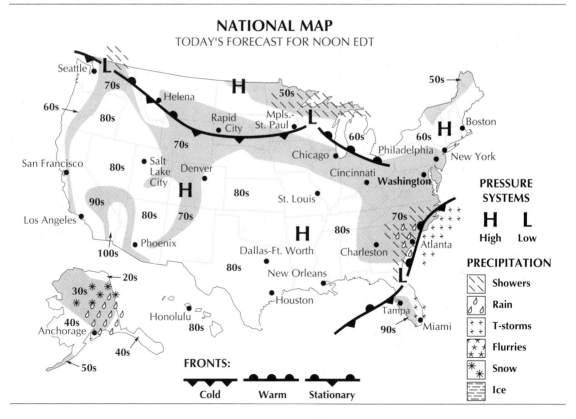

**NATIONAL MAP**
TODAY'S FORECAST FOR NOON EDT

1. What two areas of the country can expect rain today [September 30, 1996]?

   _____

2. Where will the temperatures be the highest?

   _____

3. What is the most northern state to have some temperatures in the 80s?

   _____

4. What two areas will have the coldest temperatures?

   _____

*III. Assume that you are writing a research paper on the costs of political campaigning. Scan Table 12.1 to answer the following questions. Try to complete the questions in less than one minute.*

## ■ TABLE 12.1

**Campaign for the U.S. Senate, 1992: A "Typical" Candidate's Budget of $2 Million**

| **Funds from** | **Total $** | **% of Total** |
|---|---|---|
| Political action committees (PACs) | $ 440,000 | 22% |
| Contributions from individuals | 1,200,000 | 60 |
| Political party | 300,000 | 15 |
| Candidate's own money (including family loans) | 60,000 | 3 |
| TOTAL | $2,000,000 | 100% |
| **Are Spent on** | | |
| Television (and radio) advertising | $ 800,000 | 40% |
| Staff salaries and consultant fees | 400,000 | 20 |
| Polling | 75,000 | 4 |
| Print media (literature, mail, buttons, etc.) | 60,000 | 3 |
| Canvassing/get-out-the-vote efforts | 125,000 | 6 |
| Office rent, equipment, and travel | 300,000 | 15 |
| Fund-raising expenses | 190,000 | 10 |
| Legal and accounting services | 50,000 | 2 |
| TOTAL | $2,000,000 | 100% |

O'Connor and Sabato, *American Government: Roots and Reform,* 1994

1. The table shows a typical budget for what kind of candidate?

   _____

2. The largest portion of a candidate's funds comes from what source?

   _____

3. What percent of a typical candidate's funds is obtained from PACs?

   _____

4. What is the single largest expenditure in the campaign budget?

   _____

### EXERCISE 12-3 Scanning Prose Materials

*Assume that you are doing a research project on problems with U.S. elections. Your textbook contains the box insert shown in Figure 12.6. Scan the material to answer the questions below. Do not read the passage; search aggressively just to answer the questions below. Try to answer the questions in less than one minute.*

1. What was the percentage of voter turnout in the 1988 U.S. presidential

   election? _____

2. What is the percentage of voter turnout in Japan? _____

3. What is the length of time of campaigns before an election in Britain?

   _____

4. Are campaigns given paid television time in Germany? _____

## ■ SKIMMING

**Skimming** is a strategy for getting an overview of the ideas contained in a particular piece of writing. When you scan, you search for specific information; when you skim, you overlook details to learn just the "gist" or main ideas of the work.

Skimming is like scanning, though, in two important ways. First, both reading strategies depend upon your understanding of the organization of the work and your ability to use that knowledge to find what you need.

■ **FIGURE 12.6**

Global Insights

## Getting a Better Turnout: How Other Nations Run Their Elections

The voter turnout for the presidential election of 1988 was around 50 percent of these registered to vote. Some critics argue that the problem rests with the way U.S. elections are organized and the process of voter registration. Can changes be made to improve voter turnout? Here are the models used by some other countries that have produced better voter activity.

### Italy—88.8 Percent Turnout

While voting is not compulsory, the system allows for the public disclosure of who votes and who does not. All parties receive campaign funding from the government. In addition, the government provides each party television time on state stations; time is allocated based on party membership. A party can purchase unlimited time on commercial television.

### West Germany—84.4 Percent Turnout

Campaigning is limited to the ten-month period prior to election day. There is no limit on campaign spending and the primary sources of money are party members and the state. The parties are allocated paid television time on government stations; the amount of time is determined by the number of legislative seats held by the particular party.

### Israel—79 Percent Turnout

In most cases, the duration of campaigns is between three and four months. Each of the parties is provided state campaign funds proportionally to representative seats, but overall spending is not limited. Television time is also allocated according to the number of seats a party holds.

### Britain—75 Percent Turnout

Once it is decided that an election will be called, campaigning is usually limited to a three-week period. In national elections, campaign spending is not limited and free radio and television time is provided based on the last election performance.

### Japan—71.4 Percent Turnout

Virtually all citizens are registered voters, since at the age twenty, those who register at ward offices for social benefits (including education) are automatically made eligible. There are strict guidelines on spending with the amount being determined by district size. All candidates are allocated five free six-minute television appearances and three six-minute segments on radio.

*Source:* Adapted from *New York Times,* 13 November 1988:E1, E3.

Curran and Renzetti, *Social Problems,* 3rd ed.

Second, both strategies are *alternatives* to reading for full comprehension, the reading you will use for most of your college work. Neither skimming nor scanning alone will produce success when you are reading to learn, but both can make you more efficient if you use them appropriately.

When is skimming a useful reading strategy?

**1. Skim some newspaper and magazine articles.** Even though you are busy with classes, you want to keep up with current events or a special interest or hobby. You can skim most of a paper or magazine, giving more time to one or two articles that especially interest you.

**2. Skim some research materials.** When you are reading several sources for a research paper, you will discover that some become repetitive.

Start to skim some of the articles, looking only for new information. Combining skimming and scanning with some full reading will enable you to cover many sources for your project.

**3. Skim supplementary readings.** Some instructors place additional readings on reserve in the library and expect you to know them thoroughly. Others put works on reserve for you to "look over" or be generally familiar with. In the second situation, skimming can be used to give you a quick page or two of notes on each required reading. The boxed inserts in many textbooks can also be included in this category. If your instructor tells you to "just be familiar with the boxes," then skim those sections of your text.

**4. Skim to locate articles for an assignment.** Sometimes you may be asked to find an article to respond to in writing, perhaps an editorial or an article in a collection of readings. If you try to read each one thoroughly, you may never get around to choosing and writing your essay. Skim until you find an article that seems interesting and meets the guidelines of the assignment. Then read that article carefully.

**5. Skim to preview a work before reading it carefully.** You have already been practicing this use of skimming each time you prepare to read a work.

**6. Skim to review a section or chapter after you have read it.** Some students like to reread assigned chapters in addition to reviewing their notes as preparation for testing. You may find that skimming, instead of a complete rereading, will jog your memory sufficiently to provide a good review.

In sum, there are three reasons to skim:

1. as part of preparing to read,
2. as part of reviewing for tests,
3. as an alternative to reading for full comprehension, when a general familiarity is appropriate.

Here are some guidelines for skimming.

---

### Guidelines for Skimming

1. **Establish your goal in skimming.** Know why you are skimming and how much of an overview of main ideas you need to obtain. Are you skimming an issue of *Sports Illustrated* for pleasure, or are you skimming supplementary readings that will be discussed in class?

2. **Identify the type of work and study its organization.** Identify the type of work, note signs of organization such as headings, and try to anticipate the writer's primary writing strategy.

3. **Skim newspaper articles by reading the first two paragraphs and then moving your eyes quickly down the center of each column.**

Main ideas are found in the opening paragraphs of newspaper articles. After reading them, let your eyes skim each column for additional interesting material.

4. **Skim magazine articles by reading the first one or two paragraphs and then skimming the rest of the article.** Glance at headings and words in bold or italic type. Look over charts, pictures, and diagrams. Then "read" aggressively, letting your eyes glide over the words, noting repeated key terms, lists, or steps in a process.

5. **For textbook prereading or reviewing and for supplementary readings,** skim by following the guidelines in Chapter 2.

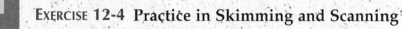

## EXERCISE 12-4  Practice in Skimming and Scanning

*Your biology instructor has announced that the textbook's boxes should be "looked over" but not learned in depth. Skim the following box, underlining as you skim, and then respond with a T (true) or F (false) to the statements that follow.*

### Sexually Transmitted Disease: A Growing Concern

One consequence of America's sexual revolution during the 1970s and 1980s has been a dramatic rise in the incidence of *venereal diseases*—diseases of the genital tract and reproductive organs caused by bacteria and viruses. These diseases are part of the broader category of *sexually transmitted diseases (STDs)*—infectious diseases of any body region that can be passed to a partner through sexual contact. A person with multiple sex partners has a substantial risk of contracting a sexually transmitted disease. Over 10 million cases are treated each year in the United States. And if undetected or untreated, such diseases can lead to severe complications.

The most common STD is *chlamydia,* an infection by the bacterium *Chlamydia trachomatis* picked up through sexual contact with an already infected person. A woman may have no symptoms of chlamydia at all, or she may experience pelvic pain, painful urination, vaginal discharge, fever, and swollen glands near the groin; a man may have a discharge from the penis or painful urination. The infection can be simply and effectively treated with antibiotics, but if undetected or untreated, it can lead to severe infection of the reproductive organs and even sterility. Because a person with chlamydia may have no symptoms, pregnant women can unknowingly pass the infection to their newborns. This STD, in fact, is the most common infection in newborns, with 100,000 cases per year.

The second most common STD is *herpes genitalis*, caused by the herpes simplex virus type 2 (HSV 1 causes cold sores and fever blisters). At least 20 million Americans have herpes, and 300,000 to 500,000 new cases arise annually. The virus causes watery blisters to form around the genitalia; these break and form painful open sores that eventually heal. The virus can be dormant for weeks, months, or years. Then, stimulated by sunlight, emotional stress, or sexual intercourse, the virus can break out once again and cause a new cycle of pustules and sores. Right now, there is no cure for herpes, and only partially effective antiviral drugs are available. If birth coincides with an active herpes phase in the mother, the newborn can suffer death or damage to the brain, liver, or other organs.

The fastest-spreading, and in many ways most worrisome, STD is *venereal warts*, caused by the papilloma virus. These small, painless, cauliflower-like bumps grow around the sex organs, rectum, or mouth and are passed through skin-to-skin contact. Getting rid of the warts is usually no problem, they can be burned or frozen off or surgically removed. More ominously, however, researchers are finding that the papilloma virus (which can remain in the body even after the warts are removed) has been present in 90 percent of the cervical cancer tissues studied so far.

Perhaps the best-known STDs are *gonorrhea* and *syphilis*. Both are caused by microorganisms; both are contracted through sexual activity with an infected person; both can have mild initial symptoms (a discharge or painless sore) or no symptoms at all; and both can be successfully treated with antibiotics. As in chlamydia, failure to find and treat gonorrhea at an early stage can lead to severe infection of reproductive organs or sterility. Failure to treat syphilis can also result in widespread damage to the heart, eyes, and brain and can result in severe damage or death to an unborn child.

Other STDs include pubic lice (crabs), scabies (parasites that burrow under the skin), certain types of vaginal yeast infections, trichomonas (flagellated protists that infect the vagina or penis), and acquired immune deficiency syndrome (AIDS).

Clearly, sexually transmitted diseases have become a serious threat. Planned Parenthood recommends that sexually active adults (particularly those with numerous sex partners) use condoms to prevent the passing of infections; be alert to sores, bumps, discharges, painful urination, or pelvic pain; and get tested regularly for STDs. This is especially important before or during pregnancy.

---

Postlethwait, Hopson, and Veres, *Biology! Bringing Science to Life*

_____ 1. STD stands for *sexually transmitted diseases.*

_____ 2. STDs are not a serious medical problem.

_____ 3. The second-most common STD is *herpes,* a virus affecting 20 million Americans.

_____ 4. The best-known STDs are *gonorrhea* and *syphilis.*

_____ 5. Condoms do not help reduce the spread of sexually transmitted diseases.

*Return to the box on sexually transmitted diseases and scan to answer the following question. Try to find the answer in less than one minute.*

Is there a cure for herpes? _____

## ■ IMPROVING VISUAL SKILLS—3

In Chapters 1 and 9 you performed some rapid word recognition and meaning recognition drills to help reduce vocalization and regressions, two reading habits that slow us down and make us less efficient readers. It is time to practice these drills again to build more control of the visual part of reading. These drills also provide a good warm-up to the timed readings that follow.

Your instructor may use these drills and readings in class, or you may be asked to time yourself at home. If you are on your own, do take the time to work the drills. Try the timed readings, too. Make it a game of testing yourself to see if you can improve your times from one drill to the next and to see if you are faster now than you were earlier in the term. Remember: the only thing you have to lose is time—time that would have been spent in future reading assignments!

## ■ EXERCISE 12-5 Rapid Word Recognition

*Move your eyes quickly across each line. Make a check over each word that is the same as the first word in **bold** type. Use a stop watch or a clock with a second hand to time each set. Do not look back over a line. Look only from left to right. Try not to say the words. Just look for each repetition of the word in bold.*

*Set II*          *Begin timing.*

1. **height**    high       heft        height     height     fight
2. **charge**    charge     change      cage       charge     cage
3. **trend**     tend       trend       tanned     spend      trend
4. **remain**    remiss     remark      ramble     remain     remake
5. **withdraw**  withdraw   withdrawn   withdrew   withdraw   withheld
6. **scarce**    scope      scan        scarce     scarce     scrape
7. **lately**    lazy       largely     lily       lately     lately
8. **clamp**     chomp      clamp       clamp      close      chomp
9. **soften**    sifter     soften      solve      soften     safety
10. **reality**  realty     regular     reality    reaching   reality
11. **ignite**   ignoble    ignite      inch       igloo      ignite
12. **command**  compote    command     common     demand     common
13. **distrust** dismay     disease     distress   disdain    dismal
14. **informed** inform     informed    informal   inflame    inform
15. **brave**    brave      bravely     brave      bravo      brace

*End timing. Your time:* _____ *Number checked:* _____

*Set II*          *Begin timing.*

1. **dismiss**   dismal     remiss      dismiss    dismiss    dismay
2. **worry**     marry      wormy       worry      wary       worry
3. **position**  position   positive    propose    pretense   posit
4. **message**   massage    message     message    massage    manage
5. **station**   sanction   stoppage    stopping   station    station
6. **verbal**    verbatim   verbal      herbal     verbal     vacant
7. **identity**  intensely  identify    identity   identity   indent
8. **million**   trillion   million     malady     million    missile
9. **human**     human      humane      humble     hopeful    humane
10. **lethal**   legal      lethal      legal      legal      lethal
11. **dinner**   dinner     diner       donor      dinner     diner
12. **vision**   version    vision      revision   visual     vision
13. **poison**   passion    poison      poison     passive    passion
14. **noise**    nose       noisome     nasal      noose      noise
15. **muddle**   middle     waddle      muddle     middle     muddle

*End timing. Your time:* _____ *Number checked:* _____

| *Set III* | *Begin timing.* | | | | |
|---|---|---|---|---|---|
| 1. **council** | council | counsel | counsel | consult | council |
| 2. **trample** | tremble | trample | treble | topple | trample |
| 3. **wretch** | wrest | witch | wrench | wretch | witch |
| 4. **ponder** | pander | ponder | ponder | poacher | pander |
| 5. **candid** | candid | cancel | corded | candid | cordial |
| 6. **nature** | nurture | nature | nature | natural | nurture |
| 7. **smash** | small | smoke | smash | smack | smash |
| 8. **reduce** | remiss | renown | reduce | deduce | remiss |
| 9. **forgive** | forgave | forgiven | forgave | forgiven | forfeit |
| 10. **effort** | effort | effect | affect | effort | effete |
| 11. **anger** | angle | ranger | anger | anger | ankle |
| 12. **proud** | prod | prank | proudly | proud | prod |
| 13. **frank** | frank | fraught | frank | fork | fraught |
| 14. **easily** | easy | easily | messily | eerily | easy |
| 15. **stake** | stoke | stack | stake | stake | stoke |

*End timing. Your time:* _____ *Number checked:* _____

| *Set IV* | *Begin timing.* | | | | |
|---|---|---|---|---|---|
| 1. **lightly** | lightly | likely | loosely | likely | lightly |
| 2. **wince** | whence | quince | win | wince | wrench |
| 3. **manage** | manger | manage | meager | manage | manger |
| 4. **bribe** | bribe | bride | bread | bribe | bride |
| 5. **witch** | wench | which | witch | witch | which |
| 6. **teacher** | teacher | preacher | thicker | toaster | teacher |
| 7. **dinner** | diner | dinner | damper | dinner | diner |
| 8. **sleeper** | sleepy | sleeping | sleeper | sleeping | sleepy |
| 9. **bought** | bought | bought | brought | brought | boater |
| 10. **opting** | opening | option | optical | opting | option |
| 11. **ageless** | eyeless | ageless | aging | absence | ageless |
| 12. **include** | incline | include | insane | incline | include |
| 13. **clause** | cause | clause | close | clause | close |
| 14. **rapid** | vapid | roped | razor | rapid | rabid |
| 15. **umpire** | uphill | vampire | umpire | umpire | vampire |

*End timing. Your time:* _____ *Number checked:* _____

## Rapid Phrase Recognition

Your eyes can read the words on the page only when they stop to look at the words. Each stop is called a "fixation." One way to increase reading speed is to make each fixation as brief as possible to take in the visual information—the printed word. Another way to increase reading speed is to see more words at each fixation. When you read the word *individual,* your eyes take in the whole word in one fixation. Of course when you first learned the word, you probably sounded out each syllable, but now you can take in the word all at once because you know it. Look at how much your eyes can now take in:

in / di / vid / u / al

If you can read five syllables with one fixation, why couldn't you read a phrase in one fixation? This phrase, for example,

when / to / re / spond

has fewer syllables than the word *individual.* You can increase your reading speed without losing comprehension if you will practice expanding the number of words you take in with each fixation. Let your eyes "collect" two or three words that make up a unit of thought and read them at one stop. The following exercises will help you practice expanding fixation.

### EXERCISE 12-6  Rapid Phrase Recognition

*Read from left to right across each line, looking for each repetition of the key phrase. Mark the key phrase each time it appears. Do not go back over any line. Try not to sound out any of the words; just look at each phrase to see if it is the key phrase to be marked.*

| Set I | Key phrase: when to respond | Begin timing. |
|---|---|---|
| when to go | when to dance | what a delight |
| wet your whistle | waiting for dark | when in doubt |
| wondering out loud | what's happening | when to respond |
| what's happening | when in doubt | washing the window |
| when in doubt | when to respond | wondering out loud |
| when to respond | wager a bet | when to respond |
| wet your whistle | wondering out loud | winter wonderland |
| waiting for dark | when to respond | when in doubt |

| | | |
|---|---|---|
| washing the window | winter wonderland | when to respond |
| wet your whistle | wondering out loud | wager a bet |

*End timing. Your time:* _____

*Number of key phrases marked:* _____ *out of 7*

---

*Set II*  Key phrase: *coping with stress*  *Begin timing.*

| | | |
|---|---|---|
| climbing the tree | coping with crime | careful with sticks |
| coping with anger | coping with stress | charging ahead |
| caring for pets | charging ahead | concern for others |
| coping with stress | challenging others | coping with stress |
| climbing the tree | coping with stress | caring for pets |
| concern for others | coping with stress | challenges ahead |
| cereal to eat | climbing the tree | coping with anger |
| caring for pets | climbing the tree | coping with stress |
| careless whispers | caring for pets | challenging others |
| coping with stress | cereal to eat | coping with anger |
| coping with crime | careless whispers | coping with stress |

*End timing. Your time:* _____

*Number of key phrases marked:* _____ *out of 8*

---

*Set III*  Key phrase: *better and faster*  *Begin timing.*

| | | |
|---|---|---|
| bargain basement | better with cream | bridges with lights |
| brighter and faster | bigger and faster | better and faster |
| better and faster | bridges with lights | butter with bread |
| baskets of fruit | better and faster | better than others |
| butter with bread | better than others | bigger than life |
| better and faster | bargain basement | bridges with lights |
| brains and heart | better with cream | brighter and faster |
| bowls and cups | bigger than life | better and faster |
| best and brightest | butter with bread | better than others |
| better and faster | bigger and faster | baskets of fruit |
| best and brightest | better with cream | better and faster |

*End timing. Your time:* _____

*Number of key phrases marked:* _____ *out of 7*

| Set IV | Key phrase: a safe place | Begin timing. |
|---|---|---|
| a soft spot | a safe haven | a safe place |
| a softer place | a sandy spot | a shady place |
| a silly idea | a safe place | a soft spot |
| a silk purse | a safe peace | a safe haven |
| a strong peace | a sandy spot | a salt lick |
| a safe place | a solid plank | a shady place |
| a softer place | a sandal strap | a soft spot |
| a silly idea | a silk purse | a safe place |
| a showy piece | a strong peace | a safe haven |
| a safe place | a shady place | a sandy spot |
| a silk purse | a safe place | a sandal strap |

End timing. Your time: _____

Number of key phrases marked: _____ out of 8

 ### Exercise 12-7  Rapid Phrase Recognition in Paragraph Form

*In the following sets the phrases are spaced to more closely resemble paragraphs. Read from left to right across each line, looking for each repetition of the key phrase. Mark the key phrase each time it appears. Do not go back over any line. Try not to sound out any of the words; just look at each phrase to see if it is the key phrase to be marked.*

| Set I | Key phrase: strive to retain | Begin timing. |
|---|---|---|

strike while hot    strive to withhold    strive to retain    under the
bridge    start the race    the other side    of the massage    strike
while hot    strength with grace    now or never    strike while hot
stop to receive    strive to retain    start the race    strike the nail
knowing the past    strive to retain    at the left    the other side
strike while hot    strive to retain    start the race    seek the strength
to some extent    ask the question    strive to retain    now or never
seek the strength    strive to withhold    under the bridge    long
and slender    in the sea    in many places    strive to retain    stop
to receive    stretch the rope    strike the nail    through the water
try to relate    strive to retain

End timing. Your time: _____

Number of key phrases marked: _____ out of 7

---

*Set II* *Key phrase: the living present* *Begin timing.*

who gets what     reactions to them     the living present     as a tool
the living past     an extra step     the living place     a new form     the
starship Enterprise     the living present     in both charts     in the sea
the best of times     the other side     a continuing change     the best of
life     the living present     the desert sand     the birthday present
laughter past     an extra step     the best of life     a past life     the future king     the living present     this present time     past lives     the
living present     present good times     reactions to them     now or
never     time flies     the living present     a future goal     present
lives     the living place     the living present     the best of life     another time     the living past

*End timing. Your time:* _____

*Number of key phrases marked:* _____ *out of 7*

---

*Set III* *Key phrase: promote the view* *Begin timing.*

promote the future     long and slender     through the water     promote the view     in the sea     pass the vases     program the PC     the
vantage point     promote the view     play the violin     in many
places     praise the victory     click the mouse     warp the impact
the vision thing     promote the view     proclaim the future     take
the journey     carry the torch     grasp the future     graph the curve
sing the praises     promote the view     program the PC     the basic
foundation     in both charts     try to rank     promote to captain     at
the right     proclaim the right     promote the view     try to rank
promote the view     a continuing change     change the view     promote the future     as a tool     make sense of     promote the view
play the flute

*End timing. Your time:* _____

*Number of key phrases marked:* _____ *out of 7*

## ■ EFFICIENT READING THROUGH AGGRESSIVE READING

You are taking a course in how to read *better,* not *faster.* Comprehension, not
speed, is your primary goal. Still, if you can maintain comprehension *and*
use your reading time more efficiently, that's a double benefit. As you have
learned in this chapter, two ways to use reading time more efficiently are to
skim and scan when those strategies are appropriate to your purpose in
reading. A third way to improve reading efficiency is to avoid bad habits
such a regression or vocalization. A fourth way is to expand eye fixations.
Expanding fixations will make you a faster reader. What else can you do?

How fast you can read *and* comprehend material depends in part on your general vocabulary and on your particular knowledge of the subject. The more you know about the subject, the faster you can read with understanding. You can increase your vocabulary and background knowledge if you keep reading.

Beyond these strategies, the only other way to be more efficient is to practice reading faster. If you practice, you will pick up the pace of your reading without losing comprehension. To practice, you need to read aggressively. Think of yourself as attacking the book or magazine. Do not let your eyes leave the page or your mind leave the subject. Do not let anything interrupt your concentration until you finish. The reading selections that follow will give you chances to practice.

## Calculating Your Reading Speed

To see how fast you read and if you are improving, you need to time your reading—and also see how well you have comprehended. You calculate reading speed—words per minute—by going through the following steps.

1. Record your starting time.

    Ex. 3:15 and no seconds

2. Record your ending time.

    Ex. 3:22 and 20 seconds

3. Subtract the starting time from the ending time to determine the number of minutes and seconds you were reading.

    Ex. 22 min. 20 sec.

    15 min.   0 sec.

    7 min. 20 sec.

4. Turn minutes and seconds into all seconds. (Remember: There are 60 seconds in every minute.)

    Ex. 7 min. 20 sec = $7 \times 60 + 20 = 420 + 20 = 440$

5. Find the number of words in the passage (provided at the end of each selection). Divide the number of seconds spent reading into the number of words in the passage.

    Ex. Words in selection: 1580

    Reading time in seconds: 440

    $$440)\overline{1580.00} \quad 3.59$$

6. Multiply the answer found in step 5 by 60 to determine the number of words read per minute.

    Ex. $3.59 \times 60 = 215.4 = 215$ words per minute

▣ Timed Reading I

*Directions: Take no more than 30 seconds to skim the selection. Now answer these questions:*

1. What do you expect the article to be about?

   _____

2. How many principles are covered?  _____

*Now begin timing and read aggressively to the end of the selection.*

**Starting time:** _____ **min.** _____ **sec.**

## Some Principles of Communication

by **J. A. DeVito,** *Essentials of Human Communication*

1    Communication is a process. Communication is always in motion; it is a process, an activity. Everything in communication is in a state of constant change. We are constantly changing, the people with whom we are communicating are changing, and our environment is changing. Nothing in communication ever remains static.

**Communication Is Inevitable**

2    Communication often takes place even though a person does not intend or want to communicate. Take, for example, a student sitting in the back of the room with an expressionless face, perhaps staring out the window. Although the student might claim not to be communicating with the teacher, the teacher may derive any of a variety of messages from this behavior. Perhaps the teacher assumes that the student lacks interest, is bored, or is worried about something. In any event, the teacher is receiving messages even though the student might not intend to be sending any. In an interactional situation, you cannot *not* communicate (Watzlawick, Beavin, and Jackson 1967). This does not mean that all behavior is communication. For instance, if the student looked out the window and the teacher did not notice, no communication would have taken place. The two people must be in an interactional situation for the principle of inevitability to operate.

3    Further, when you are in an interactional situation you cannot *not* respond to the messages of others. For example, if you notice someone winking at you, you must respond in some way. Even if you do not respond actively or openly, that lack of response is itself a response, and

it communicates. You cannot *not* respond. Again, if you don't notice the winking, then obviously there was no communication.

### Communication Is Purposeful

4   You communicate for a purpose. When you speak or write or paint, you are trying to send some message to another and trying to accomplish some goal. Four purposes may be emphasized: to discover, to relate, to persuade, and to play.

### Communication Is Irreversible

5   You can reverse the processes of only some systems. For example, you can turn water into ice and then turn the ice back into water. And you can repeat this reversal process as many times as you wish. Other systems, however, are irreversible. You can turn grapes into wine but you cannot turn the wine back into grapes. The process can go in only one direction. Communication is also an irreversible process. Once you communicate something, you cannot uncommunicate it. You can, of course, try to reduce the effects of your message. You can say, for example, "I really didn't mean what I said." Regardless of how hard you try to negate or reduce the effects of your message, the message itself, once it has been sent and received, cannot be taken back. In a public speaking situation in which the speech is recorded or broadcast, inappropriate messages may have national or even international effects. Here, attempts to reverse what one has said (in, say, trying to offer clarification) often have the effect of further publicizing the original statement.

6   This principle has several important implications for communication. In interpersonal interactions you need to be careful not to say things you may be sorry for later. Especially in conflict situations, when tempers run high, you need to avoid saying things you may wish to withdraw. Commitment messages—the "I love you" messages and their variants—need also to be monitored. Otherwise, you might commit yourself to a position you may not be happy with later. In public and in mass communication situations, when the messages are heard by hundreds, thousands, and even millions of people, it is especially crucial to recognize the irreversibility of communications.

607 words

**Finishing time:** _____ min. _____ sec.

**Starting time:** _____ min. _____ sec.   (subtract)

**Reading time:** _____ min. _____ sec. = _____ sec.

**No. of words ÷ reading time (in seconds) × 60 =** _____ **wpm**

## Comprehension Check

*Select the letter of the phrase that best completes the statement, or select either T (true) or F (false).*

_____ 1. Communication is a process because

   a. nothing is important.
   b. nothing changes.
   c. nothing remains static.

_____ 2. Communication can occur when

   a. we no not intend it.
   b. we do not see someone's behavior.
   c. there is only one person in the room.

_____ 3. Communication can be just a game without purpose.

_____ 4. Communication is a process that

   a. can be reversed or "taken back."
   b. cannot be reversed or "taken back."
   c. can be reversed when clarified.

_____ 5. Political leaders should be aware that

   a. they can reverse what they say by clarifying it.
   b. their speeches can have significant effects.
   c. their speeches can have effect only if others choose to respond.

**Comprehension score:  # right × 20 = _____ %**

## Timed Reading II

*Directions: Take no more than 30 seconds to skim the selection. Now answer these questions.*

1. What do you expect the article to be about?

   _____

2. The driver of the four-wheel-drive vehicle called the author:

   _____

*Now begin timing and read aggressively to the end of the selection.*

**Starting time: _____ min. _____ sec.**

# The Rude Awaken

by **Jeanne Marie Laskas,** the *Washington Post*, February 4, 1996

1    God forbid you should make a mistake. To err these days is subhuman.

2    I was driving late one night alone. This was not easy. My car is not good in the snow. The heck with what lane I was in. I was just trying to keep my car pointed forward.

3    A guy behind me in a fancy four-wheel-drive vehicle began flashing his headlights. I figured he knew something I didn't—that some danger was ahead, or that something was wrong with my car. So I slowed down. He kept flashing. I slowed down some more. He pulled up beside me, craned his neck to get a look at me. I could tell from the way he was trying to talk through the car windows that he had something really, really important to say. So I stopped and rolled down the passenger-side window.

4    "DON'T YOU KNOW HOW TO USE A TURN SIGNAL?" he said, spitting his words into the crisp winter air.

5    My weenie impulse was to answer him with a pathetic, "Yes."

6    "WHAT ARE YOU, STUPID?" he said. "WHAT ARE YOU, AN IDIOT?" Then he used a lot of curse words to characterize my driving, my heritage and my sexual history. He was still yelling when I rolled my window up and drove off.

7    I wished I hadn't bolted like a scared cat. I wished I had stayed and hissed at him. Then again, he seemed like the type to hoard firearms.

8    I was worked up the whole way home. Yes, I know tempers flare in winter—especially with two feet of snow on the ground. And I know that some people are, in fact, so breath-takingly important that their lives cannot be interrupted by some wacky indulgence on the part of Mother Nature. And yes, I know humans have a need to feign powerfulness when they are faced with their own powerlessness.

9    But please. Isn't there some jail we can put rude people in?

10    No, there isn't. And this is why the rude people are taking over.

11    I am not talking about just one jerk on a snowy highway. I am talking about the jerks you run into more and more often and in more and more places. I am talking about the jerk my friend Michelle met in a department store.

12    It has been Michelle's personal challenge this winter to survive with a broken ankle. Imagine. Okay, so recently she went on her first shopping expedition, and there she was, balanced on crutches, looking through a rack of dresses. She felt some pressure. She felt a push. She looked up to see a woman at the same rack, nudging her out of the way.

13    "Um," said Michelle, "I think there's room for both of us here?"

14     The lady looked at her. The lady said: "Get out of my way unless you want your other leg broken."

15     What does a normal courteous person do in a situation like this? Michelle's impulse was not to hiss, nor to run away. Instead, she reported the incident to the store manager, pointing out that the store was about to lose a good customer on account of this bully. She said people like this should be kicked out of the store.

16     The manager said there was nothing she could do. Not unless there was actual physical contact and a store employee witnessed it. "Store policy," she told Michelle. "Rude people like that are just the type to sue."

17     Suing. Shooting. The rude people seize all the power. The normal courteous people get none. This is what Michelle and I were concluding as we tried to think of a way to combat the bullies. "Solidarity!" we were saying. Take back the public places! Take back the stores, the buses, the parking spaces, the crisp winter air!

18     We imagined laws against rudeness. We considered mandatory Valium prescriptions for rude people. We envisioned support groups for the victims of rudeness. We wondered: Are we getting old?

19     For a while I walked around thinking that's probably it. You're supposed to think the world is getting uglier as you age.

20     Later I went over to a friend's house where a lot of neighborhood boys were playing. Most were about 9 years old, and they were playing rough, as boys do. But one was different. A rude person in training. For no apparent reason, this kid kicked my friend's dog, then made an obscene gesture at it. I looked at Tom, my 14-year-old nephew. "Kids are getting meaner," Tom said. "Definitely." He said maybe we should go upstairs and get a hot dog.

21     Just then, Katie, my 3-year-old niece, finished twirling around in her own personal time of glee and plopped down in the rude kid's seat. She didn't know it was his seat

22     "Get up, bitch," the boy said, "before I kick you, too."

23     I looked at Katie. I wanted to scoop her up, carry her away. I wanted to shield her forever from the generations of bullies her future held.

24     But Katie straightened her back. She folded her arms. She looked the boy square in the eye. She said: "You are rude."

25     The room went quiet. The boy retreated.

26     I'm telling you, it's a start. Try it. All together now: "You are rude."

886 words

**Finishing time:** _____ **min.** _____ **sec.**

**Starting time:** _____ **min.** _____ **sec.** (subtract)

**Reading time:** _____ **min.** _____ **sec.** = _____ **sec.**

**No. of words ÷ reading time (in seconds) × 60 =** _____ **wpm**

### Comprehension Check

*Select the letter of the phrase that best completes the statement.*

_____ 1. The best main-idea statement is:

     a. Rude people should be told they are rude and not be allowed to get away with bullying others.

     b. Older people always think young people are rude.

     c. Rude people should be put in jail.

_____ 2. The writer's friend Michelle experienced rudeness while

     a. she was visiting a friend.

     b. she was shopping on crutches.

     c. she was driving in snow.

_____ 3. We are to infer that the author

     a. believes that her age explains her sense of more rude people.

     b. does not believe that her age explains her sense of more rude people.

     c. believes that nothing can be done about rudeness.

_____ 4. The author believes that

     a. rude people are bullies.

     b. rudeness starts in childhood and continues unless corrected.

     c. both (a) and (b).

_____ 5. The author wants

     a. rude people sent to jail.

     b. courteous people to tell rude people they are being rude.

     c. rude people to take Valium.

**Comprehension score:   # right × 20 = _____ %**

### Timed Reading III

*Directions: Take no more than 30 seconds to skim the selection. Then answer these questions.*

1. What do you expect the article to be about?

_____

2. What is the subject of the list in the last section of the work?

_____

■ **Vocabulary Alert**

*Here are definitions to some words appearing in the selection that may give you trouble.*

rationalization (2): a comfortable but incorrect explanation

substantially (2): considerably

lethargic (4): inactive, sluggish

bolster (4): buoy up, reinforce

maladjustment (5): faulty or poor adjustment

alleviate (5): remove, eliminate

*Now begin timing and read aggressively to the end of the selection.*

**Starting time:** _____ **min.** _____ **sec.**

# Coping, Health, and a Positive Attitude

by **Lefton and Valvatne**, *Mastering Psychology*

1    Applied psychologists claim that simply maintaining a positive attitude can have beneficial effects on coping with stress and reducing physical symptoms. People who feel that they have control over their lives, health, and well-being are more relaxed than those who do not (Rodin, 1986). An upbeat mood, a positive sense of personal control, and even a self-serving bias can facilitate worthwhile behaviors, such as helping others and evaluating people more favorably. Some researchers suggest that people who have positive attitudes may even live longer. People say, "Look on the bright side," with the aim of reframing a situation to make it appear better, and to change a person's attitude and thus his or her behavior.

2    Sometimes, reframing or rethinking a situation is a rationalization to make it less anxiety-producing. Taking a positive approach and believing in your own abilities helps you to ward off stress and to avoid the fear and arousal that come from feelings of despair and low self-esteem (Bandura et al., 1988). Seligman (1988) argues that optimism helps people achieve goals and cope more effectively—for example, optimistic salespeople substantially outsell their pessimistic colleagues.

3    People can develop a positive attitude by conserving resources. Hobfoll (1989) suggests that people strive to retain, protect, and build

resources because the potential or actual loss of these valued resources is threatening. A person's home, marriage, or status as a community leader are all resources; and from Hobfoll's view, when these resources are under attack, people try to defend themselves against these attacks. They attempt to ward off the attack or replace the loss of resources by seeking a new marriage or new leadership position, or by gaining some new area of competence or financial strength. Treatment might mean shifting a person's focus of attention and reinterpreting the threat, replacing the lost resources (e.g., finding a new job), and reevaluating the threat. Hobfoll argues (1989) that a new more modern view of stress should go beyond the idea of stress as a reaction. His alternative is the conservation-of-resources model.

4    One effect of a positive approach is that it may harness the body's own defense mechanisms. Recent studies . . . have shown that the immune system (which fights disease) responds to a person's moods, stress, and basic attitudes about life. According to . . . researchers, the brain provides information to the immune system about how and when to respond. The two systems seem to be linked together, with each producing substances that alter the other's functions. The brain sends signals to the immune system that trigger its disease-fighting ability. The immune system sends signals to the brain that alter its functioning (Glaser & Kiecolt-Glaser, 1988). Thus, the immune system of a person with a positive, upbeat attitude responds better and faster than that of a person who is depressed and lethargic, whose depressed immune system slows down (Kiecolt-Glaser & Glaser, 1988). Consider people who have recently lost loved ones to death; they consistently show higher rates of illness. Today, many AIDS patients are provided counseling to bolster their immune systems by improving their attitudes, which may help them live longer.

5    Some psychologists find it difficult to accept the fact that the immune system responds to mental attitudes. The concept is not behavioral, in the sense that it can easily be trained, shaped, or measured. Researchers, however, are beginning to acknowledge that people can harness the power of positive thinking (O'Leary, 1990). Though positive attitudes and illusions can be beneficial, they can only go so far (DeAngelis, 1988) and help some people (Manuck, et al., 1991). Sometimes, having a positive attitude and practicing hypnosis, meditation, and the other traditional techniques fail to reduce stress. Sometimes, it is because they are tried halfheartedly; at other times, they are attempted inexpertly. More often, people just lack coping skills or even knowledge that such skills exist. Wearing rose-colored glasses from time to time can be beneficial, but continuous self-deception can lead to maladjustment, lies, and a truly distorted view of reality. Unfortunately, some individuals turn to

chemical substances to alleviate their pain, stress, fatigue, and anxiety—and these substances often lead to abuse.

6 **Effective coping strategies:** There are a number of steps you can take to cope, manage stress, and stay healthy.

- **Increase exercise.** People cope better when they improve physical fitness, usually through exercise. In addition, increased exercise will lower blood pressure, reducing the risk of heart disease.
- **Eat well.** People fell better and cope better when they eat well and have a balanced diet. This also means not being overweight.
- **Sleep well.** People react better to life when they have had a good night's sleep—reaction time improves, as does judgment.
- **Learn to relax.** In our fast-paced society, few people take the time to relax and let uncomfortable ideas and feelings leave them. Learn meditation, yoga, or deep breathing. Schedule some time each day for yourself.
- **Be flexible.** Our lives are unpredictable; accept that fact, and day-to-day surprises will be easier to handle.
- **Keep stress at school or the office.** Work-related pressures should be kept in a work environment. Bringing stress and pressure home will only make the problem worse; people are more likely to be involved in substance abuse and domestic violence when they bring stress home with them.
- **Communicate.** Share your ideas, feelings, and thoughts with the significant people in your life. This will decrease misunderstanding, mistrust, and stress.
- **Seek support.** Social support from family, friends, and self-help groups helps you to appraise a situation differently. Remember, you have to appraise a situation as stressful for it to be stressful—social support helps you keep stressful situations in perspective.

926 words

## Comprehension Check

*Select the letter of the phrase that best completes the statement, or select either T (true) or F (false), or complete the list.*

_____ 1. The best main-idea statement is:

    a. A positive attitude has little effect on health.
    b. Immune systems work better in people with positive attitudes.
    c. A positive attitude can help reduce stress and improve physical health.

_____ 2. Optimism—positive thinking—can help

    a. people achieve goals.
    b. make situations less anxiety producing.
    c. both (a) and (b).

_____ 3. One researcher argues that stress comes when

    a. we think positively.
    b. we are successful.
    c. our resources (such as marriage and job) are threatened.

_____ 4. Your immune system helps your body fight disease.

_____ 5. Having a positive attitude can lead to

    a. less stress.
    b. a distorted view of reality.
    c. both (a) and (b).

    6. Four strategies for coping include:

    a. _____

    b. _____

    c. _____

    d. _____

**Comprehension score:    # right × 16 =** _____ **%**

## Chapter Review Quiz

_Complete each of the following._

  1. Scanning is an efficient reading strategy when you are

    _____.

  2. Skim read when you want just _____
    of a work.

  3. To scan or skim successfully, you need to know how a work is

    _____.

  4. Skimming is also part of the _____
    step in your three-step reading strategy.

5. Improving visual perception in reading will help get rid of bad reading habits such as _____.

6. To calculate your reading rate (words per minute), you need to divide the number of words read by _____.

7. If you practice reading aggressively, you can increase your reading

_____.

8. Rapid Phrase Recognition

   *Key phrase: with the aim*          *Begin timing.*

| with the goal | with the aim | with the idea |
|---|---|---|
| when to aim | which to air | witches' brew |
| willing and able | when to aim | wrench the arm |
| which to air | witches' brew | with the aim |
| without air | wrench the arm | with the goal |
| with the aim | with the idea | with the aim |
| witches' brew | willing and able | which to air |
| when to aim | with the goal | without air |
| with the idea | with the aim | with the aim |
| without air | which ancient | willing and able |
| with the aim | wrench the arm | which to air |

   *End timing. Your time:* _____

   *Number of key phrases marked:* _____ *out of 7*

# CHAPTER 13

## Responding to Expressive Writing

**In this chapter you will learn:**

- The characteristics of expressive writing

- To recognize connotation and figurative language and read poems

- To read descriptive and narrative essays

- To read short fiction

### ■ PREPARE TO READ

Read and reflect on the chapter's title and objectives. Glance through the chapter, observing headings, to see what is covered. Now answer these questions:

1. What do you expect to learn from this chapter?

_____

_____

2. What do you already know about the chapter's topic?

_____

_____

3. What two or three questions do you want answered from reading this chapter?

_____

_____

_____

_____

Let's begin this chapter by comparing two brief passages. Read both and think about what each writer wants to accomplish. Then answer the questions that follow.

I. Generally, the trees that grow farthest north are conifers. These have needlelike leaves and seeds that grow in woody cones rather than in nuts or berries. (The word "conifer" means cone-bearing.)

Michael Scott, *Ecology*

II. About a mile farther, on a road I had never travelled, we came to an orchard of starved appletrees writhing over a hillside among outcroppings of slate that nuzzled up through the snow like animals pushing out their noses to breathe. Beyond the orchard lay a field or two, their boundaries lost under drifts.

Edith Wharton, *Ethan Frome*

1. In the first passage, what is the author's purpose?

_____

2. In the second passage, what is the author's purpose?

_____

3. How does the second author want you to feel after reading this passage?

_____

The first passage is straightforward, specific, and objective. The author's purpose is to *inform* us about the trees that can be found in the northernmost forests. The second passage also includes specific details—about a winter New England scene. But were you aware of differences in the two pieces of writing? In the second passage, Wharton wants us to see and feel the place she describes, to sense the emptiness and loneliness of the winter landscape. Her primary purpose is not to inform—what you find in textbooks and most of the newspaper. Rather, her purpose also includes engaging our feelings and helping us see beyond the literal landscape of trees and snow. We call this kind of writing *expressive* writing. In a third type of writing—*persuasive* writing—the author's primary purpose is to convince us to share his or her views. Newspaper editorials are primarily persuasive. It is certainly true that textbook authors care deeply about their topics and persuasive writers try to engage our emotions to convince us. It is also true that expressive writers provide information and want to persuade us to their views of life. Still, there are some differences, as you can see from the passages you compared, that are helpful for readers to understand.

## ■ CHARACTERISTICS OF EXPRESSIVE WRITING

**1. Expressive writing appeals to the senses.**   In writing to inform, details are used to help explain ideas. In expressive writing, details help us see and feel—and even taste and smell—the person or object or place under discussion.

**2. Expressive writing brings out feelings.**   Writing that informs appeals primarily to our intellect. We want to understand the ideas, facts, and processes that are presented. In expressive writing, ideas may be important too, but they are developed through the awakening of feelings.

**3. Expressive writing invites reflection on what it means to be human.**   We learn much about being human when we study a biology or psychology text: how the body creates energy, how memory works. Expressive writing, by contrast, invites us to reflect on both broader and more basic subjects: on the delight of springtime flowers, on betrayal and loss, on the joys and heartaches of childhood.

**4. Expressive writing is often subtle and indirect—imaginative—in its presentation of ideas and attitudes.**   Textbooks are organized around specific topics in a field of study. The persuasive essayist presents a thesis, examines the arguments of others, and takes a stand on an issue. But the expressive writer paints a picture, creates a character, tells a story. The subject matter is either made up or drawn from personal experience, and the first task of the expressive writer is to paint a compelling picture or tell an interesting story. The thoughts and feelings for reflection come to us indirectly, through emotionally charged language, details, and events.

## Why Write Indirectly?

Readers sometimes complain about expressive writing. Why can't authors just say what they mean, they ask. The answers to this question are important to consider.

*Variety.* Life would be boring indeed if all writers were required to write in the same style and tone.

*Pleasure in language itself.* The essays of humorists such as Dave Barry are categorized as expressive writing. It is fun just to play with language, as we find in many jokes and the books of Dr. Seuss, for example. On a more serious note, we are moved by the beautiful words in religious or patriotic songs.

*Power.* Stinging or caressing words, or the dramatic pictures created through metaphors, give power to the writer's ideas. Suppose that President Lincoln had said the following words in dedicating the Gettysburg cemetery:

> We are here today to dedicate this cemetery. We are really sorry that so many soldiers died here, and we are really upset that there is a civil war going on, and the nation may not survive as a result.

Would anyone remember "The Gettysburg Address" if Lincoln had said those words instead of the following:

> It is rather for us here to be dedicated to the great task remaining before us—that from these honored dead we take increased devotion to that cause for which they gave the last full measure of devotion; that we here highly resolve that these dead shall not have died in vain; that this nation, under God, shall have a new birth of freedom; and that government of the people, by the people, for the people shall not perish from the earth.

What Lincoln actually said is composed of difficult sentences, but powerful ones that have stirred readers for more than one hundred years.

## ▪ CONNOTATION

One way that expressive writers move their readers is through their choice of words. Words with similar meanings have similar *denotations.* Their dictionary definitions are similar, and they are considered synonyms. Some words with similar denotations do not, though, have similar connotations. A word's *connotation* is what the word suggests, what we associate the word with. For example, the words *house* and *home* both refer to a structure in which people live. These words have a similar denotation. But the word *home* suggests or is associated with ideas and feelings of family and security and comfort. So, the word *home* has a strong positive connotation. By contrast, the word *house* doesn't bring to mind anything but the physical structure because the word does not carry any "emotional baggage." Many words do not have connotations, but those that do often carry powerful associations. Studying a writer's use of emotionally charged words is an important way to understand a writer's attitude toward his or her subject.

Since we are familiar with the connotations of many common words, we may read "right over" key words without being aware of the writer's choice of language to direct our attitudes and affect our feelings. As you read, try to be especially sensitive to a writer's choice of words.

## EXERCISE 13-1 Becoming Alert to Connotation

*A. For each of the following pairs of words, check the one that has the more positive connotation. The first has been done for you.*

1.  quiet        _____ withdrawn

2. _____ miserly        _____ economical

3. _____ stubborn        _____ persistent

4. _____ naive        _____ trusting

5. _____ child        _____ brat

6. _____ hard        _____ brittle

7. _____ laid back        _____ lazy

8. _____ female parent        _____ mom

9. _____ pushy        _____ assertive

10. _____ neat        _____ neat freak

*B. Select one of the two words provided to complete each of the following sentences. Briefly explain why you did not select the other word.*

1. Some events in my brother's life have been quite _____.
(amazing/bizarre)

_____

2. Madonna has become _____ for her sexual openness.
(notorious/famous)

_____

3. Mary buys her clothes at sales because she is _____.
   (smart/cheap)

   _____

4. Tony's plan to buy out his chief competition showed a _____
   business sense. (shrewd/cunning)

   _____

5. Helena studies hard all the time; she must be a _____.
   (nerd/serious student)

   _____

## ▪ FIGURATIVE LANGUAGE

Sometimes the most effective way to express an idea and create a feeling is to take ordinary words but put them together in ways that do not make sense *literally.* When you read an expression that seems to make no sense, you may be reading a *figure of speech.* Figurative language isn't found only in poetry; it is actually quite common. For example, we say we are on pins and needles over a test grade and complain about the rat race. Now these two examples of figurative language are called *clichés,* because they are worn out from over use. Understanding figurative language in expressive writing can be difficult at first because the figures of speech are new. The first step to understanding is to recognize the figurative language and not take the statement literally. Momma's son in the comic strip below has some trouble with figurative language. Look at the cartoon and then answer the following questions.

Reprinted with permission

1. Why has Momma's son been fired?

_____

2. Why is he confused by the boss's statement?

_____

_____

## Metaphors

A *metaphor* is a comparison of two things that are not alike but seem alike in some significant way. The boss in the comic strip has used a metaphor to describe his problem with the young man. The young man is not *really* a rotten apple; he is *like* a rotten apple.

There are several ways to express a metaphor, and some of these ways have their own names, but they all fit the basic definition. Here are the most common.

**Simile:** A leader is like a mirror.

Think of the expression as having two terms, one literal and one figurative, as if it were an equation: $X$ (leader) = $Y$ (mirror). (Because a leader is a person, not an object with a reflective surface, the expression is figurative, not literal.) In a simile the "equals" sign is spelled out with "like" or "as."

**Metaphor:** A leader mirrors the desires of his or her followers.

This metaphor makes the same point as the simile does; it just doesn't spell out the comparison with "like." In some metaphors, only one of the terms is stated. The other part of the comparison is implied.

**Metaphor** (figurative term implied): A leader reflects the desires of his or her followers.

Even though the term "mirror" is not stated, the *idea* of a mirror is there in the word "reflects."

**Personification:** The daffodils tossed their heads in sprightly dance.

Personification is a metaphor in which the $Y$ term is always a person. When an idea, animal, or object is personified, it is given human qualities. In the example above, the daffodils are compared to humans who can toss their heads and dance. Actually, the daffodils are being blown by the wind but appear to the poet to be dancing.

To respond to metaphors, follow these steps:

1. Recognize that you are reading a metaphor.
2. Recognize the two terms being compared. Know what is the X and what is the Y of the comparison.
3. Reflect on the point of the comparison and the emotional impact of the comparison. How are we to take the metaphor? (Would you want to be called a "rotten apple"?)

### EXERCISE 13-2  Understanding Metaphors

*I. Reread the Edith Wharton passage on p. 397. Then answer the following questions.*

1. What metaphor is used to describe the orchard of apple trees?

   _____

2. What *type* of metaphor has Wharton used?  _____

3. What metaphor is used to describe the outcroppings of slate?

   _____

4. What *type* of metaphor has Wharton used?  _____

5. How do Wharton's metaphors make us feel? What do they add to the passage?

   _____

*II. Read the following poem by Langston Hughes and then answer the questions that follow.*

## Dreams

Hold fast to dreams
For if dreams die
Life is a broken-winged bird
That cannot fly.

5    Hold fast to dreams
For when dreams go
Life is a barren field
Frozen with snow.

1. Explain the metaphor in lines 3 and 4. What is being compared? What point is made?

   _____

   _____

2. Explain the metaphor in lines 7 and 8. What is being compared? What point is made?

   _____

   _____

3. Is it good or bad if dreams die? _____

4. What is the idea of the poem? What does the poet want us to understand about dreams?

   _____

   _____

## Irony

Another figure of speech often found in expressive writing is irony. *Irony* is a discrepancy between what we expect to happen and what actually happens, or what a writer says and what the writer means. In narratives (stories, plays, narrative poems), the characters and action may lead us to expect events to end in a particular way. Sometimes the author surprises us with events that are quite different from what we expected. This is irony of situation.

Verbal irony occurs when writers write the opposite of what they mean. Somewhere in the context of the work are clues to help us understand the use of irony. We also use verbal irony in speech. For example, if you see a friend dashing in to an early class with clothes that don't match and hair uncombed, you might say, "You're looking great this morning." Of course you—and your friend—understand that you are really commenting on how awful she looks.

Metaphors and irony are two effective figures of speech. Using them, a writer can play with words or move us with a powerful picture or lead us to reflect on the surprises in life.

## EXERCISE 13-3  Understanding Figures of Speech

*Read and reflect on each poem and then answer the questions that follow. Analyze each poet's use of figurative language but also think about what each poem says to readers.*

## Taxi

by **Amy Lowell**

When I go away from you
The world beats dead
Like a slackened drum.
I call out for you against the jutted stars

5    And shout into the ridges of the wind.
Streets coming fast,
One after the other,
Wedge you away from me,
And the lamps of the city prick my eyes
So that I can no longer see your face.

10    Why should I leave you,
To wound myself upon the sharp edges of the night?

1. What is the "situation" in the poem? What event or activity does the speaker in the poem describe? (Don't overlook the title.)

_____

_____

2. Explain the metaphor in the first three lines. What are the two items being compared?

_____

_____

Is the speaker happy?  _____

Why or why not?

_____

3. Explain the metaphor in the last line. What are the two items being compared?

_____

Is the metaphor positive or negative?    _____

4. List some words in the poem that have a negative connotation in this context.

_____

5. State briefly the main idea and feelings of the poem.

_____

_____

_____

_____

# In the Morning, In the Morning
## by A. E. Housman

In the morning, in the morning,
   In the happy field of hay,
Oh they looked at one another
   By the light of day.

In the blue and silver morning
   On the haycock as they lay,
Oh they looked at one another
   And they looked away.

1. What tone or feeling do the rhymes and rhythm of the poem help to create? Is the initial feeling as you read happy? Sad? Angry? Lighthearted? Something else?

_____

2. How is the ending of the poem a surprise? How does what you read differ from what you expected to read?

_____

_____

3. What figurative language does the poet use? _____

4. What, briefly, does the poet want us to think about?

_____

_____

## ■ READING DESCRIPTIVE ESSAYS

Descriptive essays paint a picture in words. They bring to life people, places, even objects. In descriptive essays, words are used to appeal to our senses, and we are likely to find connotation and figurative language.

Since descriptive essayists, like all essayists, have a main idea or thesis to support, you need to think about the writer's purpose and main idea as you read. Keep asking yourself: "Why is the writer showing me this scene?" or "Why is the writer describing this person in this way?" REMEMBER: DETAILS ARE USED TO SUPPORT IDEAS.

Sometimes in expressive writing, the main idea is implied rather than stated. You will need to infer the writer's ideas from the details provided. Pay particular attention to connotation, to figurative language, and to the choice of details. Analyzing the writer's use of these strategies will guide you to what the writer wants you to understand and feel. Let's practice with the following passage.

In an essay in *Time* magazine, Lance Morrow describes his experiences on safari in East Africa. Read the following paragraph from that essay, reflect on the picture Morrow creates, and then answer the questions that follow. You may want to work on this with your class partner.

In Masai Mari [in Kenya], vultures wheel dreamily in the air, like a slow motion tornado of birds. Below the swirling funnel, a cheetah has brought down a baby wildebeest. The cheetah, loner and fleet aristocrat, the upper-class version of the hyena, has opened up the wildebeest and devoured the internal organs. The cheetah's belly is swollen and its mouth is ringed with blood as it breathes heavily from the exertion of gorging. A dozen vultures flap down to take their turn. They wait 20 yards away, then waddle in a little toward the kill to test the cheetah. The cheetah, in a burst, rushes the vultures to drive them off, and then returns to the baby wildebeest.

1. What *type* of metaphor is used to describe the vultures?

_____

2. What are the two items (the *X* and *Y*) being compared?

_____

3. Does the metaphor create a positive or negative picture of the vultures?

_____

4. What is the author's attitude toward the cheetah? What words are used to characterize the cheetah?

_____

_____

5. The details of the kill are vivid. What is the author's purpose? What picture of wildlife in East Africa do we get?

_____

_____

## EXERCISE 13-4  Understanding Descriptive Details

*Read each of the paragraphs and answer the questions that follow. Try to picture what the writer describes and sense how the writer wants you to feel.*

I. My favorite place in the whole world was a big rock in the backyard that looked like the back of a buried elephant. . . . I would squat on that rock, my stick legs poking through the openings of my dirt-stained bloomers, my birdlike head turning from side to side, my gaze, unblinking, focusing up, down, in front of me, in back of me, now zooming in on the lower yard, then penetrating deeper into the garden, then rising up ever so slightly to where the corn was planted on the hill. I was in the center of life and I didn't miss a thing; nothing slipped by unobserved or unnoted.

Mary E. Mebane, *Mary: An Autobiography*

1. What metaphor is used to describe the big rock?

_____

What message of size and color comes to us from the metaphor?

_____

2. What metaphor does the author use to describe herself?

_____

What characteristics of the author are suggested by the metaphor?

_____

3. What can you conclude about Mary's childhood? Where did she live? What kind of youngster was she?

_____

_____

II. The world stills, for the longest time. Then, at the edge of sleep, the hyenas come to giggle and whoop. Peering from the tent flap, one catches in the shadows their sidelong criminal slouch. Their eyes shine like evil flashlight bulbs, a disembodied horror-movie yellow, phosphorescent, glowing like the children of the damned. In the morning, one finds their droppings: white dung, like a photographic negative. Hyenas not only eat the meat of animals but grind up and digest the bones. The hyenas' dung is white with the calcium of powdered bones.

Lance Morrow, "Africa," _Time_

1. In the second sentence, what _type_ of metaphor is used?

_____

What image of the hyenas is presented through the metaphor?

_____

2. What image is created in the third sentence?

_____

Is the connotation positive or negative?  _____

3. Explain the metaphor in sentence 4.

_____

_____

4. How do the details of the white dung add to our view of the hyenas?

_____

5. How does the figurative language add to the description of the hyenas? How are we to view these animals?

_____

_____

## ■ READING NARRATIVE ESSAYS AND SHORT FICTION

A *narrative* relates a series of events using chronology or time sequence. If the narrative relates events that are made up out of the writer's imagination, the narrative is *fiction*. If the narrative relates events that have taken place, it is *nonfiction*. Nonfiction narration is found in history, biography, newspaper articles, and narrative essays. So, narration will be found in writing designed to inform as well as in expressive writing.

In some works, the distinction between fiction and nonfiction blurs. One example is the historical novel—fiction, but somewhat controlled by the realities of a particular time and place. Narrative essays draw on the writer's experiences to develop a main idea, but the author may leave out some details and enlarge others to support the main idea. In description the writer highlights telling details; in narration the writer focuses on telling events.

Often in narrative essays and usually in fiction, the main ideas are implied rather than stated directly. In fiction, the cluster of ideas about life and human experience implied by the story are called the story's *theme* or themes. As you read, ask yourself: "Why is the writer telling me about these events?" And "How does the narrator seem to feel about the events?" And "How does the narrative make me feel?"

When reading narrative essays, also think about the "voice" you hear. Is the narrator telling about events as they occur, or is the narrator reflecting on events from an earlier time? When reading fiction, think about who the narrator is. Are the words coming from an all-knowing narrator or from one of the characters in the story? If a character is telling the story, are we to accept that character's views on other characters and events, or should we doubt the character? Sometimes characters speak for the author, but in other works the characters do not represent the views of the author. (This discrepancy is another form of irony.)

Mike Rose's use of autobiography in his book on teaching, *Lives on the Boundary* (1989), gives us an example of the use of narration.

All the hours in class tend to blend into one long, vague stretch of time. What I remember best, strangely enough, are two things I couldn't understand and over the years grew to hate: grammar lessons and mathematics. I would sit there watching a teacher draw her long horizontal line and her short, oblique lines and break up sentences and put adjectives here and adverbs there and just not get it, couldn't see the reason for it, turned off to it. I would hide by slumping down in my seat and page through my reader, carried along by the flow of sentences in a story. She would test us, and I would dread that, for I always got Cs and Ds. Mathematics was a bit different. For whatever reasons, I didn't learn early math very well, so when it came time for more complicated operations, I couldn't keep up and started daydreaming to avoid my inadequacy. This was a strategy I would rely on as I grew older. I fell further and further behind. A memory: The teacher is faceless and seems very far away. The voice is faint and is discussing an equation written on the board. It is raining, and I am watching the streams of water form patterns on the windows.

1. Are the events being told as they are developing, or are they coming to us from the perspective of an older voice?

   _____

2. Why did the writer turn to daydreaming?

   _____

3. What is important about the memory Rose recounts at the end?

   _____

4. What can you conclude about the writer's attitudes toward school when he was in class?

   _____

5. Why is Rose telling about his school experiences? What is his purpose?

   _____

   _____

### EXERCISE 13-5 Understanding Narration

*Read each of the passages and answer the questions that follow. Try to become engaged in the event and reflect on what it means.*

I. There was a path made of wooden ammo casings that led back to his tent. He walked on it like a man on a tightrope, it was so dark and so very hard to see. A couple of times he stumbled on the wooden boxes. It was quiet as he opened the tent flap, as quiet and dark as it had been outside the major's bunker. He dragged in carrying his rifle in one hand and the map case in the other. They were all asleep, all curled up on the cots, inside their mosquito nets. He walked up to his rack and sat down, his head sinking down to the floor. Panic was still rushing through him like a wild train, his heart still raced through his chest as he saw over and over again the kid from Georgia running toward him and the crack of his rifle killing him dead.

Ron Kovic, *Born on the Fourth of July*

1. What has the "he" in the passage recently done?

   _____

2. How does "he" feel about what has happened? What details support your conclusion?

   _____

   _____

3. Find and explain two similes in the passage.

   _____

   _____

   _____

   _____

4. Once you read the entire passage and learn what has happened, how does your knowledge give added meaning to the first simile?

   _____

   _____

5. What is the writer's purpose? What does he want us to feel and to understand from reading this passage?

_____

_____

II. We set out for the gallows. Two warders marched on either side of the prisoner, with their rifles at the slope; two others marched close against him, gripping him by arm and shoulder, as though at once pushing and supporting him. The rest of us, magistrates and the like, followed behind. Suddenly, when we had gone ten yards, the procession stopped short without any order or warning. A dreadful thing had happened—a dog, come goodness knows whence [from where], had appeared in the yard. It came bounding among us with a loud volley of barks and leapt round us wagging its whole body wild with glee at finding so many human beings together. It was a large wooly dog, half Airedale, half pariah [social outcast]. For a moment it pranced around us, and then, before anyone could stop it, it had made a dash for the prisoner, and jumping up tried to lick his face. Everybody stood aghast, too taken aback even to grab the dog.

George Orwell, "A Hanging"

1. What is about to take place? _____

2. Is the narrator a part of the scene or not? _____

   How do you know?

   _____

3. Why is it important that the dog is half pariah?

   _____

4. Why does the narrator say that the dog's appearance was "a dreadful thing"? Why was everybody "aghast"?

   _____

   _____

   _____

5. What type of figurative language does Orwell use in this narrative? (Hint: Is the dog's appearance in this particular scene unexpected and out of place?)

_____

_____

6. What does the narrative comment on? What does Orwell want us to understand about hangings?

_____

_____

## Mrs. Zajac

### by **Tracy Kidder**

Tracy Kidder is the author of several nonfiction books, including *Among Schoolchildren* (1988), a compassionate study of a year he spent observing Mrs. Zajac's fifth-grade classroom. The following excerpt is from this book.

### Prepare

1. Identify the author and the work. What do you expect the author's purpose to be?

_____

2. Preread to identify the subject and make predictions. What do you expect to read about?

_____

1    She was thirty-four. She wore a white skirt and yellow sweater and a thin gold necklace, which she held in her fingers, as if holding her own reins, while waiting for children to answer. Her hair was black with a hint of Irish red. It was cut short to the tops of her ears, and swept back like a pair of folded wings. She had a delicately cleft chin, and she was short—the children's chairs would have fit her. Although her voice sounded conversational, it had projection. She had never acted. She had found this voice in classrooms.

2      Mrs. Zajac seemed to have a frightening amount of energy. She strode across the room, her arms swinging high and her hands in small fists. Taking her stand in front of the green chalkboard, discussing the rules with her new class, she repeated sentences, and her lips held the shapes of certain words, such as "home-work," after she had said them. Her hands kept very busy. They sliced the air and made karate chops to mark off boundaries. They extended straight out like a traffic cop's, halting illegal maneuvers yet to be perpetrated. When they rested momentarily on her hips, her hands looked as if they were in holsters. She told the children, "One thing Mrs. Zajac expects from each of you is that you do *your* best." She said, "Mrs. Zajac gives homework. I'm sure you've all heard. The old meanie gives homework." *Mrs. Zajac.* It was in part a role. She worked her way into it every September.

## Comprehension Check

*Fill in the blanks to complete each of the following statements.*

1. Although Mrs. Zajac is thirty-four, she describes herself to her students as an _____.

2. Although her voice sounded conversational, it also had _____.

3. Mrs. Zajac emphasizes to her students that she gives _____, and she expects them to do their _____.

4. Mrs. Zajac had a frightening amount of _____.

## Expanding Vocabulary

*Review the following words in their contexts and then write a brief definition or synonym for each word.*

projection (1) _____

karate (2) _____

maneuvers (2) _____

perpetrated (2) _____

holsters (2) _____

## Analysis of Strategies and Structures

1. What are three details about Mrs. Zajac that you would call *telling* details? Why are they especially telling?

_____

_____

_____

_____

_____

2. Find and explain two metaphors in paragraph 1.

_____

_____

_____

_____

3. In paragraph 2, Kidder compares Mrs. Zajac's actions to three different kinds of people. Explain each comparison. How do they help to describe Mrs. Zajac?

_____

_____

_____

_____

_____

4. What is Kidder's attitude toward his subject? Does he portray Mrs. Zajac in a positive or negative way? As a good or bad teacher? Explain.

_____

_____

_____

_____

■ **For Discussion and Reflection**

1. Would you have enjoyed being in Mrs. Zajac's fifth-grade class? Why or why not?
2. Mrs. Zajac stresses being proud of your work, of doing your best. Is it ever too early to teach this idea? Is it ever too late?

## How the Sun Came

**Cherokee**

All cultures have myths, stories we tell to one another about how the world came into being, how and why it is the way we find it, and what will happen to us when we die. All American Indian tribes had some version of a "sun-catching" (how the world came to have light) story. The following myth is from the Cherokee Nation. It was published in *Eastern Cherokee Folktales,* compiled by Jack Frederick and Anna Gritts Kilpatrick and published in 1966.

■ **Prepare**

1. Identify the author and work. What do you expect the author's purpose to be?

   _____

2. Preread to identify the subject and make predictions. What do you expect to read about?

   _____

1    There was no light anywhere and the animal people stumbled around in the darkness. Whenever one bumped into another, he would say, "What we need in the world is light." And the other would reply, "Yes, indeed, light is what we badly need."

2   At last, the animals called a meeting, and gathered together as well as they could in the dark. The red-headed woodpecker said, "I have heard that over on the other side of the world there are people who have light."

3   "Good, good!" said everyone.

4   "Perhaps if we go over there, they will give us some light," the woodpecker suggested.

5   "If they have all the light there is," the fox said, they must be greedy people, who would not want to give any of it up. Maybe we should just go over there and take the light from them."

6   "Who shall go?" cried everyone, and the animals all began talking at once, arguing about who was strongest and ran fastest, who was best able to go and get the light.

7   Finally the 'possum said, "I can try. I have a fine big bushy tail, and I can hide the light inside my fur."

8   "Good! Good!" said all the others and the 'possum set out.

9   As he traveled eastward, the light began to grow and grow, until it dazzled his eyes, and the 'possum screwed his eyes up to keep out the bright light. Even today, if you notice, you will see that the 'possum's eyes are almost shut, and that he comes out of his house only at night.

10   All the same, the 'possum kept going, clear to the other side of the world, and there he found the sun. He snatched a little piece of it and hid it in the fur of his fine bushy tail, but the sun was so hot it burned off all the fur, and by the time the 'possum got home his tail was as bare as it is today.

11   "Oh, dear," everyone said. "Our brother has lost his fine bushy tail, and still we have no light."

12   "I'll go," said the buzzard. "I have better sense than to put the sun on my tail. I'll put it on my head."

13   So the buzzard traveled eastward till he came to the place where the sun was. And because the buzzard flies so high, the sun-keeping people did not see him, although now they were watching out for thieves. The buzzard dived straight down out of the sky, the way he does today, and caught a piece of the sun in his claws. He set the sun on his head and started for home, but the sun was so hot that it burned off all his head feathers, and that is why the buzzard's head is bald today.

14   Now the people were in despair. "What shall we do? What shall we do?" they cried. "Our brothers have tried hard; they have done their best, everything a man can do. What else shall we do so we can have light?"

15   "They have done the best a man can do," said a little voice from the grass, "but perhaps this is something a woman can do better than a man."

16    "Who are you?" everyone asked. "Who is that speaking in a tiny voice and hidden in the grass?"

17    "I am your Grandmother Spider," she replied. "Perhaps I was put in the world to bring you light. Who knows? At least I can try, and if I am burned up it will still not be as if you had lost one of your great warriors."

18    Then Grandmother Spider felt around her in the darkness until she found some damp clay. She rolled it in her hands, and molded a little clay bowl. She started eastward, carrying her bowl, and spinning a thread behind her so she could find her way back.

19    When Grandmother Spider came to the place of the sun people, she was so little and so quiet no one noticed her. She reached out gently, gently, and took a tiny bit of the sun, and placed it in her clay bowl. Then she went back along the thread that she had spun, with the sun's light growing and spreading before her, as she moved from east to west. And if you will notice, even today a spider's web is shaped like the sun's disk and its rays, and the spider will always spin her web in the morning, very early, before the sun is fully up.

20    "Thank you, Grandmother," the people said when she returned. "We will always honor you and we will always remember you."

21    And from then on pottery making became woman's work, and all pottery must be dried slowly in the shade before it is put in the heat of the firing oven, just as Grandmother Spider's bowl dried in her hand, slowly, in the darkness, as she traveled toward the land of the sun.

725 words

## Comprehension Check

*Fill in the blank with the word or phrase that best completes each sentence.*

1. The animals call a meeting because they want to obtain _____.

2. The first animal to try to bring light is the _____.

3. The buzzard tried to bring light back on his _____ and that is why the buzzard is _____ today.

4. Grandmother Spider suggests that perhaps this job is one for a _____.

5. Grandmother Spider takes a _____ with her to hold the light.

6. The animals travel _____ [east/west/north/south] to find light.

7. The Spider is _____ [successful/unsuccessful] in bringing back light.

8. Spiders always spin their webs in the _____.

9. Pottery making became _____ work.

## Analysis of Structures and Strategies

1. The fox suggests that they steal light. Why is it appropriate for this suggestion to come from the fox? What trait do we associate with the fox?

   _____

2. The buzzard believes that he has more sense than the 'possum. Does he?

   _____

   What point is the story making about the best ways to be successful?

   _____

   _____

   _____

## For Discussion and Reflection

1. How does this story differ from the story of creation in the Bible?
2. What did you like best about this story? Why?

## Early Autumn

### by **Langston Hughes**

Langston Hughes was a journalist, fiction writer, and poet, the author of more than sixty books. He was also the first African American to support himself as a professional writer. Known as "the bard of Harlem," Hughes became an important public figure and voice for black writers. "Early Autumn" comes from his short fiction collection *Something in Common* (1963).

## Prepare

1. Identify the author and work. What do you expect the author's purpose to be?

   _____

2. Preread to identify the subject and make predictions. What do you expect to read about?

   _____

When Bill was very young, they had been in love. Many nights they had spent walking, talking together. Then something not very important had come between them, and they didn't speak. Impulsively, she had married a man she thought she loved. Bill went away, bitter about women.

Yesterday, walking across Washington Square, she saw him for the first time in years.

"Bill Walker," she said.

He stopped. At first he did not recognize her, to him she looked so old.

"Mary! Where did you come from?"

Unconsciously, she lifted her face as though wanting a kiss, but he held out his hand. She took it.

"I live in New York now," she said.

"Oh"—smiling politely. Then a little frown came quickly between his eyes.

"Always wondered what happened to you, Bill."

"I'm a lawyer. Nice firm, way downtown."

"Married yet?"

"Sure. Two kids."

"Oh," she said.

A great many people went past them through the park. People they didn't know. It was late afternoon. Nearly sunset. Cold.

"And your husband?" he asked her.

"We have three children. I work in the bursar's office at Columbia."

"You're looking very . . . " (he wanted to say *old*) " . . . well," he said.

She understood. Under the trees in Washington Square, she found herself desperately reaching back into the past. She had been older than he then in Ohio. Now she was not young at all. Bill was still young.

"We live on Central Park West," she said. "Come and see us some-time."

"Sure," he replied. "You and your husband must have dinner with my family some night. Any night. Lucille and I'd love to have you."

The leaves fell slowly from the trees in the Square. Fell without wind. Autumn dusk. She felt a little sick.

"We'd love it," she answered.

"You ought to see my kids." He grinned.

Suddenly the lights came on up the whole length of Fifth Avenue, chains of misty brilliance in the blue air.

"There's my bus," she said. He held out his hand, "Good-by."

"When . . . " she wanted to say, but the bus was ready to pull off. The lights on the avenue blurred, twinkled, blurred. And she was afraid to open her mouth as she entered the bus. Afraid it would be impossible to utter a word.

Suddenly she shrieked very loudly, "Good-by!" But the bus door had closed.

The bus started. People came between them outside, people cross-ing the street, people they didn't know. Space and people. She lost sight of Bill. Then she remembered she had forgotten to give him her address—or to ask him for his—or tell him that her youngest boy was named Bill, too.

420 words

## Comprehension Check

*Fill in the blank with the word or phrase that best completes each sentence, or selct either T (true) or F (false).*

1. When Mary and Bill were young, they were _____.

2. Both characters now live in_____;

   both are _____ and have _____.

3. Bill thinks that Mary looks _____.

4. Mary gets on her bus without getting Bill's _____.

|  | T | F |
|---|---|---|
| 5. Mary is upset when she gets on the bus. | ___ | ___ |
| 6. Bill is upset when he parts from Mary. | ___ | ___ |
| 7. Mary still loves Bill. | ___ | ___ |

## Analysis of Strategies and Structures

1. What is Bill's reaction to seeing Mary?

   _____

   What specific details support your inference?

   _____

   _____

2. What can we infer from Mary's response to the question: "And your husband?"

   _____

3. What is happening to Mary when the "lights . . . blurred, twinkled, blurred"?

   _____

4. Why did the author call the story "Early Autumn"? (Look at the details of the scene—the time of year, the time of day, the activity around Mary and Bill.)

   _____

   _____

5. Briefly state the story's theme.

   _____

   _____

   _____

## For Discussion and Reflection

1. Have you done anything impulsively that you ended up regretting? If so, is there anything you can do now to undo what you did? If not, what is probably the only thing you can gain from the experience?

2. How important is it to know who we are? What are some things we can do to understand ourselves better?

## Chapter Review Quiz

*Complete each of the following statements.*

1. Writing can be placed in one of three categories based on the author's primary purpose for writing. These categories are:

    a. _____

    b. _____

    c. _____

2. Four characteristics of expressive writing are:

    a. _____

    b. _____

    c. _____

    d. _____

3. The *connotation* of a word is what the word _____.

4. A *metaphor* compares two _____.

5. Her hair was "swept back like a pair of folded wings" is a figure of speech called a _____.

6. *Irony* is a discrepancy between

    _____.

7. A *narrative* relates events in

    _____.

8. Read and reflect on the following poem by William Wordsworth and then answer the questions that follow.

# I Wandered Lonely as a Cloud

by **William Wordsworth**

I wandered lonely as a cloud
That floats on high o'er vales and hills,
When all at once I saw a crowd,
A host, of golden daffodils;
5   Beside the lake, beneath the trees,
Fluttering and dancing in the breeze.

Continuous as the stars that shine
And twinkle on the milky way,
They stretched in never-ending line
10   Along the margin of a bay:
Ten thousand saw I at a glance,
Tossing their heads in sprightly dance.

The waves beside them danced; but they
Outdid the sparkling waves in glee;
A poet could not but be gay,
15   In such a jocund[1] company;
I gazed—and gazed—but little thought
What wealth the show to me had brought:

For oft, when on my couch I lie
20   In vacant or in pensive[2] mood,
They flash upon that inward eye
Which is the bliss of solitude;
And then my heart with pleasure fills,
And dances with the daffodils.

a. What experience did the speaker in the poem have?

_____

b. Is the speaker in the midst of the experience or recalling a previous experience? _____

How do you know?_____

_____

[1]Merry
[2]Wistfully thoughtful

c. How was he feeling when he had the experience? _____

d. How did the experience make him feel?

_____

e. What can he continue to gain from the experience after it is over?

_____

_____

f. Find and explain two similes in the poem.

_____

_____

_____

_____

g. Find and explain one example of personification.

_____

_____

h. Briefly state the poem's main idea.

_____

_____

# CHAPTER 14

## Responding to Persuasive Writing

**In this chapter you will learn:**

- What it means to read and think critically
- The difference between fact and opinion
- To distinguish among kinds of opinions
- To recognize your biases
- To evaluate arguments and take a stand

## ■ PREPARE TO READ

Read and reflect on the chapter's title and objectives. Glance through the chapter, observing headings, to see what is covered. Now answer these questions:

1. What do you expect to learn from this chapter?

   _____

   _____

2. What do you already know about the chapter's topic?

   _____

   _____

3. What two or three questions do you want answered from reading this chapter?

_____

_____

_____

_____

Suppose you read the following argument in your newspaper's Letters to the Editor column:

> We are losing the war on drugs. Making drug use illegal has caused more problems than it has solved. We are not controlling the flow of illegal drugs or drug-related crime. Illegal drugs are only serving to make criminals rich. It is time to legalize drugs and take drug sales out of the hands of criminals.

How would you evaluate this argument? Is it convincing? What would be the consequences of legalizing drugs? This argument looks only at the criminal activity in the sale of drugs. Think what would happen to the crime rate over-all, if more people were using now-legal drugs such as cocaine or heroin.

To understand the argument and then think beyond what is said, to bring in other information relevant to the issue, and then to reach a decision on the issue is to read—and think—critically. When reading argumentative or persuasive writing, you first need to understand the writer's position. Then you need to evaluate the argument: Do the facts and reasons build a convincing case for the writer's position? Finally, you need to decide on your position on the issue.

When we speak of reading *critically*, we emphasize the important role of evaluating or judging ideas, not just passively taking them in. How can you develop critical reading skills? First, let's think about the characteristics of the critical reader and then develop those characteristics in ourselves.

## Characteristics of the Critical Reader

A critical reader is:

- **skeptical**
  (Just because it's in print doesn't mean it is right.)

- **fact-oriented**

  (Give me the facts and convince me that they are the relevant ones.)

- **analytic**

  (How has the work been organized? What strategies has the writer used?)

- **open-minded**

  (Prepared to listen to different points of view; not restricted by personal biases.)

- **questioning**

  (What other conclusions could be supported by the evidence?)

- **creative**

  (What are some entirely different ways of looking at the problem or issue?)

- **willing to take a stand**

  (Is the argument convincing? What is my position on the issue?)

## ■ DISTINGUISHING FACT FROM OPINION

What do these statements have in common?

My reading class meets in 116 Gray Hall.

Los Angeles is north of San Diego.

The Earth is in the Milky Way galaxy.

These statements are all facts. *Facts* are verifiable. That is, we can count or measure or confirm them through observation or by turning to trusted sources. If you want to find your reading class, you check the schedule and then confirm the location by going to the classroom when the class meets. You can confirm the second fact on a map and the third one in an astronomy textbook.

In an argument over facts, one person has the facts, the other does not. Some people think they have facts, but they have misinformation instead, what we can call false facts. When readings statements that sound like facts, be alert to the possibility that the "facts" are incorrect. Why would anyone pass on false facts? Sometimes the "facts" change as we learn more about the world we live in. Sometimes people pass on what they have been told without thinking critically about that "information." And, unfortunately, some writers present facts in an incomplete or distorted way to advance their own goals. When facts are incomplete or distorted, the total impact of the writing is false. Advertisements, including political ads during elections, come to mind as examples of messages containing false facts.

### EXERCISE 14-1  Distinguishing Between Facts and False Facts

*Mark each of the following statements as either F (fact) or FF (false fact). If you are unsure, indicate in the margin how you could verify the fact. If you are unsure of three or more statements, look them up in your dictionary or an encyclopedia in your library.*

F        FF

_____ _____    1. A healthy diet should include plenty of meat and eggs.

_____ _____    2. Egg whites have no cholesterol.

_____ _____    3. Dallas is the capital of Texas.

_____ _____    4. The Ukraine is a member of the Russian Republic.

_____ _____    5. The Saab 900 was rated a "Best Buy" by *Consumer's Digest* in 1995.

_____ _____    6. HIV-infected mothers may give birth to infected babies.

_____ _____    7. The Andromeda galaxy is larger than our galaxy.

_____ _____    8. You can become HIV-infected by attending class with an HIV-infected person.

_____ _____    9. The earth is 5,000 years old.

_____ _____    10. Over 90 percent of American homes have a television set.

Critical readers remain skeptical of "facts." If a statement doesn't sound quite right to you, then check it out before accepting as a fact.

Now, what do these statements have in common?

My reading instructor is cool.

San Diego is a nicer place to live than Los Angeles.

The Milky Way galaxy was formed about 10 billion years ago.

These statements are not facts. They are all opinions, so they are open to debate. Most writing combines facts and opinion, sometimes in the same sentence. You need to be able to tell the difference so that you can evaluate the opinions and judge if the facts support them. Keep in mind that conclusions (opinions) are found in writing to inform (such as textbooks) as well as in persuasive writing. Often the main idea in a paragraph or section is opinion. Authors sometimes (but not always) use signal words to distinguish between facts and opinions, so be alert to these guides to reading. The following are some of the words and phrases signalling opinions:

| | |
|---|---|
| consequently | in conclusion |
| as a result | this suggests |
| in my view | most experts agree that |

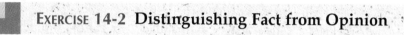

## Exercise 14-2  Distinguishing Fact from Opinion

*Mark each of the following statements as either F (fact) or O (opinion). If you are uncertain, indicate in the margin how you could confirm the fact.*

F      O

_____  _____  1. Smoking is prohibited on all flights in the continental United States.

_____  _____  2. Many Americans have lost confidence in their elected officials.

_____  _____  3. The best way to lose weight is to reduce the amount of fat in one's diet and to exercise regularly.

_____  _____  4. *Tom Sawyer* was written in the nineteenth century.

_____  _____  5. Americans are fascinated by movie stars and sports figures.

_____  _____  6. The dinosaurs may have died out because of a change in climate.

_____  _____  7. I would rather eat frozen yogurt than ice cream.

_____  _____  8. It is discourteous to talk during a movie or lecture.

_____  _____  9. Americans have become less courteous.

_____  _____  10. Because of its violence, boxing should be banned.

Did this exercise help you "hear" the difference between a fact and a statement of opinion? Did the exercise make you aware that opinions do not all sound the same? We need to make distinctions among several kinds of opinions because how we respond depends on the type of opinion.

## "Just" an Opinion

Some people use the word *opinion* to say that a statement has little value. They say, "That's just your opinion," as if that is a sufficient reason to reject the statement. In this context, *opinion* seems to mean a bias or prejudice—and one with which the speaker disagrees. Suppose, for example, that the opinion just rejected is the statement that secondhand smoke is a health hazard. Is this "just" personal opinion, or is this a view held by most scientists and doctors? Smokers may wish to dismiss the opinion as prejudice against them, but smokers probably should think about the health risks to which they expose friends and family. Many opinions actually have strong factual support and cannot be easily dismissed "just" because someone prefers not to accept them.

## Personal Preferences

Others—sometimes students—have been known to say, "Well, that's *my* opinion," as if that is a sufficient reason to justify the statement. If it's *my* opinion, I can believe it if I want to, and I do not have to defend it in a discussion. Are there some opinions that you may hold without having to defend them? Yes, you do not need to defend *personal preferences.* If you prefer frozen yogurt to ice cream, that's fine. You can like your biology class the best, while a friend prefers psychology. The problem comes when we turn personal preferences into debatable opinions but then refuse to defend them. If you prefer rock and roll to jazz music, that's fine, until you claim that rock and roll is a better kind of music than jazz. Now you are no longer expressing your preferences. You have stated an opinion that can—and should—be debated. Expect jazz fans to argue with you and prepare your defense.

## Judgments

Your claim about rock and roll music is a *judgment,* an opinion based on values and beliefs. Judgments are about what is good or bad, right or wrong, better or worse. Judgments can be challenged and must be defended with facts and reasons. If you say that you like to watch the Dallas Cowboys, that is your personal preference. But when you say that the Dallas Cowboys are the best football team, you must give evidence to support your judgment. The following statements are examples of judgments.

Jack Nicklaus is the best golfer ever to play the game.

The sunrise was beautiful.

Congress should balance the federal budget.

Smoking should be prohibited in all public facilities.

## Inferences

There is one more type of opinion to identify: inferences. An *inference* is an opinion based on facts, or on a combination of facts and simpler inferences. You have already learned to draw inferences when you read a paragraph with an unstated main idea. You also draw inferences from the details, events, and figurative language that you find in expressive writing.

Inferences vary from those closely tied to facts to those that are highly debatable. Here are four inferences.

Jack Nicklaus has been one of golf's most consistent players.

The sun will rise tomorrow.

Balancing the federal budget will result in either cutting or abolishing many popular programs.

Secondhand smoke is a health hazard.

Notice that these four inferences are about the same subjects as the four judgments given above, but the statements in each case are quite different. The inference about Nicklaus can be supported with facts from golf records—the number of tournaments won, consistent finishes in the top ten, and so forth. The second inference may sound like a fact, but until the sun actually rises, we can only assume that it will.

Observe that the third inference does not state whether it is good or bad to balance the budget. The sentence only asserts what the facts seem to indicate: To balance you have to cut. However, this inference is based on an assumption that can be challenged. Can you think of a way to balance the budget and not cut programs? Of course. We can raise taxes. The writer assumes a consistent tax base. Remember: Critical readers ask, "What other conclusions can be drawn? What is another way to look at the issue?" You may not think that raising taxes is a good idea, but it is an alternative to the opinion stated in the above inference.

Inferences are found in all kinds of writing. How do we separate reasonable inferences from those with little factual or logical support? Here are some guidelines for thinking critically about inferences.

## Guidelines for Evaluating Inferences

1. **Evaluate the writer's expertise.** People without special knowledge and training can have good ideas, and experts can be wrong. In general, though, experts are likely to present facts to support opinions. In textbooks, writers usually indicate the issues over which the experts disagree.

2. **Compare the experts and know the facts.** Read more than one work on a topic to see if similar views are shared. Compare your instructor's discussion with the textbook's. The more you know, the less likely you are to accept unsupported and questionable opinions.

3. **In science, distinguish between hypotheses and theories.** A hypothesis is a tentative idea, a possible inference based on some observation or logic, but one that needs testing. A theory is an inference based on many facts and reasoning from those facts. Theories are supported by most experts in a field.

4. **Be skeptical of generalizations.** There are few generalizations about all human beings that are true statements. Consider: Teenagers are reckless drivers. Is this a sound inference? Of course not. There are many safe teenaged drivers. What is fact is that drivers between 16 and 24 have the greatest number of accidents. However, it is incorrect to infer, from this fact, that all teens are reckless drivers.

5. **Don't trust inferences drawn from unidentified sources.** Sometimes you will read "Studies show that . . ." something or other is true. Don't believe it. Trustworthy writers always identify the sources of their information.

6. **Analyze and evaluate the evidence provided.** Question and debate with yourself as you read. Does the inference follow from the facts? Is it the only logical conclusion? If other facts were considered, would the inference have to be changed? For example:

   Professor Brown's students received all As and Bs. She must be a great teacher.

   Does the inference follow from the facts? Is it the only possible inference? No. Professor Brown could be an easy grader. The students could have been good to begin with. We do not have enough facts to decide among the possible inferences.

To evaluate arguments, you need to do more than distinguish between fact and opinion. You need to recognize the type of opinion presented and then decide if the support is convincing.

 **EXERCISE 14-3 Workshop on Recognizing Types of Opinions**

*I. With your class partner, reread each statement in Exercise 14-2 and then decide on the correct category for each. Is the statement a fact, personal preference, inference, or judgment? The first one has been completed for you.*

1. *fact* _____

2. _____

3. _____

4. _____

5. _____

6. _____

7. _____

8. _____

9. _____

10. _____

*II. Read each of the passages and answer the questions that follow. Debate answers with your class partner.*

A. Jennifer: "I just read an interesting study showing that people who watch a lot of TV are more fearful and more suspicious of other people than those who don't watch much TV.

Jim: "Oh, you can't believe all those studies. They are just used to take all the good shows off TV. I watch lots of TV, and I'm not violent."

Jennifer: "But this study wasn't just about violence making us more violent. It was about TV distorting our view of reality. That's serious. Maybe we should demand more realistic and less violent programming."

Jim: "Well, that's your opinion. I can have my opinion, too."

1. What type of opinion was the study's conclusion (expressed by Jennifer)?

_____

2. What type of opinion is expressed by Jim at the end of the dialogue?

_____

3. Who is the better critical thinker? Why?

_____

_____

B. According to a study from the National Center for Health Statistics, more than one-fourth of children twelve to thirteen years old said they have had at least one alcoholic drink. This number increases to two-thirds of mid-teens and nearly 90 percent of young adults. Although males and females are equally likely to have tried alcohol, males over seventeen were more likely to be currently drinking. Males are also more likely to be binge drinkers. The study shows that alcohol is widely used among young people.

1. What is the paragraph's main idea?

_____

2. What type of opinion is the main idea?

_____

3. What kind of support is provided for the main idea?

_____

4. Are you surprised, or are the details consistent with your knowledge of teens?

_____

C. American society has become more violent in the last twenty-five years. People seem more ready to use violence to solve problems. According to Adam Smith, each year in America about 10,000 people die from gun deaths, in contrast to three in Great Britain and seventeen in West Germany. An increasing number of victims are children and teenagers who are settling quarrels over shoes or girlfriends by shooting. According to the *Washington Post*, in the first three months of 1989 in Washington D.C., over one hundred people were murdered. The majority of murders are committed by people who know their victims, not strangers. For example, a young man in Maryland shot both parents in a quarrel over money. We have to conclude that "average" citizens, not crooks, are increasingly resorting to violence.

1. What is the main idea of the paragraph?

_____

2. What type of opinion is the main idea?

_____

3. In your view, do the facts support the writer's opinion?

_____

4. Is the opinion consistent with your knowledge and experience?

_____

D. According to medical research, each year over 400,000 people die of smoking-related diseases. The most directly connected to smoking are lung cancer and emphysema; smoking also increases the risk of heart disease and stroke. Secondhand smoke kills about 90,000 people each year, and leads to more illness—colds and asthma—among children of parents who smoke. The time has come to ban all smoking in public facilities, all cigarette advertising, and all vending machines—the primary source of cigarettes for minors. In addition, the federal government should stop subsidizing tobacco farmers.

1. What is the main idea of the paragraph?

_____

2. What type of opinion is the main idea?

_____

3. In your view, do the details in the paragraph support the conclusion?

_____

If you disagree with the argument, explain why.

_____

_____

## ▪ RECOGNIZING YOUR BIASES

Just as writers hold strong views and want to convince their readers, so readers sometimes bring strong opinions to their reading. Often when we don't know much about a topic and therefore don't have strong feelings, we are willing to "listen and learn" from the writer. On other topics, however, our strong opinions can affect the way we read. We may get angry when we read, or dismiss the argument as "just the writer's opinion."

But critical thinkers are open-minded. They can patiently follow an argument, including one that expresses a position different from theirs. They may even be convinced by facts and sound reasons to change their position. One way to become a better critical reader is to be more aware of your strongly held positions or attitudes. Then use your self-knowledge to keep your biases and emotions in check as you read. The following exercise will help you identify some of your biases and strong opinions.

### EXERCISE 14-4  Recognizing Biases and Strong Opinions

_I. Complete each of the following sentences by writing what you think of first. Finish this part of the exercise as quickly as you can. Then read and reflect on what you have written._

1. Politicians are _____

2. Asians are _____

3. Teachers are _____

4. Drivers of red sports cars are _____

_____

5. Parents are _____

6. Drug users are _____

7. People on welfare are _____

_____

8. Football players are _____

9. Police officers are _____

10. Poets are _____

II. *Compare your responses with classmates and discuss the class's various reactions. Do you have strongly positive or strongly negative feelings about some of the groups listed?*

III. *Read and react to each of the following brief statements, stating whether you agree or disagree and how strongly you feel. Compare your responses with classmates. Do you have good evidence to support your views? Finally, look at some information on these issues provided at the end of the chapter.*

1. The federal government just keeps getting bigger and bigger. Most of my tax money goes to Washington, but what do I get back? We need to reduce the size of the government in Washington.

_____

_____

2. Big cities are stressful and dangerous and generally unhealthy places. Life is much better in rural areas.

_____

_____

3. Our country is becoming divided by the "haves" and "have nots." The rich keep getting richer and the poor are getting poorer, but that's the way our system works.

_____

_____

## ▪ UNDERSTANDING THE WRITER'S POSITION

Persuasive writers want to change our thinking on an issue, make us aware of a problem, even get us to change the way we live. Before we can evaluate the writer's facts and reasons, we need to understand the writer's position. What, exactly, is the writer's point? Putting aside for the moment our own strongly held views, we need to pay careful attention to the writer's word choice and "tone of voice." Some persuasive writers stress facts and reasons in a calm tone. Other persuasive writers want to stir our emotions or shock us into seeing their viewpoint. As critical readers, we need to analyze each argument and make certain that we understand exactly what has been written. The following brief arguments will give you some practice.

### EXERCISE 14-5  Analyzing Strategies and Understanding Attitude

*Read and answer the questions for each of the following passages.*

I. The city energizes the people who live there. The noises wake them and urge them to get going. There is excitement "pounding the pavement" with all the others forming that energetic force of workers heading for offices. The tall buildings, the honking of taxis, the dense crowds, the opportunities to fulfill ambitions: All add to the thrill of living in the city.

1. What is the writer's subject? _____

2. What is the writer's position on the subject?

   _____

3. What particular words help you understand the writer's attitude?

   _____

4. What is the writer's tone—angry, excited, somber, something else?

   _____

II. How can you even think about restricting smoking on your flights to Europe and Asia? Don't you know how long those flights are? What do you think smokers are going to do all those hours without a cigarette? Whether you like it or not, smoking is an addiction; we *have* to have a cigarette—and we will, damn it! What are you going to do about it? Throw us out of the plane?

1. What is the writer's subject?  _____

2. What is the writer's position on the subject?

_____

3. What particular words help you understand the writer's attitude?

_____

4. What is the writer's tone—angry, excited, sad, something else?

_____

5. Is the writer's approach a persuasive one? Why or why not?

_____

_____

III. Modern technology has isolated us from one another. Television restricts games and conversation. In many homes there are several TVs, so the family no longer even watches the same show. Children play electronic games by themselves rather than playing with each other. Teenagers plug in their Walkmans and tune out the rest of the world.

1. What is the writer's subject?  _____

2. What is the writer's position on the subject?

_____

3. What is the writer's tone—angry, thoughtful, excited, something else?

_____

4. Is the writer's approach a persuasive one? Why or why not?

_____

_____

IV. In a nation of 40 million handguns—where anyone who wants one can get one—it's time to face a chilling fact. We're way past the point where registration, licensing, safety training, waiting periods, or mandatory sentencing are going to have much effect. Each

of these measures may save some lives or help catch a few crimi-
nals, but none—by itself or taken together—will stop the vast majority of handgun suicides or murders. A "controlled" handgun
kills just as effectively as an "uncontrolled" one.

Josh Sugarmann, "The NRA Is Right, But We Still Need to Ban Handguns"

1. What is the writer's subject?  _____

2. What is the writer's position on the subject?

   _____

3. What words are important in expressing the writer's attitude?

   _____

4. Does the writer's position seem reasonable to you?  _____

   _____

5. Is your answer to question 4 influenced by the writer or by your
   strongly held opinions?

   _____

## ■ EVALUATING ARGUMENTS AND TAKING A STAND

Critical readers are open-minded—while they read. When you read an argument that takes a stand with which you disagree, try to continue to read
thoughtfully to the end of the argument. You will gain understanding of the
views of others, and you may find some common ground with those on the
other side.

Critical readers evaluate arguments and take a stand—after they finish
reading. You may find weaknesses in some arguments you read; you may
also need to revise your thinking after reading a convincing discussion.
What you don't want to do is remain indifferent. Try to decide on your
views *every* time you read. It is a cop-out to say that one opinion is as good
as another. To support this idea, you have to agree that a decision to murder is just as valuable as a decision to help your neighbors. Surely you
would not try to support such a position. We all need to have the courage
to make informed judgments.

With some complicated arguments, you may feel that you do not know
enough to evaluate the argument and take a stand. Try to have a position
on the parts of the issue you do understand. For example, you may not

know exactly how the tax code should be changed to make it more fair. Still, you could take a stand on the issue of tax loopholes for the rich. Are they fair? What do you think?

You have already studied guidelines for evaluating inferences, opinions based on facts. Evaluating judgments can be more difficult because judgments also involve values—and strong emotions. Whatever the type of opinion under debate, you still need to think about the reliability of the facts and the logic of the argument. You can find flaws in many bad arguments if you recognize some often-used patterns of bad logic. These patterns— called logical fallacies—are so common they have been given names. Test every argument you read against the following logical fallacies.

## Recognizing Logical Fallacies

*Overstatement:* An overstatement is an error in generalizing. The inference, if qualified, may be supported by the evidence. But if the inference is stated as a broad generalization, it becomes illogical. Overstatements can often be recognized by the use of such words as *all, every, always, never,* and *none.* Remember: There are very few statements about all people or all students that can be supported with evidence. People are just too different. You can challenge overstatements by thinking of exceptions to the generalization. For example:

High school students hate school.

(Think of students from your school who worked hard and were excited about new ideas.)

*Non Sequitur:* This Latin term means, literally, "it does not follow." In this type of bad argument, the "glue" that connects evidence to conclusion is missing. It can be missing because the writer does not make the connection clear to the reader. It can also be missing because the writer's glue is based on false assumptions. You challenge the *non sequitur* by pointing out the false assumptions. For example:

Javier will definitely get a good grade in physics; he loved biology.

(If Javier is not good at math, he will not love physics. It is a false assumption to believe that success in one science course means the student will be successful in other science courses. The needed skills may differ.)

*Slippery Slope:* This type of bad argument says that we should not take step A because if we do, then the terrible consequences X, Y, and Z will follow. This type of argument oversimplifies by assuming, without evidence, that X, Y, and Z must follow from A, even though it's a long way from A to Z. Persuasive writers get on the slippery slope because they really do not want the first step (A) to take place. For example:

> If we allow the government to control handgun purchases, it will restrict rifles and then ban all guns, so only criminals will have guns.

*Do you see how this argument goes down the slippery slope from one action to many unwanted actions?* (Handgun control will not necessarily lead to banning. We restrict and register cars and planes. We do not ban them. The United States is a democracy with free elections.)

*False Dilemma:* A false dilemma occurs when one argues that there are only two possible actions or solutions, when there are clearly more than two. If the writer gives us only two choices, and one of those is unacceptable, then the writer can push us toward the preferred choice. You challenge a false dilemma by showing that there are other choices. For example:

> Either we legalize drugs, or we will never get rid of the country's drug problem.

(These are not the only two possibilities. The anti-drug programs have made a difference. We can also get tougher with countries supplying the drugs.)

*Post Hoc Fallacy:* This term (literally, "after this") refers to an error in reasoning about causes. In this fallacy a time relationship is confused with a causal relationship. The 3:00 plane takes off before the 4:00 plane; the 3:00 plane does not cause the 4:00 plane to leave. You challenge illogical causal arguments by explaining more likely causes. For example:

> Teenage pregnancy is on the increase. It must be the result of all those sex education classes in high school.

(The classes are not a cause but an attempted solution to the problem. The classes may not be helping much because the real causes remain powerful influences in teenagers' lives: poverty, single parenting, social needs.)

*Bandwagon:* To argue that an action should be taken or a position accepted because "everyone is doing it" is illogical. The majority is not always right. For example:

> There is nothing wrong with fudging on your income taxes. Everybody does it, and the government expects everyone to cheat a little.

(First, not everyone cheats on taxes. Second, if it is wrong, it is wrong no matter how many people do it.)

 ### EXERCISE 14-6 Recognizing Logical Fallacies

*After reading each passage, explain what is illogical about the argument. Then state the type of fallacy.*

I. We should stop giving handouts to the homeless. The poor of this world, of which we have all been a part at some time, have pride and work hard to improve themselves. The homeless have no pride and do not try to work.

_____

_____

_____

_____

II. The basic freedoms of America's smokers are at risk today. Tomorrow, who knows what personal behavior will become socially unacceptable, subject to restrictive laws and public ridicule? Could travel by private car make the social engineers' hit list because it is less safe than public transit? Could ice cream, cake and cookies become socially unacceptable because their consumption causes obesity? What about sky diving, mountain climbing, skiing and contact sports? How far will we allow this to spread?

Stanley S. Scott, "Letter," *New York Times*

_____

_____

_____

_____

III. College doesn't seem to make people better. In fact, it seems to make them worse. Think of the "unabomber." Although he is a college graduate and was a college professor, he sent bombs through the mail to kill people. And then there are the lawyers, using all that education to cheat clients by overcharging them. Maybe we should close down the colleges so they can't do any more harm.

_____

_____

_____

_____

## Taking a Stand

You may have been cautioned not to "rush to judgment." That is good advice. Decisions should be based on study and thoughtful consideration. Still, at some point, you need to make decisions. As you read for this course and in your other courses, listen, learn, reflect, and then take a stand.

### EXERCISE 14-7 Taking a Stand

*Study the following pieces of evidence from a survey conducted by* Zillions *magazine. Then decide if allowances are good or bad. Write your own brief argument, using the evidence given and your own ideas, to support a position on allowances.*

- About 50 percent of youngsters ages nine to fourteen get a weekly allowance.
- The average weekly allowance for youngsters nine and ten was $3; for kids 11 to 14, it was $5.
- Those getting allowances actually ended up with an average of $20 for youngsters thirteen and fourteen, so they are managing to get additional money out of their parents or others.
- Children receiving allowances were more likely to save.
- Youngsters without allowances receive almost the same amount of money each week from parents or other sources.
- Kids who receive allowances usually have chores to do and lose some money if they do not complete chores.
- Youngsters getting allowances said they were happier with that arrangement than those not receiving allowances.

*Your argument for or against allowances:*

_____

_____

_____

_____

_____

_____

_____

_____

_____

## Ban Boxing Now

by **Nat Hentoff**

Nat Hentoff is the author of articles and books on jazz and education and has been a staff writer of the *Village Voice* for many years. He is probably best known for his syndicated newspaper columns that are usually on First Amendment issues. In the following column, published October 26, 1996, Hentoff refers to the Eighth Amendment in his argument about boxing.

### Prepare

1. Identify the author and the work. What do you expect the author's purpose to be?

   _____

   _____

2. Preread to identify the subject and make predictions. What do you expect to read about?

   _____

   _____

3. What do you already know about the subject?

   _____

   _____

   _____

4. Raise two questions that you expect the article to answer.

   _____

   _____

   _____

1    In a current policy statement, the American Medical Association "encourages the elimination of both amateur and professional boxing, a sport in which the primary objective is inflict injury"—particularly "chronic brain damage." For years, Dr. George Lundberg of the AMA has been writing articles under the standing title "Boxing should be banned in civilized countries."

2    For nearly 10 years in Boston, I broadcast boxing bouts—sometimes doing blow-by-blow and sometimes color between rounds. I saw a young, extraordinarily graceful boxer who seemed choreographed. His name was Cassius Clay.[1] And I remember such equally swift and precise combatants as Sugar Ray Robinson and Willie Pep.

3    They were boxers, not brutal machines like the latter-day Mike Tyson.

4    Most of the bouts I broadcast, however, were between club fighters—professionals who could put on a good, often bloody show for the fans but would never make the big time.

5    I especially remember two of them. Young and eager at first, they looked, over time, as if they were throwing punches on an assembly line. They kept taking a lot of each other's punches, more each year.

6    By the time I left ringside to go to New York and cover jazz, the speech of those once-ardent young men had slowed. And they were not alone among the veteran gladiators who, by then, were in time zones of their own.

7    One of the last bouts I broadcast was between two fighters who had clobbered each other so hard in the early rounds that, neither being able to deliver a knockout blow, they more or less clung to each other. The disgusted crowd, cheated of the chance to see one of them fall unconscious, mockingly started to sing, "I'll Always Be in Love With You"—in waltz time.

8    Watching the deprived sports fans, a venerable sportswriter said to me, "Once you leave this place, kid, you'll never go to see another boxing bout."

9    He was right. I don't go to the fights. I don't watch them on television. Friends of mine—journalists, lawyers, nearly all of them men—make festive evening of boxing events. They too are disappointed if all that happens is bloodless boxing with nobody on the canvas with his lights out.

10   Daniel Kornstein, a lawyer and boxing fan, writes in the *New York Law Journal*: "Maybe there is something less than satisfying for a big fight to be decided by a disqualification than a knockout or a TKO. Without some form of knockout, there is no catharsis [for the fans]."

[1]The original name of Muhammad Ali.

11      I have heard defenders of the death penalty claim that each execution creates a catharsis in the surrounding community. Why not, then, televise executions—with Don King, Mike Tyson's mentor and promoter, deciding which "dead man walking" merits prime time? There would then be a national catharsis from this entertainment.

12      Don King wasn't around when I, in Boston, would visit dressing rooms before a bout to pick up some stories to use between rounds. My partner, a senior sports announcer at the radio station, warned me not to name on the air some of the portly men with cigars backstage who seemingly owned the fighters. "They don't like publicity," he said, "and for good reason." They didn't like me either, just for being there. Most of them, I expect, are gone now, but—sportswriters tell me—others like them have taken their place.

13      Occasionally, I do see reports concerning boxing on news shows. For instance, the increasing number of professional bouts between women. And Patti Davis—daughter of former sportscaster Ronald Reagan—has written a screenplay about women boxers. "They're not oddities," she told the *New York Post*. "They're athletes, and can be good looking."

14      Not for long. As the AMA's Dr. Lundberg notes, the chronic brain damage that eventually is suffered by boxers "who have had many fights . . . results from repetitive subconcussive blows over multiple training sessions and matches. . . . A major purpose of a sports event is to win. When the surest way to win is by damaging the opponent's brain, and this becomes standard procedure, the sport is morally wrong."

15      And constitutionally wrong. Boxing is licensed by the states, and the Eighth Amendment in the Bill of Rights forbids the infliction of "cruel and unusual punishment." Battering an opponent into unconsciousness, and worse, is not a sport. Not in a civilized country.

16      The defensive rationale for professional boxing is that it allows youngsters at the bottom of society to get a chance and fame and fortune. That works for some, but most of those I've seen wind up with chump change and a funny look.

765 words

## ■ Comprehension Check

*Answer the following with a, b, or c to indicate the phrase that best completes the statement.*

_____ 1. The American Medical Association would like

a. professional boxing banned.

b. chronic brain damage banned.

c. amateur and professional boxing banned.

_____ 2. For ten years the author

    a. was a boxer.

    b. broadcast boxing matches.

    c. was a member of the AMA.

_____ 3. The author saw two boxers

    a. develop slowed speech.

    b. in time zones of their own.

    c. both (a) and (b).

_____ 4. Being in a time zone of your own means

    a. living in your own time zone.

    b. living right between two time zones.

    c. being confused and disconnected from reality.

_____ 5. According to Hentoff, many boxing fans want

    a. front-row seats.

    b. to see blood and a knockout.

    c. to go to New York.

_____ 6. Hentoff describes the boxers' owners as

    a. portly.

    b. cigar smoking.

    c. both (a) and (b).

_____ 7. Hentoff believes that boxing is

    a. unconstitutional.

    b. exciting.

    c. a way for poor people to make money.

_____ 8. The author does not believe that

    a. Ronald Reagan was a sportscaster.

    b. boxing belongs in a civilized society.

    c. the AMA is right.

### Expanding Vocabulary

_Match each word in the left column with its definition in the right column by placing the correct letter in the space next to each word._

_____ inflict (1)

_____ chronic (1)

_____ choreographed (2)

a. created movements of a dance

b. those trained to entertain by engaging in mortal combat in Roman arenas

c. pounded with great force

_____ combatants (2)

_____ ardent (6)

_____ gladiators (6)

_____ clobbered (7)

_____ venerable (8)

_____ festive (9)

_____ catharsis (10)

_____ portly (12)

_____ subconcussive (14)

_____ chump (16)

d. short of producing concussions by heavy blows

e. commanding respect by age or position

f. impose, hand out

g. purging of the emotions

h. continuing over a long period, recurring

i. those fighting one another

j. a dupe, a fool

k. passionate, fiery

l. overweight, stout

m. merry, joyous

## Analysis of Structures and Strategies

1. What does the author gain by referring to his years as a boxing sportscaster? Why does he include this information?

_____

_____

_____

2. In paragraph 12, when Hentoff describes the apparent owners of the boxers as cigar smoking and hanging around in the dressing rooms, what are we to infer about them and about the game of boxing?

_____

_____

3. What is one argument in support of boxing?

_____

Why does Hentoff think that this is not a good argument? What strategy for challenging the argument does he use?

_____

_____

_____

4. Why, according to Hentoff, should boxing be banned?

_____

_____

_____

### For Discussion and Reflection

1. Does Hentoff provide a good challenge to one argument supporting boxing? Why or why not?
2. Does Hentoff provide good evidence and reasons to support his position on boxing? Why or why not?
3. If you disagree with Hentoff, what arguments would you use to support your position?

### Your Reading Assessment

1. How accurately did you predict what you would read about?

_____

2. Did the selection answer your questions? _____

If not, why do you think that it did not?

_____

3. What comments or questions do you have in response to your reading?

_____

_____

_____

## Self-Serving Society

by **Ellen Goodman**

A feature writer at the *Boston Globe*, Ellen Goodman became a syndicated columnist in 1976. Her columns have appeared in over 250 newspapers, and many have been collected into three books. Goodman has won a Pulitzer Prize for distinguished commentary. The following column appeared October 19, 1996.

## Prepare

1. Identify the author and the work. What do you expect the author's purpose to be?

   _____

   _____

2. Preread to identify the subject and make predictions. What do you expect to read about?

   _____

   _____

3. What do you already know about the subject?

   _____

   _____

   _____

4. Raise two questions that you expect the article to answer.

   _____

   _____

   _____

1   BOSTON—It is 8:30 in the morning and I am standing at a gas station in a silk suit with an unusual fashion accessory dangling from my right hand. This metal and rubber accouterment looks exactly like a gasoline hose. In fact it is a gasoline hose.

2   I am poised (for disaster) at this establishment that boasts of self-service—which is to say, no service—because there is no longer any station on my corner that has "full service," which is to say, any service.

3   At precisely 8:33, as if on cue, the hose balks, the gas leaps from its point of destination and proceeds to decorate my skirt in a fashion familiar to Jackson Pollack fans.

4   The transfer of gasoline to silk is accompanied by expletives that will be deleted for the family newspaper. It is followed by a return home, a change of clothes, a trip to the cleaners and a delayed start of more than an hour.

5   Normally I would spare you the details of a gasoline-splattered morning. But this event was accompanied by a reverie about the brave, new economy. We all know the joke about the job market of the 1990s. An economist exclaims about the millions of new jobs and a worker counters, "I know, I have four of them."

6   In my variation on this theme, another economist brags about jobs in the service industry, and the consumer says, "I know, I'm doing them all."

7   The fastest-growing part of the economy is not the service industry. It's the self-service industry. The motto of the new age is: Help Yourself.

8   The generic story is that of the company phone operator whose job has been outsourced to customers. The Great American Gripe is about the endless minutes spent wending our way through multichoice listings before we get to the person or information we want. (Press 9 for Frustration.)

9   But that's just the beginning.

10   We now have a supermarket that allows us not only to pick our food from the shelves but to scan it ourselves at the checkout counter. We have telephone companies where so-called "directory assistance" forces us to shout the town and name we are after into an electronic void.

11   Across the country, home delivery is increasingly replaced by pickup. If you buy something, u-haul. If you break it, u-haul it back. And if it's a refrigerator, you sit home at the convenience of the truck driver.

12   Even in the world of alleged health care, once house calls went the way of milkmen we learned to haul each body part to a separate specialist. But now we are sent home from hospitals with instructions on self-care that stop just short of a do-it-yourself appendectomy.

13   I am not opposed to the self-help ethic. I am still amazed and delighted that an ATM in Seattle will give $100 to a woman from Boston.

14   But I rebel at the casual ways corporations have downsized by replacing employees with consumers. Did anyone ask us if we want to moonlight for them?

15   Of course, this is all done, or so we are told, in the name of competition, lower prices and the American way. When Southwest Airlines initiated a policy of BYO food and had passengers transfer their own bags, the airline bragged of low fares. But sooner or later, competitors will pare down, fares will creep up, and we will be left toting the bag.

16      Where are the economists who tally up the cost-shifting of time and money and energy from them to us?

17      When companies boast that we pay less for gas, do they include the cost of our labor, not to mention dry cleaning? Do companies add up the wages lost while the country's on hold? (Press 8 for Outrage.) And do they include the cost to us of being hassled?

18      I hear that a modest rebellion is encouraging a few new businesses—even an oil company—to advertise their latest frill: people. But the whole trend of the new economy is some perverse play on the great American can-do spirit. That we *can do* everything on our own, and without ever encountering another human being.

19      Before my gas tank runs dry again, may I suggest a rallying cry from those who only serve themselves: Help!

711 words

## ■ Comprehension Check ·

*Answer the following with a, b, or c to indicate the phrase that best completes the statement.*

_____ 1. The author mentions spilling gasoline on her suit to show that

    a. silk has to be dry cleaned.
    b. there should be more full-service gas stations.
    c. companies are providing less and less service.

_____ 2. The fastest-growing part of the economy is

    a. the self-service industry.
    b. the service industry.
    c. the natural gas industry.

_____ 3. An example of the shift to self-service is

    a. electronic directory assistance.
    b. businesses' recorded guidelines instead of people answering the phone.
    c. both (a) and (b).

_____ 4. According to the author, making consumers do more is one way

    a. that companies have found to downsize.
    b. to encourage people to help themselves.
    c. to make service faster.

_____ 5. Economists should

    a. ban Southwest Airlines.
    b. include the costs of the work that is shifted from company workers to consumers.
    c. increase hospital stays.

_____ 6. The author thinks that many people

    a. believe in the "can-do" spirit.

    b. like hauling things themselves.

    c. feel hassled by having to serve themselves.

_____ 7. The author implies that people should

    a. start demanding more service.

    b. cry.

    c. be more careful at gas stations.

## Expanding Vocabulary

*Match each word in the left column with its definition in the right column by placing the correct letter in the space next to each word.*

_____ accessory (1)          a. standing, ready to act

_____ accouterment (1)       b. musing, daydream

_____ poised (2)             c. descriptive of an entire group

_____ expletives (4)         d. reckon, count

_____ reverie (5)            e. bothered, troubled

_____ generic (8)            f. a supplementary item

_____ void (10)              g. meeting

_____ tally up (16)          h. piece of equipment

_____ hassled (17)           i. emptiness

_____ perverse (18)          j. exclamations or oaths

_____ encountering (18)      k. persisting in an error or fault

## Analysis of Structures and Strategies

1. What is Goodman's position, the main idea of her argument?

_____

_____

2. What is the primary strategy she uses to develop her argument?

_____

3. In paragraph 13, Goodman states that she is "not opposed to the self-help ethic" and thinks ATM machines are amazing. These statements seem to run counter to her argument. Why does she make them? What does she gain?

_____

_____

4. In paragraph 5, Goodman tells the joke about economists bragging about all the new jobs and a worker responding that he or she has four of them. Why does a worker have four jobs? What is the author's point?

_____

_____

## Questions for Discussion and Reflection

1. Have you been frustrated by having to do so many tasks for yourself, or listening to recorded menus instead of getting a person to answer the phone? Would you like to have more service? Why or why not?

2. There are many advantages to the advances in communications and electronics, for example, ATM machines. What are some of the disadvantages that Goodman points out, or implies?

## Your Reading Assessment

1. How accurately did you predict what you would read about?

_____

2. Did the selection answer your questions? _____

If not, why do you think that it did not?

_____

3. What comments or questions do you have in response to your reading?

_____

_____

## Chapter Review Quiz

*Complete each of the following statements.*

1. Three characteristics of a critical reader are:

    a. _____

    b. _____

    c. _____

2. A fact is a statement that can be _____.

3. Three types of opinions are:

    a. _____

    b. _____

    c. _____

4. Identify each of the following statements as fact (F), inference (I), or judgment (J).

    a. We need campaign finance reform now.                     _____

    b. Bill Clinton has been elected to two terms as U.S. president.  _____

    c. Voter turnout is lower in the United States than in Germany.  _____

    d. The "religious right" has considerable influence in the Republican Party.                                           _____

    e. Many Americans have a low opinion of politicians.        _____

5. Three types of logical fallacies are:

    a. _____

    b. _____

    c. _____

*The following words have appeared in the chapter or in the reading selection. Circle the letter next to the word or phrase that is the best definition of the word.*

1. inference

    a. opinion based on strong values and beliefs
    b. opinion based on facts
    c. fact

2. bias

   a. opinion that restricts openmindedness, prejudice
   b. judgment
   c. critical thinking

3. expertise

   a. enterprise zones
   b. expectations
   c. special skill or knowledge

4. inflict

   a. illicit
   b. impose, hand out
   c. infighting

5. perverse

   a. persisting in a right idea
   b. prevail
   c. persisting in an error or fault

6. generic

   a. descriptive of generations
   b. descriptive of an entire group
   c. general advice

## Information Relevant To Exercise 14-4, Section II.

1. The number of federal employees decreased in 1981 (from 1971) but grew again by 1991. The great majority of federal employees work outside Washington, D.C. (See Table 10.1; p. 274.)

2. Cities, in general, provide better medical services and education, in addition to better employment opportunities (both more jobs and higher wages). Studies have shown that mental health rates are higher for urban populations. (In other words, rural life can be stressful, too—if jobs are limited and you feel trapped.)

3. The relative number of rich and poor in the United States has varied throughout the twentieth century. Since 1970, the rich have been getting richer and the poor poorer, but since that is not the only trend, it is not tied to a "system." A country chooses to redistribute its wealth according to its values. (See Figure 10.5; p. 287.)

# ADDITIONAL READINGS

The following additional readings will give you practice in improving reading rate without losing reading comprehension. Remember: You adjust your reading rate based on your purpose in reading and the difficulty of the material. To improve your reading speed of textbooks and other nonfiction works such as newspapers, practice by really concentrating on the reading task, by pushing your eyes across the lines, and by seeing phrases rather than individual words. But do not substitute skimming for reading for comprehension. There is a comprehension check after each reading. You always want to evaluate your reading rate in relation to your comprehension score. You may time yourself for practice, or your instructor may use these readings for timed exercises in class.

## Plate Tectonics and the Breakup of Pangaea

Adapted from **Helena Curtis** and **N. Sue Barnes**

The following selection is adapted from Curtis and Barnes's textbook, *An Invitation to Biology* (4th ed., 1985). Both authors are college professors who have written other books in addition to *An Invitation to Biology*.

### Prepare

1. Identify the author and work. What do you expect the author's purpose to be?

   _____

   _____

2. Preread to identify the subject and make predictions. What do you expect to read about?

   _____

3. What do you already know about the subject?

_____

_____

_____

4. Raise two questions that you expect the article to answer.

_____

_____

_____

1   Most scientists now accept the theory of plate tectonics. According to plate tectonics, the outer layer of the earth is divided into a number of sections, or plates. The continents rest on the plates, but the plates are not stationary. They slide around the surface of the earth, moving in relation to one another.

2   Sometimes the moving plates collide. Where plates bump into each other, volcanic islands may be formed. Also, mountain ranges such as the Andes or the Himalayas are created. At the boundaries where plates are separating, volcanic material wells up to fill the space. Plates may also move along their boundaries but in opposite directions, or in the same direction but at different speeds. These actions lead to earthquakes.

3   About 200 million years ago, all the major continents were locked together in one supercontinent called Pangaea. Several drawings of Pangaea have been suggested. One is shown on page 462. Scientists generally agree that Pangaea began to break up about 190 million years ago. This is about the same time that the dinosaurs were dominating the earth and the first mammals began to appear. First, the northern group of continents, called Laurasia, split apart from the southern group (Gondwana). Later, Gondwana broke into three parts: Africa–South America, Australia–Antarctica, and India. India drifted northward and bumped into Asia (the part of Laurasia to the right). This collision started the uplift of the Himalayan mountains. These continue to rise today as India continues to push northward into Asia.

4   About 65 million years ago, South America and Africa separated enough to form half of the South Atlantic Ocean. Also, Europe, North America, and Greenland began to drift apart. However, final separa-

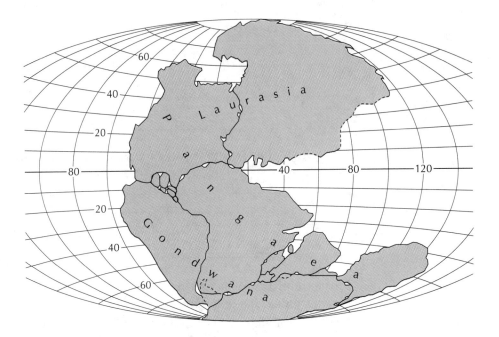

tion between Europe and North America–Greenland did not occur until about 43 million years ago. At this same time, Australia finally split from Antarctica and moved northward to its present location. Later North and South America were joined at Panama, which was created by volcanic action.

5    One of the earliest and most convincing pieces of evidence supporting continental drift was the discovery of fossils of the same reptile (*Mesosaurus*) along the coasts of both Brazil and South Africa but nowhere else. Also, in 1982, scientists found the first fossil of a land mammal—a marsupial—in Antarctica. This supports the theory that marsupials migrated by land from South America (still home of the opossum) across Antarctica to Australia before the two continents separated, about 55 million years ago. The best known marsupials living in Australia today are the kangaroos.

417 words

**Finishing time:**  _____ min. _____ sec.

**Starting time:**  _____ min. _____ sec.

**Reading time:**  _____ min. _____ sec. = _____ sec.

**No. of words ÷ reading time (in seconds) × 60 = _____ wpm**

■ **Comprehension Check** ·

*Answer the following with a, b, or c to indicate the phrase that best completes each statement.*

_____ 1. The theory of plate tectonics is that
 a. the outer layer of the moon is composed of moving plates.
 b. the inner layer of the Earth is composed of moving plates.
 c. the outer layer of the Earth is composed of moving plates.

_____ 2. Colliding plates may cause
 a. volcanic islands.
 b. mountain ranges.
 c. both (a) and (b).

_____ 3. Plates moving in opposite directions or at different speeds
 a. create new continents.
 b. cause earthquakes.
 c. happened only 200 million years ago.

_____ 4. The supercontinent is called
 a. Pangaea
 b. Gondwana
 c. Asia

_____ 5. The supercontinent began to break up when
 a. mammals dominated the Earth.
 b. the dinosaurs dominated the Earth.
 c. the dinosaurs died out.

_____ 6. When India broke off, it moved northward and bumped into
 a. Australia.
 b. South America.
 c. Asia.

_____ 7. North and South America were joined at Panama as a result of
 a. South America bumping into North America.
 b. earthquakes.
 c. volcanic action.

_____ 8. Fossils of the same reptile have been found in
 a. both Brazil and South Africa.
 b. both Panama and Greenland.
 c. both Antarctica and North America.

**Comprehension score:   no. right** _____ **× 12.5 =** _____ %

# Conformity

## by **Vincent Ryan Ruggiero**

Vincent Ruggiero is a professor of humanities at the State University of New York at Delhi as well as a writer and education consultant. The following excerpt is from his textbook, *The Art of Thinking* (2nd ed., 1988).

### ◼ Prepare

1. Identify the author and work. What do you expect the author's purpose to be?

   _____

   _____

2. Preread to identify the subject and make predictions. What do you expect to read about?

   _____

   _____

3. What do you already know about the subject?

   _____

   _____

4. Raise two questions that you expect the article to answer.

   _____

   _____

   _____

1    Not all conformity is bad. We put our out-of-town letters in the out-of-town post office slot, say hello instead of goodbye when we answer the phone, try to spell correctly and not violate the rules of grammar, and stop for red lights when driving. Such actions, and thousands of others like them, are a sensible kind of conformity. If we were to try nonconformity in such matters, we would merely waste valuable time,

confuse or annoy those around us, or threaten the safety of ourselves and others.

2    Harmful conformity is what we do instead of thinking, in order to belong to a group or to avoid the risk of being different. Such conformity is an act of cowardice, a sacrificing of independence for a lesser good. In time it makes us more concerned about what others think than about what is right and true and sensible. Once we begin to conform, we quickly find ourselves saying and doing not what we believe is best, but what we believe others want or expect us to say and do. That focus dulls our ability to think creatively and critically.

3    It's not always easy to avoid conforming. Our friends, families, and associates may exert considerable pressure on us. It takes courage to say, "I disagree," or "That's wrong," when the group is firm in its view. If you've ever tried it, you know how painful that why-must-you-be-such-a-traitor look can be. That's why so many people give in again and again until they have completely surrendered their individuality. One widely repeated laboratory experiment documented this surrender dramatically. The experiment involved two subjects, who were told they were participating in a memory test. One assumed the role of teacher; the other, the role of student. When the student gave a wrong answer, the teacher was supposed to deliver an electric shock. With each wrong answer the shock increased.

4    The situation, of course, was rigged. There was really no electric shock, and the student was really an actor instructed to say he had a heart condition, to plead with the teacher to stop, and even to claim chest pains. At the highest level of shock, he remained silent, and, since he was in another room, the teacher must have considered the possibility that the shock killed him.

5    The result of the experiment? Fully 65 percent of the teachers administered the shocks up to the highest level. Most protested to the experimenter that they didn't want to inflict pain on the student, but when the experimenter insisted, they obeyed.

6    Perhaps we would behave differently in that experiment. Perhaps not. In any case, the effects of conformity are all around us. Abraham Maslow observed:

> Too many people do not make up their own minds, but have their minds made up for them by salesmen, advertisers, parents, propagandists, TV, newspapers and so on. They are pawns to be moved by others rather than self-determining individuals. Therefore they are apt to feel helpless, weak, and totally determined; they are prey for predators, flabby whiners rather than self-determining persons.

7    It would be a mistake to fight conformity by refusing to believe and act as others do, to be different for the sake of being different. That is

no more thoughtful than mindless conformity. The right way to fight conformity is to think for yourself and not worry about whether others agree with you.

567 words

**Finishing time:** _____ **min.** _____ **sec.**

**Starting time:** _____ **min.** _____ **sec.**

**Reading time:** _____ **min.** _____ **sec.** = _____ **sec.**

**No. of words ÷ reading time (in seconds) × 60 =** _____ **wpm**

## Comprehension Check

*Answer the following with a, b, or c to indicate the phrase that best completes each statement.*

_____ 1. An example of appropriate conformity is

    a. stopping for red lights.
    b. saying what our families want us to say.
    c. doing what an authority figure tells us to do.

_____ 2. Harmful conformity is

    a. saying hello when answering the phone.
    b. following grammar rules.
    c. not thinking for ourselves.

_____ 3. Harmful conformity limits our

    a. number of friends.
    b. critical and creative thinking skills.
    c. ability to get along with family.

_____ 4. Conformity often seems easier than

    a. disagreeing with colleagues.
    b. thinking for oneself.
    c. both (a) and (b).

_____ 5. Conformists have their minds made up for them by

    a. advertising and propaganda.
    b. thinking for themselves.
    c. both (a) and (b).

_____ 6. Abraham Maslow argues that conformists are

    a. self-determining individuals.
    b. critical thinkers.
    c. likely to feel weak and helpless.

_____ 7. The author implies that

    a. resisting conformity is easy.

    b. resisting conformity is not easy.

    c. people like nonconformists.

**Comprehension score:  no. right** _____ **× 14 =** _____ **%**

## Who Wins? Who Cares?

by **Mariah Burton Nelson**

Mariah Nelson has a Master's in Public Health, has been a professional basketball player, is an advocate for women's sports and feminist issues, and is author of _Are We Winning Yet? How Women Are Changing Sports and Sports Are Changing Women_ (1991) as well as other books and articles. The following article appeared in the July/August 1990 issue of _Women's Sport and Fitness_ magazine.

### Prepare

1. Identify the author and work. What do you expect the author's purpose to be?

    _____

    _____

2. Preread to identify the subject and make predictions. What do you expect to read about?

    _____

    _____

3. What do you already know about this subject?

    _____

    _____

4. Raise two questions that you expect the article to answer.

_____

_____

_____

1    Competition can damage self-esteem, create anxiety and lead to cheating and hurt feelings. But so can romantic love. No one suggests we do away with love; rather, we must perfect our understanding of what love means.

2    So too with competition. "To compete" is derived from the Latin competere, meaning "to seek together." Women seem to understand this. Maybe it's because we sat on the sidelines for so long, watching. Maybe it's because we were raised to be kind and nurturing. I'm not sure why it is. But I've noticed that it's not women who greet each other with a ritualistic, "Who won?"; not women who memorize scores and statistics; not women who pride themselves on "killer instincts." Passionate though we are, women don't take competition that seriously. Or rather, we take competition seriously, but we don't take winning and losing seriously. We've always been more interested in playing.

3    In fact, since the early part of this century, women have devised ways to make sport specifically inclusive and cooperative. Physical educators of the 1920s taught sportswomanship as well as sport skills, emphasizing health, vigor, high moral conduct, participation, respect for other players and friendship. So intent were these women on dodging the pitfalls of men's sports that many shied away from competition altogether.

4    Nowadays, many women compete wholeheartedly. But we don't buy into the "Super Bull" mentality that the game is everything. Like Martina Navratilova and Chris Evert, former "rivals" whose rapport has come to symbolize a classically female approach to competition, many women find ways to remain close while also reaching for victory. We understand that trying to win is not tantamount to trying to belittle; that winning is not wonderful if the process of play isn't challenging, fair or fun; and that losing, though at times disappointing, does not connote failure. For women, if sports are power plays, they're not about power over (power as dominance) but power to (power as competence). Sports are not about domination and defeat but caring and cooperation.

5    "The playing of a game has to do with your feelings, your emotions, how you care about the people you're involved with," says University of Iowa basketball coach C. Vivian Stringer.

6 Pam Shriver has said of Steffi Graf, "I hope in the next couple of years that I get to be friends with her because it's just easier. It's more fun. I don't think it affects the competitive side of things."

7 Friendship has been a major theme of my sporting life as well, along with physical competence, achievement and joy. Though I've competed in seven sports from the high school to the professional level, I have few memories of victories or losses. I don't think winning taught me to be a gracious winner. I don't think losing readied me for more serious losses in life. Rather, my nearly 30 years of competition have taught me how to *play*, with empathy, humor and honesty. If another player challenges me to row harder, swim faster or make more clever moves toward the basket, the games take on a special thrill. But the final score is nearly irrelevant. Chris Evert once said the joy of winning "lasts about an hour."

8 I'm choosy about whom I compete with, and how. I don't participate in games in which "losers" are no longer allowed to play. Monopoly, poker, musical chairs, and single-elimination tournaments are a few examples. If playing is the point, then exclusion never makes sense. I also eschew competitions that pit women against men; they only serve to antagonize and polarize. I no longer injure myself in the name of victory. Nor, as a coach, will I allow players to get that carried away.

9 Some women, scarred by childhood exclusion, shamed by early "defeats," or sickened by abuses such as cheating and steroid use, still avoid competition. They're right to be wary. Although these things are more visible in men's sports, female athletes and coaches can also succumb to the "winning is the only thing" myth, committing myriad ethical and personal offenses, from recruiting violations to bulimia, in the name of victory.

10 But once one understands the spirit of the game, it's not a matter of *believing* that winning and losing aren't important, it's a matter of noticing that they're not. Women seem to notice. Most women can play soccer, golf, or run competitively and enjoy themselves, regardless of outcome. They can play on a "losing" team but leave the court with little or no sense of loss. They can win without feeling superior.

11 I think it's the responsibility of these women—and the men who remain unblinded by the seductive glow of victory—to share this vision with young players. Children, it seems to me, naturally enjoy comparing their skills: "How far can you throw the ball? Farther than I can? How did you do it? Will you show me?" It's only when adults ascribe undue importance to victory that losing becomes devastating and children get hurt.

12 Adults must show children that what matters is how one plays the game. It's important that we not just parrot that cliché, but demon-

strate our commitment to fair, participatory competition by paying equal attention to skilled and unskilled children; by allowing all children to participate fully in games, regardless of the score; and by caring more about process than results. This way, children can fully comprehend what they seem to intuit: that competition can be a way to get to know other people, to be challenged, and to have fun in a close and caring environment. To seek together.

13    Some of my best friends are the women and men who share a court or pool or field with me. Together we take risks, make mistakes, laugh, push ourselves and revel in the grace and beauty of sports. Who wins? Who cares? We're playing *with,* not *against* each other, using each other's accomplishments to inspire.

14    At its best, competition is not divisive but unifying, not hateful but loving. Like other expressions of love, it should not be avoided simply because it has been misunderstood.

947 words

**Finishing time:** _____ min. _____ sec.

**Starting time:** _____ min. _____ sec.

**Reading time:** _____ min. _____ sec. = _____ sec.

**No. of words ÷ reading time (in seconds) × 60 =** _____ wpm

## Comprehension Check

*Answer the following with a, b, or c to indicate the phrase that best completes each statement.*

_____ 1. The best main-idea statement for the article is

a. competition is bad for self-esteem.
b. men and women should enjoy competing, but not put too much emphasis on winning.
c. women were taught to be kind and nurturing.

_____ 2. The author asserts that women who compete are

a. not seeking power over others.
b. seeking power over others.
c. only interested in victory.

_____ 3. Tennis player Chris Evert said that the joy of winning lasts

a. many hours.
b. a lifetime.
c. about an hour.

_____ 4. The author objects to

    a. women playing against men.

    b. getting injured in an attempt to win.

    c. both (a) and (b).

_____ 5. Adults need to show children that

    a. winning is everything.

    b. what matters is how you play the game.

    c. losing is devastating.

_____ 6. Children playing sports get hurt from the experience when

    a. adults don't care what happens.

    b. their friends don't play.

    c. adults are too concerned about their winning.

_____ 7. The author believes that, at its best, competition is

    a. unifying.

    b. divisive.

    c. dumb.

_____ 8. Readers can infer that the author believes that

    a. women were taught different values than men.

    b. men care too much about winning.

    c. both (a) and (b).

**Comprehension score:   no. right** _____ **× 12.5 =** _____ **%**

## A New Day for Alfred

by **James Herriot**

A veterinarian in Yorkshire, England, James Herriot wrote a number of best-selling books about his experiences, including *All Creatures Great and Small* and *Every Living Thing* (1992), from which the following is taken.

### Prepare

1. Identify the author and work. What do you expect the author's purpose to be?

_____

_____

2. Preread to identify the subject and make predictions. What do you expect to read about?

_____

_____

3. What do you already know about the subject?

_____

_____

_____

4. Raise two questions that you expect the articles to answer.

_____

_____

_____

1    My throat was killing me. Three successive nocturnal lambings on the windswept hillsides in my shirtsleeves had left me with the beginnings of a cold and I felt in urgent need of a packet of Geoff Hatfield's cough drops. An unscientific treatment, perhaps, but I had a childish faith in those powerful little candies that exploded in the mouth, sending a blast of medicated vapour surging through the bronchial tubes.

2    The shop was down a side alley, almost hidden away, and it was so tiny—not much more than a cubby hole—that there was hardly room for the sign, GEOFFREY HATFIELD, CONFECTIONER, above the window. But it was full. It was always full, and, this being market day, it was packed out.

3    The little bell went "ching" as I opened the door and squeezed into the crush of local ladies and farmers' wives. I'd have to wait for a while but I didn't mind, because watching Mr. Hatfield in action was one of the rewarding things in my life.

4    I had come at a good time, too, because the proprietor was in the middle of one of his selection struggles. He had his back to me, the silver-haired, leonine head nodding slightly on the broad shoulders as he surveyed the rows of tall glass sweet jars against the wall. His hands, clasped behind him, tensed and relaxed repeatedly as he

fought his inner battle, then he took a few strides along the row, gazing intently at each jar in turn. It struck me that Lord Nelson[1] pacing the quarter deck of the *Victory* and wondering how best to engage the enemy could not have displayed a more portentous concentration.

5      The tension in the little shop rose palpably as he reached up a hand, then withdrew it with a shake of the head, but a sigh went up from the assembled ladies as, with a final grave nod and a squaring of the shoulders, he extended both arms, seized a jar and swung round to face the company. His large Roman senator face was crinkled into a benign smile.

6      "Now, Mrs. Moffat," he boomed at a stout matron, holding out the glass vessel with both hands, inclining it slightly with all the grace and deference of a Cartier[2] jeweller displaying a diamond necklace, "I wonder if I can interest you in this."

7      Mrs. Moffat, clutching her shopping basket, peered closely at the paper-wrapped confections in the jar. "Well, ah don't know. . . ."

8      "If I remember rightly, madam, you indicated that you were seeking something in the nature of a Russian caramel, and I can thoroughly recommend these little sweetmeats. Not quite a Russian, but nevertheless a very nice, smooth-eating toffee." His expression became serious, expectant.

9      The fruity tones rolling round his description made me want to grab the sweets and devour them on the spot, and they seemed to have the same effect on the lady. "Right, Mr. Hatfield," she said eagerly. "I'll 'ave half a pound."

10     The shopkeeper gave a slight bow. "Thank you so much, madam, I'm sure you will not regret your choice." His features relaxed into a gracious smile and as he lovingly trickled the toffees onto his scales before bagging them with a professional twirl, I felt a renewed desire to get at the things.

11     Mr. Hatfield, leaning forward with both hands on the counter, kept his gaze on his customer until he had bowed her out of the shop with a courteous "Good day to you, madam." Then he turned to face the congregation. "Ah, Mrs. Dawson, how very nice to see you. And what is your pleasure this morning?"

12     The lady, obviously delighted, beamed at him. "I'd like some of them fudge chocolates I 'ad last week, Mr. Hatfield. They were lovely. Have you still got some?"

13     "Indeed I have, madam, and I am delighted that you approve of my recommendation. Such a deliciously creamy flavour. Also, it so

[1]Eighteenth-century British admiral.

[2]Expensive jewelry store chain.

happens that I have just received a consignment in a special presentation box for Easter." He lifted one from the shelf and balanced it on the palm of his hand. "Really pretty and attractive, don't you think?"

14    Mrs. Dawson nodded rapidly. "Oh, aye, that's real bonny. I'll take a box and there's summat else I want. A right big bag of nice boiled sweets for the family to suck at. Mixed colours, you know. What 'ave you got?"

15    Mr. Hatfield steepled his fingers, gazed at her fixedly and took a long, contemplative breath. He held this pose for several seconds, then he swung round, clasped his hands behind him, and recommenced his inspection of the jars.

16    That was my favourite bit and, as always, I was enjoying it. It was a familiar scene. The tiny, crowded shop, the proprietor wrestling with his assignment and Alfred sitting at the far end of the counter.

17    Alfred was Geoff's cat and he was always there, seated upright and majestic on the polished boards near the curtained doorway that led to the Hatfield sitting room. As usual, he seemed to be taking a keen interest in the proceedings, his gaze moving from his master's face to the customer's, and though it may have been my imagination I felt that his expression registered a grave involvement in the negotiations and a deep satisfaction at the outcome. He never left his place or encroached on the rest of the counter, but occasionally one or other of the ladies would stroke his cheek and he would respond with a booming purr and a gracious movement of the head towards them.

18    It was typical that he never yielded to any unseemly display of emotion. That would have been undignified and dignity was an unchanging part of him. Even as a kitten he had never indulged in immoderate playfulness. I had neutered him three years ago—for which he appeared to bear me no ill will—and he had grown into a massive, benevolent tabby. I looked at him now, sitting in his place. Vast, imperturbable, at peace with his world. There was no doubt he was a cat of enormous presence.

19    And it had always struck me forcibly that he was exactly like his master in that respect. They were two of a kind and it was no surprise that they were such devoted friends.

20    When it came to my turn I was able to reach Alfred and I tickled him under his chin. He liked that and raised his head high while the purring rumbled up from the furry rib-cage till it resounded throughout the shop.

21    Even collecting my cough drops had its touch of ceremony. The big man behind the counter sniffed gravely at the packet, then clapped his hand a few times against his chest. "You can smell the goodness, Mr.

Herriot, the beneficial vapours. These will have you right in no time."
He bowed and smiled and I could swear that Alfred smiled with him.

22    I squeezed my way out through the ladies and as I walked down
the alley I marvelled for the umpteenth time at the phenomenon of Geoffrey Hatfield. There were several other sweet shops in Darrowby, big
double-fronted places with their wares attractively displayed in the
windows, but none of them did anything like the trade of the poky establishment I had just left. There was no doubt that it was all due to
Geoff's unique selling technique and it was certainly not an act on his
part; it was born of a completely sincere devotion to his calling, a delight in what he was doing.

23    His manner and "posh" diction gave rise to a certain amount of ribald comment from men who had left the local school with him at the
age of fourteen, and in the pubs he was often referred to as "the
bishop," but it was good-natured stuff because he was a well-liked
man. And, of course, the ladies adored him and flocked to bask in his
attentions.

24    About a month later I was in the shop again to get some of Rosie's
favourite liquorice all-sorts and the picture was the same—Geoffrey
smiling and booming, Alfred in his place, following every move, the
pair of them radiating dignity and well-being. As I collected my
sweets, the proprietor whispered in my ear.

25    "I'll be closing for lunch at twelve noon, Mr. Herriot. Would you be
so kind as to call in and examine Alfred?"

26    "Yes, of course." I looked along the counter at the big cat. "Is he ill?"

27    "Oh, no, no . . . but I just feel there's something not right."

28    Later I knocked at the closed door and Geoffrey let me into the shop,
empty for once, then through the curtained doorway into his sitting
room. Mrs. Hatfield was at a table, drinking tea. She was a much earthier character than her husband. "Now then, Mr. Herriot, you've come
to see t'little cat."

29    "He isn't so little," I said, laughing. And indeed, Alfred looked more
massive than ever seated by the fire, looking calmly into the flames.
When he saw me he got up, stalked unhurriedly over the carpet and
arched his back against my legs. I felt strangely honoured.

30    "He's really beautiful, isn't he?" I murmured. I hadn't had a close
look at him for some time and the friendly face with the dark stripes
running down to the intelligent eyes appealed to me as never before.
"Yes," I said, stroking the fur, which shone luxuriantly in the flickering firelight, "you're a big beautiful fellow."

31    I turned to Mr. Hatfield. "He looks fine to me. What is it that's worrying you?"

32    "Oh, maybe it's nothing at all. His appearance certainly has not altered in the slightest, but for over a week now I've noticed that he is not quite so keen on his food, not quite so lively. He's not really ill . . . he's just different."

33    "I see. Well, let's have a look at him." I went over the cat carefully. Temperature was normal, mucous membranes a healthy pink. I got out my stethoscope and auscultated heart and lungs—nothing abnormal to hear. Palpation of the abdomen produced no clue.

34    "Well, Mr. Hatfield," I said, "there doesn't seem to be anything obviously wrong with him. He's maybe a bit run down, but he doesn't look it. Anyway, I'll give him a vitamin injection. That should buck him up. Let me know in a few days if he's no better."

35    "Thank you indeed, sir. I am most grateful. You have set my mind at rest." The big man reached out a hand to his pet. The confident resonance of his voice was belied by the expression of concern on his face. Seeing them together made me sense anew the similarity of man and cat—human and animal, yes, but alike in their impressiveness.

36    I heard nothing about Alfred for a week and assumed that he had returned to normal, but then his master telephoned. "He's just the same, Mr. Herriot. In fact, if anything, he had deteriorated slightly. I would be obliged if you would look at him again."

37    It was just as before. Nothing definite to see even on close examination. I put him onto a course of mixed minerals and vitamin tablets. There was no point in launching into treatment with our new antibiotics—there was no elevation of temperature, no indication of any infectious agent.

38    I passed the alley every day—it was only about a hundred yards from Skeldale House—and I fell into the habit of stopping and looking in through the little window of the shop. Each day, the familiar scene presented itself; Geoff bowing and smiling to his customers and Alfred sitting in his place at the end of the counter. Everything seemed right, and yet . . . there was something different about the cat.

39    I called in one evening and examined him again. "He's losing weight," I said.

40    Geoffrey nodded. "Yes, I do think so. He is still eating fairly well, but not as much as before."

41    "Give him another few days on the tablets," I said, "and if he's no better I'll have to get him round to the surgery and go into this thing a bit more deeply."

42    I had a nasty feeling there would be no improvement and there wasn't, so one evening I took a cat cage round to the shop. Alfred was so huge that there was a problem fitting him into the container, but he did not resist as I bundled him gently inside.

43   At the surgery I took a blood sample from him and X-rayed him. The plate was perfectly clear and when the report came back from the laboratory it showed no abnormality.

44   In a way, it was reassuring, but that did not help because the steady decline continued. The next few weeks were something like a nightmare. My anxious peering through the shop window became a daily ordeal. The big cat was still in his place, but he was getting thinner and thinner until he was almost unrecognisable. I tried every drug and treatment I could think of, but nothing did any good. I had Siegfried examine him, but he thought as I did. The progressive emaciation was the sort of thing you would expect from an internal tumour, but further X-rays still showed nothing. Alfred must have been thoroughly fed up of all the pushing around, the tests, the kneading of his abdomen, but at no time did he show any annoyance. He accepted the whole thing placidly as was his wont.

45   There was another factor that made the situation much worse. Geoff himself was wilting under the strain. His comfortable coating of flesh was dropping steadily away from him, the normally florid cheeks were pale and sunken and, worse still, his dramatic selling style appeared to be deserting him. One day I left my viewpoint at the window and pushed my way into the press of ladies in the shop. It was a harrowing scene. Geoff, bowed and shrunken, was taking the orders without even a smile, pouring the sweets listlessly into their bags and mumbling a word or two. Gone was the booming voice and the happy chatter of the customers and a strange silence hung over the company. It was just like any other sweet shop.

46   Saddest sight of all was Alfred, still sitting bravely upright in his place. He was unbelievably gaunt, his fur had lost its bloom and he stared straight ahead, dead-eyed, as though nothing interested him any more. He was like a feline scarecrow.

47   I couldn't stand it any longer. That evening I went round to see Geoff Hatfield.

48   "I saw your cat today," I said, "and he's going rapidly downhill. Are there any new symptoms?"

49   The big man nodded dully. "Yes, as a matter of fact. I was going to ring you. He's been vomiting a bit."

50   I dug my nails into my palms. "There it is again. Everything points to something abnormal inside him and yet I can't find a thing." I bent down and stroked Alfred. "I hate to see him like this. Look at his fur. It used to be so glossy."

51   "That's right," replied Geoff. "He's neglecting himself. He never washes himself now. It's as though he can't be bothered. And before, he was always at it. Lick, lick, lick for hours on end. "

52 I stared at him. His words had sparked something in my mind. "Lick, lick, lick." I paused in thought. "Yes . . . when I think about it, no cat I ever knew washed himself as much as Alfred. . . ." The spark suddenly became a flame and I jerked upright in my chair.

53 "Mr. Hatfield," I said, "I want to do an exploratory laparotomy!"

54 "What do you mean?"

55 "I think he's got a hair-ball inside him and I want to operate to see if I'm right."

56 "Open him up, you mean?"

57 "That's right."

58 He put a hand over his eyes and his chin sank onto his chest. He stayed like that for a long time, then he looked at me with haunted eyes. "Oh, I don't know. I've never thought of anything like that."

59 "We've got to do something or this cat is going to die."

60 He bent and stroked Alfred's head again and again, then without looking up he spoke in a husky voice. "All right, when?"

61 "Tomorrow morning."

62 Next day, in the operating room, as Siegfried and I bent over the sleeping cat, my mind was racing. We had been doing much more small-animal surgery lately, but I had always known what to expect. This time I felt as though I was venturing into the unknown.

63 I incised through skin, abdominal muscles and peritoneum and when I reached forward towards the diaphragm I could feel a doughy mass inside the stomach. I cut through the stomach wall and my heart leaped. There it was, a large, matted hair-ball. The cause of all the trouble. Something that wouldn't show up on an X-ray plate.

64 Siegfried grinned. "Well, now we know!"

65 "Yes," I said as the great waves of relief swept over me. "Now we know."

66 And there was more. After I had evacuated and stitched the stomach, I found other, smaller hair-balls, bulging the intestine along its length. These had all to be removed and the bowel wall stitched in several places. I didn't like this. It meant a bigger trauma and shock to my patient, but finally all was done and only a neat row of skin sutures was visible.

67 When I returned Alfred to his home his master could hardly bear to look at him. At length he took a timid glance at the cat, still sleeping under the anaesthetic. "Will he live?" he whispered.

68 "He has a good chance," I replied. "He has had some major surgery and it might take him some time to get over it, but he's young and strong. He should be all right."

69 I could see Geoff wasn't convinced, and that was how it was over the next few days. I kept visiting the little room behind the shop to give

the cat penicillin injections, and it was obvious that he had made up his mind that Alfred was going to die.

70 Mrs. Hatfield was more optimistic, but she was worried about her husband.

71 "Eee, he's given up hope," she said. "And it's all because Alfred just lies in his bed all day. I've tried to tell 'im that it'll be a bit o' time before the cat starts runnin' around, but he won't listen."

72 She looked at me with anxious eyes. "And, you know, it's gettin' him down, Mr. Herriot. He's a different man. Sometimes I wonder if he'll ever be the same again."

73 I went over and peeped past the curtain into the shop. Geoff was there, doing his job like an automaton. Haggard, unsmiling, silently handing out the sweets. When he did speak it was in a listless monotone and I realised with a sense of shock that his voice had lost all its old timbre. Mrs. Hatfield was right. He was a different man. And, I thought, if he stayed different what would happen to his clientele? So far they had remained faithful, but I had a feeling they would soon start to drift away.

74 It was a week before the picture began to change for the better. I entered the sitting room, but Alfred wasn't there.

75 Mrs. Hatfield jumped up from her chair. "He's a lot better, Mr. Herriot," she said eagerly. "Eating well and seemed to want to go into t'shop. He's in there with Geoff now."

76 Again I took a surreptitious look past the curtain. Alfred was back in his place, skinny but sitting upright. But his master didn't look any better.

77 I turned back into the room. "Well, I won't need to come any more, Mrs. Hatfield. Your cat is well on the way to recovery. He should soon be as good as new. " I was quite confident about this, but I wasn't so sure about Geoff.

78 Soon afterwards, the rush of spring lambing and post-lambing troubles overwhelmed me as it did every year, and I had little time to think about my other cases. It must have been three weeks before I visited the sweet shop to buy some chocolates for Helen. The place was packed and as I pushed my way inside all my fears were rushing back and I looked anxiously at man and cat.

79 Alfred, massive and dignified again, sat like a king at the far end of the counter. Geoff was leaning on the counter with both hands, gazing closely into a lady's face. "As I understand you, Mrs. Hird, you are looking for something in the nature of a softer sweetmeat." The rich voice reverberated round the little shop. "Could you perhaps mean a Turkish delight?"

80 "Nay, Mr. Hatfield, it wasn't that . . . "

81    His head fell on his chest and he studied the polished boards of the counter with fierce concentration. Then he looked up and pushed his face nearer to the lady's. "A pastille, possibly . . . ?"

82    "Nay . . . nay.

83    "A truffle? A soft caramel? A peppermint cream?"

84    "No, nowt like that."

85    He straightened up. This was a tough one. He folded his arms across his chest and as he stared into space and took the long inhalation I remembered so well, I could see that he was a big man again, his shoulders spreading wide, his face ruddy and well-fleshed.

86    Nothing having evolved from his cogitations, his jaw jutted and he turned his face upwards, seeking further inspiration from the ceiling. Alfred, I noticed, looked upwards, too.

87    There was a tense silence as Geoff held his pose, then a smile crept slowly over his noble features. He raised a finger. "Madam," he said, "I do fancy I have it. Whitish, you said . . . sometimes pink . . . rather squashy . . . May I suggest to you . . . marshmallow?"

88    Mrs. Hird thumped the counter. "Aye, that's it, Mr. Hatfield. I just couldn't think of t'name."

89    "Ha-ha, I thought so," boomed the proprietor, his organ tones rolling to the roof. He laughed, the ladies laughed, and I was positive that Alfred laughed, too.

90    All was well again. Everybody in the shop was happy—Geoff, Alfred, the ladies and, not least, James Herriot.

2814 words

| Finishing time: | _____ min. _____ sec. | |
|---|---|---|
| Starting time: | _____ min. _____ sec. | |
| Reading time: | _____ min. _____ sec. = | _____ sec. |

No. of words ÷ reading time (in seconds) × 60 = _____ wpm

## Comprehension Check

*Answer the following with a, b, or c to indicate the phrase that best completes each statement.*

\_\_\_\_ 1. The narrative begins in

   a. Alfred's home.
   b. Geoff Hatfield's candy shop.
   c. Dr. Herriot's office.

_____ 2. Alfred is

    a. Dr. Herriot's assistant.
    b. Geoff Hatfield's brother.
    c. Geoff Hatfield's cat.

_____ 3. Alfred, just like Geoff Hatfield, had

    a. dignity and presence.
    b. playfulness.
    c. a lack of interest in customers.

_____ 4. Alfred became sick because he

    a. had been neutered by the narrator.
    b. was locked out of the candy shop.
    c. had hair balls in his stomach and intestine.

_____ 5. When Alfred became very sick,

    a. Dr. Herriot operated on him.
    b. Geoff hatfield became sick, too.
    c. both (a) and (b).

_____ 6. Readers can infer that the health of pets

    a. is not important to owners.
    b. affects the health of owners.
    c. affects one's business.

**Comprehension score:** **no. right** _____ **× 16.6 =** _____ %

# GLOSSARY

**Analysis** Dividing a work or a topic into its parts.

**Annotating** A combination of underlining and marginal notes used to guide one's study of written material.

**Bias** The position or viewpoint of the author, as revealed in the way facts are presented and strategies used to create tone.

**Cause and effect** An organizational strategy in which one or more items are shown to produce one or more consequences.

**Chronology** The arrangement of events in time sequence. A narrative or historical account organizes events in chronological order. A process analysis explains steps in their appropriate chronology.

**Cognition** The process of knowing or learning.

**Commitment** An active desire to do something well.

**Comparison** A structuring of information to show similarities between two items.

**Concentration** An active attention given to a task.

**Connotation** The associations and emotional overtones suggested by a word.

**Context clues** The language environment that gives information about the meaning of words within that environment.

**Contrast** A structuring of information to show differences between two items.

**Cornell Method** A method of taking notes from reading or from lectures. A vertical line divides each page into two parts, the left part one-third of the page and the right two-thirds. Notes are taken to the right of the line and key words and topics are placed to the left.

**Critical thinking** An organized, purposeful study of information and ideas to evaluate their usefulness.

**Definition** Explanation of a word's meaning or meanings. It can be provided in a sentence or expanded into an essay.

**Denotation** The meanings of a word, often referred to as a word's dictionary definitions.

**Description** Details appealing to the five senses that help readers to "see" the writer's subject.

**Details** Specific pieces of information that range from descriptions of people and places to statistical data and that are used by writers to illustrate and support ideas and general points.

**Evidence** Facts and examples used to support the main idea of an argument.

**Example** A specific illustration used to develop a main idea.

**Expository writing** Writing primarily designed to provide information, e.g., reporting and textbook writing.

**Expressive writing** Writing designed to produce an emotional as well as intellectual response to the subject discussed and to generate reflection on human life and experiences.

**Fact** A statement that is verifiable by observation, measurement, experiment, or use of reliable reference sources such as encyclopedias.

**Fiction** An imagined narrative; a story.

**Figurative language** Language containing figures of speech (e.g., metaphors) that extend meaning beyond the literal.

**Flowchart** A type of graph best used to depict steps in a process, or a sequence of events or ideas.

**Graphics** Methods of presenting information visually, such as graphs, maps, charts, or diagrams.

**Highlighting** The use of colored markers to make some lines of a text stand out, as an aid to studying the text.

**Inference** A conclusion drawn from related information on a given subject.

**Irony** The expression of some form of discrepancy between what is said and what is meant, what we expect to happen and what actually happens, or what a character says and what we understand to be true.

**Main idea** The central point of a passage or work.

**Mapping** A writing-to-learn strategy that displays main ideas and shows their relationships graphically.

**Metaphor** A figure of speech in which a comparison is either stated or implied between two basically unlike items. (E.g., Love is compared to red roses.)

**Monitor** Regular, purposeful checking of one's work to maintain ideal performance of a task.

**Notetaking** Paraphrasing and summarizing main ideas and key points in assigned readings as a strategy for studying the readings.

**Opinion** Statements of inference or judgment, in contrast to statements of fact.

**Organization** The structure or pattern of development of a work.

**Outlining** A strategy for summarizing and indicating the relationships of a work's main ideas, main details, and minor details by using a pattern of Roman numerals, letters, and Arabic numerals and indentation.

**Personification** A comparison that gives human qualities to something not human. (E.g., "The daffodils tossed their heads.")

**Persuasive writing** Writing primarily designed to support a position on an issue or beliefs about a given subject.

**Point of View** The perspective from which a story is told.

**Preread** A step in preparing to read that involves getting an overview by reading only key parts of a work.

**Purpose** The reason or reasons a writer chooses to write a particular work.

**Scanning** A method of quick reading that focuses on finding just the information needed from the reading material.

**Signal words** Words or phrases that make clear a passage's structure.

**Simile** A comparison between two basically unlike things stated explicitly through a connector such as *like* or *as*. (E.g., "My love is like a red, red rose.")

**Skimming** A reading strategy that focuses on obtaining an overview or "gist" of a work by searching for main ideas and skipping most details.

**Style** A writer's choice of words and sentence patterns.

**Subvocalization** Practice of sounding words in one's head as one reads.

**Summary** A condensed, objective restatement in different words of the main points of a passage or work.

**Theme** The central idea or ideas that a literary work expresses.

**Thesis** The main idea of an essay, article, or book; what a writer asserts about his or her subject.

**Tone** The way the writer's attitude is expressed. (E.g., playful, sarcastic.)

**Topic** The subject of a piece of writing.

**Topic sentence** The sentence in a paragraph that states the paragraph's main idea. (In some paragraphs, the main idea is not stated but implied.)

**Vocalization** Practice of moving one's lips or saying words aloud as one reads.

## Credits

Robert A. Ricklefs, excerpt from *Ecology* 3rd ed. Copyright © 1990 by W. H. Freeman and Co. Used with permission.

John G. Ross, photo: "The Great Sphinx." Reprinted with permission of Photo Researchers, Inc., New York.

Vincent Ryan Ruggiero, excerpt from *The Art of Thinking: A Guide to Critical and Creative Thought,* 3rd ed., pp. 40–41. Copyright © 1991 by HarperCollins Publishers, Inc. Reprinted by permission of Addison-Wesley Educational Publishers, Inc.

The Schlesinger Library, Radcliffe College. Photo of Amelia Earhart.

Michael Scott, excerpt from *Ecology,* p. 149. Copyright © 1995. Reprinted by permission of Oxford University Press.

Dorothy U. Seyler, index page from *Patterns of Reflection,* 2nd ed. Copyright © 1996 by Allyn and Bacon. Used with permission.

Sizer and Whitney, excerpts from *Nutrition: Concepts and Controversies,* 6th ed., pp. 19, 101–102, 183–184, 433. Copyright © 1994 by West Publishing Company. All rights reserved.

Jackson J. Spielvogel, excerpts from *Western Civilization,* pp. 17, 21–22, 23–24, 307, 372, 574. Copyright © 1994 by West Publishing Company. Reprinted with permission. All rights reserved.

Stock Montage, Inc., New York. Images of the Mayflower Compact, title page of Hobbes' *Leviathan,* portraits of Thomas Hobbes, John Locke, and Karl Marx.

George Tames, "The Loneliest Job" (President John F. Kennedy in the Oval Office). Copyright © 1961. Used with permission of NYT Pictures, New York.

John Vivian, *The Media of Mass Communications,* 3rd ed. Copyright © 1995 by Allyn and Bacon. Reprinted by permission.

Weather information, temperatures, and map. Copyright © 1996 *The Washington Post.* Used with permission.

Vincent Wilson, Jr. "Amelia Earhart," from *The Book of Distinguished American Women.* Copyright © 1992. Used with permission.

Wood and Wood, excerpts from *The World of Psychology,* 2nd ed., pp. 128–129, 205, 210, 457. Copyright © 1995 by Allyn and Bacon. Used with permission.

Joseph Wright, portrait of Benjamin Franklin. Corcoran Museum of Art, Washington, DC. Used with permission.

# INDEX